In Dialogue with the Agallamh

In Dialogue with the *Agallamh*
Essays in Honour of
Seán Ó Coileáin

Aidan Doyle and Kevin Murray

EDITORS

FOUR COURTS PRESS

Set in 10.5 pt on 12.5 pt Ehrhardt for
FOUR COURTS PRESS LTD
7 Malpas Street, Dublin 8, Ireland
www.fourcourtspress.ie
and in North America for
FOUR COURTS PRESS
c/o ISBS, 920 N.E. 58th Avenue, Suite 300, Portland, OR 97213.

A catalogue record for this title
is available from the British Library.

ISBN 978–1–84682–385–5

Printed in England
by Antony Rowe Ltd, Chippenham, Wilts.

Contents

Brollach/Prologue

Tá na haistí sa leabhar seo bunaithe, don chuid is mó, ar chainteanna a tugadh ag comhdháil ar *Agallamh na seanórach* i gColáiste na hOllscoile, Corcaigh, 7–8 Meán Fómhair, 2012. Eagraíodh an chomhdháil faoi choimirce Scoil Léann na Gaeilge in ómós do Sheán Ó Coileáin, iar-ollamh le Nua-Ghaeilge, chun comóradh a dhéanamh ar an méid atá déanta aige i rith a shaoil ar son an léinn agus ar son na hOllscoile.

The centrepiece of *Fiannaíocht* literature, *Agallamh na seanórach* 'The dialogue of the ancients', was chosen as the theme of the conference for two main reasons. First, the *Agallamh* survives in numerous different versions dating from the late-medieval/early-modern Irish period to the twentieth century; consequently, it is part of the scholarly field of enquiry for members of the School of Irish Learning's three constituent Departments — Roinn an Bhéaloidis, Roinn na Nua-Ghaeilge agus Roinn na Sean- agus na Meán-Ghaeilge. Second, and more importantly, Professor Ó Coileáin has made a number of seminal contributions to our understanding of the *Agallamh*, two of which are reprinted in this volume, book-ending the papers delivered at the conference. It is hoped that this collection will add significantly to the growing body of scholarship on *Fiannaíocht* which occupies such a central position in the canon of Gaelic literature.

As organizers and editors, we would like to acknowledge the financial assistance of the following within UCC: Roinn na Sean- agus na Meán-Ghaeilge, Roinn na Nua-Ghaeilge, the College of Arts, Celtic Studies and Social Sciences, and particularly Scoil Léann na Gaeilge; without these subventions, the conference could not have been held and this volume would not have been published. We are grateful to John Fitzgerald and Special Collections, Boole Library, for permission to use the manuscript image from UCC MS 96 on the cover. We would also like to thank Martin Fanning of Four Courts Press for the attention that he devoted to the production of this volume: *míle buíochas*. Last, but not least, we wish to thank the authors for their thoughtful and thought-provoking contributions.

Tá fonn orainn buíochas a ghabháil le Riona Doolan, Ciara Ní Churnáin agus Siobhán Ní Dhonghaile a thug cabhair dúinn go fonnmhar le linn na comhdhála. Thar éinne eile, áfach, tá buíochas faoi leith ag dul do Mháire Herbert a thug gach cúnamh dúinn agus muidne i mbun oibre. Those of us who have worked with Professor Ó Coileáin over the years are aware of the depth of his integrity, the range of his intellectual abilities and the extent of his generosity; this volume is a small token in return from his colleagues and friends.

Aidan Doyle / Kevin Murray,
Scoil Léann na Gaeilge,
Coláiste na hOllscoile, Corcaigh.

Noid/Abbreviations

AB	*Agallamh bheag*
ACon.	Freeman, *Annála Connacht: the annals of Connacht*
AFM	O'Donovan, *Annals of the Four Masters*
AgS	Ní Shéaghdha, *Agallamh na seanórach*
ALC	Hennessy, *Annals of Loch Cé*
AOP	*Agallamh Oisín agus Phádraig*
ARÉ	Acadamh Ríoga na hÉireann, Baile Átha Cliath
AS	Stokes, 'Acallamh na senórach'
ATig.	Stokes, 'The annals of Tigernach'
AU	Mac Airt and Mac Niocaill, *The annals of Ulster*
AU¹	Hennessy and Mac Carthy, *Annála Uladh: annals of Ulster*
BL	British Library
COC	Coláiste na hOllscoile, Corcaigh
Cott.	Freeman, *The annals in Cotton MS. Titus A. XXV*
CS	Hennessy, *Chronicum Scotorum*
DF	MacNeill and Murphy, *Duanaire Finn*
DIL	Quin (general editor), *Dictionary of the Irish language* (available online at http://edil.qub.ac.uk).
LLM	Leabhar Leasa Móir
LNÉ	Leabharlann Náisiúnta na hÉireann, Baile Átha Cliath
LS/LSS	Lámhscríbhinn/í
MS/MSS	Manuscript/s
NLI	National Library of Ireland
RIA	Royal Irish Academy, Dublin
TCD	Trinity College Dublin
UCC	University College Cork
UCD	University College Dublin

NOTE

Acallam na senórach is the spelling used throughout to refer to the earliest version of the text; later versions are referred to as *Agallamh bheag*, *Agallamh na seanórach* and *Agallamh Oisín agus Phádraig* (as appropriate). The spellings *fian/fiana*, *síd*, Finn, *fianaigeacht*, Caílte etc. are used in material dealing with the medieval period; these terms and names are rendered *fiann/fianna*, *sí/síodh*, Fionn, *fianaigheacht/fiannaíocht*, Caoilte etc. in the essays dealing with the later sources.

Tabula gratulatoria

Anders Ahlqvist
Angela Bourke
Diarmuid Breathnach
Pádraig A. Breatnach
Mícheál Briody
Neil Buttimer
Marc Caball
John Carey
Anne Connon
Valerie Kelly Curtin
Síle de Cléir
Alan Desmond
Charles Dillon
Riona Doolan
Ann Dooley
Clodagh Downey
Aidan Doyle
John FitzGerald
Kelly Fitzgerald
Joseph Flahive
Hugh Fogarty
William Gillies
Máire Herbert
Barbara Hillers
Kaarina Hollo
Colbert Kearney
Patricia Kelly
Fergus Kelly
John Koch
Máirín agus Éamon Lankford
Éanna Mac Cába
Pádraig Mac Cárthaigh
Marcas Mac Coinnigh
Máirtín Mac Conmara MSC
Mícheál Mac Craith OFM
Uáitéar Mac Gearailt
Caoimhín Mac Giolla Léith

Damian McManus
Liam Mac Mathúna
Séamus Mac Mathúna
Brent Miles
John A. Murphy
Kevin Murray
Joseph Falaky Nagy
Kuninao Nashimoto
Grace Neville
Stephen Newman
Máire Ní Annracháin
Emma Nic Cárthaigh
Próinséas Ní Chatháin
Máirín Ní Dhonnchadha
Úna Nic Éinrí
Róisín Ní Ghairbhí
Máiréad Ní Loingsigh
Máire Ní Mhaonaigh
Deirdre Nic Mhathúna
Áinéad Ní Mhuirthile
Lesa Ní Mhunghaile
Máire Ní Mhurchú
Síle Ní Mhurchú
Máire Ní Neachtain
Tríona Ní Shíocháin
Meidhbhín Ní Úrdail agus Jürgen Uhlich
Tomás Ó Briain
Seán Ó Broin
Stiofán Ó Cadhla
Diarmaid Ó Catháin and Gearóidín de Buitléir
Séamas Ó Catháin
Tomás Ó Cathasaigh
Pádraig Ó Céilleachair
Máire and Gearóid Ó Cléirigh
Fionnbarra Ó Coileáin
Séamus Ó Coileáin
Brian Ó Conchubhair
Breandán Ó Conchúir
Donnchadh Ó Corráin
Breandán Ó Cróinín
Dáibhí Ó Cróinín
Gearóid Ó Crualaoich

Séamas Ó Direáin
Caitríona Ó Dochartaigh
Patrick O'Donovan
Tadhg Ó Dúshláine
Dónall Ó Fionnáin
Tony Ó Floinn
Cathal Ó Háinle
Liam Ó hAisibéil
Donnchadh Ó hAodha
Liam Ó hÉigearta
Maeve agus Roibeárd Ó hÚrdail
Lillis Ó Laoire
Pádraig Ó Macháin
Breandán Ó Madagáin
Mícheál Ó Mainnín
Roibeard Ó Maolalaigh
Diarmaid Ó Mathúna
Nollaig Ó Muraíle
Liam P. Ó Murchú
Máirtín Ó Murchú
Tomás Ó Nialláin
Pádraig Ó Riain and Dagmar Ó Riain-Raedel
Geraldine Parsons
Erich Poppe
Pádraigín Riggs
Pól Ruiséal
William J. Smyth
David Stifter
Catherine Swift
Donna Thornton agus Niall Ó Murchadha
Alan Titley
Seán Ua Súilleabháin
Bláthnaid Uí Chatháin
Ríonach uí Ógáin
Henar Velasco López
Seosamh Watson
Máire West
Peter Woodman

Seán Ó Coileáin: 'primollam maith'

GEARÓID Ó CRUALAOICH

As Chairperson of the opening session of the Conference that provided the starting-point for the collection of articles in this book, it fell to my lot to say something bearing on the man and the career that were honoured on that occasion. This prologue is a slightly altered version of that address.

Ó chúlra de Ghaeilge agus de Ghaeilgeoireacht a shíolraíonn muintir Sheáin agus dhein sé tógáil ann féin go luath ar oidhreachtaí teanga Bheanntraí agus Bhéarra agus Chairbre mar bhonnchloch lena bhfuil d'eolas agus de chumas aige i réimsí eile den Ghaeilge abhus is thall agus aníos trí stair na teanga ó thús. Ag éisteacht leis ag léachtóireacht as Gaeilge nó ag léamh duit a chuid altanna agus aistí Gaeilge, rithfeadh sé leat nár tharla an t-athrú teanga in aon chor in Iarthar Mumhan – toisc réimeanna teanga Chairbre agus Chorca Dhuibhne tríd is tríd chomh mór san ar a thoil aige agus friotal a bhéil agus a phinn chomh dílis sin dóibh.

This faithfulness in terms of linguistic identity is mirrored in other aspects of Seán's personal and academic life. Bantry and its hinterlands remain very dear to him and he is a frequent *comhairíoch* ('funeral-goer') in the case of the passing away of friends and old neighbours from Bantry and from Caheragh. It could be said of him that he never really left Bantry behind, but brought it with him on a life journey that has taken him from his grandfather's Borlin and Coomhola to Colomane and Cork, to Harvard and back to Cork again after a second stay on the banks of the Charles River in New England.

In the course of that journey – much of it in the company of his wife Carmel and their family of four daughters – he has encountered others whose influence on him has been great and whom he has brought with him as presences that inform his academic work as well as his intellectual and emotional life. I am thinking here of such figures as John V. Kelleher or Séamus Caomhánach or Seán Ó Ríordáin who have been his teachers, his mentors and his muses in a way that remains palpable in his fund of stories about them, and in his generous acknowledgment of their influence on him and on his work.

Another trait Seán has in abundance is that of leadership; a leadership born of exceptional competence and a willingness to put that competence to the service of Irish scholarship within and without the National University. As well as being a fair-minded and facilitating Department head, he has had leading roles on the academic council and governing body of University College Cork, and on both the senate of the National University of Ireland and the council of the Royal Irish Academy. Many Irish language committees and school boards have reason to be grateful to him for his counsel. Tá Bord na Gaeilge i gColáiste na hOllscoile, Corcaigh, fé chomaoin speisialta aige as a dhúthracht ar a shon.

In all this work, Seán has displayed constant qualities of patience, tolerance and even-handedness, together with an acute comprehension of the issues at hand. All regard him as a colleague of integrity beyond any or all 'party lines' – something that UCC rewarded by enticing him into the role of Staff Ombudsman for a considerable stint. In this capacity, we can believe that Seán too had learned from his Harvard mentor the benefits of what another Harvard graduate, the esteemed essayist Roger Rosenblatt, claims that John Kelleher taught *him*: 'that the world is full of subplots, mixed motives, deceits, all piled high in a generous puzzle ... that if one stays alert to the motions of the world, it is possible to see a great deal, occasionally including things that no one else has seen before'.[1]

If this is true in regard to Seán's execution of the duties of Ombudsman, it is doubly true in respect of his scholarship. His ability to be so constantly alert to the motions of all the worlds, textual and theoretical, to which he addresses his mind is a rare gift and his publications demonstrate a masterful and creative control of a multitude of areas within his fields of interest – a control that results from this alertness and its application – qualities that have always marked his studies.

His thematic analyses of narrative tradition and the structures of the literary cycle – originally pursued at Harvard under the aegis of his other renowned teacher there, Albert Lord – have continued to set standards for the study of Irish medieval and later literature, both lyric poetry and prose, in combining a dynamic understanding of literary production with a fully informed appreciation of social and historical context. His extraordinary book on the poetry and life of Seán Ó Ríordáin is a model of how intense scholarly scrutiny of a body of poetry, in the light of an intimate knowledge of the poet's mind and circumstances, can illuminate the creativity and humanity of both subject and author in a way that is at once devastatingly honest and delicately profound. His edition of the celebrated Blasket Island autobiography *An tOileánach* achieves a level of comprehensiveness and authoritativeness rarely encountered in the modern Irish canon and gives rise to a wish in all of us for such a quality of editorial work to be widespread henceforth.

I dteannta na stuamachta gur ceann dá chomharthaí soirt é, tá idir ghéire agus mhacántacht intinne ag Seán ná ligeann dó glacadh leis an míniú ná an réiteach ginearálta simplí ar cheist ar bith. Tuigeann sé go maith chomh casta agus chomh leochailleach agus atá cúrsaí an tsaoil daonna – agus léiriú na gcúrsaí sin – sa litríocht, sa stair agus ó thaobh an chultúir de. Bíonn an mheabhair cinn agus an fuinneamh aigne ann i gcónaí ag rómhar go grinneall,

1 M.J. Bailey, 'John V. Kelleher, retired Harvard professor', *Boston Globe*, 11 January 2004.

agus solus as an nua á chaitheamh ar bhunchúinsí an ábhair a bhíonn fé chaibidil aige. Sampla maith de seo is ea an t-alt 'Oral or literary? Some strands of the argument' a d'fhoillsigh sé tríocha a cúig bliain ó shoin, agus atá luaite ag oiread san údar in oiread san alt ó shoin.[2] Sampla eile, b'fhéidir, an aiste a shíolraigh ón gcaint a thug sé ag an gComhdháil Cheilteach anso i gCorcaigh i 1999 inar innis sé an fhírinne ghlan, mar ba ró-léir dó é, i dtaobh seasaimh an stáit i leith labhairt agus léann na Gaeilge.[3] Maidir leis an dtréith seo i Seán a ligeann dó – agus a thugann air – an fhírinne ghlan, ní hamháin a insint dúinn, ach a chur siar orainn go doshéanta, símplí, galánta, samhlaím é le hurlabhraí mór suaithinseach eile na fírinne, George Orwell, agus aith-nímse comhfhriotal Sheáin i roinnt d'aistí Orwell ar nós, cuirim i gcás, 'Bookshop memories', 'Some thoughts on the common toad', nó fiú, 'In praise of English cooking'.

Professor Ann Dooley, one of the recent co-translators of *Acallam na senórach*, is the author of one of the essays in this book. Seán Ó Coileáin has written a preface to another modern translation of the *Acallam* from the hand of Professor Maurice Harmon, his friend and colleague. Therein, Seán holds the *Acallam* 'worthy to stand comparison with anything that had gone before in the long history of Irish literature' and gives a number of justifications for this claim.[4] Among these are the work's perspective on the events it relates, a perspective that incorporates ancient and apparently incompatible material into a contemporary literary canon by the process of creative cultural and textual renewal – a renewal which is, to a certain extent, continued in the translation of the *Acallam* for a modern readership today. Seán Ó Coileáin's own contribution to that general process within the fields of Irish Studies and Irish-language scholarship – in terms of always-enlightened commentary and interpretation, and in terms of flawless editorial consolidation – has been outstanding. For this and for his loyalty, his collegiality and his generosity to us all, he deserves to have the praise given to Finn in the *Acallam* applied to himself: 'had the yellow leaves that strewed the woods in autumn all been gold, Finn, in his generosity, would have given it all away'; in Seán's own words, '[i]n Gaelic society, from beginning to end, there could be no greater praise than this'.[5] It is our wish in this volume of essays to render this greatest praise to Seán himself, and to wish him the good health and long life in the company of his family and his friends, which will enable him further to fulfill his scholarly and his personal ambitions.

Go maire tú an céad, a Ollaimh!

---

2 *Studia Hibernica*, 17–18 (1977–8), 7–35.   3 S. Ó Coileáin, 'Society and scholarship: Irish in the modern world' in M. Herbert and K. Murray (eds), *Retrospect and prospect in Celtic Studies* (2003), pp 45–58.   4 S. Ó Coileáin, 'Preface' in M. Harmon, *The dialogue of the ancients of Ireland* (2009), pp ix–x.   5 Ibid., p. x.

Seán Ó Coileáin: scholar

JOSEPH FALAKY NAGY

Given the theme of this collection of essays (and of the conference on which the collection was based), the most heartfelt compliment I could pay to Professor Seán Ó Coileáin is to say that, if Seán were to assemble and lead a *fian* (and – who knows? – perhaps upon his retirement he's thinking of doing just that), I would be the first to sign up. Even if I were to be a mere *gilla* providing entertainment by jumping back and forth over the *fulacht*; or (more suitably for my age, I suppose), a Garad mac Morna assigned the task of keeping an eye on the womenfolk, and maybe playing a game or two of *fid-chell* with them – I know I would have a good time in the company of one of the best, shrewdest, and wittiest minds 'in the business'.

Like the Finn mac Cumaill of *Acallam na senórach*,[1] Professor Ó Coileáin is a model of generosity, shown over the years to students and colleagues both in Ireland and in the United States. I still vividly remember running into him in Harvard's Widener Library back in the summer following my first year of college. I sheepishly asked him whether it might be possible for me to take the introductory Old Irish course he was scheduled to teach. He responded with enthusiasm and encouragement – none of the stand-offish snobbery of academics that can be encountered even in the field of Celtic studies. Fate intervened, however, and I did not have the opportunity to learn Old Irish with Professor Ó Coileáin after all, since he was soon invited to join the faculty of University College Cork, where he became a mainstay of the Department of Irish.

I also remember the time, several years later, when Professor Ó Coileáin graciously accepted our invitation to lecture at the UCLA Celtic Colloquium conference, held in the *bruidhean* that is Los Angeles, a meeting where those in attendance heard a preview of what was to become the now-classic article on the Irish lament tradition.[2] In his various publications on a wide range of topics, as well as in his presence, one always detects an adventurous spirit in Professor Ó Coileáin, a scholar who is open to new ideas and methods, and who sagaciously chooses, tests and shares them with his readership. Who else in our field could have written, for *Studia Hibernica*, the thoughtful review of the collected works of Milman Parry, the great pioneer in the study of Homeric and Serbo-Croatian oral epic composition, and actually made Parry's

---

1 For a description of Finn's munificent nature, see my contribution below, pp 97–8. 2 'The Irish lament: an oral genre', *Studia Hibernica*, 24 (1988), 97–117. With his typical thoughtfulness, he mentions this visit in the first footnote to the piece.

achievement compellingly relevant to the kind of work that usually appears in the pages of that journal?[3] Or, who else but Ó Coileáin could have brought and woven together so cogently the wealth of critical approaches on display in one of the 'Greatest Hits' of the late seventies, 'Oral or literary? some strands of the argument'?[4] Propp, Lévi-Strauss, Frye, Lord – these and other key contributors to oral-traditional and literary criticism of the last century figure meaningfully in Ó Coileáin's work, which in turn has developed its own critique and method.

One of the outstanding features of Seán's publications, useful for now and for the future, has been his unhesitating revision of revisionist views. An example of this 'meta-revisionism', especially relevant for the study of texts centered on Finn and his *fian*, is 'The setting of *Géisid cúan*' (in the *Festschrift* dedicated to his longtime UCC colleague, Professor Emeritus Pádraig Ó Riain).[5] The same sensitivity to the subtleties of the *Acallam* on display in that article is also in evidence in the oft-cited 'Place and placename in *fianaigheacht*' of 1993,[6] which I am proud to say as a long-time member, is a written testament to Ó Coileáin's plenary lecture to the Celtic Studies Association of North America, given at the Association's meeting in Nova Scotia the previous year, under the auspices of the late Professor Kenneth Nilsen of St Francis Xavier University.

Some may disagree, but in my opinion we are on the cusp of a renaissance in Celtic studies. It is truly heartening for those of us who remember lonelier days to see and hear all the young scholars, brimming with knowledge and energy, coming from varied backgrounds, and trained at universities from both sides of the Atlantic (as well as the Pacific), at meetings such as the recent Congress of Celtic Studies in Maynooth, and the memorable conference from which the proceedings in this volume derive. Among the members of this new generation, there are aspirations to attain the scholarly virtues we associate with perpetually vibrant and relevant figures in the field such as Seán: confident control over the sources combined with an openness to new approaches and concerns in the wider world of scholarship; a dedication to 'modern' as well as 'medieval' language and literature; and a gusto for specialisation which, however, does not preclude making contributions in other areas of Celtic studies. In his retirement, I am sure that Seán Ó Coileáin will view with satisfaction this new *fian* and its fresh adventures, while the mentors of these younger *fénnidi*, when they seek guidance, will continue to point them toward the magnanimous and magisterial paradigm we are celebrating in the following pages.

---

3 Review of *The making of Homeric verse: the collected papers of Milman Parry*, ed. Adam Parry, *Studia Hibernica*, 13 (1973), 171–8. 4 *Studia Hibernica*, 17–18 (1977–8), 7–35. 5 In J. Carey et al. (eds), *Cín Chille Cúile* (2004), pp 234–48 (reprinted in this volume). 6 *Studia Hibernica*, 27 (1993), 45–60 (reprinted in this volume).

Place and placename in *fianaigheacht*

SEÁN Ó COILEÁIN

Having given due acknowledgement to John Kelleher and to Gene Haley for their assistance in identifying the various places mentioned in the *Táin*, Thomas Kinsella wittily comments that 'the strange events of the *Táin* may be pure fant[a]sy or they may have some basis in fact – it is impossible to know. But even if they never happened, we know fairly accurately where they didn't'.[1] It might equally be said of the events of the *fianaigheacht*, at least from the twelfth century onwards, that even if they had happened we would scarcely have any idea where they did. These differing geographies, and the worlds they delineate, are the subject of what follows. It is not so much a question of place as of the sense of place, and the concern is with texture rather than with texts.

Of Kinsella's remark I have said elsewhere that 'it is as useful a distinction as any between the milieu of the hero of epic and that of the adventurer of romance'.[2] Alan Bruford adverts to the inadequacy of the conventional map to describe the world of Gaelic romance: while such a map can be provided up to a limit, even that limit does not represent a real boundary between known and unknown in terms of the imaginative universe being described. Having constructed what he calls 'a sort of map which shows the principal countries', he immediately concedes that 'it should ideally be in the form of a dial, with the central pin in Ireland, a fixed section covering Western

Reprinted from *Studia Hibernica*, 27 (1993), pp 45–60, with kind permission of the editors, particularly Dr Uáitéar Mac Gearailt. The presentation and referencing system have been brought into line with the norms of the volume; a number of minor authorial changes have been made to the content of the essay. Many thanks to Ms Ciara Ní Churnáin for creating the digital copy.

This paper is substantially the same as that read at the Annual Conference of the Celtic Studies Association of North America held in Antigonish, Nova Scotia, 21–24 May 1992. I wish to express my thanks to the organisers, particularly to Dr Kenneth Nilsen; the financial assistance of An Roinn Gnóthaí Eachtracha is gratefully acknowledged.

1 Foreword to illustrated guide to placenames of the *Táin* in *Ireland of the welcomes*, 24, no. 6 (Nov.–Dec. 1975), 20. There are, of course, some placenames in the *Táin* that are unidentifiable due, among other reasons, to 'their being merely descriptive words or phrases that might apply to any number of places, or the result of a storyteller's or scribe's rationalisation or fancy': T. Kinsella (trans.), *The Táin* (1970), p. xiv. Nevertheless, the general sense of realism, of which precision of place is but one aspect, which led the Chadwicks among others to regard it as resting substantially upon historical foundations, is far greater in the Ulster Cycle; see, for example, H.M. Chadwick and N.K. Chadwick, *The growth of literature*, vol. 1 (1932), pp 179, 236, and compare G. Murphy, *Saga and myth in ancient Ireland* (1955), p. 27.   2 S. Ó Coileáin, 'Irish literature' in J.R. Strayer (ed.), *Dictionary of the Middle Ages*, vol. 6 (1985), pp 521–33 at p. 531.

Europe, and all the other names rotating around it to be used at the romancer's whim'. Of the outer fringes of this world he says:

> Orkney (*Inis Orc*, *Inis Torc*) and Thule (*Inis Tuile*) are as imaginary as *Tír fo Thuinn* and *Tír Tairngire*, the Land under the Waves of folk tale and the Land of Promise of the older stories, which are sometimes treated as real kingdoms, and vaguely described regions such as *Tír an tSneachta* (Snowland) and *Tír an Óir* (Goldland), or the races of Catheads, Dogheads and Fair Men (*Caitchinn*, *Coinchinn*, *Fir Fhinn*), which all serve to swell the list.[3]

But the failure to observe physical (including geographical) division is as much internal as external: it is not merely a matter of near and far, of real and imaginary, but of an apprehension which is not bound by any of these considerations; this is a land where the strange is always familiar and the familiar often tinged with strangeness, where things are rarely what they seem and nothing ever really is but what is not.

The first essay in Carolly Erickson's *The medieval vision* begins with an account, contained in a late thirteenth-century manuscript, of three 'Mesopotamian monks' who set out to find 'the place where heaven and earth join'. The account of their journey 'combines several dimensions of reality into a single and continuous landscape', being at once a journey backwards through time to the garden of Eden, a spiritual pilgrimage with its associated 'theological topography', and a 'physical journey through the actual and speculative geography of the known world'. Physical, spiritual and chronological blend and become as one in this entirely congruous and self-contained landscape. Speaking of the creative interdependence of these various elements, Erickson says:

> The multiform reality which forms a backdrop to the monks' journey may be likened to an enchanted world in which the boundaries of imagination and factuality are constantly shifting. At one time the observed physical limits of time and space may be acknowledged; at another they may be ignored or, from another point of view, transcended. Yet so constant and automatic is this expansion and contraction of the field of perceived reality that it goes on unnoted and unreconciled by medieval writers. It belongs to those tacit norms of all cultures which, because they are more basic than perception itself, are rarely explicitly acknowledged.[4]

---

3 A. Bruford, *Gaelic folk-tales and mediaeval romances* (1969), p. 21 (= *Béaloideas*, 24 [1966], 21).
4 C. Erickson, *The medieval vision. Essays in history and perception* (1976), pp 3–6.

Even more than the Bruford quotation above, this strikes one as being of particular relevance to the Irish situation – for instance, it would need very little
qualification to be applied to *Acallam na senórach*; where Bruford analyses and
describes she synthesises and transmutes; he is concerned for the view of the
world as it appears in the distorting mirror of romance, she for the world that
is created by it, one that is of more than mere geographical extent or significance and that must be surveyed from within on its own terms, according to
what she calls 'a different view of reality' that 'underlay medieval perception'
in general.[5] For this purpose we need not observe the usual distinction
between *fianaigheacht* and romance, since we are not concerned with the
dramatis personae, their particular setting or attributes, but with the direction
towards which the narrative tends, as described by Northrop Frye:

> One direction is called 'romantic', the other 'realistic'. The realistic
> tendency moves in the direction of the representational and the dis-
> placed, the romantic tendency in the opposite direction, concentrating
> on the formulaic units of myth and metaphor. At the extreme of imag-
> ination we find the themes and motifs of folktale ... At the extreme of
> realism comes what is often called 'naturalism'...[6]

The heroic tale would likely fall into Frye's category of 'relatively serious literature', the relationship in this instance being with *fianaigheacht*/romance,
the type he would call 'the literature designed only to entertain or amuse'.[7]
But clearly realism need not correspond to an extra-literary reality and, con-
versely, with respect to the *fianaigheacht*, Kim McCone has 'attempted to
show that the early Irish *fian* had important economic and social functions
despite ecclesiastical reservations about its role'.[8] On the whole the attempt is

---

5 Ibid., p. 6. 6 N. Frye, *The secular scripture. A study of the structure of romance* (1976), p. 37.
Frye defines displacement as 'the adjusting of formulaic structures to the roughly credible context' (p. 36). 'Myth' is here to be understood not in the generally accepted sense of 'the more
important group of stories in the middle of a society's verbal culture', as defined in the preceding essay (p. 7), a definition which he had gone on to qualify and refine (p. 21), but according to the statement that 'the imagination is the power of building unities out of units. In
literature the unity is the *mythos* or narrative' (p. 36). Likewise, 'metaphor' has here a meaning
close to that which he assigns elsewhere to 'symbol': the units out of which the imagination con-
structs the unity of literature 'are metaphors, that is, images connected primarily with each other
rather than separately with the outer world' (ibid.). In N. Frye, *The anatomy of criticism* (1957),
he had similarly said of 'symbols' that they are 'simply and literally verbal elements, or units of
a verbal structure' (p. 73); symbols, so understood, make no statement except in relation to one
another (ibid., pp 80–1). 7 *The secular scripture*, p. 21. 8 K. McCone, 'Werewolves, cyclopes,
díberga and *fianna*: juvenile delinquency in early Ireland', *Cambridge Medieval Celtic Studies*, 12
(1986), 1–22 at 22. For the progressive narrowing of generic *fianaigheacht* to a specific tradition,
we may note the observation of P. Mac Cana that 'within the period encompassed by the written literature, say from the early seventh century onwards ... the Fionn cycle was in the ascen-

a convincing one, although at the outset he seems to misrepresent Gerard Murphy's stance with regard to the question of the cultivation and preservation of *fianaigheacht* in general prior to the twelfth century, saying of it that:

> Gerard Murphy ascribed the poor showing of Fenian tales in the early literary record to their essentially popular orientation in comparison with the 'aristocratically-conditioned' Ulster sagas and so on cultivated by monastic *literati*, but this observation is hardly valid in view of the intensely aristocratic leanings of the *Agallamh*, which again and again depicts *fian*-members as the sons of kings.[9]

Professor Murphy, who knew the material better than anyone, nowhere speaks of the 'essentially popular orientation' of *fianaigheacht*; what he says, referring at first to 'tales of gods, heroes and kings', is:

> When those aristocratically-conditioned tales were being told in kings' [sic leg.] palaces and at royal *óenaige* in ninth and tenth-century Ireland, simple folk, seated by their firesides or in their fishing-boats, probably preferred to tell magically-controlled tales about Fionn mac Cumha[i]ll and his Fiana, such as their descendants have continued to tell down to the present day.[10]

Now not only can a cat look at a king but a peasant can tell tales about him and frequently does – witness the *mac rí in Éirinn* of modern folktale – though no doubt the royal figure was frequently visualised after the manner of a Werenskiold drawing. A list of references to mentions of sons of kings in the *Acallam*, such as that supplied by McCone, no more proves the aristocratic connections of those who cultivated it, or to whom it served as entertainment, than the obsession of the present-day British tabloids with royalty proves their readers (or their writers) to be of noble blood. There is frequently an inverse relationship in such things – it seemed to Frye that 'one very obvious feature of romance is its pervasive social snobbery'[11] – although what the precise relationship may have been in this case one cannot finally say.

Indeed there would seem to be a great deal of common ground, more perhaps than would appear from the above, between the theories of various scholars regarding the origin and development of *fianaigheacht*. So Eoin MacNeill would have it originate among the Gáileóin and would distinguish

---

dant as a comprehensive expression of *fianaigecht*, expanding and diversifying and assimilating to itself the traditions of the other *fiana* and their leaders': Mac Cana, '*Fianaigecht* in the pre-Norman period' in Bo Almqvist et al. (eds), *The heroic process* (1987), pp 75–99 at p. 83. 9 McCone, 'Werewolves, cyclopes, *díberga* and *fianna*', 2. 10 G. Murphy, *The Ossianic lore and romantic tales of medieval Ireland* (1961), p. 5. 11 *The secular scripture*, p. 161.

it 'from ... almost every other primitive epic in that it is the hero-lore of a subject, not a ruling race'; it 'remained in the possession of the subject races apparently until about the tenth century' when the 'prejudices of conquest had ... grown feeble', assisted in no small measure by the contribution of the Church and by a harmonising school of history which had developed a 'new theory of racial unity, of a common descent' which 'marked the final disappearance of race prejudices', leading to the adoption of the *fianaigheacht* as the 'property of the whole nation without any burden of learned prestige' and correspondingly 'open to every kind of development'.[12]

The comparative evidence impels Marie-Louise Sjoestedt to reject this theory of pre-Celtic and consequently non-Indo European origin, although she allows it to be '*a priori* probable ... that the dispossessed classes played a part in the elaboration and diffusion of these myths';[13] her final summation does not greatly differ from his in terms of the working out of the process:

> The myth of Cú Chulainn, a heritage of ordered society, of princes, scholars and clerics, after dominating for a long time the literary tradition of the propertied classes, declined and disappeared with that society and those classes. The myth of the *fiana*, relegated for centuries to the shadow of oral tradition, shares the longevity of folklore and survives to this day in the folktales of the people.[14]

From here it is no great distance to Murphy's 'simple folk' and the essential continuity of the tradition up to modern times, with the qualification that he would place particular emphasis on the political events of the twelfth century – although his presentation of these events now makes less than convincing reading – and particularly on the social upheaval following the arrival of the Anglo-Normans as a factor in the acceptance of *fianaigheacht* as a proper subject for literature.[15]

For Professor McCone, accounting for the different situations early and late,

> The evidence points ... to a marked clerical aversion to the *fían* in the early period because it embodied values which were perceived as a threat to the hierarchical, settled society of the *túath* in which the Church had a vested interest. In time this aversion seems to have diminished as the threat of the *fían* receded ...

---

12 E. MacNeill and G. Murphy (ed. agus trans.), *Duanaire Finn*, 3 vols (1908–53), i, pp xxxii–xli.   13 M.-L. Sjoestedt, *Gods and heroes of the Celts*, trans. M. Dillon (1949), p. 88; compare the remarks of P. Mac Cana, '*Fianaigecht* in the pre-Norman period', p. 94.   14 Ibid., p. 91.   15 Murphy, *The Ossianic lore*, pp 16, 30; cf. idem, 'Irish storytelling after the coming of the Normans' in B. Ó Cuív (ed.), *Seven centuries of Irish learning: 1000–1700* (1961), pp 72–86 at pp 74–7.

It is difficult to see why the clerical establishment should have campaigned so vehemently and insistently against the *fian* and what it stood for in the early Christian period unless the institution was a social reality perceived as an all too real threat to a system of law and order in which the church had a heavy vested interest.[16]

Underlying all of these positions is the premiss of two parallel traditions in the early period: higher and lower, literary and non-literary; and although the precise motives supplied for the submergence and later emergence of *fianaigheacht* in literary tradition vary with regard to emphasis, they are all clearly related to social status of one kind or another; even McCone, who assigns a prominent role to the 'clerical establishment' in the suppression of the *fian*, visualises it as doing so primarily because of its own stake in maintaining the *status quo*. (It is hardly necessary to say that, while there is obviously a connection of some sort, the persons of the *fian* are no more to be equated with the tradition-bearers spoken of earlier than the social institution is with the narrative; to do so would be to confuse the known literary with the half-known historical, the imperfectly understood fact with its oblique representation.)

T.F. O'Rahilly observed that 'unlike the heroes of the Ulidian tales, Finn mac Cumaill and the members of his *fiana* are entirely ignored by the genealogists and the authors of Lebor Gabála'.[17] Rolf Baumgarten makes a similar comment and finds in this functional lack an explanation of the poor showing of *fianaigheacht*, whether as substantial text or in vestigial tale-list form, before the very late Middle-Irish period:

> The Fenian tales ... were not of societal relevance: they had no tribal, historical, genealogical or religious function. This, possibly, explains their absence ... from the extant type of pre-Norman codices and from the tale-lists.[18]

This statement points two ways: backward to the question of origins and causes which, even if they could be securely established, would tell us little about the texts as we have them and, perhaps inadvertently, forward and inward to the imaginative world of composer and composition. Marie-Louise Sjoestedt in her remarkable little book whose potential has only recently been realised and developed, most notably by Joseph Nagy,[19] speaks of the *fianaigheacht* in terms of a 'fluid mythical world in which the species are not

---

16 McCone, 'Werewolves, cyclopes, *díberga* and *fianna*', 2, 6.   17 T.F. O'Rahilly, *Early Irish history and mythology* (1946), p. 274.   18 R. Baumgarten, 'Placenames, etymology and the structure of *fianaigecht*' in B. Almqvist et al. (eds), *The heroic process* (1987), pp 1–24 at p. 16.   19 Especially in Nagy, *The wisdom of the outlaw* (1985), passim.

separated by rigid distinctions'.[20] O'Rahilly, too, noted in a somewhat different context and style that 'the Finnian tales are much more elastic' than those
of the Ulster Cycle which are 'tied down geographically and are assigned to
a definite period of pseudo-history'.[21] Either way, this is not an area in which
one would wish to anchor one's social standing or prospects of advancement;
as it relates to the written record, it is not, I suggest, so much a matter of
cause or effect, though effect there may have been, as of the ethos being quite
other. That otherness would have been at odds with the four coordinates
sought of every composition, *locc, persa, aimser* and *fáth airicc*, in the most
fundamental possible way, at the level of conception itself. The medium, if
not the entire message, is a considerable part of it, for this is not the ordered
world of geography, history or chronology which between them would have
supplied a ready motive; motive (*fáth airicc*) there must be, but for this one
is disposed to agree with the opinion of the angels who justify the writing of
the *Acallam* to St Patrick on the grounds that it may be as 'gairdiughadh do
dronguibh 7 do degdáinib deridh aimsire éisdecht frisna scéluib sin' (*AS* ll.
301–2; cf. ll. 1062–3) – in other words nothing for the generality of scholars
ancient or modern to be too concerned about, and in this they were clearly
right. (Not so with regard to the endurance of the stories it contains for, as
Stokes comments, 'In Ireland, at least, there are now few companies and no
nobles that are able to read them', nor does the number increase with the
passing years.)[22] We recall Frye's observation that:

> any serious study of romance has to take into account its curiously pro-
> letarian status as a form generally disapproved of, in most ages, by the
> guardians of taste and learning ... The close connection of the roman-
> tic and the popular runs all through literature.

One definition of popular literature might be

> the literature that demands the minimum of previous verbal experience
> and special education from the reader ... When we apply this concep-
> tion of the popular to stories in prose, we find ourselves again close to
> folktale.

Not being of the same significance to those in authority, the romance will also
lack the complex erudition and controlled frame of reference we expect to
find in what he calls 'elite' literature.[23]

20 Sjoestedt, *Gods and heroes of the Celts*, p. 85.   **21** O'Rahilly, *Early Irish history and mythology*, pp 273–4.   **22** W. Stokes (ed. and partial trans.), 'Acallamh na senórach' in W. Stokes and
E. Windisch (eds), *Irische Texte*, iv, 1 (1900), p. xii.   **23** *The secular scripture*, pp 23, 26–7. The
main line of argument here is remarkably similar to that of Murphy, 'Irish storytelling after the
coming of the Normans', pp 73–6.

Of the coordinates mentioned above, only that of place properly concerns us here, although, in general looseness of composition and treatment, personal names frequently suggest a similar factitious process and give the appearance of being equally unlocated in respect of established pedigrees; the similarity is not surprising for the personal name is to the pedigree as the placename is to the topography. In the dissolving world of *fianaigheacht*, names of places and persons are reabsorbed by the poetics that created them and from which they had never really escaped to begin with. The most outstanding feature of the chronology of *Acallam na senórach*, the longevity of Oisín and Caílte, which underlies the text, has lately been considered in detail by Máirtín Ó Briain;[24] on the matter of chronology generally, in the *Acallam* and elsewhere, one might give as a general rule that to speak of anachronism is to be oneself anachronistic, to use inappropriate terms of reference: each text is its own contemporary, in and of its own time, and all other temporal considerations are subservient to that one. So, too, of all 'incongruity' and 'inconsistency': if the matter did not disturb the shared consciousness of author and audience, neither should it trouble the modern reader except in so far as he is obliged to appreciate that fact. We cannot insist on our own terms: knowledge, to be useful, must relate to its subject rather than stand apart from it; otherwise it becomes an impediment. History is not thereby made redundant, but more diverse and meaningful. As Alfred Nutt succinctly stated long ago, 'what the historian seeks for in legend is far more a picture of the society in which it took rise than a record of the events it commemorates',[25] although the event commemorated and the society which commemorates may be closely connected as Máire Herbert has shown for *Fled Dúin na nGéd* of which she concludes that it 'is a tale influenced by, and seeking to be influential in, its contemporary society. It chooses to represent the present in terms of the past, recreating a narrative of political events of the seventh century in order to communicate the concerns of its own day'.[26] It is, therefore, not so much a matter of the past as preserved and understood in the present (history) as the past being made serve a present purpose in narrative form (political allegory). Here what matters to the historian is the manner of translation and application in order to effect what Dr Herbert calls 'a paradigm of contemporary reality',[27] not if the allegorical details correspond to what we know of seventh-century history. And while there is an abiding tension between the facts of history and those of literature – the latter being essentially, in Frye's words,

24 M. Ó Briain, 'Some material on Oisín in the Land of Youth' in D. Ó Corráin et al. (eds), *Sages, saints and storytellers* (1989), pp 181–99 at pp 184–7.   25 A. Nutt, *Ossian and Ossianic literature* (1910), p. 11. We may compare Kenney's observation: 'Primarily, the *acta sanctorum* are sources for the times in which they were written and revised, not for those in which their heroes flourished'; J.F. Kenney, *The sources for the early history of Ireland* (1929), p. 297.   26 M. Herbert, 'Fled Dúin na nGéd: a reappraisal', *Cambridge Medieval Celtic Studies*, 18 (1989), 75–87 at 86.   27 Ibid., 87.

'always a form of "lying", that is, of turning away from the descriptive use of language and the correspondence form of truth'[28] – it does not thereby follow that bad literary criticism makes good history: if one discipline is flawed the other must inevitably be so too when used in conjunction with it.

So also, if I understand him correctly, Joseph Nagy would see the events described in *Acallam na senórach* as a general metaphor for the 'paradoxical juxtaposing of literary and oral that is the premise ... of all medieval Irish literature based on traditional materials', with all that this involved in terms of form and content.[29] Of course, like all metaphors, it cannot be applied too literally, nor in respect of every detail, and Professor Nagy is careful to acknowledge that the reality would have been a far more complicated business; the *Acallam* itself is an untraditional text fashioned in traditional prosimetrum form out of what we generally assume to have been more-or-less traditional sources, and in no wise can it, or any part of it, be regarded as raw oral literature. Incidentally, I would say here with regard to the term 'oral literature', now in general use although described by one of the most distinguished American folklore scholars of this century as rather grating every time he heard it,[30] that not only is it an acceptable term but almost invariably the only acceptable one to describe the thing: for, whether speculating on the origin of twelfth-century material or dealing with twentieth-century material of known oral origin, the oral event, in and through which it lived, or may have done so, is now past, and no amount of information, no matter how detailed or imaginative, can ever restore it. We are dealing with textual matter, albeit of a rather special kind. Given this innate contradiction, it is only fitting that we should use an oxymoron ('oral literature') to describe it.

In the introduction to his edition of the *Acallam*, Stokes comments on the difficulty caused him by the placenames: 'I have vainly tried to identify many of the localities mentioned in the *Acallam*. A Gaelic onomasticon may, I am told, be expected from Father Hogan. By one Irishman, at all events, it will be gratefully welcomed'.[31] In view of earlier comments, the fact that Hogan's *Onomasticon* has not greatly improved matters need not surprise us. Whatever other shortcomings the work might have, it could not be expected to be more precise than its sources, an imprecision that derived from the nature of the material; rather than viewing it as a matter of unfinished business, a problem still to be overcome, it turns out not to be a problem at all, or rather one of a different order. The first example below is taken not from the *Acallam* but

---

28 *The secular scripture*, p. 46.   29 J.F. Nagy, 'Compositional concerns in the *Acallam na senórach*' in D. Ó Corráin et al. (eds), *Sages, saints and storytellers* (1989), pp 149–58 at p. 157. 30 R.M. Dorson, in B.A. Stolz and R.S. Shannon III (eds), *Oral literature and the formula* (1976), p. 170. Similarly Walter Ong would regard it as a 'strictly preposterous term': W. Ong, *Orality and literacy* (1982), p. 11. For a more sympathetic view, see the comments of J. Harris in idem (ed.), *The ballad and oral literature* (1991), pp 9–12.   31 Stokes, 'Acallamh', p. xiii.

from the well-known lay on the blackbird of Doire an Chairn which, in view
of the simplicity of its language, probably dates from the very end of the
Early Modern period; following a brief account of Fionn's acquiring the bird
in Lochlainn and its transference to Doire an Chairn, there comes a catalogue
of the sounds in which the Fian delighted, commencing with the song of the
blackbird; inevitably in terms of the underlying conceit, which is a development of that on which the *Acallam* itself is based, these sounds are those of
nature which are favourably contrasted with the ringing of the church bells
that symbolise the new order.

> Sgolghaire luin Doire an Chairn,
> búithre an daimh o Aill na gCaor,
> ceól le gcolladh Fionn go moch,
> lachain ó Loch na dTrí gCaol.
>
> Cearca fraoich um Chruachain Chuinn,
> feadghail dobhráin Druim Dhá Loch,
> gotha fiulair Ghlinn na bhFuath,
> longhaire cuach Chnuic na Sgoth.
>
> Gotha gadhair Ghleanna Caoin,
> is gáir fhiulair chaoich na sealg,
> tairm na tuinne ag triall go moch
> isteach ó Thráigh na gCloch nDearg.[32]

Ostensibly this contains nine different placenames with upper-case initial, each,
with the exception of the last, listed in the index with occasional attempts at
identification. All of these may be actual placenames and some, such as
Cruachain, certainly are. Doire an Chairn itself, O'Rahilly suggests, may stand
for 'Derreenacarrin, a place half-way between Glengarriff and Adrigole, in the
Beare peninsula'.[33] And while O'Rahilly does not mention it, Loch na dTrí
gCaol was the name sometimes given to Castlemaine Harbour in the inner
reaches of Dingle Bay, where three sandspits extending from the peninsulas
on either side give rise to the effect described in the name.[34] But as well as
designating a place, if it does, each also forms part of the texture of the poem
and the cumulative effect is not so much referential as evocative; in other
words it would be quite in order to write all except Cruachain with lower case
initials, so that they point inwards to the poem and to their own contextual
relationship rather than outwards to some location beyond: we are shown the

32 T.F. O'Rahilly (ed.), *Measgra dánta* (1927), p. 55.   33 Ibid., p. 113.   34 An Seabhac
(Pádraig Ó Siochfhradha), *Triocha-céad Chorca Dhuibhne* (1939), map facing p. [1], pp 3–4, 198,
209.

wood on the mound, the cliff of the berries, the lake/inlet of the three nar-
rows, the ridge of two lakes, the glen of the spectres, the hill of the blossoms,
the beautiful glen and the strand of the red stones – everywhere and nowhere.
Necessity to choose a precise location is a factor of geography, of outside considerations; here the places have become internalised as literature with no
physical or other restriction beyond that set by the resources of the poem
itself. Places have become words, perhaps always were words. Whatever independent existence they might previously have had as places, it is clear that, if
not in some cases actually invented for the purpose, they have, at very least,
been selected and arranged to particular effect. Nobody hearing the lay would
have concerned to abstract and separately define them; not being specific to
any place, the names could be taken to refer to many and would settle unques-
tioned in the imagination. These are not the far regions of the romantic tale
of which Bruford spoke, although Lochlainn lies just beyond the horizon of
the poem, but then romance has never been a direct factor of physical distance
(for distance can also be imaginative and stylistic), but much more a matter of
the intangible of which physical distance is but one, fairly crude, aspect; here
that sense of the intangible has suffused the landscape of the poem so that,
while all around, it must remain forever unvisited.

Concluding his essay on 'Etymological aetiology in Irish tradition',
Professor Baumgarten remarks of the placename patterns he has examined in
it that 'one could say, descriptively and from a modern point of view, that
names are moved from denotation to connotation'.[35] In the context, the
agency of that move is aetiology, often working through medieval etymology,
but the effect, what he calls 'de-onymization',[36] the reduction of the locative
function, seems to me to be similar to that described above. He cites from the
Acallam such examples as *Sliab Echtge inghine Nuadha[t] Aircetlaim* (*AS* l.
1011) and *Loch Greine ingine Finn* (*AS* l. 1013) where the eponymic *Echtge*
and *Grian* is each supplemented by the patronymic extension. He comments
that 'in cases such as these the placename is de-onymized to such an extent
that it cannot be retained, as would be usual in modern editorial practice, in
its Irish form in a translation of the text'. The final example of this kind as
printed in Stokes' edition is *leathanMagh Luirg in Dagda* (*AS* ll. 1501–2). So
expanded, *Mag Luirg* has ceased to be a placename proper; Baumgarten
would dispose of the capitals and translate 'the wide "plane of the track" of
the Dagda'.[37] It is clear that the placename here verges on narrative, if it has
not actually passed over into it, as the placenames of the Doire an Chairn lay
have passed over into description. In either case, the placename is simultane-

---

35 *Ériu*, 41 (1990), 115–22, at 121.   36 Ibid., 116.   37 Ibid., 117–18. The asterisk which he
places on *Grian* is redundant since the nominative is attested elsewhere: 'Loch Gréine, Grían
ingen Find' in E.J. Gwynn (ed. and trans.), *The metrical dindshenchas*, 5 vols (1906–35), iii, p.
306.37.

ously more and less than what it purports to be: in the poem, the word picture is already painted and available for appreciation in the text, while, in the *Acallam*, there is frequently an implied narrative that remains to some degree beyond the text compelling one to draw from other sources for its completion. Whether these sources are traditionally supplied, or even whether there may have been a tradition to supply them in every instance, is a secondary question: the result is a random series of what we may call 'out-tales' in whose creation we imaginatively participate, following out, as we must, the textual allusion which can sometimes amount to what reads as a brief summary supplied by way of etiological explanation. These 'out-tales' function as loosely attached satellites of the larger narrative, itself the aggregate of a fixed series of self-sufficient in-tales.

This kind of secondary incomplete telling by allusion is also typical of the roughly contemporary prose *dinnshenchas*. That this should be so is not surprising: Gerard Murphy points out that

> The first mention of *Acallam na senórach* in Irish literature occurs in a recension of *Dinnshenchus Érenn* ('The place-lore of Ireland') belonging to the last quarter of the twelfth century. In that recension a poem on *Tonn Chlidna* is said to have been uttered by 'Caílte in the time of Patrick in the course of the Colloquy (*Acallam*) they carried on concerning the placelore (*dinnshenchus*) of Ireland'. This proves that the Acallam was in existence in the last quarter of the twelfth century and was then regarded by the learned as essentially a branch of *dinnshenchus* literature.[38]

This does not mean, of course, that one will serve to explain the other – only that we are dealing with a more widespread phenomenon. In a phrase that has been widely adopted, Marie-Louise Sjoestedt called the *dinnshenchas* 'the mythological geography of the country' just as the *Lebor gabála* was 'its mythological prehistory'.[39] Although he had not read her book at the time – he was later to dismiss it out of hand as being 'of slender value to the expert, and perhaps more likely to mislead than to enlighten the general reader'[40] – O'Rahilly's comment is apposite: 'Actually Lebor Gabála is no more a mythological treatise than it is an historical one'.[41] In terms of the work taken as a

---

38 Murphy, *The Ossianic lore*, p. 24. The reference is to the Book of Ballymote (Royal Irish Academy MS 23 P 12) 374b1–2 which Ní Shéaghdha (*Agallamh*, i, p. xi) transcribes: '*amail ro can Caílti i n-aimsir Pátraig ar an agall*aim *do-rōnsat ar dindshenchus Ér*enn'. Cf. W. Stokes (ed. and trans.), 'The prose tales in the Rennes dindshenchas', *Révue Celtique*, 15 (1894), 272–336, 418–84; and 16 (1895), 31–83, 135–67, 269–312 (vol. 15, 437–8). **39** Sjoestedt, *Gods and heroes of the Celts*, p. 1. **40** *Celtica* 1, ii (1950), 398. Her work on the mythology has worn much better than his, her superior method proving more valuable than his unrivalled mastery of detail. **41** O'Rahilly, *Early Irish history and mythology*, p. 164.

whole and viewed conventionally, O'Rahilly's judgement would still have to
be regarded as generally valid. But as we move from the event represented to
the representation of the event, from knowledge of the past in the present to
knowledge of the present in the past, another perspective becomes possible,
that described by Mark Scowcroft, speaking again of the *Lebor gabála*: 'This
fusion of fact and fiction, of native and Latin (pagan and Christian) tradition
furnishes the Irish *literati* with their own mythology – a history and re-enact-
ment of the order of things – and with a historical framework for the sagas,
the annals and chronicles'.[42] It is only in some such sense, although its terms
of reference are far less comprehensive and ambitious, that we can speak, it
seems to me, of the *dinnshenchas* as 'mythological geography', although
Sjoestedt's description is curiously reminiscent of the terms 'theological
topography', 'theological geography', used by Carolly Erickson to describe a
world that bordered on the real and sometimes mingled with it in the
medieval imagination.[43] Proinsias Mac Cana, who brings an impressive range
of primary and secondary sources to bear on the question, would generally
tend to be more generous in his appraisal, and indeed cites Sjoestedt's phrase
with approval and supporting argument.[44] To what extent and at what period
we may suppose the medieval science of etymology, through which much of
the *dinnshenchas* is mediated, to have facilitated a mythopoeic process, and
when that science comes to reproduce itself with little sense of restraint from
the subject to which it is applied, is a moot question, but it is clear that by
the period of compilation in the twelfth century, at any rate, mythopoesis has
largely become mere poesis, a matter of describing empty figures on what
might as well have been a blank page. This is not to deny that the science
itself is a defensible one (and it has recently found a stout apologist in
Professor Baumgarten),[45] or that genuine tradition undoubtedly survived the
process as well as persisting quite independently of it up to modern times; it
is a question of the relationship and its outcome as viewed in terms of its usefulness as a guide to the *status quo ante*. Professor Mac Cana is, of course,
aware of this difficulty noting that 'it is not always easy in dealing with early
written tradition to distinguish between learned pedantry and banality on the
one hand and inherited patterns of thought on the other';[46] indeed if one were
to quarrel with this statement it would only be in order to follow Baumgarten
in questioning the description of the methods of the etymologist as 'learned
pedantry and banality'.

42 R.M. Scowcroft, '*Leabhar gabhála*. Part 1: the growth of the text', *Ériu*, 38 (1987), 82–142
at 82.   43 Erickson, *The medieval vision*, pp 5, 7.   44 P. Mac Cana, 'Placenames and mythology in Irish tradition: places, pilgrimages and things' in G.W. MacLennan (ed.), *Proceedings of
the First North American Congress of Celtic Studies* (1982), pp 319–41 at p. 333.   45 Baumgarten,
'Placenames, etymology and the structure of *fianaigecht*' and 'Etymological aetiology in Irish tradition'; in addition, see idem, 'A Hiberno-Isidorian etymology', *Peritia*, 2 (1983), 225–8.   46
Mac Cana, 'Placenames and mythology in Irish tradition', p. 339.

In the same context, Mac Cana remarks on a typical feature of the place-name in *Acallam na senórach*: its seeming double identity. The text 'offers endless minor variations on the phrase "X which is now/today called Y", a constantly reiterated reminder that toponomy is in fact (sacred) history'.[47] That may be to take the model too much at its face value. Instead of being named twice, the place may not in fact be named at all. Not only is it doubt-ful that the 'earlier' name ever had any reality outside of the text, but the 'later' one also frequently serves to suggest the subject matter of a story other than that ostensibly being told. As an example, we might cite the following from O'Grady's translation:

> Touching Caeilte now: on he went northwards to the wide plain of *lorg an Daghda* ...; across *coirrléim na féinne*, which at this time is called *eas mac nEirc* or 'the water-fall of Erc's sons' [sic leg.]; northwards yet into *sliabh Seghsa* or 'the Curlieu mountains'; into *berna na gcét*, now called *céis Chorainn* or 'Keshcorann', and out upon the Corann's level lands.
>
> Here they heard a great rushing sound that came towards them, and with a glance that Caeilte threw around him he discerned nine wild stags in swift career. At these they [Caeilte and his eight] deliv-ered nine javelins, and so killed the nine deer; whereby they had that night's provision. They pack the venison on them, and bring it along to *eas meic Modairn* or 'the waterfall of Modarn's son', now called *eas dara* or 'Ballysodare'; into *críoch an chosnama*, which is called *críoch Chairbre* or 'the barony of Carbery'; past the *rinn* or 'point' of Ebha daughter of Geibtine mac Morna: the place where a tidal wave drown-ed her; skirting *druim derg*, now called *druim cliabh* or 'Drumcliff', and *áth an chomraic* or 'the fighting ford', now called *áth an daimh ghlais* or 'the grey stag's ford'. Thence they held on to *lecht na muice* or 'the swine grave', where once the wild pig killed Duibhne's grandson Dermot; and to the *tulach*'s top where *leaba Dhiarmata*, 'Dermot's bed', is. There Caeilte laid his weapons on the ground, and himself lay down on his dear comrade's grave and place of rest ...[48]

This is neither history nor geography proper, though presented under the guise of both, since there is no very good reason to think that the name underwent the supposed change or even that, in some cases, it ended up in any particular place. The formula functions as a compositional device. Here to the slight story of the stag hunt are added, almost subliminally and by stealth, numerous others. Some of these may never have had more than a potential existence, as it were, to be actualised only in the imagination of the

47 Ibid., p. 338.   48 O'Grady, *Silva gadelica*, ii, pp 137–8. The emendation *eas meic Néra* to *eas mac nEirc* is due to Stokes, 'Acallamh', p. 285, with reference to l. 1502.

hearer. So *coirrléim na Féinne* ('the prodigious (?) leap of the *Fían*'), *berna na gcét* ('the gap of the hundreds'), *críoch an chosnama* ('the land of strife'), *druim derg* ('the red ridge') and *áth an chomraic* ('the ford of battle') each has its own sub-text. The 'later' names (the 'lateness' being purely textual) tend to be more substantial, although there is little to choose between *áth an chomraic* and *áth an daimh ghlais* (wisely ignored by Hogan) in this respect. And even when the placename is a 'real' one, reality always being a relative term in this context, it still inclines towards narrative. The instance of the development of *leathanMagh Luirg in Dagda*, already discussed, refers to this passage, and *Rinn Ebha* comes already supplied not only with the extension of name but with its *senchas*. Towards the end, all pretence of distinction is abandoned: with *lecht na muice* and *leaba Dhiarmata* the place is clearly subsidiary to the name and the landmarks are now frankly those of story, the obviously already well-known one of *Tóraigheacht Dhiarmada agus Ghráinne*. Sjoestedt has observed that:

> Living on the margin of human affairs, as advanced outposts of the natural world in the supernatural world, the heroes of the *fiana* have a part in both these worlds and a double character.[49]

It is not surprising that the placenames should share in this ambivalence, which was to serve the *fianaigheacht* well in taking its place in the new world of romance.

---

49 Sjoestedt, *Gods and heroes of the Celts*, p. 85.

The Roscommon *locus* of *Acallam na senórach* and some thoughts as to *tempus* and *persona*

ANNE CONNON

Seán Ó Coileáin memorably wrote that the placenames in *Acallam na senórach* 'incline towards narrative', adding that the stories which the names suggest – the 'out-tales', to use his phrasing – were often different from those ostensibly being told.[1] This contribution takes the position that it is not only the names of places in the *Acallam* that allude to stories outside the text, but also the actual places themselves. The particular 'out-tale' to be explored here is one pieced together from places visited in the course of the three journeys made to Connacht in the *Acallam*. The composite landscapes created by these places tell a story, indeed several stories, of their own. My aim is to argue that one of the stories they tell is that *Acallam na senórach*, in the form we now have it, was written in the Augustinian house of canons regular at Roscommon.

The study is divided into three sections. The first, and by far the longest, section of the paper makes the case for Roscommon as the *locus* of composition of the *Acallam*. The shorter second and third sections present some speculative thoughts on *tempus* and *persona* that follow on from the arguments regarding place. The foundation underpinning all three sections is the pioneering work of Ann Dooley on the historical context of *Acallam na senórach*. In a 2004 article, Dooley argued that the *Acallam* was a product of Connacht, the backdrop to more journeys in the text than any other province. Suggesting that *Acallam na senórach* was composed during the reign of Cathal Crobderg Úa Conchobair as king of Connacht (*c.*1190–1200; 1202–24), Dooley highlighted the role of the Síl Muiredaig sept of Muinter Roduib – and their Aghagower connections – in the composition of the text.[2] Her observations on the significance of Muinter Roduib to *Acallam na senórach* form a central plank in my case for Roscommon as the *locus* of composition of the text. Although my conclusions ultimately take a different turn, the debt they owe to Dooley's approach and arguments is considerable.

---

1 S. Ó Coileáin, 'Place and placename in *fianaigheacht*', *Studia Hibernica*, 27 (1993), 45–60 at 59–60 (reprinted in this volume). It is an honour to contribute this piece to a collection celebrating Professor Seán Ó Coileáin, whose scholarship I so admire, and whose kindness to my family during our time in Cork was so appreciated. 2 A. Dooley, 'The date and purpose of *Acallam na senórach*', *Éigse*, 34 (2004), 97–126 at 120–2.

I. *LOCUS*

Ros Comáin, the monastery of Roscommon, takes its name from its founding
saint, Comán mac Fáelchon, a member of the east Galway people known as
the Sogain.[3] Comán's death is entered in the annals under the year 747.[4]
According to the Annals of the Four Masters, Comán was abbot of
Clonmacnoise, and this link between the two religious houses was to continue
throughout much of their history. Several of Roscommon's tenth- and
eleventh-century abbots were also abbots of Clonmacnoise, and it is possible
that Roscommon was a daughter house of Ciarán's famous monastery.[5]
Certainly both ecclesiastical institutions were intimately connected with Síl
Muiredaig, the royal house of Connacht.[6]

In the 1140s, the monastery of Roscommon became an Augustinian house
of canons, probably under the aegis of the reforming king of Connacht and
Ireland, Toirdelbach Úa Conchobair.[7] More than a hundred years later, likely
several decades after the composition of the *Acallam*, the Dominican order
also founded a priory at Roscommon. Until the sixteenth-century dissolution
of the monasteries, the two ecclesiastical houses co-existed in Roscommon
town. Today, there are still fine upstanding remains of the Dominican priory,
but the Augustinian house survives only in architectural fragments incorporated into the Church of Ireland church that stands in its place. Its name,
however, endures, not only in the name of the town, but also in the name of
a parish, barony and county.[8]

The central argument for seeing Roscommon as the place of composition
of the *Acallam* is the monastery's position as the nexus of the text's
Connacht-related interests. 'Ros Comáin' itself features as one of the sites
named in the first Connacht journey in the *Acallam*; however, the notice is
brief, mainly included as part of a 'laundry-list' type sequence of placenames
describing Patrick and Cáilte's route from Loch Cróine to Ráith Brénainn.
Rather than standing out as a single site where particularly noteworthy tales
are set, Roscommon's importance for the text is instead underlined by its centrality to whole landscapes of Connacht sites in the *Acallam*. Most significantly, it represents the intersection of the text's dynastic landscape with its
physical landscape.

---

3 ATig. 747.   4 AU 747.12; ATig. 747; Cott. [k 4]; AFM 742, 746. The Annals of the Four
Masters state that Comán was 200 years old at his death, a claim which presumably relates to the
tradition that Comán was a sixth-century bishop associated with Finnian of Clonard (P. Ó Riain,
A dictionary of Irish saints (2012), p. 216; A. Gwynn and R.N. Hadcock, *Medieval religious houses:
Ireland* (1970), p. 191).   5 CS [978] (*recte* 980); AU 1025.1, 1052.4; CS [1084] (*recte* 1088). A.
Dooley and H. Roe, *Tales of the elders of Ireland* (1999), p. 233.   6 AU 772.8, 780.14; 793.2; R.I.
Best, 'The graves of the kings at Clonmacnois', *Ériu*, 2 (1905), 163–71.   7 Gwynn and Hadcock,
Medieval religious houses, p. 191.   8 Whenever the word 'Roscommon' occurs in the text without
any qualifier, it refers specifically to the Augustinian house of canons; references to the parish,

Figure 1: Síl Muiredaig genealogy

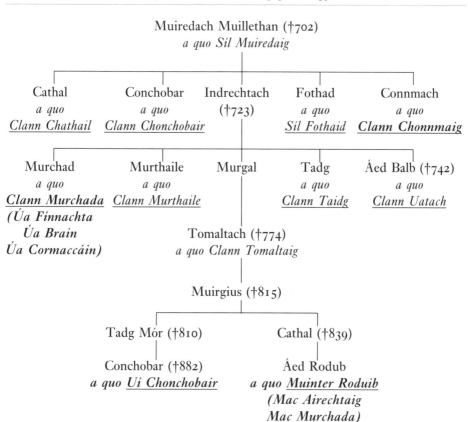

Within the Connacht sections of the text, the *Acallam* focuses upon three key dynastic groups: the dynasty of Síl Muiredaig as a whole, and, within that umbrella grouping, the Síl Muiredaig septs of Muinter Roduib and Clann Murchada (figure 1). This specific constellation of dynastic interests forms the crux of the paper's Roscommon argument since the monastery represents the one point where the interests of these particular septs meet. The following discussion will examine each dynastic grouping in turn, illustrating the ways in which they are represented in the *Acallam*, and the nature of their connection to the monastery of Roscommon.

(a) Síl Muiredaig

Síl Muiredaig, a branch of the dynasty of Uí Briúin Aí, held a near monopoly on the kingship of Connacht from the second half of the eighth century

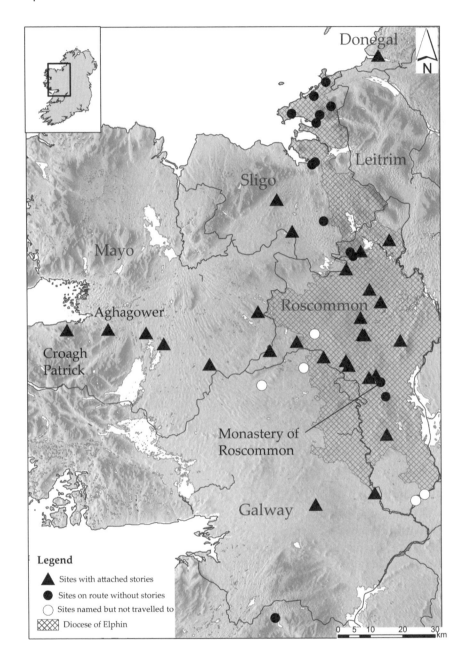

Figure 2: Connacht sites in *Acallam na senórach*

onwards. From the middle of the tenth century, their royal line was the family of Úa Conchobair. Although the power of the Uí Chonchobair kings of Connacht extended over the whole province, Síl Muiredaig's own patrimonial territory was based in eastern Connacht, in a region roughly approximating to the modern diocese of Elphin (figure 2).[9] The monastery of Roscommon lay at the heart of the diocese, and was in fact the diocesan seat for a time *c.*1152; by the end of the twelfth century, however, the Patrician church of Elphin appears to have taken over.[10] According to the *Acallam*, Elphin was the site where visitors stabled their horses when drinking at Rathcroghan (a hearty ten-kilometre walk distant);[11] the theory that the *Acallam* was written at Roscommon would help account for this rather dismissive characterisation of its triumphant rival for the bishop's seat. In addition to its ecclesiastical importance, there is also some evidence to indicate that there was a royal Úa Conchobair *caput* at Roscommon, situated at Loughnaneane (adjacent to the site of Roscommon Castle), less than a kilometre from the Augustinian house.[12] Roscommon thus appears to have been a site of considerable secular and ecclesiastical significance within Síl Muiredaig as a whole.

In the *Acallam*, the royal line of Síl Muiredaig is represented by the aptly named king of Connacht, Muiredach mac Fínnachta, and by his son and eventual heir, Áed. As Dooley points out:

> the key element is surely that the reader is directed to consider the Síol Muireadhaigh dynastic line from its founder Muiredach Muillethan (†702), through Fínshnechta (†848) to Cathal Croibhdherg (†1224) – the king almost certainly reigning at the time the *Acallam* was composed – and his son Áed.[13]

Muiredach and Áed make their debut at the opening of the first Connacht journey in the *Acallam* when Patrick, responding to messengers sent by Muiredach, travels from Munster to meet them at Loch Cróine, now Lough Croan in the parish of Cam, barony of Athlone, Co. Roscommon.[14] Highlighting the significance of Síl Muiredaig within the *Acallam*, Patrick performs

barony, town, county and Dominican priory will be flagged specifically as such. **9** The original extent of Síl Muiredaig, however, would have been larger than the current diocese of Elphin, extending into east Galway. **10** Roscommon is named as one of the dioceses of Connacht at the Synod of Kells-Mellifont in 1152 (Gwynn and Hadcock, *Medieval religious houses*, p. 95). By the very end of the twelfth century, however, the title 'bishop of Elphin' starts to appear in the annals (AU[1] 1195, ALC 1195, Cott. 379 [1195]; 'bishop of Elphin' also appears at ALC 1137, but this title is likely not contemporary, but a later gloss). **11** W. Stokes (ed. and partial trans.), 'Acallamh na senórach' in W. Stokes and E. Windisch (eds), *Irische Texte*, iv, 1 (1900), ll. 3887–92; Dooley and Roe, *Tales*, p. 117. **12** ACon. 1225.5. **13** Dooley, 'The date and purpose', 103. **14** Stokes, 'Acallamh', ll. 1051–231; Dooley and Roe, *Tales*, pp 32–8.

his most powerful miracle in the whole text here – raising the dead to life – when he revives Áed after the young prince collapses and dies following a game of hurling.

Patrick and Muiredach then eventually make their way to the Síl Muiredaig inauguration site of Carn Fraích (Carns townland, parish of Ogulla, barony of Roscommon, Co. Roscommon), stopping at several sites along the way.[15] It is at Carn Fraích that Caílte reveals to Patrick that Finn and the *fían* knew of the existence of 'the King of Heaven and Earth', the first iteration in the *Acallam* of the important theme of Finn's proto-Christianity.[16] Although Patrick does not technically inaugurate Muiredach at Carn Fraích – after all, Muiredach is already king – the text does state that Muiredach sets off from there to proclaim his kingship and rule. Patrick, meanwhile, departs from Carn Fraích 'to preach the faith and the religious life, to expel the demons and the druids from Ireland, to choose the holy and the righteous, to erect crosses, penitential stations and altars, and to destroy idols and spectres, and the arts of druidism'.[17] As Dooley notes, the passage celebrates a joint proclamation of royal and ecclesiastical power,[18] with the ceremonial Síl Muiredaig site of Carn Fraích used not only to confirm Muiredach's rule but also to inaugurate the truly active part of Patrick's mission in Ireland.[19] Nor is Caílte immune from the new sense of purpose imparted at Carn Fraích, for it is from the inauguration site that the Fenian, tired of being in one place all the time, sets off 'to search the hills and mounds and the heights' (*D'iarraid cnoc 7 céite 7 dingnadh*), looking for the places he once frequented with the *fían*.[20]

---

15 Their two stops en route are at Ráith Brénainn (see discussion on the physical landscape of Roscommon) and Úarán Garad (see discussion of Clann Murchada and the Oran episodes): Stokes, 'Acallamh', ll. 1241–450; Dooley and Roe, *Tales*, pp 39–45. 16 Stokes, 'Acallamh', ll. 1451–84 at l. 1484: *ro thuicsem rí[g] nime 7 talman*; cf. Dooley and Roe, *Tales*, pp 45–6. See Dooley, 'The date and purpose', 103–4; G. Parsons, 'The structure of *Acallam na senórach*', *Cambrian Medieval Celtic Studies*, 55 (2008), 11–39 at 30 (diagram), 33. 17 Dooley and Roe, *Tales*, p. 46 (cf. Stokes, 'Acallamh', ll. 1497–1500: *do šílad chreitmhe 7 crabaid 7 do dhíchur deman 7 druadh a hEirinn, 7 do togha naemh 7 fírén 7 [do tocbáil] cros 7 uladh 7 altoiredh, 7 do thairnemh idhul 7 arracht 7 ealadhan ndráidhechta*). 18 Dooley, 'The date and purpose', 103–4. 19 The Carn Fraích episode in the *Acallam* echoes the prevailing theme of Part II of the *Vita tripartita* which begins with a short sermon on the final part of the gospel according to Matthew: *Euntes ergo nunc docete omnes gentes, baptizantes eos in nomine Patris et Filii et Spiritus Sancti* (Mt. 28:19–20; K. Mulchrone (ed.), *Bethu Phátraic* (1939), p. 41, ll. 662–5; W. Stokes (ed. and trans.), *The tripartite Life of Patrick*, 2 vols (1887), i, p. 64). The image of Patrick and Muiredach on the hill together at Carn Fraích strongly echoes the later tradition of Patrick's blessing of Dauí Galach, the ancestor of Uí Briúin Aí (parent dynasty of Síl Muiredaig) at either Duma Selcae – the ecclesiastical site at Carn Fraích – or at Carn Fraích itself (Book of Ballymote [RIA MS 536 (23 P 12)], 89a11–27; N. Ó Muraíle (ed. and trans.), *Leabhar mór na ngenealach*, 5 vols (2003), i, 436–8, §199.1–10; M. Dillon (ed. and trans.), 'The inauguration of O'Conor' in J.A. Watt et al. (eds), *Medieval studies presented to Aubrey Gwynn* (1961), pp 186–202 at pp 188, 196). 20 Stokes, 'Acallamh', ll. 1488–90; Dooley and Roe, *Tales*, p. 46.

After the scene at Carn Fraích, Muiredach mac Fínnachta is not heard of in the *Acallam* again, but his son, Áed, returns to feature heavily in the third Connacht section of the text. Instead of the youth of the first Connacht section, though, Áed is now married and the reigning king of Connacht. Despite his marital status, the third Connacht section opens with Áed falling in love with a woman of the *síd*, Aillenn Fíalchorcra, daugter of Bodb Derg; their encounter sets the scene for the *Acallam*'s most important exploration of the theme of the sanctity of marriage.[21] Unlike his father, who is depicted as being much more on an equal footing with Patrick, Áed is seen as the junior partner throughout most of his relationship with the saint. Whether it be following Patrick's counsel when the saint bids him follow his marriage vows rather than his heart, or obeying Patrick's command to give a young couple the landed inheritance that is due to them, Áed's obedience to the man who brought him back from the dead establishes the right of the church to dictate the behaviour of kings.

Áed's presence continues throughout most of the third Connacht section, and he is there whenever Patrick and the Fenians are together, though mainly absent when Caílte and Cas Corach part company from the saint. As Caílte and Cas Corach prepare to reunite with saint and king at the end of the third Connacht section of the text, Patrick and Áed together call an assembly of all the men of Ireland at Úarán Garad (townland of Oran, in the parish of Oran, barony of Ballymoe, Co. Roscommon). In this way, Áed's kingship seems to finally mature into *gravitas*, with the joint assembly at Úarán Garad echoing the joint proclamation of Patrick and Muiredach at Carn Fraích.

Although neither Áed nor Muiredach are present in the second Connacht section of the *Acallam*, this is not to say that Síl Muiredaig is similarly absent from this section of the text. On the contrary, most of the second Connacht section is set in Mag nAí, in the heart of Síl Muiredaig territory.[22] A similar focus on Síl Muiredaig territory is found in the first and third Connacht sections of the text. The significance of Síl Muiredaig within the Connacht portions of the text can be graphically illustrated by plotting all the Connacht sites in the *Acallam* on a map and comparing their distribution pattern to the borders of the diocese of Elphin (roughly approximating to the borders of Síl Muiredaig) (figure 2). This exercise reveals a strong correlation between the two, with the majority of the Connacht episodes in the text set within, or quite close to, the diocesan limits. The one really conspicuous exception to this trend is the journey west to Croagh Patrick, on the shores of Clew Bay, Co. Mayo. As will be discussed below, this lone projection westwards represents some of the secular and ecclesiastical interests of the Síl Muiredaig sept of Muinter Roduib.

21 Stokes, 'Acallamh', ll. 6361–437, 7820–43; Dooley and Roe, *Tales*, pp 179–81, 217–18. See note 100 for secondary references to discussion of the theme of marriage in the *Acallam*.
22 Stokes, 'Acallamh', ll. 3859–4106; Dooley and Roe, *Tales*, pp 116–21.

(b) Muinter Roduib

Muinter Roduib of Clann Tomaltaig were a sept of Síl Muiredaig, descended from the ninth-century dynast Áed Ro-dub, a son of one of the proto-Úa Conchobair kings of Connacht, Cathal mac Muirgiusa (†839) (figure 1). The Muinter Roduib lords, reckoned as one of the four *ríg-thóisig* of Síl Muiredaig, were drawn from the Mac Airechtaig branch of the Úa Roduib line of Muinter Roduib. As Ann Dooley has shown, an avatar of Áed Ro-dub features in an episode in the *Acallam* that makes the text's interest in Muinter Roduib abundantly clear.

The story is found in the third Connacht section of the *Acallam*, near the beginning of the journey westwards undertaken by Patrick, Caílte and Cas Corach, and Áed mac Muiredaig.[23] Travelling from Kiltullagh, Co. Roscommon, the assembled company is forced to stop at Fírchuing ('True Yoke'), formerly called Clúain Carpait ('the Meadow of Chariot'), when the yoke of Patrick's chariot snaps. The stranded saint is rescued by Dub, a beautiful black-haired youth who offers Patrick the use of his own chariot. When Patrick asks his name, Dub identifies himself with a pedigree that, as Dooley points out, links him to the Muinter Roduib line of Síl Muiredaig.[24] This association is confirmed when Patrick says that from now Dub's descendants will be known as the Uí Raduib.[25]

Patrick then prophesies that Dub's line will have great wealth, and be associated with Fobar (Aghagower) and Crúachan (Rathcroghan, or, possibly, Croagh Patrick). Finally, the saint bestows upon Muinter Roduib a legacy of abbots and poets, of husbandry, counsel and fellowship. At the end of the episode, a chariot approaches carrying a beautiful woman, Aífe Derg daughter of Conall Costadach, a king of Connacht. Aífe had come to seek Patrick, in order to ask his advice on whom she should take as a partner. Patrick suggests Dub, and the couple agree to the match but express concern that they have no land. Patrick then presses Áed mac Muiredaig to give Dub the cantred that is due to him as his patrimony. The text hints that until Patrick came along, Dub, and thus by implication Muinter Roduib, had some difficulty in gaining or retaining their territory.[26]

Although Dub and Aífe leave the scene immediately thereafter, the Muinter Roduib associations continue for much of the remaining journey west to Croagh Patrick, albeit in a less overt fashion. Two stops after Fírchuing, the assembled company arrive at Tipra Pátraic, now Ballintober on the shores of Lough Carra, Co. Mayo.[27] The ecclesiastical site of Tipra Pátraic had been

---

23 Stokes, 'Acallamh', ll. 6632–90; Dooley and Roe, *Tales*, pp 186–7. The journey west, and its connections to Muinter Roduib, is discussed in detail in A. Connon, 'Plotting *Acallam na senórach*: the physical context of the "Mayo" sequence' in S. Sheehan et al. (eds), *Gablánach in scélaigecht* (2013), pp 69–102. 24 Dooley, 'The date and purpose', 112. 25 Stokes, 'Acallamh', l. 6649; Dooley and Roe, *Tales*, p. 186. 26 Dooley, 'The date and purpose', 115–16. 27 P. Ó

an Augustinian house of canons since 1216, and it was there that the most powerful lord of Muinter Roduib on record, Donn Cathaig mac Airechtaig Úa Roduib, died in 1224 *in ailithri*, 'on pilgrimage'.[28] It may be that he had retired there. Donn Cathaig's power was such that not only did he hold the lordship of Muinter Roduib, but he also had been granted the lordship and stewardship of the Síl Muiredaig septs of Clann Taidg and Clann Murthaile.[29] The issue of whether Muinter Roduib was able to retain control over Clann Taidg and Clann Murthaile beyond Donn Cathaig's death is potentially of relevance to the dating of the *Acallam*, and will be addressed towards the end of this essay in the section on *tempus*.

Following their stay at Tipra Pátraic, the company splits up. Caílte and Cas Corach head north with Áed mac Muiredaig to the territory of Luigne, while Patrick continues westwards, first reaching the Patrician church of Achad Fobair Umaill, Aghagower (parish of Aghagower, barony of Burris-hoole, Co. Mayo), and then the Patrician pilgrimage site of Croagh Patrick in the parish of Oughaval (barony of Murrisk, Co. Mayo).[30] Since the narrative follows Caílte rather than Patrick, these last two stops are not told as part of the narrative of the main westward journey, but are related later by Patrick when he reunites with the company at Úarán Garad.[31]

Aghagower's links to Muinter Roduib are even stronger than those of Ballintober. The 'gift of abbots' and association with 'Fobar' foretold by Patrick of Muinter Roduib is a reference to Mac Airechtaig control of the abbacy of Aghagower. The family appears to have assumed ecclesiastical power in Aghagower by the late twelfth century, but it is not certain how much earlier than that their control might have extended.[32] As for Croagh Patrick, the reference to 'Crúachan' in Patrick's prophecy about Muinter Roduib might refer to the holy mountain there, though it could alternatively be a reference to Rathcroghan. Dooely has argued that Muinter Roduib had control of the important pilgrimage to the mountain in the Middle Ages;[33] it is possible that similarities in the *Acallam*'s descriptions of Ballintober, Aghagower, and Croagh Patrick might indicate that they were all stops on the pilgrimage trail.[34] While the pre-Norman records do not link Croagh Patrick with any particular ecclesiastical family, there is evidence in later centuries to indicate Muinter Roduib involvement in the pilgrimage. The Geraghty (Mac Airechtaig) family had become the hereditary keepers of the *Clogh-dubh*, the black bell of Patrick, said in pre-Norman times to have been the property of

Riain et al., *Historical dictionary of Gaelic placenames*, fascicle 2 (2005), p. 57; Stokes, 'Acallamh', ll. 6759–826; Dooley and Roe, *Tales*, pp 189–90. **28** ACon. 1224.4. **29** Book of Lecan (RIA MS 535 [23 P 2]), 65ra; Book of Ballymote 58rd; Ó Muraíle, *Leabhar mór na ngenealach*, i, p. 504, §225.7; Dooley, 'The date and purpose', 114. **30** Stokes, 'Acallamh', ll. 6826–88; Dooley and Roe, *Tales*, pp 192–3. **31** Stokes, 'Acallamh', ll. 7760–86; Dooley and Roe, *Tales*, p. 216. **32** Dooley, 'The date and purpose', 122, n. 45. **33** Ibid., 112–13. **34** Connon, 'Plotting *Acallam na senórach*', p. 92.

the Mac Beoláin ecclesiastical family of Killower, near Tuam.[35] Tradition held
that the *Clogh-dubh* was the 'gapped bell' used by Patrick in Tírechán and the
Vita tripartita to ward off demons as he fasted on the mountain.[36] Every
Garland Sunday – the last Sunday in July, when the most popular pilgrim-
age to the holy mountain took place – it was the responsibility of the
Geraghtys to bring the bell up Croagh Patrick. In the nineteenth century,
however, the last Geraghty keeper of the bell sold it to the Royal Irish
Academy to pay for his passage to America.[37]

Her astute observation of the strong connection between Muinter Roduib
and the *Acallam*'s account of the journey to Croagh Patrick led Dooley to
suggest that the text might have been written at the Muinter Roduib-con-
trolled Patrician monastery of Aghagower.[38] However, while the ecclesiastical
arm of Muinter Roduib was based at Aghagower, the more powerful secular
arm of the sept was actually based some considerable distance east in central
Co. Roscommon. This patrimonial territory of Muinter Roduib appears to
have corresponded to the modern Co. Roscommon parishes of Kilbride,
Roscommon and Fuerty (figure 3). One of the central planks in the argument
for the Roscommon *locus* of *Acallam na senórach* is that the Augustinian house
of canons at Roscommon is located right in the heart of this territorial lordship of Muinter Roduib.

Muinter Roduib and the Augustinian house of canons at Roscommon
The chief clue to the location of Muinter Roduib's territory is found in the
late sixteenth-century *Compossicion booke of Connought*. There, the term
'Monter Raa', an anglicisation of Muinter Roduib, is given as the name for
most of the territory in the parishes of Roscommon and Kilbride. Included
under this rubric in the *Compossicion booke* are the 'Abbey of Roscommon'
and the twenty quarters of land the abbey owned in the parish of
Roscommon.[39] Also found in the *Compossicion booke* is the term 'Eraght mc
gerraght', the *airecht* or 'lordship' of Mac Airechtaig, a unit of thirty-three
quarters of land corresponding to the modern parish of Fuerty.[40] Like
Aghagower, the church of Fuerty is an ancient Patrician foundation, the
ecclesiastical site of Fidarta which features in Tírechán and the *Vita tripartita*.[41] A connection between these two Patrician churches, located a hundred
kilometres apart, is witnessed by the name of 'Aghagower' given to one of the

35 W. Wilde, *Lough Corrib, its shores and islands* (1867), pp 196–7; H.T. Knox, *Notes on the early
history of the dioceses of Tuam, Killala and Achonry* (1904), p. 146.   36 L. Bieler (ed. and trans.),
The Patrician texts in the Book of Armagh (1979), p. 152; Mulchrone, *Bethu Phátraic* (1939), pp
71–5; Stokes, *Tripartite Life*, pp 112–20.   37 Wilde, *Lough Corrib*, p. 196.   38 Dooley, 'The
date and purpose', 120–1.   39 A.M. Freeman (ed.), *The compossicion booke of Connought* (1936),
pp 152, 168; M.T. Flanagan, *Irish royal charters* (2005), p. 354, n. 16.   40 Freeman, *The compossicion booke*, p. 168.   41 Bieler, *Patrician texts*, pp 146–7; Mulchrone, *Bethu Phátraic*, p. 65;
Stokes, *Tripartite Life*, pp 104–5.

townlands in southwest Fuerty. Presumably this land was owned at one time by the church of Achad Fobair Umaill.

Although the lateness of the *Compossicion booke of Connought* might call its reliability as a source for thirteenth-century Connacht into some question, pre-Norman and medieval vernacular sources confirm its location of Muinter Roduib in central Co. Roscommon. A poem attributed to the eleventh-century poet, Urard mac Coisse, links Muinter Roduib to Ráith Brénainn, now the townland of Rathbrennan in the northwestern part of the parish of Roscommon.[42] From internal historical evidence, the poem would seem to date to before the late twelfth century. Thirteenth-century annals, meanwhile, link Muinter Roduib to secular and ecclesiastical centres in the parish of Kilbride. Under the year 1263, the Annals of the Four Masters report the death of Gilla Pátraic mac Gilla na Guisén, prior of the abbey of Doirean (Derrane) in southern Kilbride; fifteenth-century papal letters identify the family of Meic Gilla na Guisén as a branch of the Maic Airechtaig.[43] Fifteen years later, Tomaltach Mac Airechtaig, the *ríg-toísech* of Síl Muiredaig, is said by the Annals of Connacht to be 'of Cagal'; the name is preserved in the six contiguous townlands beginning 'Coggal-' in the parishes of Kilbride and Lisonuffy.[44] One can thus be reasonably confident that the 'Monter Raa' of the late sixteenth century corresponded in at least basic outline to the Muinter Roduib lands of the twelfth and thirteenth centuries, and that the Augustinian house of canons at Roscommon therefore lay within Muinter Roduib territory at the time of composition of the *Acallam*.

In order to argue that the *Acallam*'s interest in Muinter Roduib reflects a Roscommon *locus* of composition, however, it is not enough to simply show that the Augustinian house lay within Muinter Roduib territory. Instead, it is essential to explore whether the relationship between sept and monastery is reflected in the actual text, to investigate if the *Acallam* is as interested in central Co. Roscommon sites connected to Muinter Roduib as it is in Co. Mayo sites connected to Aghagower. The section of the paper dealing with Roscommon's centrality to the physical landscape of the *Acallam* will explore this issue in detail. For now, it is enough to say that in addition to a brief reference to the monastery of Roscommon itself,[45] the *Acallam* includes several

---

42 National Library of Ireland MS G131, pp 223–4. I am very grateful to Máirín Ní Dhonnchadha both for alerting me to this reference, and for giving me access to her edition in progress of the poem. 43 J.A. Twemlow (ed.), *Calendar of entries in the papal registers relating to Great Britain and Ireland*, x, 1447–55 (1915), p. 110, §179. Under the year 1143, there is a record of Murchad Úa Roduib's involvement in a land transaction made between Toirdelbach Úa Conchobair, king of Connacht and Ireland, and the abbot of Roscommon with regard to territory in the immediate vicinity of the monastery of Roscommon (ATig. 1143). Although not proof in itself of Muinter Roduib's location, the transaction would make more sense were Mac Airechtaig the lord of the region. 44 ACon. 1278.8; Ó Riain et al., *Historical dictionary of Gaelic placenames*, fascicle 3 (2008), p. 4. 45 Stokes, 'Acallamh', ll. 1238–41; Dooley and Roe,

episodes set within Muinter Roduib's territory in central Co. Roscommon. One such sequence is the quite lengthy story of the battle between Glas, king of Lochlann, and the *fiana*.[46] This tale is set at Ráith Brénainn, the site explicitly connected with Muinter Roduib in the poem attributed to Urard mac Coisse. Another relevant tale is the story of the female werewolves at Carn Bricrenn, now the townland of Carrownabrickna in the parish of Roscommon.[47] As will be discussed more fully in the physical landscape section of this paper, both episodes feature quite detailed topographical descriptions, an element absent for the most part from the episodes set in Aghagower and Croagh Patrick. It is also worth noting that while the Ráith Brénainn sequence occurs in the first Connacht section of the *Acallam*, the Carn Bricrenn story is found in the third. The text's interest in Muinter Roduib's home territory thus appears to be *Acallam*-wide. The presence of these episodes, as well as the level of local knowledge about the area implicit in them, clearly indicate that the *Acallam*'s keen interest in Muinter Roduib encompassed the sept's central Co. Roscommon territory at least as much as it did their ecclesiastical interests in Co. Mayo.

The conclusions presented thus far – that the *Acallam* is very interested in Muinter Roduib; that this interest extends to Muinter Roduib's central Roscommon territory; and that the Augustinian house of canons at Roscomon was located within that territory – are consistent with a Roscommon *locus* for the composition of the *Acallam* in the form we now have it. In order to bring the argument up to the next level, however, and make the case that the Augustinian house of canons at Roscommon is not just a plausible candidate for the *locus* of composition of the *Acallam*, but the strongest candidate, one must consider the *Acallam*'s depiction not only of the sept who controlled the territory in which Roscommon was located but also of the sept who controlled its abbacy. The following section will thus examine the Síl Muiredaig sept of Clann Murchada and their ruling family of Úa Fínnachta.

(c) Clann Murchada

One of the notable aspects of Roscommon's position within the political network of Síl Muiredaig is that although the monastery was physically located within the territory of Muinter Roduib, the sept that dominated its ecclesiastical offices was actually another branch of Síl Muiredaig altogether, the sept of Clann Murchada (see figure 1). Clann Murchada's territory, together with that of their distant cousins Clann Chonnmaig – a neighbouring Síl Muiredaig sept that had come under Clann Murchada control – lay on the western limits of Muinter Roduib in what is now the barony of Ballymoe (see figure 3). Their ruling line was the dynasty of Úa Fínnachta.

Tales, pp 38–9.   **46** Stokes, 'Acallamh', ll. 1241–1312; Dooley and Roe, *Tales*, pp 39–41. **47** Stokes, 'Acallamh', ll. 7674–725; Dooley and Roe, *Tales*, pp 212–14.

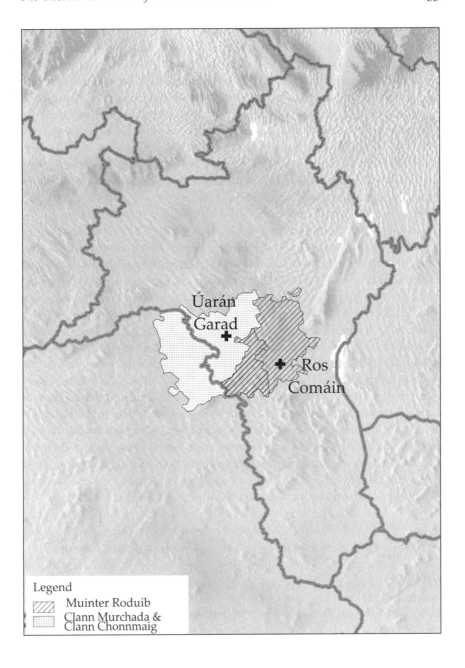

Figure 3: The Síl Muiredaig sub-kingdoms of Muinter Roduib, Clann
Chonnmaig and Clann Murchada

Like the Maic Airechtaig of Muinter Roduib, the Úa Fínnachta family were one of the four *ríg-thoísig* of Síl Muiredaig. The annals note members of their line as heads of their native Clann Murchada by the mid-tenth century, while they appear to have also taken over the lordship of Clann Chonnmaig by at least as early as the first half of the twelfth century (see figure 1).[48] Although the annals name a single Úa Fínnachta dynast as lord of both territories in 1140, later sources suggest that control of the two territories came to be divided within the family so that one line of the Úa Fínnachta sept controlled Clann Murchada while a second Úa Fínnachta line controlled Clann Chonnmaig.[49] As will be discussed shortly, the Úa Fínnachta family appears to have been of very considerable interest to the author of the *Acallam*.

The earliest evidence for Clann Murchada's association with the monastery of Roscommon is a possibly tenth-century tract on the religious affiliations of the various Síl Muiredaig septs, which claims that Clann Murchada was 'for Comán', Roscommon's founding saint.[50] The strongest evidence for the link between the sept and monastery, however, is found in the names of the individuals who controlled Roscommon's chief ecclesiastical offices. The Síl Muiredaig genealogies list four surnames associated with Clann Murchada, three of which – Úa Fínnachta, Úa Brain and Úa Cormaccáin – consistently feature in the obits of abbots of Roscommon from the late eleventh century through to the thirteenth.[51]

The earliest Clann Murchada abbot to be linked to Roscommon was Tigernach Úa Brain – the same Tigernach who gave his name to the Annals of Tigernach – who died in 1088 as the joint abbot of Roscommon and Clonmacnoise.[52] All Tigernach's known successors in the first half of the twelfth century likewise belonged to Síl Muiredaig, although only one – Máel Ísu Úa Fínnachta, who died in 1135 – also belonged to Clann Murchada. From 1152 to 1234, however, Clann Murchada held a virtual monopoly on the abbacy, with the headship of Roscommon alternating between the Úa Cormaccáin and Úa Brain families. It may have been during this period that the house of canons at Roscommon acquired the scattered landholdings in the over-lordship of Clann Murchada that are listed as being in their possession at the dissolution of the monasteries.[53]

---

48 AFM 953 [*recte* 955] – the dynast in question was the brother of the eponym of the Úa Fínnachta line; CS [971] [*recte* 973]; ATig. 1140.   49 J. Carney (ed.), *Topographical poems by Seaán Mór Ó Dubhagáin and Giolla-na-naomh Ó Huidhrín* (1943), pp 21, 98; Dillon, 'The inauguration of O'Conor', p. 189.   50 P. Ó Riain (ed.), *Corpus genealogiarum sanctorum Hiberniae* (1986), p. 60, §394.5: *Clann Murchada dino fri(?) Choman beannt o aimsir Finnachta m. Gleitnichain alle.*   51 AU 1088.3 (CS 1084); AFM 1135; AFM 1170; ATig. 1170; AFM 1200; AFM 1232; ALC 1234 (Cott. 1234); ACon. 1234.8.   52 AU 1088.3 ATig. 1088, CS [1084], AFM 1088. Tigernach's obit in CS identifies him as belonging to Síl Muiredaig. While there was also an Úa Brain family belonging to the Clann Chathail sept of Síl Muiredaig, the known association between Clann Murchada and Roscommon makes it most likely that Tigernach and his fellow Úa Brain ecclesiasts at Roscommon belonged to Clann Murchada.   53 Although most

The one break in the Clann Murchada succession during this period appears to have been at some point in the first quarter of the thirteenth century, when Máel Ísu (†1223) son of Toirdelbach Mór Úa Conchobair, brother of the reigning king of Connacht, Cathal Crobderg Úa Conchobair, became abbot. Immediately following Máel Ísu's tenure in office, Clann Murchada resumed control of the abbacy; however, after 1234 there is no further record of their direct involvement in Roscommon's affairs. Instead, the mantle of control at Roscommon appears to have been retaken by the Úa Conchobair family.[54] Nonetheless, a lingering connection between Roscommon and Clann Murchada persisted into the Early Modern period: up until the dissolution of the monasteries, the house of canons at Roscommon held the rectory of nearly all the parishes in the part of the barony of Ballymoe that lay in the diocese of Elphin, that is to say, the parishes that appear to have been situated in the combined territories of Clann Murchada and Clann Chonnmaig.[55] The link between the lordship of Clann Murchada and the Augustinian house of canons at Roscommon thus endured for over six hundred years.

Acallam na senórach and Úa Fínnachta
With Clann Murchada's link to the monastery of Roscommon established, discussion will now turn to the sept's connections to the *Acallam*. An intriguing, but unfortunately undateable, connection between *fianaigecht* tradition and the Úa Fínnachta lords of Clann Murchada and Clann Chonnmaig actually comes from outside the *Acallam*. This is a verse enumerating the four *ríg-thoísig* of Síl Muiredaig, which has been interpolated into a variant copy of the thirteenth-century prose tract on the 'Inauguration of Ó Conchobhair'. Each of the four lines of the verse names and very briefly describes one of the four lords. The line pertaining to Úa Fínnachta refers to him simply as a *féin-nid*, 'a member of a *fian*'.[56] The rest of the evidence linking the Úa Fínnachta family to the *Acallam*, however, is very much from within the pages of that

---

of the house of canons' landholdings were in the parish of Roscommon itself, the townlands of Tobermakee and Dromatemple in the parish of Dromatemple, a constituent part of Úa Fínnachta territory, also belonged to them. The Dominican priory at Roscommon, meanwhile, owned large chunks of the parish of Oran, a key Clann Chonnmaig location in the *Acallam* (National Archives of Ireland MS RC 9/15, §§4, 23).   **54** Book of Ballymote 105bb51, Book of Lecan 64rc45, Ó Muraíle, *Leabhar mór na ngenealach*, i, p. 496, §222.11; ACon. 1244.11, 1245.12, ALC 1258. It is interesting to note that Clann Murchada control of the monastic house at Roscommon appears to have ended at almost exactly the same time as the Anglo-Normans built a castle within their territory at Dunamon (ACon. 1232.5).   **55** TCD MS 1066, p. 496; *The Irish fiants of the Tudor sovereigns*, 4 vols (1994), ii, p. 299, §2295, and p. 427, §3134; M.C. Griffith (ed.), *Calendar of the Irish patent rolls of James I* (1965), p. 154.   **56** Dillon, 'The inauguration of O'Conor', p. 189 n 4. Internal evidence dates the main recension of the prose inauguration tract to the thirteenth century: K. Simms, '"Gabh umad a Fheidhlimidh": a fifteenth-century inauguration ode', *Ériu*, 31 (1980), 132–45 at 141. The manuscript containing the interpolated verse – RIA MS C i 1 (935), fo. 28 – dates to the seventeenth century.

work. In contrast to the *Acallam*'s explicit recognition of Muinter Roduib, though, the text's emphasis on the Úa Fínnachta lords of Clann Murchada and Clann Chonnmaig is more subtle, though arguably more pervasive. The case for the *Acallam*'s interest in the Úa Fínnachta family rests on two pillars: the first is the text's emphasis on the Úa Fínnachta name, the second is its emphasis on Úa Fínnachta territory.

Ann Dooley first drew attention to the possible significance of the patronymic bestowed by the *Acallam* upon the king of Connacht, Muiredach mac Fínnachta, suggesting that the name might bear further exploration.[57] Following up this line of enquiry has indeed proved fruitful. The marked repetition of the name 'Fínnachta' in the *Acallam* bears witness to its importance in the text. Throughout the *Acallam*, the most common way to introduce a character is by his or her first name followed by a patronymic, that is to say as 'X son or daughter of Y'. While the introduction of the king of Connacht, Muiredach mac Fínnachta, follows this formula, Muiredach's children are consistently introduced by reference not only to their father but also to their grandfather: thus we meet throughout the course of the text 'Áed mac Muiredaig meic Fínnachta', 'Bé Bind ingen Muiredaig meic Fínnachta' and 'Échna ingen Muiredaig meic Fínnachta'.[58] In this way, the name Fínnachta appears considerably more frequently than if the usual patronymic paradigm had been invoked.

Now, it must be said that Muiredach's children are not the only characters in the *Acallam* to be introduced as the descendant of both their father and their grandfather. While a naming formula that spans three generations is definitely in the minority in the text, it would be misleading to characterise it as entirely rare: of the hundreds of characters in the *Acallam*, there are approximately thirty who are identified by their grandfather as well as by their father. What is unique about one particular descendant of Fínnachta, however, is the frequency with which the tri-generational naming formula occurs. Áed mac Muiredaig meic Fínnachta, king of Connacht, is referred to as the grandson of Fínnachta (and son of Muiredach) no less than six times in the *Acallam*. Such repetition stands in contrast to the rest of the small tri-generational group, roughly two thirds of whom are never again referred to by all three names.[59] Of the remaining third, most are referred to by all three names only twice in the text, while two characters are referred to thus on three occasions. The six references to Áed as the grandson of Fínnachta thus constitute a highly unusual naming pattern.

57 Dooley, 'The date and purpose', 114 n. 32.   58 Stokes, 'Acallamh', ll. 1230 (in UCD Franciscan MS A4 only; not in Dooley and Roe, *Tales*), 2066, 6359, 6393–4, 7419, 7729, 7842; Dooley and Roe, *Tales*, pp 64, 179, 180, 207, 215, 218.   59 The relevant characters either are never again mentioned in the text, or are referred to on subsequent occasions only by first name or by first name plus patronymic.

The most important Fínnachta in Síl Muiredaig history was the childless ninth-century king of Connacht, Fínnachta mac Tomaltaig (†848), who abdicated the throne in order to become an anchorite.[60] This Fínnachta was the sole member of his dynasty to attain the status of saint.[61] Since the first Connacht section of the *Acallam* draws a parallel between the role of saint and king – with Patrick beginning his proselytising career in earnest from Carnfree, and Muiredach setting off from the same site to proclaim his kingship and rule[62] – it would not be implausible to consider that the choice of 'Fínnachta' as Muiredach's patronymic may have been intended to evoke the one Síl Muiredaig dynast who combined the roles of saint and king. However, while such connotations may have been a useful secondary consideration, I would argue that the initial choice of 'Fínnachta' as the name of Muiredach's father, and the subsequent pointed repetition of his name, relates primarily to a desire to highlight the ruling Úa Fínnachta family of Clann Murchada and Clann Chonnmaig (descendants of a quite different Fínnachta: Fínnachta mac Gleitnecháin; see figure 1). The prime position which the Úa Fínnachta dynasty occupied in the hierarchy of the *Acallam*'s interests is signalled by the marked attention which the text pays to their lands.

The composite Úa Fínnachta territory of Clann Murchada and Clann Chonnmaig was said to have comprised forty-eight *bailti* on either side of the River Suck.[63] These lands likely corresponded to the region known in the medieval and early modern periods as 'Clan Conway' or 'Clan Conoo', which, from the late thirteenth century onwards, was the territory of the branch of the de Burgos known as the Mac David (or Mac Davy) Burkes. Their holdings are now represented by the portion of the modern barony of Ballymoe that lies in the diocese of Elphin.[64] Although an Anglicisation of 'Clann Connmaig', I think it likely that the placename 'Clan Conway' came to designate both parts of the former Úa Fínnachta territory, expanding the scope of its meaning to include Clann Murchada's original territory as well.[65]

Multiple different sites within the Úa Fínnachta lordships appear within the *Acallam*, including two of the locations on the *fian*'s favourite hunting trail. In the third Connacht section of the *Acallam*, Caílte sits at Suide Finn on top of Slíab Formaíle (O'Flynn's Mountain, parish of Kiltullagh, Co.

---

60 AU 848.2; CS [848]; Ó Riain, *Corpus genealogiarum sanctorum Hiberniae*, p. 61, §399; Dooley, 'The date and purpose', 103.   61 Ó Riain, *Corpus genealogiarum sanctorum Hiberniae*, p. 61, §399; AU 848.2; CS [848].   62 Stokes, 'Acallamh', ll. 1495–500; Dooley and Roe, *Tales*, p. 46. 63 Dillon, 'The inauguration of O'Conor', 190; Ó Muraíle, *Leabhar mór na ngenealach*, i, p. 542 §240.5; H.S. Sweetman (ed.), *Calendar of documents relating to Ireland, 1252–84* (1877), p. 489, §2115.   64 Knox understood Clan Conway to designate Drumatemple, Cloonygormican, Oran, Dunamon, Kilbegnet, Ballynakill, and Kilcroan: H.T. Knox, 'Occupation of the county of Galway by the Anglo-Normans after 1237', *Journal of the Royal Society of Antiquaries of Ireland*, 31 (1901), 365–70 at 365.   65 'Clann Murchada' does not appear to have survived as a territorial placename.

Roscommon) and reminisces about the trail, briefly naming Inn Airm and the closeby ecclesiastical site of Cell Chaímín amongst the sites on the route.[66] Both locations were situated in land controlled by the Clann Chonnmaig sub-sept of Clann Cheithernaig, whose territory lay in the modern parish of Kilkeevin in west Co. Roscommon (outside the traditional limits of Clan Conway). Another *Acallam* setting within Úa Fínnachta territory was Áth Moga, an important ford on the River Suck (parish of Drumatemple, barony of Ballymoe, Co. Roscommon). As the destination of a high-stakes race between an old hag and the trio of Oisín, Díarmait úa Duibne and Caílte, Áth Moga features in the second Connacht section of the *Acallam*.[67] The attention that these three sites receive is trivial, however, compared to the *Acallam*'s deep interest in the part of Úa Fínnachta territory corresponding to the parish of Oran, several parishes west of the parish of Roscommon.

The Oran episodes in *Acallam na senórach*
Oran takes its name from Úarán Garad, 'the Spring of Garad', a marvellous well at the hill of Garad that was famed in both the secular and hagiographical literature of early medieval Ireland. In one of the *remscéla* of the *Táin*, Úarán Garad was the site where the white bull, Findbennach, was 'conceived', after a cow from Medb's herd drank water containing a magical worm into which the cowherd, Rucht, had been transformed.[68] In Patrician hagiography, meanwhile, the well was said to have sprung forth under the aegis of Patrick, who praises its virtues in several verses in the *Vita tripartita*.[69] Úarán Garad features prominently in the *Acallam*, as does another site in the same parish, Ráith Medba, 'the Fort of Medb', sometimes referred to as Ráith Chaerech Medba, 'the Fort of the Sheep of Medb'. Ráith Medba gave its name to the Oran townland of Rathmew, situated on the next hill over from Úarán Garad, less than two kilometers west of the spring.[70] The 'fort' itself

---

66 J.H. Lloyd, '*Formaoil na bhfiann*: a country of the Clann Morna', *Journal of the Galway Archaeological and Historical Society*, 9 (1915–6), 112–14; Stokes, 'Acallamh', ll. 6541–3; Dooley and Roe, *Tales*, p. 183. Inn Airm and Cell Chaímín are both located in the modern townland of Arm in the parish of Kilkeevin, barony of Ballintober West, Co. Roscommon. For a fuller discussion of the locations on this trail, see Connon, 'Plotting *Acallam na senórach*', pp 75–80. For evidence indicating that Clann Cheithernaig were a sub-sept of Clann Chonnmaig, see P. Ó Macháin, 'Two documents relating to Ó Conchubhair Donn', *Ériu*, 57 (2007), 113–19 at 116. 67 Stokes, 'Acallamh', ll. 3968–72; Dooley and Roe, *Tales*, p. 118. 68 'De chophur in dá muic-cida', R.I. Best et al. (ed.), *Book of Leinster*, 6 vols (1954–83), ll. 32990–1; U. Roider (ed. and trans.), *De chophur in da muccida* (1979), p. 38, l. 81. Úarán Garad also appears in *Togail bruidne Da Derga* as the only well from which Mac Cécht is able to obtain water for the dying Conaire Már: E. Knott (ed.), *Togail bruidne Da Derga* (1975), p. 44. The triads further feature Úarán Garad as one of the three chief wells of Ireland: K. Meyer (ed. and trans.), *The triads of Ireland* (1906), pp 6–7. 69 Bieler, *Patrician texts*, pp 146–7; Mulchrone, *Bethu Phátraic*, p. 66; Stokes, *Tripartite Life*, pp 106–7. 70 E. Hogan, *Onomasticon Goedelicum locorum et tribuum Hiberniae et Scotiae* (1910), p. 574. In the following discussion, 'Oran' refers to the general parish, while Úarán Garad refers to the specific ecclesiastical site.

is presumably the very large barrow located on Rathmew's western border.[71] Collectively, Úarán Garad and Ráith Medba give the Oran area the highest topographical profile in the entire *Acallam*. More discrete episodes are set in this two kilometre strip than at any other location in the text, with one or another of the sites, sometimes both, featuring in each of the three Connacht sections. As will be discussed below, the author's interest in the region is evident not just from the frequency of the Oran episodes within the text, but also from the significance of the role played by these particular episodes within the *Acallam*.

The first of the Oran episodes occurs mid-way through the initial Connacht section of the *Acallam*.[72] After spending a night at Ráith Brénainn, the assembled entourages of Patrick, Caílte and the king of Connacht, Muiredach mac Fínnachta, make their way to Imaire meic Connrach (the ridge on which Ráith Medba was situated) and to the hill at Úarán Garad, setting up camp at the latter. Patrick proclaimed that the site was one of the eighteen burial places that would be dear to him in Ireland and then, mindful of the need for water, Patrick (as in the *Vita tripartita*) struck the ground with his staff and caused three streams to spring forth. Patrick blessed the well at Úarán Garad such that anyone who drank its water would receive protection, cure from illness, and, if they were to die shortly thereafter (presumably not of an illness), heaven. Furthermore, even if all the other water in Ireland were to be destroyed at the end of the world, it would be possible to maintain the whole island from the well.[73]

Patrick then asked Caílte for a story, and the Fenian related the tale of how, in the time of Finn, the *fian* were nearly destroyed at Úarán Garad as a consequence of a game of *fidchell*. Finn's servant, Gúaire Goll, had challenged the noble Finn Bán, one of the four best *fidchell* players in the world, to a series of games. After Gúaire Goll repeatedly lost, the servant viciously insulted Finn Bán until the latter finally struck him. When Finn mac Cumaill heard that his retainer had been struck, he was about to kill Finn Bán and his men in retaliation; however, Oisín's cooler head prevailed and peace was made after the reality of the situation was made clear to Finn.

Caílte then segues from the tale of Finn Bán and Gúaire Goll to another tale involving *fidchell*: the tale of Garad and the women of the *fian*, set twenty years later in time from the tale of Finn Bán. Here, the old retainer, Garad mac Morna, is left to guard the women at Druim Criad while the *fian* go hunting. The women try to cajole Garad into playing *fidchell* with them, but he refuses, citing as his excuse the tale of Finn Bán and Gúaire Goll and the

71 Sites and Monument Record RO034–035. 72 Stokes, 'Acallamh', ll. 1314–450; Dooley and Roe, *Tales*, pp 41–5. 73 There is a possible allusion here to *Togail bruidne Da Derga*, when Conaire Már is dying of thirst. The only place in all of Ireland where Mac Cécht can find water for him to drink is Úarán Garad: Knott, *Togail bruidne Da Derga*, p. 44.

tragedy that had almost ensued at Úarán Garad two decades earlier. He then proceeds to tell the women the tale. When the women subsequently mock him, teasing him that all he is good for in his old age is lighting fires and playing *fidchell*, Garad lights a great fire in the hall, locks all its doors, and recites a long poem retelling the Finn Bán and Gúaire Goll story. Later versions of the episode of Garad and the women, which stand as tales independent of the *Acallam*, relate that after locking all the doors of the hall, Garad sets it on fire and mercilessly burns the women to death in revenge for their teasing; however, the outcome of the *Acallam* version is more ambiguous, with the end of Garad's poem suggesting that he shows the forebearance required of a good retainer and refrains from violence.[74]

The importance of this first Oran sequence within the *Acallam* has been noted by several commentators. They have emphasised its role in the story of the rivalry between Clann Morna and Clann Baíscne, and have highlighted its pertinence to the theme of how a king's *airecht* should act in terms of relationships between figures from different classes.[75] Particular emphasis has been placed on the way in which the episode signals the design of the *Acallam*'s narrative structure. Geraldine Parsons and Rory McTurk have pointed out how the layered narrative structure of *Acallam na senórach* is mirrored in microcosm by the set of stories within stories in the two *fidchell* tales. Just as the narrator of the *Acallam* tells the story of the frametale in which Caílte relates stories of the Fenian past, so Caílte tells the story of 'Garad and the Women' in which Garad relates the tale of 'Finn Bán and Gúaire Goll'.[76]

An additional factor that might have contributed to the complex narrative structure of the two *fidchell* tales may have been the author's desire to pun on place and person, having Caílte tell the Fenian cycle's most significant story about Garad mac Morna at a place that contains Garad in its name. The difficulty with making such a pun, however, is that the *Acallam* usually employs the device of mutual location to link the frametale with tales from the Fenian past; however, while the story of Finn Bán and Gúaire Goll is set at Úarán Garad, the story of Garad and the women is not. Instead, it is set at Druim Criad, said to be somewhere in the territory of the Uí Thairrsig of Leinster.[77] In comparing this incident from the *Acallam* with the later stand-alone versions that end so badly for the women, Proinsias Mac Cana has suggested that

74 Dooley, 'The date and purpose', 106; Parsons, 'The structure', 20–1; J.F. Nagy, *The wisdom of the outlaw* (1985), p. 74 has a darker interpretation of the ending, feeling that the women were burnt to death.   75 Parsons, 'The structure', 20; Dooley, 'The date and purpose', 106. 76 Parsons, 'The structure', 18–20; R. McTurk, '*Acallam na senórach* and Snorri Sturluson's *Edda*' in S. Ó Catháin (ed.), *Northern lights* (2001), pp 178–89 at p. 179.   77 While the Uí Thairrsig are associated with Leinster in the *Acallam*, the 'Boyhood deeds' associates them with Corcu Ochae in Munster: K. Meyer (ed.), 'Macgnimartha Find', *Revue Celtique*, 5 (1881–3), 195–204 at 197 §1; Nagy, *The wisdom of the outlaw*, p. 209. Dooley and Roe, *Tales*, p. 234, suggest that the site is to be equated with Druim Criaich in Mide.

'another and perhaps fuller version of the conflagration tale was available to the author of the *Acallam*'.[78] Were this to be the case, then Druim Criad might already have been established as the setting of the tale (albeit the later versions do not stipulate its location), and the author of the *Acallam* might have felt constrained not to change it. Telling the story of Garad and the women within the context of another Fenian tale set at Úarán Garad would get around the problem, and still allow the author to indulge in word play.

In the absence of a mutual location, *fidchell* becomes the narrative device used to link the two stories; however, it is striking that in the later independent versions of Garad and the women, *fidchell* does not feature at all. In these versions, the women earn Garad's wrath by tying his hair and beard to stakes in the ground as he lies sleeping and then startling him awake so that he effectively scalps himself.[79] The absence of *fidchell* in the later independent versions suggests the possibility that it may not have been present in the hypothesised original version either, but was deliberately chosen and inserted by the author of the *Acallam* as a way to link the two stories together. Scenes in which Finn plays *fidchell* in the eleventh- or twelfth-century 'Boyhood deeds' indicate that the game was no stranger to pre-*Acallam fianaígecht* tradition,[80] and since the medium of *fidchell* was an effective way to bring together the disparate class elements involved in the Finn Bán and Gúaire Goll story, the choice of *fidchell* as the linking mechanism does not necessarily require any additional explanation. That said, the possibility that there is something further behind the author's use of *fidchell* as a narrative device arises when one considers that in addition to these two *fidchell*-related tales in the first Oran episode, the third Oran sequence also contains a *fidchell*-based tale: this is the episode where Áed mac Muiredaig and Caílte attempt to play *fidchell* at Úarán Garad but, upon discovering that the set is missing three pieces, Caílte goes to Slíab Badgna to recover three magnificent *fidchell* pieces from the hidden set of Goll mac Morna. We thus have a situation where three out of the five *fidchell* games played in the *Acallam* are set at Úarán Garad, and the possibility that the author of the *Acallam* altered the story of Garad and the women in order to make *fidchell* a central plot point within it. It would seem that the link between *fidchell* and Úarán Garad in the *Acallam* was not purely coincidental.

A simple explanation of the emphasis on *fidchell* here is that it was a way for the third Oran episode to reflect the first one, another of the many mirrors at work in the *Acallam*'s narrative structure.[81] An examination of the

---

78 'The *ingen moel*', *Ériu*, 52 (2002), 217–27, at 218 n. 2.   79 E.J. Gwynn (ed. and trans.), 'The burning of Finn's house', *Ériu*, 1 (1904), 13–37; J.F. Campbell, *Leabhar na feinne* (1872), pp 175–80.   80 Meyer, 'Macgnimartha Find', 200 §14; Nagy, *The wisdom of the outlaw*, p. 212. 81 For discussion of the mirror device in the *Acallam*'s narrative structure, see Parsons, 'The structure', 13; Dooley, 'The date and purpose', 105.

genealogies, however, suggests that prominence of *fidchell* may have been the crux of yet another placename pun, albeit one several orders of subtlety more understated than the Úarán Garad one. In terms of the political geography of Síl Muiredaig, Úarán Garad was almost certainly located in the Clann Chonnmaig section of Úa Fínnachta territory.[82] The Clann Chonnmaig genealogies ascribe three sons to their eponymous ancestor Connmach: Donn Garad, Ceithernach and Fithchellach.[83] Fithchellach, whose name is sometimes written as Fichellach, translates as '*fidchell* player'. While the genealogies note lines descended from all three sons, only the descendants of Ceithernach and Fithchellach are named as distinct septs: Clann Cheithernaig and Clann Fithchellaig.[84]

As seen in the discussion of Muinter Roduib territory, the names of distinct Síl Muiredaig septs and sub-septs very often were used as placenames to refer to the territories they (once) controlled. As both Clann Chonnmaig and its sub-sept of Clann Cheithernaig were being used as placenames up until the Early Modern period, it seems reasonable to suggest that the sub-sept of Clann Fithchellaig might similarly have given their name to a region within Clann Chonnmaig.[85] We do not know the location of the territory which Clann Fithchellaig once occupied, but it is not implausible that it might have been in the Oran area, particularly since the territory of the other Clann Chonnmaig sept, Clann Cheithernaig, is traditionally located further west, in the parish of Kilkeevin.[86] If so, then with his stress on *fidchell* and *fidchellaig* in the Oran episodes, the author of the *Acallam* may have been punning on the hypothesised regional placename of 'Clann Fithchellaig'.[87]

---

82 Clann Chonnmaig's link to Úarán Garad is suggested by a number of different pieces of evidence. The first is the name 'Donn Garad' given to one of the sons of Connmach, the eponym of the sept (see note 83). The second is the explicit association made between Clann Chonnmaig and the Patrician church in a possibly tenth-century tract on the religious affiliations of the Uí Briúin Aí (Ó Riain, *Corpus genealogiarum sanctorum Hiberniae*, p. 60, § 394.6). As Clann Chonnmaig is one of only two Síl Muiredaig septs linked to Patrick in the tract, the reference is most plausibly explained as a nod to Úarán Garad as the chief ecclesiastical site of Clann Chonnmaig. These inferences are backed up by the more solid evidence of a late thirteenth-century Anglo-Norman record outlining the demise of certain lands 'in the Theodum of Clonconewy on each side of the water' (Sweetman, *Calendar of documents of Ireland, 1252–84*, p. 289, §2115).   83 TCD MS 1298 (formerly H.2.7) 31a38; Book of Lecan 68vd10; Book of Ballymote 103ac22; Ó Muraíle, *Leabhar mór na ngenealach*, i, p. 542, §240.7.   84 Book of Ballymote reads, 'Clann Fichellaigh annso'. In the Book of Ballymote genealogies, the heading '[X] annso' is usually found in association with a list of the lines descended from [X], rather than simply a list of the children of [X].   85 See note 64 for 'Clanconway'. 'Clankearney' referred to 44 quarters of land in the north of the parish of Kilkeevin (Freeman, *The compossicion booke*, p. 156).   86 It is not clear, however, if the Kilkeevin territory, once originally part of Ciarraige, had been associated with Clann Cheithernaig since their emergence as a distinct sept, or if Clann Cheithernaig had been relocated there, either after Clann Murchada took over Clann Chonnmaig territory some time before the mid twelfth century, or perhaps after the Anglo-Normans took over Ballymoe *c.*1232 (ACon. 1232.5).   87 Rather than use the more

Were such a pun to have been made, the inclusion of wordplay that hinges on the name of a fairly obscure Clann Chonnmaig sept suggests that the author of the *Acallam* possessed local knowledge about the Oran area.[88]

The second, much shorter, Oran episode acts as the opening sequence of the second Connacht section of the *Acallam*.[89] Here, the *mise-en-scène* shifts abruptly from east Ulster to east Connacht, as Patrick and Caílte arrive at Ráith Medba from Dál nAraidi. This is the first time that Ráith Medba appears in the text as 'Ráith Medba' *per se*;[90] however, Imaire meic Connrach, the ridge with which the *Acallam* later equates the fort, features in the first Oran sequence (see above).[91] Ráith Medba also appears as the setting of several different stories in the third Oran sequence (see below), thereby earning the title of the single most featured monument in the *Acallam*. From the perspective of the text's interest in the Úa Fínnachta family, it is worth noting that the townland in which Ráith Medba is situated lies directly north of the Oran townland of Killinraghty Big. The latter contains the no longer visible ruins of an ecclesiastical site known locally in the 1950s as 'Killfinerty', the 'church of Úa Fínnachta'.[92]

When Patrick inquires as to the identity of the Medb who gave her name to the fort, Caílte tells him that Medb daughter of Eochaid Feidlech, queen of Connacht, used to come there on the feast of Samain. When Caílte added that she would arrive in her chariot with nine chariots in front of her, nine behind her, and nine on either side so that her new robes would not get spattered by mud, Patrick comments: 'That is a silly business' (*'Adhbur subhach sin!' ar Pátraic*).[93] Caílte then tells Patrick the tale of how the field they were standing in received the name 'Gort ind Fostáid' ('the Field of the Prevent-

common medieval spelling of *fidchell*, the Laud manuscript of the *Acallam* uses the forms *fichell* (genitive *fichle*) and *fithchell* in all but one instance. While these forms probably just represent a more 'phonetic' spelling, reflecting devoicing of [ð] by following [x], it is nevertheless worth noting the possibly intentional parallel with the form of the name 'Clann Fithchellaig'. *Fichell* and *Fithchell* are also the forms used in the first Oran episode in the Rawlinson B. 487 version of the text, and in at least some parts of the Fransiscan A 4 manuscript (I am grateful to Geraldine Parsons for checking the spelling for me in the Rawlinson manuscript). I have yet to investigate the forms used in the rest of the manuscripts. 88 Centuries later, a visual version of this pun was made in a seventeenth-century depiction of the fifteenth-century scholar Muris Ó Fithcheallaigh (Maurice O'Fihely) in a fresco in the Aula of the Irish College in Rome. There, the standard black and white tile floor depicted in the twin portrait of Aodh Mac Aingil has been altered so that in Ó Fithcheallaigh's portrait it resembles a chessboard. I am grateful to Geraldine Parsons and Mícheál Mac Craith for this reference. 89 Stokes, 'Acallamh', ll. 3859–86; Dooley and Roe, *Tales*, pp 116–17. 90 Stokes, 'Acallamh', ll. 3859–60; Dooley and Roe, *Tales*, p. 116. 91 Stokes, 'Acallamh', l. 1315; Dooley and Roe, *Tales*, p. 41. For identification of Ráith Medba with In Mairtine meic Conrach, see Stokes, 'Acallamh', ll. 7730–1; Dooley and Roe, *Tales*, p. 215. 92 Field notes compiled by Michael Moore regarding Sites and Monument Record RO034–059001 at http://webgis.archaeology.ie/NationalMonuments/FlexViewer/; query: Killinraghty Big, Co. Roscommon. 93 Stokes, 'Acallamh', ll. 3861–70; Dooley and Roe, *Tales*, p. 116.

ing'), after Finn used his powers of persuasion there to prevent a member of the *fían* from leaving the band.[94] It is noteworthy that although Caílte possesses vast knowledge about every hill, plain and stream in Ireland, this episode is the only instance in the *Acallam* which relates the story behind the name of a field. Following this short tale, Caílte and Patrick journey several parishes north, moving on from Oran to Elphin.

Although Caílte's identification of Medb explicitly acknowledges only her lineage and title, the audience of the *Acallam* could not fail to be aware of the queen's seminal role in the *Táin* and Ulster Cycle narratives. The Ráith Medba passage is one of a series of allusions to the Ulster Cycle that led Ann Dooley to characterise the *Táin* as a 'sleeper cell in the heart of the *Acallam*'.[95] One notable aspect of these allusions is that both of the explicit references to the *Táin* in the Connacht sections of the *Acallam*, and several of the implied references there, all occur within Oran-based episodes. The Oran episode in the first Connacht section refers to the ridge on which Ráith Medba stands as Imaire meic Connrach, 'the Ridge of the Son of Connra', adding that it was formerly called Ré Carpuit Fearghusa, 'the Chariot Course of Fergus'.[96] Here, the son of Connra in question would seem to be the Fir Domnann king of Connacht, Tinne mac Connrach Cais, who is identified as a former husband of Medb by the Middle-Irish tale *Cath Bóinde* (also known as *Ferchuitred Medba*).[97] Likewise, the chariot-racing Fergus is likely to be Medb's lover, the Ulster warrior, Fergus mac Róich.

A final Oran-linked Ulster Cycle reference occurs in the third Connacht section of the *Acallam* in relation to Fert in Gedig, 'the Grave of Gedech', a grave on the hill of Úarán Garad. There, the *Acallam* identifies the eponymous Gedech as either the bishop of the household of Patrick (the Cethiacus of Tírechán and the *Vita tripartita*) or as the druid of Medb and Ailill.[98] The double identification reinforces Úarán Garad's duality in earlier literature as a site that features in both Patrician hagiography and secular tales set in the legendary past. This multivalency of Christian and pre-Christian assocations lies at the very heart of the *Acallam*, except that therein the pagan and Christian connotations of Úarán Garad are no longer an either/or proposition. Instead, the author has invested the well, and indeed all of Patrick and Caílte's mutual itinerary, with interlaced Patrician and *fianaígecht* connotations.

94 Stokes, 'Acallamh', ll. 3871–86; Dooley and Roe, *Tales*, p. 117.   95 Ann Dooley, 'The *Táin bó Cúailgne* and *Acallam na senórach*', paper read at the Irish Conference of Medievalists, National University of Ireland, Galway, June, 2011.   96 Stokes, 'Acallamh', ll. 1314–15; Dooley and Roe, *Tales*, p. 41.   97 K. Meyer (ed.), 'Ferchuitred Medba' in O. Bergin et al. (eds), *Anecdota from Irish manuscripts*, v, (1913), p. 19; J. O'Neill (ed. and trans.), 'Cath Boinde', *Ériu*, 2 (1905), 173–85 at 178–9.   98 Stokes, 'Acallamh', ll. 7727–9; Dooley and Roe, *Tales*, p. 215. For Cethiacus, see Bieler, *Patrician texts*, p. 146; Mulchrone, *Bethu Phátraic*, p. 66; Stokes, *Vita tripartita*, pp 106–7. The *Vita tripartita* says that the grave of Cethiacus was at Úarán Garad. Fert Gédig is mentioned as a placename in ATig. s.a. 1177.

The third set of Oran episodes is an extended sequence, set at both Ráith Medba and Úarán Garad, that forms the conclusion to the third and longest Connacht section of the *Acallam*. It is there that Patrick, Áed mac Muiredaig and the duo of Caílte and Cas Corach reunite after their travels, and it is there that the group is joined soon afterwards by the men of Connacht, as Patrick and Áed hold the great assembly at Úarán Garad. The choice of Oran as the site of the assembly, rather than the more traditional sites of Rathcroghan or Carnfree, highlights the elevated status accorded to the area by the author. The company remains there for six weeks, affording both king and saint ample opportunity to listen to Caílte's tales of the past, recounted in a secret house set up between Áed's *longphort* and Patrick's tent at Úarán Garad. The position of Caílte's house, which literally marks a halfway point between the Christian and the secular, again underlines the duality of Úarán Garad as a site that figures in both hagiography and secular literature.

Despite the multitude of tales related there by Caílte, however, only one of his stories of the Fenian past is also told to the readers of the *Acallam*: the story of the accidental killing of a detachment of Finn's men by their own people at Úarán Garad, and the subsequent retrieval of a royal pillar stone (*ríg-lia cloiche*) from Ráith Medba with which to commemorate the dead.[99] Otherwise, the sequence remains firmly in the 'present' of Patrick and Caílte, thereby allowing the resolution of several storylines in the frametale. Chief amongst them is the love story between the king of Connacht, Áed mac Muiredaig, and the otherwordly woman, Aillenn daughter of Bodb Derg. After the king's human wife conveniently dies at Ráith Medba, Áed and Aillenn are finally free to be married, just down the road at Úarán Garad, in the first marriage ceremony performed by Patrick in Ireland. Here, the marriage of Áed and Aillenn marks the culmination, not only of their individual love story, but also of a key theme in the *Acallam*: the importance of monogamous, church-sanctioned marriage.[100] The thematic significance of the third Oran episode to the *Acallam* thereby parallels the thematic, as well as structural, importance of the first and second Oran episodes to the text.

An interesting aspect of the depiction of Úarán Garad and Ráith Medba in this final Oran sequence is that the sites are consistently portrayed as discrete locations: Áed mac Muiredaig first sets up camp at Ráith Medba and only later, with the arrival of Patrick, moves to Úarán Garad; meanwhile,

---

99 Stokes, 'Acallamh', ll. 7844–77; Dooley and Roe, *Tales*, p. 218.   100 For a discussion of marriage in the *Acallam* and its relationship to the reformers' concerns, see Dooley, 'The date and purpose', 104–5; H. Roe, '*Acallamh na senórach*: the confluence of lay and clerical oral traditions' in C.J. Byrne et al. (eds), *Celtic languages and Celtic peoples* (1992), pp 331–46 at p. 341; John Carey's contribution to this volume (pp 86–7); G. Parsons, 'A reading of *Acallam na senórach* as a literary text', Unpublished PhD (Cambridge, 2007), pp 204–9; I am indebted to Dr Parsons for providing access to her dissertation.

Caílte and Oisín go to Ráith Medba to find the pillar stone and then bring it back to the hill at Úarán Garad to erect above the graves of the *fian* members accidentally killed there. This depiction of the two sites as distinct is in spite of their being close enough to one another that the Annals of Connacht refer to Imaire meic Connrach, the ridge on which Ráith Medba was located, as 'Imaire Úaráin', a placename that suggests the two sites were viewed as part of a unified landscape.[101] The way that the *Acallam* distinguishes between the two nearby, but separate, locations, rather than telescope them together like someone unacquainted with the area might, gives a sense that the author probably had personal knowledge of the area. This sense of local character in the third Oran episode echoes the geographical familiarity inherent in the possible *fidchell/*Clann Fithchellaig pun in the first Oran episode, and is further underlined by Caílte's naming of the field in which Ráith Medba is located in the second Oran episode. While it cannot be confirmed that 'Gort ind Fostáid' was an actual placename, the intimacy of scale involved in naming topography at the field level – a practice found nowhere else in the *Acallam* – once again hints that the author knew the Oran area well.[102]

The sense that the author of the *Acallam* had first-hand knowledge of the Úa Fínnachta territory of Oran, taken together with the significance and sheer number of episodes set there, copperfastens the idea that the highlighting of the name 'Fínnachta' in the text mainly reflects the *Acallam*'s interest in the ruling family of Clann Murchada and Clann Chonnmaig – the same family who controlled the abbacy of the Augustinian house of canons at Roscommon. With regard to the Connacht sections of the text, the Augustinian house at Roscommon thus forms the nexus of the *Acallam*'s dynastic landscapes, positioned at the juncture of the text's general concern with Síl Muiredaig, its pointed notice of the sept who ruled the territory in which Roscommon was located, and its abiding interest in the sept who controlled Roscommon's abbacy.

***

It is not only the dynastic landscape of the *Acallam*, however, that features Roscommon as a key nodal point. The physical landscape of the *Acallam* likewise reflects a keen interest in, and local knowledge of, sites that were linked to the monastery of Roscommon in terms of geographical proximity and territorial possessions.

---

101 ACon. 1468.23.   102 The only other two 'field' names in the *Acallam* are Achad Bó (Aghaboe, Co. Laois) and Achad Fobair Umaill (Aghagower, Co. Mayo): Stokes, 'Acallamh', ll. 699–701, 7763–4; Dooley and Roe, *Tales*, pp 23, 216. However, although the names of these sites derive from the word *achad* 'field', they are not invoked in the *Acallam* as the names of actual fields *per se*, but, rather, as well-known ecclesiastical sites which took their name from the fields in which they were founded. *Achad* is very common as a generic in ecclesiastical sites: see Ó Riain et al., *Historical dictionary of Gaelic placenames*, fascicle 1 (2003), pp 9–24.

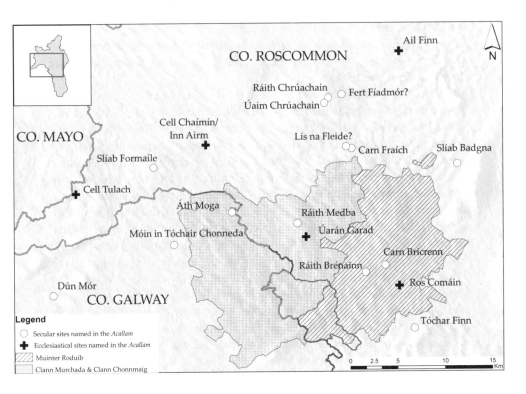

Figure 4: Sites in close proximity to the Augustinian house of
canons regular at Roscommon

The earlier discussion of the *Acallam*'s interest in Síl Muiredaig touched
upon the close relationship between the distribution of Connacht sites in the
Acallam and the limits of Síl Muiredaig/the diocese of Elphin (figure 2).
Within that distribution, the heaviest concentration of sites is in the central
Co. Roscommon area. This area of concentration approximates to the ancient
territorial unit of Mag nAí, near to whose southern limit the monastery of
Roscommon lies. Admittedly, this density of sites is partly due to the promi-
nence in the *Acallam* of the ceremonial landscapes of Rathcroghan and
Carnfree, both of which were situated in Mag nAí, and it could be argued
that their ritual significance would have warranted their inclusion in the
Acallam regardless of where in Connacht the text was written.[103] Even leaving the ceremonial landscapes out of the equation, however, there is still a

---

103 Stokes, 'Acallamh', ll. 7597–691; Dooley and Roe, *Tales*, pp 45, 210–13. It is also possible
that the site of Fert Fíadmór in Mag nAí, where Caílte relates the tale of the death of Fíadmór,
son of the king of Scotland, belongs to one of the ceremonial landscapes (Stokes, 'Acallamh', ll.
6438–529; Dooley and Roe, *Tales*, p. 181). The *Acallam* calls this site Suidhi Pátraic ('the Seat

notable cluster of sites near the monastery of Roscommon that feature as settings in the *Acallam* (figure 4). As will be seen below, these sites are often
described in terms of specific topography and monuments, thereby acquiring
a certain local colour.

In the first Connacht section of the *Acallam*, Lough Croan, located
approximately twenty kilometres due south of Roscommon (and thus outside
Mag nÁí), provides the setting for the initial meeting between Patrick, Caílte
and the king of Connacht, Muiredach mac Fínnachta, and his son Áed.[104]
From there, the assembled company is said to have travelled north towards
Roscommon via Tóchar Finn.[105] I would identify this causeway with the now
obsolete townland of 'Togharfin', which corresponds roughly to the modern
townland of Bolinree in the parish of Kilmeane.[106] Bolinree is directly south
of the southern border of the parish of Roscommon (formed by the Hind
River), and less than five kilometres south of the Augustinian house at
Roscommon.

From Tóchar Finn, the saint and Fenians passed briefly through Ros
Comáin, the site of the monastery of Roscommon itself.[107] Unlike some of the
other locations in close proximity to the monastery, there is no full tale
attached to Ros Comáin. Instead, the *Acallam* simply states that the former
name of Ros Comáin was Ros na Fingaili, 'the Wood of the Kin-slaying', and
explains that it received this name when the nine sons of Úar son of Indast
killed one another there. Although the *Acallam* makes no further mention of
Úar's nine sons in relation to Ros Comáin, three of them appear again
towards the end of the *Acallam*, in the climax to the longest-running story arc
in the *Acallam*: the saga of the wondrous sons of the king of Irúaith. In this
episode, also centring around *fingal*, the king of Irúaith's sons use a charm
that expells three sons of Úar son of Indast into the sea from Slíab Mis in Co.
Kerry, and compels them to commit *fingal* by driving their swords into one
another's heads.[108] While the repetition of the story is hardly likely to be accidental, the connection between the Ros Comáin and Slíab Mis episodes is
unclear. Perhaps there is some link to the Augustinian house of canons at
Killagh (St Mary of Bello Loco), founded *c.*1216, which is located very near
the foot of the southern side of Slíab Mis.

---

of Patrick'), an epithet which the *Vita tertia* of Patrick applies to the grave of Eithne and
Fedelm at the well of Clébach on the side of Rathcroghan: L. Bieler (ed.), *Four Latin lives of
Saint Patrick* (1971), pp 155–6. The *Tripartite Life*, meanwhile, places *suide Pátraic* at Duma
Selcae, part of the landscape of Carnfree: Mulchrone, *Bethu Phátraic*, p. 67; Stokes, *Tripartite
Life*, p. 100. **104** Stokes, 'Acallamh', ll. 1014–1236; Dooley and Roe, *Tales*, pp 33–8.
105 Stokes, 'Acallamh', ll. 1237–8; Dooley and Roes, *Tales*, p. 38. **106** W. Petty, *Hiberniae
delineatio: atlas of Ireland*, Map of Roscommon (1685); Down Survey map of barony of Athlone,
in R. Simington, *Books of survey and distribution … vol. 1: County of Roscommon* (1949), p. 122.
107 Stokes, 'Acallamh', ll. 1239–41; Dooley and Roe, *Tales*, p. 38. **108** Stokes, 'Acallamh', ll.
6146–269; Dooley and Roe, *Tales*, pp 172–6.

From Ros Comáin, the assembled company travel approximately five kilometres north of the monastery to the mound and fort at Ráith Brénainn. The
conjoined monuments there give their name to the modern townland of
Rathbrennan (parish of Roscommon), the setting for the story of Glas, king
of Lochlann. In an epic battle between the *fían* and the men of Lochlann,
Glas was killed by Finn mac Cumaill at Ráith Brénainn, to which the *Acallam*
gives the older name of Ráith Glais. Following the battle, Finn and his men
found nine massive pillars of gold which they hid in the 'red moor' (*móin
ruaidh*) on the northern side of the fort.[109] Here, the *Acallam*'s description of
the moor corresponds closely to the location of the boggy ground in the townland of Cams, Rathbrennan's immediate neighbour to the north and west.
These topographically accurate details suggest that the Ráith Brénainn episode
is based upon familiarity with the area, an impression which recalls the strong
sense of local character that permeates the Oran episodes discussed earlier.[110]
The details of the Oran sequences need no further rehearsing, but, in terms
of the physical landscape in the vicinity of the monastery of Roscommon, it
is worth noting that Oran parish, situated just across the bog from Cams
townland, is located only twelve kilometres to the northwest.

Directly to the east of Rathbrennan is the townland of Carrownabrickna
(parish of Roscommon). 'Carrownabrickna' is an anglicised form of Carn
Bricrenn, the setting for the 'werewolf' story in the third Connacht section of
the *Acallam*.[111] There, Caílte and Cas Corach together put an end to the three
sisters from the cave of Crúachu, who had been raiding the lands of the king
of Ireland's steward in the form of she-wolves. Cas Corach had gone to the
wolves' resting place at the hill of Carn Bricrenn, but soon realised that he
would not be able to kill the sisters while they were in animal form. After Cas
Corach used his music to lure them into discarding their wolf shapes (*conricht*), Caílte thrust a spear through the women and killed them. From this,
says the narrator of the *Acallam*: 'the valley running north from Cairn
Bricrenn is even now called Glenn na Conricht to this day'.[112] As with Ráith

---

109 Stokes, 'Acallamh', ll. 1241–312; Dooley and Roe, *Tales*, pp 39–41. **110** At the dissolution
of the monasteries, the Augustinian house at Roscommon actually owned Rathbrennan; however, it did not come into possession of it until 1282, i.e. probably at least half a century after
the composition of the *Acallam* (Sweetman, *Calendar of documents of Ireland, 1252–84*, p. 458).
The possibility of discord between the monastery of Roscommon and the land-owners of Ráith
Brénainn is hinted at by the metrical version of the story of Finn Bán and Gúaire Goll. There,
Garad compares the bad behaviour of Gúaire with that of several other servants, one of whom
is named as a certain Comán who insulted a certain Glas. Comán would seem to be a reference
to Ros Comáin through its saint, while Glas, the king associated with Ráith Brénainn in the
Acallam, might be a reference to the Mac Airechtaig rulers of Muinter Roduib (Stokes,
'Acallamh', 40, ll. 1433–5; Dooley and Roe, *Tales*, p. 44). **111** Ó Riain et al., *Historical dic-
tionary of Gaelic placenames*, fascicle 3, p. 65. **112** Dooley and Roe, *Tales*, pp 213–14; cf.
Stokes, 'Acallamh', ll. 7716–17: *Conid Glenn na Conricht ainm in glenna i l-leith ituaid do Charnn
Bricrenn o sin anall gus aniu.*

Brénainn, the *Acallam*'s description of Carn Bricrenn reflects a familiarity with local topography. The townland of Carrownabrickna, situated less than four kilometres northwest of Roscommon, contains a hill (surmounted by a row of four barrows), with a valley running northwards from it. Although there is no cairn on the hill today, its one-time presence there is attested by the Early Modern form of the townland name, 'Carnebrickny'.[113]

The final two locations to be discussed in this investigation of the physical landscape of Roscommon are the ecclesiastical sites of Cell Chaímín, 'the Church of Caímín', said to be 'on the [River] Suck' and Cell Tulach, 'the Church of Hills', in the westernmost part of Co. Roscommon. The two sites are named near the beginning of the third Connacht section of the *Acallam* in the episode set at Slíab Formaíle.[114] There, the weeping Caílte rhymes off the names of the two churches in a list-like description of the stops on the favourite hunting circuit of the *fian*. The list also includes the supposed 'former' names of the churches, with Cell Chaímín given the alternative name of Dún Saltráin Sálfata, 'the Fortress of Long-heeled Saltrán', and Cell Tulach the alternative name of Clúain na Damraide, 'the Meadow of the Stags'.

Immediately after the Slíab Formaíle sequence, Clúain na Damraide is named again, this time as the setting for the tale of an encounter between the rival *fiana* of Finn mac Cumaill and Goll mac Morna.[115] When Goll and his men were encamped on the ridge at Clúain na Damraide in order to make raids on Finn and his men, Clann Baíscne surprised them and surrounded Clann Morna while they were preoccupied with their meal. From that, Cell Tulach/Clúain na Damraide was said to have earned the further alternative name of Clúain Imdergtha, 'the Meadow of Shame'. At the end of the episode, Finn made a prophecy after washing his face and hands in a white gold basin filled with water, and putting his thumb 'under his tooth of wisdom'. There, Finn foretold that in time the site would become a peaceful church on a ridge (*druim*) above a lake, and later a royal site.

Cell Chaímín is the ecclesiastical site of Kilkeevin, situated in the modern townland of Arm in the parish of Kilkeevin (barony of Castlerea, Co. Roscommon).[116] Cell Tulach/Clúain na Damraide/Clúain Imdergtha is the Patrician church of Kiltullagh situated in the townland and parish of Kiltullagh (barony of Castlerea, Co. Roscommon);[117] the parish of Kiltullagh is located to the immediate south of Kilkeevin. As with Carn Bricrenn and

---

113 Simington, *Books of survey and distribution: Roscommon*, 32.   114 Stokes, 'Acallamh', ll. 6542–3; Dooley and Roe, *Tales*, p. 183.   115 Stokes, 'Acallamh', ll. 6606–31; Dooley and Roe, *Tales*, pp 185–6.   116 The quarter of Arm, one of the ecclesiastical lands of Kilkeevin church (Simington, *Books of survey and distribution: Roscommon*, 14), is also mentioned by the *Acallam* in the Slíab Formaíle circuit.   117 Kiltullagh's status as a Patrician church is indicated by its inclusion in a list of Connacht Patrician sites whose control was contested by Armagh and the Archbishop of Tuam in the early thirteenth century: W.H. Bliss (ed.), *Calendar of entries in the papal registers relating to Great Britain and Ireland*, i: 1198–1304 (1893), p. 40.

Ráith Brénainn, the *Acallam*'s description of Cell Chaímín and Cell Tulach corresponds closely to the topographical situation of the sites. Kilkeevin is located on the shore of the Suck River, as mentioned in the text, while the description of Cell Tulach being on 'a ridge over a lake' (*druim os loch*) accords with Kiltullagh's hill-top position overlooking what is now a turlough. Where Kilkeevin and Kiltullagh differ from Carrownabrickna and Rathbrennan, however, is that they are located considerably further away from the house of canons at Roscommon. Kilkeevin is approximately thirty kilometres distant from the monastic house, while Kiltullagh is approximately forty. Their inclusion in the present account of *Acallam* sites associated with the monastic house at Roscommon is owed not to proximity, but instead to their status as possessions of the two religious houses at Roscommon. Kilkeevin and its associated three quarters of land was owned by the Dominican priory at Roscommon, while Kiltullagh and its associated two quarters of land were owned by the Augustinian house of canons at Roscommon.[118]

Kiltullagh is unusual in this regard, for although the possessions of the monastery of Roscommon included considerable landholdings, as well as the rectories of numerous Ballymoe churches, 'the churchton of Kiltullagh' and its attendant lands are the only ecclesiastical site beyond the house of canons itself that the monastery actually owned (as opposed to simply controlled the tithes of) at the dissolution of the monasteries.[119] Kiltullagh's unusual status within the holdings of Roscommon is paralleled by its unusual treatment amongst the many ecclesiastical sites numbered within the pages of the *Acallam*. Cell Tulach and Cell Chaímín are two of only three ecclesiastical sites in Connacht mentioned in the text whose placename explicitly acknowledges their status as a church.[120]

Cell Tulach is further distinguished by the role it plays in the prophecies of Finn mac Cumaill. Finn's ritual of predicting the future through his 'tooth of wisdom' occurs seven times in the *Acallam*, with the prophecy about the future church at Kiltullagh being the final revelation obtained in this way. The prediction about Kiltullagh is the endpoint in the evolution of Finn's

---

118 Griffith, *Calendar of Irish patent rolls of James I*, p. 154. While the Dominican priory of Roscommon was likely founded later than the date of the *Acallam*, its link to Kilkeevin is still worth noting, particularly since it also owned a considerable amount of land in the parish of Oran, the region of such significance in the Connacht sections of the *Acallam*. Kiltullagh lay within the territory of the Úa Flainn lords of Síl Maíl Rúain, a sept of Uí Briúin Aí. It is possible that Kiltullagh came under Roscommon's control during the mid-thirteenth-century abbacy of the Síl Maíl Rúain ecclesiast, Gilla na Náem Úa Flainn (ATig. 1143). 119 The Dominican priory at Roscommon owned the parish church of Roscommon, as well as chapels at Emlaghmore in Oran and Cloneenbaun in Cloonygormican (Griffith, *Calendar of Irish patent rolls*, p. 154). 120 The third site is Cell Búadnatan (perhaps in townland Keelty, parish of Drumcliff, barony of Carbury, Co. Sligo): Stokes, 'Acallamh', ll. 6894–5. For the near absence of Christian placenames in the *Acallam*, see J.B. Arthurs, 'The legends of placenames', *Ulster Folklife*, 1 (1955), 37–42 at 40; see also Parsons, 'A reading of *Acallam na senórach*', p. 96.

prophecies, marking their progression from the revelation of purely secular information at the beginning of the text to visions that are wholly ecclesiastical/eschatological by the end.[121] In contrast to the relatively minor church of Kiltullagh, however, the other religiously linked predictions all involve key ecclesiastical sites – Clonmacnoise, Glendalough, Ferns, St Mullins and Cashel – that were highly important monasteries and, in many cases, post-reform diocesan seats. The inclusion of Kiltullagh amidst such lofty company would certainly seem to signal a special interest on the part of the author. Were the *Acallam* to have been written in Roscommon, Kiltullagh's status as a possession of the monastery provides a plausible context for the highlighting of the church in this fashion.

Although devoting only limited attention to the site of Ros Comáin itself, the *Acallam* thus pays significant, topographically detailed and locally coloured attention to sites that were either in close physical proximity to the monastery of Roscommon, part of its landed possessions, or linked to the dynastic septs that controlled it. The way in which the Augustinian house of canons at Roscommon thereby stands at the intersection of the *Acallam*'s physical and dynastic landscapes of Connacht argues strongly for the monastery as the text's *locus* of composition. Adding further weight to the argument is the long-standing reputation of Roscommon's scriptorium as a centre of secular and religious learning, noted from the ninth century through to its incarnation as a reformed Augustinian house.[122] Boasting several abbots renowned as a master (*suí*) of *senchas* – one before and one after the monastery assumed the Augustinian rule – Roscommon was precisely the type of institution where one might expect a text like the *Acallam* to be written.[123] The issues that may have arisen in trying to accommodate – and perhaps rationalise – an interest in *senchas* within a reformed monastery might account for Patrick's somewhat conflicted attitude towards Caílte's entertaining, but pagan, tales.[124]

If Roscommon is where one might expect the *Acallam* to have been written, the next questions are 'when?' and 'by whom?' Below are some speculative thoughts on the *tempus* and *persona* of *Acallam na senórach* that arise out of the arguments relating to *locus*.

***

121 Stokes, 'Acallamh', ll. 202–5, 1831–56, 2406–33, 2602–25, 2657–87, 5411–19, 6626–31; Dooley and Roe, *Tales*, pp 9, 56, 74, 80, 81, 151, 186. 122 AU 874.1; AFM 1043; AU 1088.3, ATig. 1088, AFM 1088; AFM 1097, 1232, 1234; K. Meyer (ed. and trans.), *The vision of Mac Conglinne* (1892), pp 8–9. In the latter part of the thirteenth century, the Dominican and Franciscan priories at Roscommon were involved in the production of Latin manuscripts: B. Williams (ed.), *The 'Annals of Multyfarnham': Roscommon and Connacht provenance* (Dublin, 2012); B. Hazard and K.W. Nicholls, *Annales Dominicani de Roscoman* (www.ucc.ie/celt/published/L100015A). 123 AFM 1088, 1232. 124 Stokes, 'Acallamh', ll. 127–9, 286–303, 3471–86, 3988–94; Dooley and Roe, *Tales*, pp 6, 11–12, 105–6, 119; M. Ní Mhaonaigh, 'Pagans and holy men: literary manifestations of twelfth-century reform' in D. Bracken and D. Ó Riain-Raedel (eds), *Ireland and Europe in the twelfth century* (2006), pp 143–61 at pp 147, 151–5; J.F.

II. *TEMPUS*

The starting point for this discussion of the date of composition of *Acallam na senórach* is Dooley's comment that the choice of 'Muiredach' as the name of the king of Connacht, and the choice of 'Áed' as the name of his son, was meant to recall 'the Síol Muireadhaigh dynastic line from its founder Muiredach Muillethan (†702), through Fínshnechta (†848) to Cathal Croibhdherg (†1224) – the king almost certainly reigning at the time the *Acallam* was composed – and his son Áed'.[125] Implicit in Dooley's comment is the idea that Muiredach mac Fínnachta was a literary stand-in for Cathal Crobderg Úa Conchobair, king of Connacht (*c*.1190–1200 and 1202–24), and that Muiredach's son and heir, Áed mac Muiredaig, likewise represented Crobderg's son and heir, Áed mac Cathail Úa Conchobair, king of Connacht *c*.1224–8.

Beyond the parallel of each having a son and heir by the name of Áed, there is a second correspondence in royal offspring to support the identification of Muiredach with Cathal Crobderg. In the *Acallam*, Muiredach mac Fínnachta has a daughter, Bé Binn (one of the many women of this name in the text), who is the wife of Conall Mór mac Néill, king of Cenél Conaill.[126] Likewise, Cathal Crobderg had a daughter, Lasairfhína (†1282), who appears to have been the wife of Domnall Mór Úa Domnaill (†1242), king of Cenél Conaill.[127]

The theory that Muiredach mac Fínnachta represents Cathal Crobderg could potentially help explain why the *Acallam* set Patrick's initial meeting with Muiredach and Áed at Loch Cróine, now Lough Croan in the parish of Cam in southern Co. Roscommon.[128] Although there is a certain symmetry with Patrician hagiography in that Loch Cróine is one of the first Connacht sites mentioned in the *Vita tripartita*, the decision to set this pivotal encounter at the lough – rather than, say, Rathcroghan or another site intimately connected with Síl Muiredaig kingship – still seems to be an unusual choice for an author usually so attuned to the nuances of Connacht political geography.[129] A hint as to why the *Acallam* chose this location may lie in the fact that several, now obsolete, placenames very close to the lough appear to have

Nagy, *Conversing with angels and ancients* (1997), pp 320–1. **125** Dooley, 'The date and purpose', 103. **126** Stokes, 'Acallamh', ll. 2065–7; Dooley and Roes, *Tales*, p. 64. **127** A verse in Lasairfhína's obit in the Annals of Loch Cé identifies her as the wife not of Domnall Mór Úa Domnall, but of his son Domnall Óg (†1279 [ALC *s.a.*]); however, this appears to have been an error since she is identified as the wife of Domnall Mór not only in her obit in AFM (*s.a.* 1282), but also in an entry detailing a donation she made to Holy Trinity (ALC 1239, AU¹ 1239). A poem by Gilla Brigde Mac Con Midhe, beginning 'Rogha na cloinne Conall', similarly depicts Domnall Óg as her son and not her husband: N. Williams (ed. and trans.), *The poems of Giolla Brighde Mac Con Midhe* (1980), pp 82–95. **128** Stokes, 'Acallamh', ll. 1014–1236; Dooley and Roe, *Tales*, pp 32–8. **129** Mulchrone, *Bethu Phátraic*, p. 53; Stokes, *Tripartite Life*, p. 86.

incorporated a reference to *dún Cathail*, 'the fort of Cathal'. 'Ballydooncahill' (either 'the *baile* or *belach* (pass) of Cathal's *dún*') lay along the southern shores of the lough (within the [obsolete] denomination of Lisrockeda), while 'Derrydooncahell' ('the oak forest of Cathal's *dún*') lay a little further to the east.[130] If Muiredach mac Fínnachta did represent Cathal Crobderg, the *Acallam*'s introduction of him at a setting that evoked Cathal's name may have been another of the author's word games. Nor is it impossible that Cathal Crobderg was himself the eponym of these *dún Cathail* names, and that the decision to set the episode there reflects its possible status as a contemporary royal centre.[131]

Given the parallels between their children (and the possible allusion to Cathal in the choice of setting of the Lough Croan episode), as well as the agreement seen by Dooley between the values promoted in the *Acallam* and those of Cathal Crobderg's reign,[132] there seems to be a reasonable case for the identification of Cathal Crobderg with Muiredach mac Fínnachta. In terms of dating the *Acallam*, the most salient point about this equation is that, by extension, Áed mac Muiredaig is to be identified with Áed mac Cathail Úa Conchobair. Since (a grown-up) Áed mac Muiredaig was the ruling king of Connacht by the end of the *Acallam*, the implication is that by the time the final Connacht section of the *Acallam* was written, Áed mac Cathail Úa Conchobair had succeeded his father.[133] If this theory is correct, then at least the final Connacht section of the *Acallam* likely dates to the years of Áed's rule: 1224 to 1228. It may be that the writing of the *Acallam* spanned the reigns of Cathal Crobderg and his son,[134] or that the whole text was written after 1224.

130 Petty, *Hiberniae delineatio*: map of Roscommon; Down survey map of barony of Athlone, in Simington, *Books of survey and distribution: Roscommon*. For the position of Ballydooncahill/Balladooncahill within Lisrockeda, see British Library MS Add. MS 47052 77r; Simington, *Books of survey and distribution: Roscommon*, p. 100. Lisrockeda, and thus Ballydooncahill, likely lay in the modern Cam townland of Cornalee, while Derrydooncahell would seem to have lain in the western half of the present Cam townland of Coolagarry. 131 It is notable that Áed mac Muiredaig is introduced in his role as king of Connacht at the known Úa Conchobair castle of Dún Leóda, now Ballinasloe (ATig. 1124). That a castle existed at some point on the shores of Lough Croan is indicated by the placename 'Castlebregy' which early modern sources list as part of the same denomination of land that contained Ballydooncahill (Simington, *Books of survey and distribution: Roscommon*, p. 100; Add. MS 47052 77r). The castle in question would appear to be the archaeological remains locally referred to as 'O'Kelly's Castle', situated near the eastern shore of Lough Croan in the northern end of the townland of Cornalee (field notes compiled by Michael Moore regarding Sites and Monument Record RO048–001 at http://webgis.archaeology.ie/NationalMonuments/FlexViewer/; query: Cornalee, Co. Roscommon). 132 Dooley, 'The date and purpose', esp. 98–9, 105–7, 118–21. 133 It should be noted, though, that Áed mac Cathail had been designated as his father's heir at least fourteen years before his father died (ALC 1210). It is thus not impossible that the depiction of Áed as king was written before his actual succesion to the throne. 134 Ann Dooley (personal comment).

There are several other pieces of historical evidence that are in line with dating the *Acallam* to the period of Áed mac Cathail's kingship. The first relates to the famous mention at the opening of the *Acallam* to the monastery of Mellifont, the first Cistercian abbey in Ireland.[135] Mellifont was founded in 1142, and the reference to it in the *Acallam* has been used as a *terminus post quem* for the dating of the text.[136] While Myles Dillon raised the possibility that the Mellifont reference may have been a later gloss, there are a number of hints in the *Acallam* to indicate that interest in the Cistercian houses of Ireland may have been a running theme throughout the text.[137] Consequently, it is very interesting to note that in 1224, the first year of Áed mac Cathail's reign, he pledged to donate five silver marks annually to the Cistercian mother house of Cîteaux, through the offices of the abbot of Mellifont.[138]

The second piece of evidence supporting the dating of the *Acallam* to Áed's rule is related to one of the signatory witnesses to the 1224 Cîteaux charter. This was Donn Cathaig mac Airechtaig Úa Roduib, the lord of Muinter Roduib who also controlled the Síl Muiredaig septs of Clann Taidg and Clann Murthaile. His lordship over the latter septs was said by the genealogies to have generated 'great pickings never before won by any of his kin'.[139] Later that year, Donn Cathaig died and was succeeded by his son, Donn Bó, creating a situation where both the lord of Muinter Roduib and the king of Connacht, Áed mac Cathail Úa Conchobair, were new to their positions. The next year, 1225, Donn Bó rebelled against Áed mac Cathail, in part because the king of Connacht had deprived him of his lands, his *ferann 7 aicidecht.*[140]

Elsewhere, I have argued that Fírchuing – the setting for the key meeting in the *Acallam* between Patrick and Dub, the representative of Muinter Roduib – may have been located in one of the two Síl Muiredaig septs that Donn Cathaig had acquired control over, most likely Clann Murthaile.[141] I further made the case that the property problems facing Dub and his new

---

135 Stokes, 'Acallamh', l. 53; Dooley and Roe, *Tales*, p. 4. **136** M. Dillon, *Stories from the Acallam*, (1970), p. 25; K. Murray, 'Interpreting the evidence: problems with dating the early *fianaigecht* corpus' in S. Arbuthnot and G. Parsons (eds), *The Gaelic Finn tradition* (2012), pp 31–49 at p. 44. **137** For example, two of the longest episodes in the text are set in the *síd* at Ess Rúad, Assaroe near Ballyshannon, Co. Donegal: Stokes, 'Acallamh', ll. 1559–867, ll. 6898–7287; Dooley and Roe, *Tales*, pp 48–57, 194–204. While the inclusion of these episodes might be owed to Ess Rúad's status as both a Patrician site and a traditional *síd* location, it cannot be overlooked that it was also the site of an important Cistercian monastery: Gwynn and Hadcock, *Medieval religious houses*, p. 127. **138** Flanagan, *Irish royal charters*, pp 350–1. Cathal Crobderg was also a notable supporter of the order, responsible for founding the Cistercian house of Abbeyknockmoy (*Collis Victoriae*), his own burial place (ACon. 1224.2; Gwynn and Hadcock, *Medieval religious houses*, p. 124). **139** Book of Lecan 65rb28–31: *ro gob siden forgobail móir nachar gab neach roimhe da chenél* (cf. Book of Ballymote 97db26; Ó Muráile, *Leabhar mór na ngenealach*, i, p. 504, §225.7); see Dooley, 'The date and purpose', 114. **140** ALC 1225, ACon. 1225.4. **141** Connon, 'Plotting *Acallam na senórach*', pp 81–90, 97.

bride before Patrick's intervention with Áed mac Muiredaig may thus have been a reference to problems which Donn Bó faced during the reign of Áed mac Cathail in making his father's control over the additional Síl Muiredaig septs hereditary.[142] If this supposition is accurate, then the Fírchuing episode could be considered further evidence in dating at least the third Connacht section of the *Acallam* to Áed's reign, most likely to the earlier part *c.*1224–5. This notion is in agreement with Nuner's linguistic analysis of the verbal forms in the *Acallam* which led him to date the text to the period 1200–25, with an emphasis on the 1225 end of the scale as the most probable date of composition.[143]

III. *PERSONA*

In light of the argument for Roscommon as the *locus* of composition for *Acallam na senórach*, and *c.*1224 as a possible *tempus* for the text, two individuals stand out as candidates to fill the role of *persona*. Both of these possible identifications for the author of the *Acallam* are drawn from the list of Clann Murchada personnel who dominated the ecclesiastical offices at the Augustinian house of Roscommon. The first is Máel Petair Úa Cormaccáin, who died in 1234 as *magister* of Roscommon.[144] Not only would the head of the monastic school at Roscommon potentially have been capable of writing something like the *Acallam*, but his Clann Murchada ancestry would be in keeping with the *Acallam*'s strong interest in the Úa Fínnachta line. Furthermore, he would have possessed intimate knowledge of the Roscommon landscape, as well as the local knowledge that appears to illuminate the episodes set around Oran: the *caput* of the Úa Cormaccáin family was Clúain Úa Cormaccáin, now the townland of Clogher in the parish of Cloonygormican, barony of Ballymoe, Co. Roscommon. Clogher is very close to Úarán Garad, bordering directly on the eastern boundary of the parish of Oran.

Attractive though Máel Petair might be as a potential author of the *Acallam*, more attractive still is the second candidate: Tipraite Úa Brain, abbot of Roscommon, who died in 1232.[145] Like his colleague Máel Petair,

---

142 Ibid., p. 97. One possible explanation behind the confiscation of Donn Bó's land was that Donn Bó might have seen his father's unprecedented control of Clann Taidg and Clann Murthaile as an hereditary right that he expected henceforth to continue within the Muinter Roduib lordship. Áed mac Cathail, on the other hand, might not have seen matters this way, and he may have taken Clann Taidg and Clann Murthaile away from Donn Bó, either to award them to someone else, or keep them for himself. This argument builds upon the initial connection made by Dooley, 'The date and purpose', 117, between the land confiscated from Donn Bó and the problems facing Dub with regard to his patrimonial land.   143 R.D. Nuner, 'The verbal system of the *Agallamh na senórach*', *Zeitschrift für celtische Philologie*, 27 (1958–59), 230–310 at 308–9; Murray, 'Interpreting the evidence', p. 45.   144 ACon. 1234.8.   145 AFM 1232.

Tipraite was tied strongly to Roscommon, belonged to one of the Clann Murchada families, and thus would have been native to the Ballymoe area. Unfortunately, we do not have a more specific site for the Úa Brain *caput*: the only clue to the family's precise location is that the topographical poems of Ó Dubhagáin place them by the unidentified Loch Gealgosa.[146] It is worth noting that the sole Roscommon O'Brene (anglicisation of Úa Brain) named in the Elizabethan fiants is said to be from Oran, but the late date and single instance of the name do not constitute enough evidence to confidently link the family to thirteenth-century Úarán Garad.[147]

Where Tipraite Úa Brain has the edge over Máel Petair in the authorship stakes is that his obituary calls him, *saoí cléircechta, sencusa, 7 breithemhnassa*, 'a master of clerical life [or, possibly, monasticism], lore and judgement'.[148] The *Acallam*'s interest in judicial decisions is manifest in several episodes in the text,[149] while the relevance to the *Acallam* of mastery over *senchas* needs no explanation. Tipraite's obit in AFM goes on to say that he died *in ailithre*, 'on pilgrimage', at Inis Clothrann, the island of Inchcleraun on Lough Ree. The reference to 'pilgrimage' may suggest that Tipraite had retired from Roscommon to Inis Clothrann before his death;[150] Inis Clothrann itself had a renowned monastic school, and, were Tipraite to have been the author of the *Acallam*, it is not impossible that he might have written it on the island in his retirement.[151] Against this notion, though, is the apparent absence of any reference to Lough Ree within the text.

An identification of Tipraite Úa Brain as author of the *Acallam* would further make sense of an odd placename change on the route westwards to Aghagower and Croagh Patrick. As noted in the discussion on Muinter Roduib, the last stop before Aghagower was Tipra Pátraic, the Augustinian house of canons at Ballintober.[152] The unusual thing about the name Tipra Pátraic, though, is that the *Acallam* is the only one to refer to it as such. All other vernacular sources that refer to Ballintober unanimously call it some variation on Topar Pátraic, Baile Topair Pátraic, or Baile an Topair (in Latin, it is called [Monasterium] de Fonte Sancti Patricii).[153] *Tipra* and *Topar* (later

---

I am grateful to Kevin Murray who first spied Tipraite's authorship potential as we scanned a list of Roscommon-based Clann Murchada ecclesiasts for potential links to the *Acallam*. **146** Carney, *Topographical poems*, p. 23. **147** *The Irish fiants of the Tudor sovereigns*, iii, p. 47. **148** AFM 1232. **149** Stokes, 'Acallamh', ll. 1355–61, 2834–5, 3017–40, 6329–58; Dooley and Roe, *Tales*, pp 42, 73, 92, 175. **150** The abbacy of Máel Ísu Úa Conchobair (†1223), although unrecorded in the annals, would have been situated somewhere between the abbacy of Máel Eóin Úa Cormaccáin (†1200 [AFM *s.a.*]) and Tipraite's. It might be that Máel Ísu had displaced Tipraite and forced him into retirement at Inis Clothrann. Were this the case, one wonders if the *Acallam*'s references to *fingal* at Roscommon were linked to any feelings of betrayal occasioned by Máel Ísu's abbacy. **151** ATig. 1160. **152** Stokes, 'Acallamh', l. 6760; Dooley and Roe, *Tales*, p. 189. **153** Ó Riain et al., *Historical dictionary of Gaelic placenames*, fascicle 2, pp 19, 57; Twemlow, *Calendar of papal registers*, x, 1447–55, p. 632.

spelt *tibra* and *tobar*) mean essentially the same thing, and are often used
interchangeably when referring to 'well' or 'spring' as a common noun.[154] The
Vita tripartita, for example, refers to the same well on the side of Rathcroghan
as *topar* in one sentence and then as *tipra* in the next.[155] When it comes to
topar and *tipra* in placenames, however, the pattern appears to be very different. In the vast majority of cases, specific placenames consistently use
either *tipra* or *topar*, but almost never both interchangeably.[156] Calling
Ballintober Tipra Pátraic instead of Topar Pátraic was so unusual, in fact, that
it might have been one reason why the scribe of the Laud manuscript of the
Acallam glossed the episode as 'Topur Patraic' in the margin.[157]

Nor is a preference for *tipra* over *topar* just limited to the name for Tipra
Pátraic. In the just under fifty instances of the two words in the *Acallam*,
tipra occurs over four times more often than *topar* (the exact split is 40:9);
furthermore, it may be significant that two-thirds of the relatively few uses of
topar occur in poetry.[158] As a point of comparison, the *Vita tripartita* – the
Acallam's sources for much of the material dealing with wells – is evenly split
as regards its use of the two terms. The *Acallam*'s preference for the form
tipra is thus striking and unusual. Were, however, the author of the text to
have been Tipraite Úa Brain – whose name is homonymous with the genitive
singular of *tipra*, meaning 'of the well' – the *tipra* pattern could be explained
as a gleeful pun on himself: the author of the *Acallam* may have quite literally inserted himself into the text! Such word games could also help explain
the *Acallam*'s great emphasis on wells in general, providing a further reason
for their inclusion in the text beyond their relevance to the theme of baptism
and their importance in Patrician hagiography.[159]

The notion that Tipraite Úa Brain, functioning as a living Tipra Pátraic,
was the source of *Acallam na senórach* in the form we now have it thus fits

---

154 *DIL* 'T', cols 186, 250.   **155** Mulchrone, *Bethu Phátraic*, pp 60–1; Stokes, *Tripartite Life*,
p. 98.   **156** Using Hogan's *Onomasticon Goedelicum* (pp 634–5, 639–41) as a rough guide to pro-
portional use – of the approximately 180 placenames incorporating the 'well' element in the
Onomasticon, there appear to be only three instances where *tipra* and *topar* are used interchangeably in a placename: *Tipra Arann/Tobar da rann*; *Tipra Finn/Tobar Finn*; and *Tipra
Segsa/Tobar Segsa* (I am excluding here the cases of *Tipra Phátraic* and *Tipra Ailbe* from the
Acallam).   **157** Stokes, 'Acallamh', l. 6758. I am grateful to Eystein Thanisch for drawing my
attention to the Laud glosses.   **158** The six references to *topar* that occur in poetry are found
at Stokes, 'Acallamh', ll. 91, 101, 103, 807, 2683, 6776; Dooley and Roe, *Tales*, pp 5–6, 27, 190.
The first three references are all within the same poem beginning 'A thobuir Trágha dhá bhan'.
The fourth reference occurs within the poem beginning 'Turus acam dia háine', which originally may have been an independent poem worked into the *Acallam*: G. Parsons, '*Acallam na
senórach* as prosimetrum', *Proceedings of the Harvard Celtic Colloquium*, 24–5 (2004–5), 86–100
at 95. The three instances of *topar* within a prose context occur at Stokes, 'Acallamh', ll. 81–2
(within the introduction to the poem beginning 'A thobuir Trágha dhá bhan'), 2331, and 2811;
Dooley and Roe, *Tales*, pp 5, 72, and 84.   **159** For the importance of baptism in the *Acallam*,
see Ní Mhaonaigh, 'Pagans and holy men', p. 152.

with an array of internal and external evidence relating to the composition of the text. Since the nature of that evidence is mostly circumstantial, though, the theory of Tipraite's authorship cannot be removed entirely from the realm of speculation. The same is true of the thoughts expressed here regarding the period *c.*1224 as the likely date of the *Acallam*'s composition. The argument made for the Augustinian house at Roscommon as the place of composition of *Acallam na senórach*, however, stands on a firmer foundation. Grounded in the topographical and dynastic interests of the Connact sections of the text, the 'out-tales' told by the *Acallam*'s western landscapes make a strong case for Roscommon as its *locus* of composition.[160]

160 I wish to thank the Moore Institute (NUI Galway), the Higher Education Authority and the Discovery Programme, for funding the research underpinning this article.

The European context of *Acallam na senórach*

ANN DOOLEY

Re-reading Seán Ó Coileáin's wonderful piece in *Cín Chille Cúile* has got me thinking once again about aspects of the *Acallam* to which I have done very little justice thus far.[1] How to frame a medieval European context for the work has long been my concern – as it has for other scholars – but, for me, it took this article of Sean's to bring it to a head. I am grateful then for this chance to engage in an '*agallamh*' about the *Acallam* with a master. In this latest work he deftly demolishes Carney's theories about the relation of prose to verse in the tale of Cáel and Créide; he re-establishes it as an integral romantic tale and not a piece of pre-existing professional eulogistic poetry stuck inappropriately in a make-shift and unprofessional setting of a soft tale of tragic love. The demolition of Carney's argument based on careful *dinnshenchas* observation, however, is secondary to that thread of his argument that identifies the essential dynamic of this mini-saga in particular and, by extension, the *Acallam* as a whole. He returns many times with evocative phrases such as 'the emotional effect is generated among the story personae' and 'in selecting (or inventing) the placenames to serve his poetic purpose he was not constrained by more mundane considerations'. More acutely still, he observes, that in a departure from *dinnshenchas* form

> placename has become text; ... but the appeal must always be not to logical consistency in term of the author's conceit as viewed from beyond the affective range of the text, but to the sensibilities of those who, while sharing in that conceit, share also in the less definable knowledge of the freedoms and limitations with which it will be allowed to function in the totality of their imaginative experience.

Finally, he notes: 'It is not so much the lack of detailed evidence as of [Carney's] approach being overly deterministic, as appears to me: a fluid world cannot be mapped in a conventional way'.[2]

It is a great privilege to have been invited to contribute to this volume in honour of Professor Ó Coileáin. I treasure the memory of his kind words to me many years ago – at that time a diffident novice in Celtic Studies who sorely needed encouragement. How many times have we not gone back to seminal works of his like 'The structure of a literary cycle' (*Ériu*, 25 (1974), 88–125) only to marvel anew at the range and depth of its argument, the mastery of its subject, and the elegant succinctness of its style.
1 'The setting of *Géisid cúan*' in J. Carey et al. (eds), *Cín Chille Cúile* (2004), pp 234–48 (reprinted in this volume). 2 Ibid., pp 244, 248.

So felicitous a phrase as 'mapping a fluid world' redirects the reader of the *Acallam* to reconsider the value of imagination and what it is that gives life to stories. By way of trying to understand how one might respond to the imaginative richness of the many streams of narrative in the *Acallam*, an analogy for this organisational dilemma comes to mind from a modern *dinnshenchas* maker, Tim Robinson, who also works in the area of commonly-shared imagination, in the complex interaction between the personally-experienced reality of landscape and the cultural memory of its inhabitants:

> Where to start, though, in presenting this land and its unquenchable talk of itself, and how to proceed are problems. There is no overarching story other than the dominance of story itself, no dominating theme but the multiplicity of themes. I have notes of hundreds of placenames, legends of saints and strong men of ancient times, curious incidents unforgotten through the centuries – but how do I link them together? Topographically [as a geologist] ... Chronologically ... Thematically [as a folklorist would] ... Or by improvisation and association? ... I think of the man whose story I began with, who walks one morning across familiar hills to witness a visionary re-enactment of an event out of a dateless past. His trajectory has the rugged reality of bog and granite, but begins in a dream of a place he [thinks he] recognises, and ends with a forbidden attendance at an incursion of the otherworld into his everyday.[3]

Some of the solutions to managing multiplicity and fluidity of stories must, as the *Acallam* author also recognised, lie in simply getting a work so palimpsested with layers of time and space, from here to there by way of a paratactic threading of small stepped individual stories. And on the microlevel of each individual tale we respond to what Walter Benjamin, in a classic essay on storytellers, describes as the moving power of a story: 'an intelligence coming from afar' – in his understanding, from a forgotten world of tradition or an unknown land.[4] Particular attention, however, should be paid to the points in the narrative where the narrator adopts a hypotactic style and creates an interlaced string of extended stories all of which relate to the 'present' Patrician time of the action.[5]

The *Acallam* was composed at the very beginning of the thirteenth century and as such shares a common chivalric literary landscape with the great

---

3 *Connemara, a little Gaelic kingdom* (2011), pp 110–11.   4 W. Benjamin, 'The storyteller' in D.J. Hale (ed.), *The novel* (2006), pp 362–77 at pp 364–5.   5 The use of these terms for narrative styles is from E. Auerbach, *Mimesis* (1968).   6 I use this term which has some currency among French scholars in order to re-direct and expand the more common medieval literary term, 'The Matter of Britain'.

products of contemporary medieval romance. I think we would all agree that the great unknown land from which medieval vernacular narrative literatures drew their vitality was precisely that world of the 'Matter of Celtia' that opened up freshly for them from the mid-twelfth century on.[6] For the most part, however, such romance authors as Chrétien de Troyes were still shaped by a power culture of the book and so received a British model of Arthur and his court somewhat different to that developing in native British popular tradition.[7] Their work is already shaped and rendered decorous by an actual literary source work, Geoffrey of Monmouth's pseudo-history, and, behind it, the *mise en abyme* fictive shadow of another clerical written *auctoritas*, the British book of Archdeacon Walter of Oxford.[8] Thus for medieval romance the values of invention and imagination, though frequently grounded in a Celtic story base, are bounded by ideas of the decorous inherited from received high literary sources. Chrétien is anxious to separate his work from that of the mere jongleurs.[9] The *Acallam* author by contrast employs an inclusive formula for his imagined audience, 'so that listening to those stories may provide entertainment for companies and lords to the end of time'.[10]

How do we think about that value of the imagination that Seán Ó Coileáin saw rightly as being the unique gift of the *Acallam*? Current literary criticism shies away somewhat from this term and the only full discussion is that of Wolfang Iser. As he sees it, every fictional representation rests on 'two forms of boundary-crossing: elements of external "reality" are repeated in the literary text, but not simply for their own sake. In the context of the fictional world, the replicated reality becomes itself a sign and takes on other meanings'.[11] On the other hand, the 'imaginary' – which Iser somewhat awkwardly describes as 'tend[ing] to manifest itself in a somewhat diffuse manner, in fleeting impressions that defy our attempts to pin it down in a concrete and stabilised form' – is given body through its representation in the medium of fiction, thereby achieving a determinacy which it did not previously possess. 'Reproduced reality is made to point to a "reality" beyond itself, while the imaginary is lured into form'.[12] Further, Iser says, the intentionality of a literary text 'is not to be found in the world to which the text refers, nor is it

7 O. Padel, *Arthur in medieval Welsh literature* (2000). See J. Carey, *Ireland and the grail* (Aberystwyth, 2007).   8 For *Historia Regum Brittaniae*, see L. Thorpe, *The history of the kings of Britain* (1966). For further recent work, see S. Echard (ed.), *The Arthur of medieval literature* (2011).   9 Preface to *Erec et Enid: D'Erec, le fil Lac, est li contes, / que devant rois et devant contes / depecier et corronpre suelent / cils qui de conter vivre veulent* ('The tale is of Erec, son of Lac, which those who are wont to recite orally before kings and counts mutilate and corrupt'). Text from Dictionnaire Électronique de Chrétien de Troyes (www.atilf.fr/dect/); translation my own.   10 W. Stokes (ed. and partial trans.), 'Acallamh na senórach' in W. Stokes and E. Windisch (eds), *Irische Texte*, iv, 1 (1900), ll. 301–2: *budh gairdiugudh do dronguibh 7 do degdáinibh deridh aimsire éisdecht frisna scéluib sin*; translations from the *Acallam* are my own.   11 W. Iser, *The fictive and the imaginary* (1993), p. 3.   12 Ibid.

simply something imaginary; it is the preparation of an imaginary quality for use – a use that remains dependent on the given situation within which it is to be applied'.[13]

How would this dual dynamic work if applied to the *Acallam*? How would a typical replication of a social reality – the familiar materials of a traditional tale-telling – mesh with material that seems to be uniquely new, a wonder to be sure, but also beyond the bounds of anything encountered before in the matrix of pre-existing literary tradition? I will take an extreme example of imaginative strangeness, the interlaced tale of the three brothers and their magical hound, itself part of the long story-telling session with the king of Munster.[14] Three brothers and their magical dog come from Irúaith seeking Finn's friendship. They offer their night-vigilance skills, thus removing from the *fian* themselves their normal human fear of night attack. At first their obvious non-humanness poses unease; they request privacy because they do not wish to reveal that one or the other of them actually dies each night and comes back to life in the morning. This secretiveness clashes with one of Finn's own *gessa* concerning open generosity. Cash-flow problems with importuning poets reveals their dog's real value; she vomits gold and thereby relieves Finn's social embarrassment concerning payment for poems. Where the intoxicating drink supplied by the brothers to the *fian* comes from is glided over by the narrator to be revealed later. Human curiosity inevitably gets the better of the guards of Finn's camp and they spy on the brothers. A fart from the dog is enough to deprive them of their weapons, they are killed by the brothers, and the dog's breath reduces their bodies to dust and ashes, to utter annihilation.

Already we can see some aspects of the way the story with its audacious imaginary is trending here. There is a real anxiety building about overly fluid boundaries of the human and non-human: these brothers are unknown entities and, however benign, their very presence and their non-human magical powers disturb deeply on the level of the body. Part of that anxiety of opening up to the manifestly and marginally human other, revealed in confusing sensual derangement, finds its focus in this novel imaginary, the dog herself. Humans are being socially and bodily sustained, intoxicated, but also annihilated by the canine's extra-body, projectile effluences. False plenitude and

---

13 Ibid., p. 6. Iser devotes a major section of his study to the imaginary, mapping the history of the term 'imagination' from the seventeenth-century recapitulation of Aristotle conception of fantasy, through Coleridge who coupled the imagination with the self-constituting subject, to Sartre and finally, with approbation, to Castoriadis' formulation of the radical imaginary in social context: 'the imaginary signification achieves two things: it institutes society, and it makes society into a possibility of its own self-transformation' (ibid., p. 215). 14 Stokes, 'Acallamh', ll. 5447–514, 5555–88, 6083–289. Cf. the comment (ll. 5589–91) of the king of Munster: *nir' indis duind riam ... scél budh inganta 7 budh diamra ina sin*, 'you have never told us ... a more marvelous or mysterious tale than that'.

nothingness, animal pollution, human abjection and death – these are the inverse powers of this attractive magic and the question arises as to how the author, in so dangerous a game, will bring this tale to its conclusion?

The story resurfaces with the *fian* publicly requesting the three's banishment and Finn's refusing; in his judgment, their reformulated gifts of healing, generosity and music align them more closely to an acceptable 'other'. The weird dog returns in the story, no less strange, now seducing Finn, licking him and surrounding him with her fragrant breath. The parameters of good and evil are then re-positioned and the story moves on through a narrative replication act when another trio of brothers, now clearly poisonous enemies of Finn's, arrive from the Túatha Dé Danann. By this narrative splitting off of the unremitting and vengeful destructiveness of the new trio, the debate on the relative *olc* of the original three (ll. 6108–14) can be resolved in their favour. At king Cormac's request, they pronounce an impressive curse on the evil trio – 'the brood of Herod' – in language that situates and relates the power of the curse to conscious reverence for the 'true and glorious god and the lord of all mankind' at the moment of Christ's redemptive sacrifice. By acting now on behalf of the good justified king at this clearly signalled stage of pagan/Christian transition, they join the ranks of the *Acallam*'s justified Otherworldly ones. The evil trio are disposed of by the dog at her most entertaining: she foul-farts them away into the sea; in magical logic this act would have banished them to primal chaos, but in this case the cycle is not complete.[15] In Patrician time, that is, in historic time, evil again comes to Ireland from the North and thus the same evil trio can still be destructively active in another guise. And it is Caílte's invocation, which repeats Dub's curse while firmly adding the invocation of Patrick's god, that finally sees them off and out of the story.

We see how fluid both the deployment of reality and the imaginary – and in Iser's terms, the uses of the imaginary, are. Otherworld marauders, dogs and destroying birds are two a penny in the *Acallam*. But this tale lifts a huge load: the author has combined models of cyclic and teleological historic time; he has moved the myth of the Otherworld and old heroic time into as fantastic a model as is possible; he has destabilised heroic action and eschewed a straightforward linear telling of the tale; and we have come out into an identifiable real world in the author's own time, of agricultural anxieties and

---

15 This is itself an inverse evocation of Patrick's banishment of the demon birds from Crúachain Aigle in the *Vita tripartita* and in the Leabhar Breac homily on Patrick: W. Stokes, *Three Middle-Irish homilies on the lives of saints Patrick, Brigit and Columba* (1877), pp 36–7: *Canaid patraic psalmu escaine forru. 7 ciid. 7 … Techit nademnu fachétoir ead radaircc forsinfairgi. 7 nosbaidet fen isininudsin. 7 nitaraill demun tir nerenn osin cocend .uii. lathi. 7 uii. mís 7 uii mbliadan:* 'Patrick sings psalms of cursing against them, and he weeps and … The devils flee at once upon the sea, as far as eye can reach, and drown themselves in that place, and no devil visited the land of Ireland from that time to the end of seven days and seven months and seven years'.

their popular remedies vetted and monitored by an increasingly powerful church. All this beautifully managed narrative pivots, I would suggest, on the single-most daring act of authorial imagination, the invention of the magical dog. Invention is, to give it its medieval value, the ability to adapt extant material to one's own artistic purpose. As a possible source for the dog with the ability to reduce people to ashes, there are some references in this segment of storytelling that imply knowledge of *Immram curaig Máele Dúin*.[16] I suggest that the marvelous cat there that possesses the same powers may be a model, suitably transposed into a more heroic and Fenian animal.[17]

We have been so accustomed to the pervasive presence of animals in continental romance tales of the period that we sometimes forget to question how they get there. In the *Lais* of Marie de France, say, magical animals purporting to belong to popular Breton tales could be expected to come from outside 'clerical purview'.[18] Contemporary critics of Marie are concerned with this inherent ambiguity in the *Lais*: they conduct otherness and novelty through their origins in oral and Celtic tradition but they are also subsumed as part of the text's *ordo* around which writers trained in classical rhetoric – as Marie de France undoubtedly was – build meaningful narrative description.[19] If Marie is one of the few continental writers whose work deliberately embraces the popular oral and traditional tales from the Celtic fringes of the Angevin empire, she does so only to re-mediate them for a courtly secular world quite different from popular British and Irish cultural concerns. Her swan, werewolf, hawk/knight and speaking deer are striking enough to engage an audience by their novelty and engender a limited debate on the human/animal boundary; but the *Acallam* dog as a narrative device takes its audience deeper into the structure of these body relations and embodied values, both through its striking novelty and through the more daring social and personal destabilisation caused by a concentration on deconstructed heroic and animal body essences.

Again I return to the question of what adds to the fluidity of stories. How are stories mediated and what aids their portability? Some are so fixed in their attachment to specific places and heroes that they have limited valency except

---

16 H.P.A. Oskamp (ed. and trans.), *The voyage of Máel Dúin* (1970). I have explored some of these references in a forthcoming article on popular beliefs in the *Acallam*, in J. Borsje et al. (eds), *Celtic cosmology* (2013).   17 Máirtín Ó Briain has explored the theme of burning and consigning to the waters in his comprehensive 'Snáithín san uisge: loisc agus léig a luaigh le sruth' in M. Ó Briain and P. Ó Héalaí (eds), *Téada dúchais* (2002), pp 245–72 at pp 257–8. He also connects Bran (pp 261–4) with the burning of the pigs in the *Agallamh bheag*.   18 The phrase is from M.T. Bruckner, 'Speaking through animals in Marie de France's *Lais* and *Fables*' in L.E. Whalen (ed.), *A companion to Marie de France* (2011), pp 157–85 at p. 185.   19 S. Kinoshita and P. McCracken, *Marie de France, a critical companion* (2012), p. 26: 'Deploying her God-given gifts of "*escïence*" and "*eloquence*" (*Prologue*, ll. 1–2) in novel ways, the narrator transforms (into French) and preserves (in writing) the evanescent eloquence of Celtic oral tradition'. For a discussion of animals and their Celtic contexts, see ibid., pp 144–58.

within this zone and locality. They become paradoxically more fixed by the act of writing even if, to a contemporary medieval writer like Marie de France, writing – and translating – is the liberating key that opens up the small world of Breton oral narrative performances to a wider audience. Even a totalising genre project like the Irish *dinnshenchas* may not be useful for this purpose. It achieves wide appeal by its pan-Irish mapping but it hews strongly to a conservative clerical literary pool of source material. The weak penetration of less literary Fenian tales in this latter genre signals that the bulk of this work was probably in place before the rise of any *fianaigecht* collections. For remembering and performing in a Fenian mode in the later twelfth century, a way must be found to create a new work of substantial weight that validates hitherto unexplored but current cultural 'hot' Fenian media. The way forward is through an old text, the *Vita tripartita*, and it may be significant that Patrician texts had been opening a vista on the world of the heroic *fian* past since Tírechán's *Vita*. In addition, narrative production in the eleventh and twelfth centuries favoured prosimetrum compositions and so could accommodate the short verse narrative of the Fenian tale. The discursive frame of such a work is, however, fluid both in its conception by the author and in its subsequent performance and afterlife in the minds of its audience. Fenian lore is not the only place in Irish tradition where something popular circulates below the radar of written clerical media. Sermons can yield references to elements of popular tradition which serve to embed them in the minds of their hearers. Thus – to digress into non-Fenian material briefly – the Patrician sermon in Leabhar Breac preserves an account of the five mountain guardians with one at Slieve Donard/Slíab Slánga.[20] Giraldus Cambrensis picks up on this same local tradition of one of the three sons of Parthalón who is buried on the mountain, and in rationalising the legend of Slánga's immortality attests to the vitality of oral beliefs: 'These three, in leaving traces of their names on certain things still existing, have acquired an immortal memory, and, so to speak, a continual and living presence'.[21]

To engage what Seán Ó Coileáin calls an audience's 'totality of ... imaginative experience' in an affective bond in the sum of *fianaigecht* imaginary, and also to allow stories to move between cultural registers and worlds – in other words, to describe also the creative impulse that caused western Europe to embrace the matter of Celtia so ardently – two elements in Ireland and Angevin Europe at this time are crucial: music and memory. Let me try to annotate these in turn in attempting to build a context for the Celtic turn in

---

20 See M. MacNeill, *The festival of Lughnasa* (1962), pp 84–96.   21 J.J. O'Meara, *The topography of Ireland by Giraldus Cambrensis* (1949), p. 111. Text from idem (ed.), 'Giraldus Cambrensis in Topographia Hibernie. Text of the first recension', *Proceedings of the Royal Irish Academy*, 52C (1948–50), 113–178 at 157: *Qui cum nominum suorum inditia rebus largirentur extantibus, perpetuam sui memoriam et quasi uiuacem quandam presentiam sunt inde sortiti.*

European literature. But first, a general remark: nowadays we have difficulty in thinking about the transfer from one culture to another of linguistic products. However, in an earlier world, as in the world of contemporary pop culture, language difference and plurality is accepted more readily if music accompanies it.

MUSIC

We are familiar with the broad outlines of the circulation of tales and music in the Irish Sea province from 1100 on. Gruffudd ap Cynan, the most Irish of Welsh princes, had an Irish harper and *pencerdd*, Gellán.[22] Arthur of Britain makes an isolated appearance in the *Acallam* and his character there is Welsh rather than courtly. Irish heroic tales – Ulster and Fenian in the same list as the two Essylts [Isolde] – in some form or another seem to have been known in Wales by the mid-twelfth century if the most recent dating of *Culhwch and Olwen* to *c*.1160 is accepted, with its mention of 'Conchobar mac Nesa, Cú Roí mac Dáiri, Fergus mac Róich, Lóegaire Búadach, Conall Cernach ... Caílte the lightfooted'.[23] From the 1140s, Geffrei Gaimar's epilogue to his *Estoire des Engleis* speaks of the book of a certain David who supplied content and music for a work honouring the feats of Henry I:

> Ke unkes Davit ne fist escrivere / ne la reine du Luvain / N'en tint le lievere en sa main. / Ele en fist fere un lievere grant, / le primer vers noter par chant. / Ben dit Davit e bien trovat, / E la chançon bien asemblat.[24]

> Things that David never wrote and whose book the Queen of Louvain [Henry's second wife] never held in her hand. She had a large book of these things made; the first verse was annotated with music. David performed well, created well, and put together the song well.[25]

This David (†1139) has been identified as an Irish monk from Würzburg, later made bishop of Bangor and this is the first reference to a vernacular manuscript with musical notation in the period.[26] We do not know the con-

22 See P. Sims-Williams, *Irish influence on medieval Welsh literature* (2011) for the most sustained and skeptical discussion of relations between the two countries; Gellán is cited at p. 18 but it is claimed that the name 'was naturalised in Wales (and Brittany) by Gruffudd's time'. 23 J.G. Evans, *Llyfr Gwyn Rhydderch* (1973), col. 460: *Chnychwr mab nes. a chubert .m. daere. a fercos .m. poch. a lluber beuthach. a choruil beruach / bernach ... a Scilti scawntroet.* For the most recent discussion, see Sims-Williams, *Irish influence*, pp 167–72, 173–80. 24 A. Bell, *L'estoire des Engleis by Geffrei Gaimar* (1960), p. 205. 25 Translation with minor changes from J. Haines, *Satire in the songs of Renart le Nouvel* (2011), pp 95–7. The speaker goes on to address David familiarly and to urge him to emphasise more the festival aspects of the court. 26 See Haines,

tent of these versified episodes of Henry's life but they come very close to the Breton lays that Marie de France offers as models where the Breton sung *aventures* could be either actual biographical segments or legendary lore.

The Welsh Mabinogi tale of *Branwen* also adds to the Irish Sea interchange, not just the possible transmission of tale themes – a possibility rejected by Sims-Williams – but rather as an important reference to the ongoing rivalry about the relative merits of Welsh and Irish harpers. In *Branwen*, music moves from Britain to Ireland: 'And then he [Bran] moved all the stringed instruments on his back to the land of Ireland'.[27] From the Welsh princely courts of Gruffudd ap Cynan on, there is a persistent tradition of Irish musicians, and Giraldus Cambrensis notes with Cambro-Norman appreciativeness the special performance aptitude of Irish string players and the veneration shown St Kevin's harp at Glendalough. Granted, the traditions that associate the reform of Welsh music to the twelfth century and to Glendalough are attested later but their sheer persistence gives an ultimate twelfth-century date a certain validity.[28]

Constance Bullough-Davies collected some important descriptions of the playing of Breton lays.[29] From the *Tristan* of Gottfried von Strassburg, I take this one example: Tristan, after tuning the harp, plays some runs on it that seem a marvel to the audience. Then he begins:

> alse ez ie ze staten kam, / so lie der tungendriche / supz' unde wunneliche / sine schanzune flegen in. / er sanc diu leichnotelin / britunsche und galise. Latinsche un franzoise / so suoze mit den munde / daz nieman wizzen kunde / weders suezer waere / oder baz lobelare, / sin harphen oder sin singen.

> as he came to the places, the wonderful youth let his songs come flying in sweetly and wonderfully. He sang the *lai* airs/songs in four different languages, Breton, Welsh, Latin and French. So sweetly did he sing them with his mouth that no one could say whether his harping or his singing was sweeter or more praiseworthy.[30]

'The lay of the strand', on William the Conqueror's stay in Brittany, which survives only in Icelandic, gives a time-frame 1070–1150, within which the Breton *lai* might be presumed to have spread into the Angevin world, and the

Satire in the songs of Renart le Nouvel, pp 97–102.   **27** D.S. Thomson (ed.), *Branwen Merch Lyr* (1961), p. 10: *Ac yna y kerdwys ef ac a oed gerd arwest ar y geuyn e hun, a chyrchu tir Iwerdon.* **28** For different opinions to Sims-Williams on the antiquity of this tradition, see S. Harper, 'So how many Irishmen went to Glen Achlach? Early accounts of the formation of *Cerdd Dafod*', *Cambrian Medieval Celtic Studies*, 42 (Winter, 2001), 1–25; D. Klausner (ed.), *Wales* (2005), pp 278–86, 232–7.   **29** C. Bullough-Davies, 'The form of the Breton lay', *Medium Ævum*, 42 (1973), 18–31.   **30** A.T. Hatto (trans.), *Gottfried von Strassburg: Tristan* (1967), ll. 3620–31.

story of this *lai*'s composition adds to Bullough-Davies' contention that the essence of the Breton *lai* genre was its music.

The etymology of the Anglo-Norman word *lai*, its possible connection with Irish *laíd* and the corresponding rise of the Fenian *laidh* narrative genre in the twelfth century is too large a topic to treat in detail here. The term in Irish first appears in a list of six degrees of poets which Liam Breatnach has suggested belongs to a seventh-century period even before the fixing of the seven grades of *fili* in the early eighth, harking back to 'an earlier state of affairs where the *bard* and *fili* were not so sharply distinguished'.[31] Thus, the term's survival is possibly as a genre descriptive relating to a bard's performance rather than as a product tied to the world of the *fili* and of writing. As it develops in saga, its range is that of interpollatory, or direct speech, or dialogue utterance in verse; and in the first recension of *Táin bó Cúailnge*, for example, it is more frequent in the later Fer Diad incident than elsewhere (the proportion is 5 out of 8). The term becomes widespread in twelfth-century saga redactions including the Book of Leinster *Táin*.[32] Its association with Fenian 'ballads' may be exemplified in the *Acallam* by the verse tale of Cnú Deróil, Finn's little harper, which is called a *laíd*.

It is obvious that music is a major interest of the *Acallam* as a whole, and if one compares the description of performing a Breton *lai* above with the description of Cas Corach's music, similarities are apparent: 'He took up his *timpán*, tuned it and played on it until he produced a run of melody on it'.[33] His stated purpose in joining Caílte is to learn how to combine his own skill in music, epitomised in his soubriquet *corach* 'melodius', to the acquisition of stories and Fenian adventures: 'This is what has brought me: to learn knowledge and true accounts, storytelling and the great warrior adventures of the *fian* from Caílte mac Ronáin'.[34]

Cas Corach's progress mirrors other Túatha Dé Danann figures and not just in the *Acallam*. He makes his act of faith in God to Patrick and is blessed by him; but he is also endorsed as fully and corporally human by Caílte when he undertakes manly heroic duels under his sponsorship. The endorsement of his art by Patrick at the second feast of Tara implies an assertion of the validity of his mixed, and by implication, Fenian performance art. Such figures,

---

31 L. Breatnach (ed. and trans.), *Uraicecht na ríar* (1987), p. 100. For the earlier *Bretha Nemed* six-fold division where performance of *laíd* is mentioned, see Tracts BN I (p. 23): *do-fuasluice laid laogha* 'a *laíd* releases calves [as reward]' (l. 65); *firlaoda la hemuin / dligid marsai mís* '[of a] true *laíd* and an *emain*, a great sage is entitled to a month's [protection]' (ll. 70–1); BN IV (p. 36): *Sloinde lanlaidhe, labru cin esbuid* 'the declaration of a full *laíd*, utterance without defect' is what is proper to a *lethcerd* (ll. 6–7) (translations from Breatnach with minor changes). 32 Though not in the greatly expanded Fer Diad section. 33 Stokes, 'Acallamh', ll. 3465–6: *tuc a thimpan cuice 7 ra gles hí 7 do tseind hí co tucastar cairchi cíuil urrí.* 34 Ibid., ll. 3353–5: *iss ed ro m-imluaid, d'foglaim fessa 7 fíreolais 7 scélaigechta 7 morgnim gaiscid na Féinne ó Chailti mac Ronain.*

drawn into ecclesiastical or regional kings' retinues – and in the *Acallam*, even dreaming upmarket, to royal status marriages at the end of the twelfth century – imply a brief widening of the pool of literary patronage before the relegation of Fenian performers to a lesser status by the thirteenth century.

MEMORY

In all of the above references to the European scene of performance, there is a background context of royal feasting that both Norman (Gaimar) and Welsh (tradition of Gruffudd ap Cynan) sources see as somehow originary for the period.[35] The *Acallam* is suffused with this spirit of enhanced socialising, both regionally and nationally. Indeed, both church and court emphasise their separate spheres of discourse: for the one feasting, odes, and storytelling with status clerics and regional kings; for the other, the sermon and the liturgy. The compositional innovation that Michelle O'Riordan saw in bardic praise poems, and ascribed to the implied influence of the new *artes dictandi* from the Continent, may be turning up first in the model of sermon composition as popularised and disseminated after the Fourth Lateran Council of 1215.[36] *Betha Cholmáin Ela* most likely belongs to a later period of fifteenth-century active reform but the parallels with the *Acallam* and Patrick's preaching there are instructive. This is a description of clerics praying and preaching to the aesthetic appreciation of the people, appreciation which echoes the *Acallam* endorsement of listening to Fenian tales:

> Ocus do tionnsgnadh senmóir agna cléircibh sin; 7 do bhadar leabair lán-áille laidíanda aca ann, 7 iatt ag solas-ghabhail a leighinn, 7 acc adhmoladh an Duilemhain go dasachtach. Ocus ba gairdiuccadh menman 7 aiccenta leisna sluagaibh, beith oc eisteacht friu.

> And these clerks began their preaching, and they had fair Latin books with them, and they recited their reading clearly, and praised the Creator fervently. And it was recreation of mind and heart to the hosts to listen to them.[37]

The ensuing verse counsels the clergy to explain scripture both to the religious community and to the people:

---

35 Bell, *L'estoire des Engleis*, p. 206, ll. 6504–12: *Mes s'il uncore s'en volt pener, / des plus bels fias pot vers trover: / ... de boscheier e del gaber / E de festes e des noblesces, / ... D'iço devreit hom bien chanter / nient leissir ne trespasser* ('But if he [Gaimar] wanted to go to the trouble he could make verses about some of the greatest deeds ... the parties and excesses, the feasts and entertainments ... of all this one should sing well and let none of it be forgotten'). 36 *Irish bardic poetry and rhetorical reality* (2007). 37 C. Plummer (ed. and trans.), *Bethada naem nÉrenn*, 2 vols (1922), i, p. 168 §5; ii, p. 162.

Gach fersa gabus tú díbh, / Minigh a texa go min; / Labhair it aignedh co becht, / Ocus saigh ionnta t'inntleacht; ... Gabh let go min, milis, mall (*restoring MS reading*), / Th'urnaighthe ocus do leighend, / Minigh a lLaidin gan ceilcc, / Is cuir do paider i nGaoideilg ... Cuir senmóir 'sna tuatadhaibh.

Every verse of them that you recite, expound their texts minutely; speak from your mind exactly, and apply your mind to them; ... Recite softly, sweetly and slowly, your prayers and your reading. Explain their Latin precisely, and translate your prayer into Irish ... preach to the lay-people.[38]

In the *Acallam*, Caílte is amazed and fascinated by the sight of this same Colmán Ela and his monks as they sing their Hours in a context that brings performance and books together: 'Seldom have my ears heard reading across water ... for one with a pen it would take a long time to write it. Sad am I now, many the marvel I experienced'.[39] Patrick, as we know, is famously addicted to Fenian tales but develops a bad conscience about the distraction of listening to them after the tale of Artúir: however, his guardian angels, 'Little Flame' (Aibelán) and 'Light of Judgement' (Solusbreathach) speak their famous dictum:

'A anum, a naimchléirigh', ar siat, 'ní mó iná trian a scél innisit na sen-laich út ar dáig dermait 7 dichuimhne. Ocus scribhthar letsa i támlorguib filed 7 i mbriatraibh ollaman, ór budh gairdiugudh do dronguibh 7 do degdáinibh deridh aimsire éisdecht frisna scéluibh sin'.[40]

'Dear holy cleric', said they, 'these old warriors tell you no more than a third of their stories, because of forgetfulness and failing memory. Have these stories written down in poets' tablets and in literary language so that listening to these tales will be comfort and entertainment to both lords and commons in latter times'.

In the Laud version, there is a variant of this formula for the king of Ulster storytelling segment which brings it closer to the idea of a Fenian miscellany: *scribtar libh in scél út i tamlorgaib filed 7 il-lechtaib fiann.*[41]

Thus in this schema, a schema that probably owes as much to common medieval ideas of the value of written and fully scripted tales as it does to

---

38 Ibid., i, p. 170 §11 (translation my own; cf. ibid., ii, p. 164).   39 Stokes, 'Acallamh', ll. 2892–5: *Ba hannam re hó mo chind . cloistecht re léigind os lind, / ... / Gebé nech ica mbiad pend . fada do biad 'ga scribenn, / is truag mar atussa bos . is mor d'ingantaib fuarus.*   40 Ibid., ll. 297–302.   41 Ibid., ll. 3105–6: 'let this story be written by you in poetic tablets and in Fenian monuments'.

native Irish tradition, a history of oral performance, itself constantly enacted intra-diegetically in the work, is already being supplemented by writing, precisely because of the need to establish a future life and circulation for the tales beyond the present. It also conjures up a refined written work, probably a self-referential gesture towards the *Acallam* itself, a step up from Fenian balladry, just as Chrétien de Troyes in his first romance, *Erec et Enide*, feels the need to distance himself from the itinerant oral jongleurs who had the story in their repertoire. Marie de France in her versions of Breton lays had presented the oral/written re-mediation in these conventional terms in her Prologue:

> Des lais pensai k'oï aveie; / … Ke pur remambrance les firent / Des aventures k'il oïrent / Cil ki primes les comencierent / E ki avant les enveierent. / Plusurs en ai oïconter, / Nes voil laisser në oblïer; / Rimez en ai e fait ditié, / Soventes fiez en ai veillié.[42]

> So I thought of lays which I had heard … that were composed by those who first began them and put them into circulation, to perpetuate the memory of adventures they had heard. I myself have heard a number of them and do not wish to overlook or neglect them. I have put them into verse, made poems of them, often working late into the night.[43]

Though Marie ascribes the first act of memorial salvage of great deeds of the past to the ancient Britons who witnessed them and composed oral lays, it is clear that the end result is Marie's own written volume, the sole and necessary preserver of earlier oral performances.

As we have already seen, the deeds of the *fían* are recessed in a background of oral performance, with Caílte as the figure of memory, Cas Corach as the contemporary figure of oral performance, and the clerics as the scribal textual recorders. These, however, must also be rendered courtly, reconstituted through acts of gathering, rewriting and official dissemination at its most authoritative in the royal national assembly of nobles and clerics at Tara. The closest contemporary analogy to this process of transitioning from orality to writing is to be found in the *Lais* of Marie de France. Here, however, unlike the *Acallam*, the court scenario with the figure of the sole author and Henry II as the sole patron is fore-grounded, and Marie is active in her own text in a way foreign to the Irish work: 'I set myself to collect lays, to compose and re-tell them'.[44] Her famous *Prologue*, probably the last thing to be written by her, grounds her presentation in the practice of the ancients and

---

42 J. Rychner (ed.), *Les lais de Marie de France* (1969), p. 2, §§3–42.   43 Translation with minor variation from L.E. Whalen, 'The prologues and the epilogues of Marie de France' in Whalen (ed.), *A companion to Marie de France* (2011), pp 1–30 at p. 14.   44 Ibid., p. 15, Prologue ll. 47–8: *M'entris des lais assembler, / Par rime faire e reconter.*

their grammatical commentators like Priscian: medieval *inventio* places memory as one of its fundamental parts. As Whalen notes with respect to Marie's insistence on the term, memory is an important step in the process of *inventio* as formulated by the author of the *Ad Herennium*:

> Sunt igitur duae memoriae: una naturalis, altera artificiosa. Naturalis est ea, quae nostris animis insita est et simul cogitatione nata; artificiosa est ea, quam confirmat inductio quedam et ratio praeceptionis.

> There are, then, two kinds of memory: one natural, and the other the product of art. The natural memory is that memory which is embedded in our minds, born simultaneously with thought. The artificial memory is that memory which is strengthened by a kind of training and system of discipline.[45]

Marie seems to endorse the truth claims of the prior Breton lays and the spirit of their 'natural' remembrance agenda; but she seems to be unwilling either to break the connection with the idea of remembrance embodied in her source material, or to rely solely on it. Is it the old Breton artifact that is reliable or is remembrance ensured only by the literary sophistication and artistic value of her new composition?[46] As in the *Acallam*, memorability is only ensured by the written word, and the Fenian 'ballad' and old performed Breton lay sit in deformed subordination to the major written work.

The process of recovery through memory of old materials from the past through the device of the unbroken chain of witnesses relates directly to the work of *inventio*. In the *Acallam*, the adventures and old stories are carried by the device of living witnesses, Caílte and Oisín, so the process seems simpler. But there is actually an even more daring device employed in the Irish work, that of extra-human inspiration. Towards the end of the collection, the process of invention is itself de-constructed and laid bare by a narrative sequence that takes us from Patrician literacy back to an originary Otherworld legitimation, an assertion of transcendent truth comparable to the invocation to the Muses of epic composition. The old Fenian hero asks Patrick to be allowed to resort to the pagan Otherworld of the Túatha Dé Danann in order to be healed of the many bodily ailments incurred throughout his long warrior life. Patrick, in gallant comradeship, and sure of his returning reminds him of their bond of personal friendship. Once there, the gift of youth is offered to him by the people of the Otherworld. But he refuses the tempta-

---

45 H. Caplan (ed. and trans.), *Cicero: rhetorica ad Herennium* (1954), pp 24–5; see Whalen, 'The prologues and the epilogues of Marie de France', p. 5.   46 On this ambiguity, see M.T. Bruckner's remarks on the Prologue to *Eliduc* in Whalen, *A companion to Marie de France*, p. 148.

tion; he does not wish to compromise his human integrity because this would negate the contract of Christian belief that he had already made with Patrick. They yield and agree to patch up the old mortal body which he presents to them. When they clean him out through a succession of humor-based pharmacal purges, an inverse teleology of tale-telling – firmly based in the matter of the body – is the result. Caílte vomits up the stuff of his tales composed out of all his experiences: experiences of key locations in the natural world, experiences marked permanently in the body through the wear and tear of hunts, battles, emotional pain at the loss of his fellow companions, and, finally a combination of all of these:

> 'Now it is time to heal me', said Caílte, 'because I am weary from waiting'. … Then Bé Binn entered the men's hall in the company of her two sons, and a healing bed of rushes was there laid out for Caílte. An oval vessel of white gold filled with water was brought to her and a vat of crystal. She put herbs in the basin breaking them over the water, and put it into Caílte's hands. He drank a great draught from it and threw up a greenish vomit. 'Woman dear', said Caílte, 'what likeness do you find in this?' 'A pooling of blood brought about by the cataracts and rivers, and estuaries and early morning hunts', she said. 'Drink again'. He drank again and vomited up a reddish bloody liquid. 'What is this vomit, girl?' he asked. 'Bloody pools from the poison of all the spears and blades that wounded you in every combat you were ever in', she replied. He took another drink from it and vomited a jet-black stream. 'What do you make of that?' he asked. 'It comes from the blood of your companions, your foster-brothers, your lord and your captain, Finn mac Cumaill'. He drank another, a fourth drink and vomited up a yellow stream. 'What is that liquid, girl?' he asked. 'The residue and clotting from every poison and bleeding that still remain. Drink the last mouthful'. 'I loathe it', said Caílte, 'for I never found anything more difficult to do in any battle or attack or combat that ever I was in than drinking that stuff'. However, he drank it and he vomited up a multi-coloured stream containing traces of every colour. 'How is that, girl?' asked Caílte. 'The mixture comes from every run and every exertion, and every deed you have ever done on every mound and hill and rock, but the colour of blood on top is from your own body and flesh, and that is a sign of your healing'. And the girl gave him a drink of milk and he drank it, but he remained weak from all his vomiting for three days and three nights. … 'Now I must leave, and my blessing on you, people of the *síd*. There is a meeting of the men of Ireland in Tara at the end of the year, and I must go there to converse with my comrade and joint-fosterling, Oisín mac Finn, and also because I am summoned by Patrick, the Adze-Head, who ordered

me to go tell the nobles of the men of Ireland, all assembled there, of the exploits and the great deeds of valour and prowess of the *Fían* and of Finn mac Cumaill, and of the men of Ireland as well, so that the scholars and the sages may preserve the tales that we tell them until the end of time'. 'Here is some help for you from us', said Bé. 'What help might that be?' asked Caílte. 'A drink that we give you to take to Tara for the remembrance of lore, so that you may be able to recall at will every cataract or river or estuary that you meet, along with its attendant battles and combats'. 'That is the help of friends and of a true family!' said Caílte.[47]

In this way, a classic medieval dream of a free literary zone is established: the body of the heroic tale-teller is now separated from the burden of the tales formerly experienced and graphed on the body and the heart – heroic adventure as before language, and before memory. Now separated from this grief-filled burden through the purgative healing gift of the Otherworld, all is restored to Caílte. The ability to remember and tell tales is now perceived as a gift from the muses, here the Irish immortal Otherworld, where everything is perpetually present and perpetually seen. Inspiration as the gift of the gods replaces witness. The marvel is that this gift does not, however, compromise human culture and its constantly developing cultural media. The benefits of a Christian order with its technology of literacy is that it has the means to record tales efficiently and future-project them, but it is not itself their source. It is an extraordinary way of arriving at the same place as European secular literature did, using very different resources. As Fergus was for the *Táin*, so too Caílte is for the *Acallam*, a figure from an unreachable past made marvelously present and translucent: Benjamin's traveller, who can be summoned to witness to that past and, in so doing, enhance for the audience of the present their awareness of their own cultural riches.

---

47 My translation (cf. A. Dooley and H. Roe, *Tales of the elders of Ireland* (1999), pp 200–4); original text in Stokes, 'Acallamh', ll. 7138–262.

Acallam na senórach: a conversation between worlds

JOHN CAREY

There could scarcely be a less controversial pronouncement concerning *Acallam na senórach* than to say that it is a tale preoccupied with time. Its central narrative conceit is the bringing together of the protagonists of one time – the conversion period, dominated by the apostolic figure of Saint Patrick – with the survivors of another – the vanished age of the pagan heroes of the *fiana*, represented by Caílte and Oisín. To these two eras must, of course, be added the time of the text's composition, separated from both Patrick and the Fenians by an interval vastly greater than that which divides them from one another. The emotional climate of the *Acallam* is largely governed by feelings about the past: the eager curiosity of Patrick and the Christian kings, and the nostalgia and elegiac regret of Caílte and his companions. Also important, albeit more sporadic, are foreshadowings of the future: references to the longer-term effects of Patrick's missionary work, to the establishment of the Cistercian monastery of Mellifont, and to John de Courcy's cult of the triple burial of Patrick, Brigit and Colum Cille at Down;[1] and also the prophecy – the non-fulfilment of which, as Whitley Stokes rather cynically observed, is the saddest thing about the whole wistful work – that Caílte's tales would be a source of entertainment for 'populace and nobles in the final days'.[2]

When we look more closely at the *Acallam*'s treatment of time, however, it is almost immediately evident that it is not at all straightforward. While we might have a half-unconscious predisposition to associate the text's 'pagan past' and 'Christian present' respectively with myth (to whatever extent modified by transmission and reinterpretation) and with history (to whatever extent idealised and reconstructed), in fact the latter is at least as fabulous as the former. There was a nearly monolithic consensus concerning the events of Patrick's career, beginning with the seventh-century *uitae* by Muirchú and Tírechán, comprehensively synthesised in the *Tripartite Life*, and continuing thereafter throughout the whole of the Middle Irish period: everyone knew that Patrick came to Ireland in 432, and that the king of Tara in his time was

---

1 On this reference and its significance, see A. Dooley, 'The date and purpose of *Acallam na senórach*', *Éigse*, 34 (2004), 97–126 at 101 n. 11. 2 W. Stokes (ed. and partial trans.), 'Acallamh na senórach' in W. Stokes and E. Windisch (eds), *Irische Texte*, iv, 1 (1900), p. xii: 'Sadder even than these is the non-fulfilment of the prophecy … that the tales of the Fian will be a pastime to the companies and nobles of the latter time. In Ireland, at least, there are now few companies and no nobles that are able to read them'.

Lóegaire mac Néill Noígíallaig; and there were stories of his encounters with the ancestors of other important dynasties. But this whole familiar framework melts away when we step into the *Acallam*. Nearly all of the kings whom it names are otherwise unknown to history or pseudohistory; and the ruler in Tara is not Lóegaire but Díarmait mac Cerbaill, who lived in the middle of the following century. Even within the context of the story itself, there are temporal anomalies so glaring that they can scarcely be inadvertent: thus Áed mac Muiredaig, a key figure of whom I shall have more to say below, is a young boy when he first enters the story, but Patrick officiates at his second marriage less than a year-and-a-half later; and when Caílte calls upon Patrick's knowledge of computistics, so that the actual mechanics of time-reckoning enter the narrative, we get such chimerical gobbledygook as the notion of 'a month which contains three moons' (*mí congeib tri héscca*).[3]

One would be less inclined to expect consistency in the area of *fianaigecht*, fragmentary and marginal as it is in the earlier literature; but here too the *Acallam* recklessly diverges from such comparanda as are available.[4] For instance, the story of Garad mac Morna and the women of the *fian*, elsewhere portrayed as a misogynistic massacre, is here transformed (at some cost to narrative clarity) into an exemplary anecdote of prudent self-restraint.[5] Other aspects of the pre-Patrician past fare no better: out of many examples, I will give just two. **(a)** Túathal Techtmar, his father Fíachu Findfolaid and his grandfather Feradach Findfechtnach are three crucial characters in the dynastic mythology of the Uí Néill, Feradach being the addressee of the celebrated 'Mirror for Princes' *Audacht Morainn*, while Túathal is portrayed as having defeated the provincial rulers who had slain his father, before carving out the fifth of Mide as a demesne of the Tara kings. But the *Acallam*, while it is aware of these well-known associations, can choose to ignore them: in one anecdote Fíachu and Túathal are brothers, not father and son, and their father Feradach bequeaths to them the settled and wild parts of Ireland respectively in a fable which has been well described as 'a kind of founding charter for the *Fían* institution and ruling dynasties', but which is certainly subversive of the unequivocal royal propaganda normally associated with these figures.[6] **(b)** Lí Ban, daughter of Eochaid mac Maireda of the drowned realm

3 Stokes, 'Acallamh', ll. 6292–304 at l. 6296. Translations throughout are my own.   4 Thus James Carney describes the author as 'anything but a strict traditionalist': 'Language and literature to 1169' in D. Ó Cróinín (ed.), *A new history of Ireland*, i (2005), pp 451–510 at p. 490. 5 Stokes, 'Acallamh', ll. 1362–48. See the comments of A. Dooley and H. Roe, *Tales of the elders of Ireland* (1999), p. 234 (43), and of Anne Connon in her contribution to this volume (pp 38–46).   6 Thus Dooley and Roe, *Tales*, p. 237, who note the story's untraditional character; but contrast Stokes, 'Acallamh', ll. 4127–32, where a story also found in the *Bórama* portrays Túathal, his father and his grandfather in their traditional roles. Marie-Louise Sjoestedt was mistaken, as in her reading of the *Acallam* generally, in regarding this story as a reflection of 'the native tradition': *Gods and heroes of the Celts*, trans. M. Dillon (1949), p. 107.

of Líathmuine, becomes the daughter of a king of Ireland, Eochaid mac
Eógain maic Ailella, of whom there seems to be no trace in any other source.[7]
Her story, like that of Túathal, was generally known,[8] as was the traditional
sequence of Ireland's legendary kings: a man as well-informed as the author
of the *Acallam* evidently was would not make such changes inadvertently, nor
would he expect them to go unnoticed by his audience.

The text's temporal discrepancies have also, needless to say, been noticed
by modern scholars. Thus the late Máirtín Ó Briain gave a lucid survey of
the anachronisms and fabrications of the *Acallam*'s depiction of the conversion period, observing that:

> the author ... was consciously engaged on a literary work of fiction ...
> Although this work exhibits his vast knowledge of Irish literature, both
> secular and ecclesiastical, he pays scant heed to the accepted or
> received chronology of Patrician Ireland.

He went on to offer the persuasive suggestions that the substitution of Díarmait
for Lóegaire as king of Tara was made because of the former's prominent role
as 'a preserver of traditional lore' in other texts; and that the fictitious
Muiredach mac Fínnachta, king of Connacht, represents the Ó Conchobair
dynasty which ruled Connacht at the time of the text's composition, a family
derived from the earlier royal lineage of Síl Muiredaig.[9] Ann Dooley has taken
this historicist line of speculation considerably further, arguing that the 'enduring present' constituted by the *Acallam*'s 'blatantly artificial frame of anachronistic but aesthetically pleasing rapport' expresses events and concerns specific
to Connacht in the early decades of the thirteenth century; and suggesting an
even more specific provenance in the milieu of a relatively minor branch of Síl
Muiredaig known as the Mic Oireachtaigh.[10] Joseph Nagy too holds that the
Acallam's picture of Patrick's Ireland is constructed 'with so little regard for
chronology that it is clearly meant to stand in for the world of the audience of
the text'.[11] His emphasis is however semiotic rather than political:

---

7 Stokes, 'Acallamh', ll. 3219–20, 3247–8. 8 The sources are comprehensively documented and
discussed by R. de Vries (ed. and trans.), *Two texts on Loch nEchach* (2012). 9 'Some material
on Oisín in the Land of Youth' in D. Ó Corráin et al. (eds), *Sages, saints and storytellers* (1989),
pp 181–99 at pp 185–6. 10 'Date and purpose'; the quoted phrases are taken from pp 100 and
97, and Dooley's own more detailed analysis of Muiredach mac Fínnachta is given on p. 103.
Valuable and illuminating as her suggestions are, other aspects of this complex text naturally
remain to be accounted for. Dooley's argument for seeing Muiredach's son Áed in the *Acallam* as
representing Áed the son of Cathal Crobderg Úa Conchobair (†1228) is based on parallelism
between the names of the fictitious Áed's father and grandfather and those of various of the historical Áed's dynastic ancestors; in purely onomastic terms, however, a more obvious counterpart
for the thirteenth-century prince would be Áed Álainn mac Cétaig Crobdeirg, the murderous giant
from the Land of Men who is mentioned below (Stokes, 'Acallamh', ll. 5964–5), see Anne
Connon's contribution (above pp 53–6). 11 'Life in the fast lane: the *Acallam na senórach*' in H.

> Caílte and his companions transcend time and sequence, paralleling the
> innumerable anachronistic references to placenames which they and the
> text make ... The key to the miracle, which both makes the miracle
> happen and provides its matter, is simply talk.[12]

All of these perspectives are astute and illuminating, and there is room for
all of them in interpreting this intricate and many-layered work. But I do not
think that any of them quite exhausts the 'strangeness', to use Ann Dooley's
term,[13] of a story about the weight and pathos and consequences of time in
which time's realities are so flamboyantly made light of. Nor are the anachronisms and inventions of which I have so far spoken the only instances of this:
the very survival of the *fénnidi* into Patrick's day is another. We are constantly
being reminded that they are old; but how old are they? Some passages suggest that two or three generations have passed since the disbanding of the
fían: the young warrior Donn is the grandson of Caílte's contemporary Garad
mac Morna; and later in the text Caílte enjoys the hospitality of the grand-
daughter of a man whose generosity was celebrated in the days of Finn and
Cormac.[14] Yet while Caílte repeatedly bemoans the feebleness of his old age,
he is still unequalled in feats of strength and skill. This may be no more than
the rhetoric of a vanished 'heroic age' – if Caílte is still so mighty as a cente-
narian, what must he have been like in his youth? – but other scenes in the
Acallam cannot be accounted for in this way. Eógan Flaithbrugaid, hospitaller
of Cairpre Lifechar, tells Caílte that he and his wife are two hundred years
old; but they are described as 'a radiant fair-hued couple'.[15] The three sons
of the king of Ulster, who have been carrying out raids on the *síde* for a hundred years, appear also to have suffered no ill effects from the passage of
time.[16] On at least one occasion the interval seems to slip past virtually unnoticed: Cormac mac Airt's champion Lám Lúath kills one of his brothers, and
then goes to Patrick to do penance.[17] Various explanations for all of this are
possible;[18] what is striking is that the author feels no need to supply one, or
even to account for how Caílte and Oisín have been spending their time since
their warrior days.[19]

Fulton (ed.), *Medieval Celtic literature and society* (2005), pp 117–31 at p. 118.   **12** *Conversing with
angels and ancients* (1997), p. 321.   **13** 'Date and purpose', 102.   **14** Stokes, 'Acallamh', ll. 1955,
3249–328.   **15** Ibid., ll. 1870–8. The author appears here to be adapting, with characteristic
audacity, a story of how Patrick encountered on a remote island a couple to whom Christ had
granted eternal youth as a reward for their generosity: K. Mulchrone (ed.), *Bethu Phátraic* (1939),
pp 18–19. For analysis of the use of Patrician sources in the *Acallam*, see A. Dooley, 'The deployment of some hagiographical sources in *Acallam na senórach*' in S.J. Arbuthnot and G. Parsons
(eds), *The Gaelic Finn tradition* (2012), pp 97–110 at pp 98–104.   **16** Stokes, 'Acallamh', l. 7115.
17 Ibid., ll. 7475–96; cf. the comments of Dooley and Roe, *Tales*, p. 243.   **18** As Ó Briain, 'Some
material', pp 186 and 196 n. 53, points out, the *Acallam* states that Finn lived to be two hundred
and thirty, and his followers may have been gifted with similar longevity.   **19** As Joseph

While time is clearly of the utmost significance to the author, accordingly, it seems to have a different place in his mental universe from that which it occupies in ours. How did he conceive it? I am not sure that I can solve this puzzle, but I would at any rate like to think about it further. To this end, we can consider three passages in the *Acallam* that articulate the idea of figures belonging to different times.

The first of these forms part of the celebrated scene in which the *fénnidi* first encounter Patrick and his followers. We are told that: 'the clerics saw them approaching; and horror and fear seized them at the big men, together with their big dogs, for they were not folk of the same era and the same time as themselves'.[20] We are then given some sense of the size of the warriors: even when they are seated, the tallest of the clerics stands only as high as their waists or their shoulders. That the men of former times were far larger than ourselves is a widespread notion, and one not limited to Ireland;[21] this instance may be more specifically compared to a famous episode in Tírechán's *Collectanea*, in which Patrick's companions are similarly described as feeling overwhelming fear (*timor*) at a huge revenant whom the saint has brought back from the pagan past;[22] and also with modern topographic folktales, in which Finn figures as a giant.[23]

I suggest however that more may be involved in the *Acallam*'s portrayal of the men of old as being so dramatically different from those of the present. Considerably later in the text Caílte's former lover Scothníam, a woman of the *síd*, comes to demand the *coibche*, a term usually translated 'bride-price', which he had once promised her.[24] Patrick exclaims at the contrast in the pair's appearance.

'INgnad lind mar atchiamait sibh', ar Pátraic, '.i. inn ingen as í óc ildelbach 7 tusa, a Cailti', ar Pátraic, 'at senoir chrin chrotach crom-

Nagy remarks, 'No explicit reason is ever given in the text for why or how the Fenian survivors lived on till the age of Patrick': 'Compositional concerns in the *Acallam na senórach*' in D. Ó Corráin et al. (eds), *Sages, saints and storytellers*, pp 149–58 at p. 154. 20 Stokes, 'Acallamh', ll. 61–3: *atconncatar na cléirigh dá n-indsaighi iat-sum, 7 ro ghabh gráin 7 egla iat roimh na feraibh móra cona conaibh móra leo, uair nír' lucht coimhré na comhaimsire dóibh iatt.* 21 Thus the skull of Eochaid mac Luchta, 'the size of a large cauldron', was said to have been dug up in the year 1157: J. O'Donovan (ed. and trans.), *Annala rioghachta Eireann*, 7 vols (1848–51), ii, pp 1126–9. As the editors have reminded me, the similarly huge skull of a Fenian warrior is exhumed in the *Acallam* itself (Stokes, 'Acallamh', ll. 2077–9); cf. H. Roe, '*Acallamh na senórach*: the confluence of lay and clerical oral traditions' in C.J. Byrne et al. (eds), *Celtic languages and Celtic peoples* (1992), pp 331–46 at pp 335–6. Cf. the even more extravagant midrashic account of the thigh-bone of Og of Bashan: L. Ginzberg, *The legends of the Jews*, trans. H. Szold, 7 vols (1909), iii, p. 344 and vi, p. 119. 22 L. Bieler (ed. and trans.), *The Patrician texts in the Book of Armagh* (1979), pp 154–5. 23 D. Ó hÓgáin, *Fionn mac Cumhaill* (1988), pp 305–10. 24 While 'bride-price' is certainly the usual sense, *coibche* can also be paid to women outside wedlock. Thus Lambert McKenna (ed.), *Dioghluim dána* (1938), p. 533, suggested that it may on occasion designate a *tuarasdal méirdrighe* ('payment to a prostitute'). 25 Stokes, 'Acallamh', ll.

liath'. 'Do fuil a adhbhur sin acum', ar Cailte, '7 ni lucht comaimsire sind, 7 do Tuathaib dé Danann iss í, 7 nemirchradach iat sein, 7 missi do clannaib Miled, 7 dimbuan irchradach iat'.[25]

'It is strange for me to see you thus', said Patrick: 'the girl young and beautiful, and you, Caílte', said Patrick, 'a withered stooped bent grey old man'. 'I have reason to be so', said Caílte, 'and we are not folk of the same time. She is of the Túatha Dé Danann, and they are unfading; and I am of the descendants of Míl, and they are impermanent and subject to decay'.

The statement that Scothníam is not 'of the same time' as Caílte can be understood in terms of the framework of Irish legendary history, as articulated in such texts as *Lebor gabála*: the supernatural Túatha Dé Danann were held to have ruled Ireland prior to the coming of the Gaels, who conquered it from them under the leadership of the sons of Míl Espáine. Indeed, when Caílte refers to his own people as 'the descendants of Míl' he is invoking precisely this doctrine. We could compare Scothníam's relationship to Caílte with Caílte's relationship to Patrick: even as the Túatha Dé Danann were obliged to submit to the invading Gaels, so the pagan Gaelic order was obliged to submit to Christianity. But there is an obvious difference between the two cases, and a paradoxical one. In this contrast, articulated in terms of time, the one who belongs to the earlier time is free from time's effects. Even more clearly than in the scene of Caílte's meeting with Patrick, a difference in time is also a difference in order of being.

The third passage to be considered in this connection is found within one of Caílte's tales of the Fenian past. He tells of an occasion when, as Finn and his *fian* were out hunting, they were joined by a woman of great beauty and unnerving dimensions:

co faccamar in t-aenduine dar n-indsaigid, 7 suidhis ar in tulaig-seo inar farrad, 7 ben do bói ann, 7 leine do tśroll rig re cnes, 7 brat cimsach corcarglan uimpi, 7 delg oir ann, 7 inar fannclechtach [sic leg.] forórda uimp[i] cona uchtchlar ordaigi ann, 7 mind óir fa cenn. Ocus ní suaill in ní ris fa samalta lind hí .i. re séolcrand luingi lánmoire as ardmullach [*reading* os murloch lánadbul *with Franciscan MS A 4*], 7 rob' uathad accaind nech nar' gab gráin 7 ecla 7 uruamain re febus delba na mná 7 ar a mét. Uair nír' lucht comaimsire di sinde, uair ba mó issi co mór.[26]

3904–9: Cf. the copy of the *Acallam* in the Book of Lismore, where Caílte uses the phrase *ni lucht coimdhine na comaimsi[re] sinn* ('we are not folk of the same generation or the same time'), and says of the Túatha Dé Danann: *neimhircradhach iat- sein 7 suthain a sæg-* 'they are unfading and their life is eternal' (facs. fo. 225v; S. O'Grady [ed. and trans.], *Silva gadelica*, 2 vols [1892], i, p. 180). **26** Stokes, 'Acallamh', ll. 5919–27.

we saw a lone person approaching us, who sat on this hill in our company. And it was a woman, with a garment of royal silk next to her skin, and she wore a fringed mantle of pure purple with a brooch of gold in it, and she had on a soft pleated golden tunic with a golden yoke on it, and a crown of gold on her head. And not puny was the thing to which we likened her: the mast of a very great ship above a vast estuary of the sea. And there were few of us whom horror and fear and great terror did not seize on account of the excellence of the woman's form, and of her size. For we were not folk of the same time as she, for she was much bigger.

She tells them that she is Bé Binn, daughter of the king of the 'Land of Maidens' (Tír na nIngen) beyond the sea, and that she has come to seek Finn's protection against her unwanted fiancé, a son of the king of the 'Land of Men'. He too soon arrives, proving to be a giant even larger than Bé Binn; in Finn's despite, he gives her a fatal wound with his spear and then escapes.

There is a great deal which could be said about this tragic episode, so damaging to the honour of Finn and his men. Thus it appears to be based, with typically inventive variation, on an account of a giant maiden from the sea in the 'Life of Brendan';[27] also interesting is the deceptive narrative strategy employed by Caílte, who manipulates his audience's expectations by first temporarily concealing the stranger's sex, and then her size.[28] For present purposes, however, I shall confine my attention to the passage's points of resemblance to the two scenes which we have already considered. These are evident enough: not only is Bé Binn's difference from the *fían* accounted for, like the surviving *fénnidi*'s difference from the clerics, and Scothníam's from Caílte, by the statement that they are not 'of the same time'; but 'horror and fear' (*gráin 7 egla*) seize the *fían* at sight of her, just as they seize the clerics at sight of the pagan warriors.

Interpretation of these parallels, however, is rather more difficult. Bé Binn is like the Fenian survivors in being a giant; and she is like Scothníam in being Otherworldly, a beautiful visitor from an overseas land of women like those in *Echtrae Chonnlai* and *Immram Brain*.[29] But neither of these resem-

<hr />

27 Here too a giant woman from the sea is killed by a spear, and the episode centres on her placing herself under the protagonist's protection; it may be significant that this protection is effective in the saint's case, but not in the hero's. For the text, see C. Plummer (ed.), *Vitae sanctorum Hiberniae*, 2 vols (1910), i, p. 135; and cf. K. Meyer (ed.), 'Stories from the Edinburgh MS. XXVI (Kilbride Collection No 22)' in O. Bergin et al. (eds), *Anecdota from Irish manuscripts*, iii (1910), pp 7–10 at p. 10.   28 In this he goes one better than the author of *Immram curaig Maile Dúin*, who misleads his readers into at first assuming that a woman is a man: H.P.A. Oskamp (ed. and trans.), *The voyage of Máel Dúin* (1970), pp 154–5, where the translation does not convey the deceptive phrasing of the original. This is not the only indication that the *Acallam*'s author was familiar with this text; but this is a subject for another study.   29 K.

blances, on the face of it, accounts for the statement that Finn's *fian* are not 'folk of the same time as she': there is nothing explicit to associate her, like Scothníam, with an earlier epoch.

However we are to understand this, it seems that the *Acallam* is identifying the native supernatural as a whole, whether localised in the *síde* or beyond the sea, as being in some sense another 'time'.[30] Conceivably, this reflects the association of the native immortals with humanity before the Fall: an idea which can be detected in some of the earliest Irish tales, and which resurfaces in literature of the Middle Irish and Early Modern Irish periods.[31] That Otherworldly beings experience time differently from mortals, or may seem to be outside time altogether, may also have some connection with these references to them in terms of chronological disparity. But whatever the correct explanation may be, and whether or not we are able to arrive at it, the text unequivocally presents the gulf which divides ordinary mortals from the dwellers in the *síde* in the same terms as that which divides pagans from Christians. The people of the *síde*, the *fénnidi* and the emerging Irish church are situated at three points on a single temporal axis. The dialectic of the second and third of these points, personified in the relationship of Caílte and Patrick, has always been recognised as being central to the *Acallam*. But this is only part of a larger structure: the warriors of the *fian* exist in confrontation not only with a Christian future, but also with a magical 'past' – a past which, to the extent that it eludes mortal time, has never departed. As Joseph Nagy has aptly noted, 'the *síd* and its multifarious denizens … constitute as important a part of the past depicted in the *Acallam* as the Fenian heroes themselves'.[32] They do; but in a significantly different way. What this is, and how it functions in the argument of the *Acallam* as a whole, are attractive objects of exploration.

That the *Acallam* is constructed in terms of three 'times', or worlds, and not simply of two, is signalled at the very beginning of the text. When the two *fénnidi*, Caílte and Oisín, emerge from their orgy of reminiscent melancholy with Finn's fostermother Cáma, each has a distinct destination. Caílte proceeds to his encounter with Patrick: toward a Christian future which, with

McCone (ed. and trans.), *Echtrae Chonnlai* (2000), p. 121; S. Mac Mathúna (ed. and trans.), *Immram Brain* (1985), pp 33, 46.   **30** This association – and the further association with giant size – did not originate with the *Acallam*. An anecdote of perhaps eleventh-century date, preserved in Liber Flavus Fergusiorum, describes a woman of the *síd* as follows: 'All of the beauty of the women of the world was in her form; in size she was huge and immeasurable, beyond the women of her time' (*Aille do mnaibh an domain a dealb; ba mor 7 ba diairmhe a met seoch mnaib a haimsire*): K. Meyer (ed.), 'Mitteilungen aus irischen Handschriften', *Zeitschrift für celtische Philologie*, 8 (1912), 102–20, 195–232, 559–65 at 559; translation in J. Carey, 'The finding of Arthur's grave: a story from Clonmacnoise?' in J. Carey et al. (eds), *Ildánach ildírech* (1999), 1–14 at 7, with discussion of dating at 8–10.   **31** Discussion in J. Carey, *A single ray of the sun* (2nd ed., 2011), pp 27–36.   **32** 'Life in the fast lane', p. 118.

the celebrated allusion to the foundation of Mellifont, hints at the yet more remote future of the story's composition and reception. Oisín, by contrast, goes to the *síd* which is the dwelling of his fairy mother. Later, after Caílte has himself spent time in the *síd* of Assaroe with Oisín's maternal grandfather, he returns to find that Oisín is now in Patrick's company. The symmetry seems deliberate. It recalls another symmetry: that of the story – attested only in the modern period, but surviving in such widely varying versions that it is easy to believe that it is much older – in which Oisín first leaves the familiar world of the *fian* to sojourn in the Otherworld, then returns after unnoticed ages to the Ireland of Saint Patrick.[33]

If the pagan Gaels and the Túatha Dé Danann, 'the two equal companies in Ireland',[34] represent two kinds of past time, the heterogeneity of these pasts is underlined throughout the *Acallam*. Although the author, as we have seen, does not take the time of his narrative entirely seriously, the idea that one age has given place to another is fundamental to his story: with a few mischievous exceptions, the Gaels of the old days are all long dead apart from Caílte and Oisín and their followers. But the Túatha Dé Danann are not only still alive; they are unchanged, and unchanging. We have already considered the contrast between Scothníam and Caílte; Aillenn, one of Scothníam's many sisters and a figure who comes to play a significant part in the story, subsequently explains to Patrick that 'every one among us who was drinking at the feast of Goibniu ... no weariness or sickness comes to them'.[35] Immediately after Caílte has finished telling a story of long-ago adventures with Donn mac Midir, Donn himself appears to offer Patrick the hospitality of his *síd*.[36]

Perhaps surprisingly, the idyllic condition of the ever-living is not regarded as an enviable one. Caílte's former comrade (and Oisín's grandfather) Derg Díanscothach, dwelling in the *síd* of Assaroe, is richly adorned and still youthful but for all that deeply discontented: 'We have no scarcity of food or of clothing ... and [all the same], those three whose life was worst in the *fian* ... I would rather be in their life than to be in the life in which I am in the *síd*'.[37] Elsewhere, the wealth of the *síde* appears as an alternative to the winning of spoils by conquest;[38] but Derg can scarcely be fretting at unheroic idleness here, as his *síd* is embroiled in war with another. Rather, surely, it is the companionship of his fellow *fénnidi* for which he is pining, even if at this point that could only be companionship in death.

33 For the text, see B. O'Looney (ed. and trans.), 'Tír na n-Óg: the Land of Youth', *Transactions of the Ossianic Society*, 4 (1859), 227–79; T. Ó Flannghaile (ed. and trans.), *Laoi Oisín ar Thír na n-Óg* ([1910]).   34 Stokes, 'Acallamh', l. 399: *dá airecht chudrama a n-Eirinn*. 35 Ibid., ll. 6402–3: *Cach áen ro bói ac ól fleide Goibnind acaind ... ni thic saeth na galur ríu.* 36 Ibid., ll. 5366–82.   37 Ibid., ll. 1571–6: *Ní fuil a n-uiresbaid duin do biudh na d'étach ... 7 ba hiat triar is mesa betha búi isin Féin ... ro badh fearr lim-sa beith 'na mbethaid sin iná bheith isin bethaidh a fuilim isin tsídh.*   38 In the story of the sons of Lugaid Menn: ibid., ll. 357–444.

The stakes are different for Caílte, whose baptism by Patrick has brought him the promise of a different kind of immortality. The people of the same *síd* of Assaroe heal him of various wounds and afflictions, but also offer to share their own condition with him:

> '7 dogentar linde sódh crotha duit', ar siat, 'co rabais fa luth 7 fá lán-choibled, 7 sóermacanacht Túaithe dé Danann duit leis sin'. 'Truag dono sin', ar Cailte, '7 missi do gabail deilbe druidechta umum. Ní géb acht in delb tuc mo Déntaid 7 mo Dúilem 7 in firDia fororda dam, 7 iris chreidme 7 crabaid in Táilgind intí tarrus a nEirinn'. Ocus adubradur Túath dé Danann: 'Guth fírlaich 7 fírgaiscid sin!' ar siat, '7 is maith in ní ráidi ...'.[39]

> 'and we will make a changing of form for you', said they, 'so that you may be in vigour and full activity; and you will have the noble youthfulness of the Túath Dé Danann'. 'That would be grievous', said Caílte, 'for me to take a shape of wizardry upon me. I will take only the shape that my Maker and my Creator and the true golden God gave to me, together with the faith of belief and devotion of the Adzehead, the one who has come into Ireland'. And the Túath Dé Danann said, 'That is the voice of a true warrior and a true fighter!' said they. 'And good is what you say ...'.

The phrase 'shape of wizardry' recalls the fairy maiden Aillenn's protest that 'I am not a bewitching woman of the *síde*; but [I am] of the Túath Dé Danann, with my own body';[40] in the latter passage the casuistical distinction between woman of the *síde* and woman of the Túatha Dé Danann, denying a clear equivalence which is unambiguously present throughout the rest of the *Acallam*, appears to reflect the old debate as to whether such beings were devilish spirits or supernaturally gifted humans.[41] The rest of Caílte's speech, however, brings out the real issue: the perpetual life of the *síde* is a snare, in that it precludes the true immortality of the Christian hereafter. Patrick himself makes this point when promising to protect a young prince, who has escaped after having been kidnapped by *síd* women, from falling again under the control (*comus*) of the Túatha Dé Danann: 'He will have the death which the King of heaven and earth has appointed'.[42]

---

39 Ibid., ll. 7037–44. 40 Ibid., ll. 6380–1: *Ni ben tširrachtach tšidhe mé, acht mad do Thuaith dé Danann 7 mo chorp fēin umum.* It is hard to know how best to render *acht mad* (literally 'except it be') here; unfortunately, the fragmentary condition of all manuscripts of the *Acallam* has the consequence that this passage appears only in the Laud 610 copy. Stokes translated the clause in question as 'but one of the Tuath dé Danann' (ibid., p. 246); Dooley and Roe's 'Though I am of the *Túatha Dé Danann*' does not seem grammatically feasible (*Tales*, p. 179). 41 Carey, *A single ray*, pp 14–21. 42 Stokes, 'Acallamh', ll. 4928–9: *IN bás ro ordaig Rí nime*

The Fenian past is past: all that Patrick needs to do with respect to the *fénnidi* is to baptise them, to rescue some of their friends and relatives from hell, and – most important of all, and with angelic authorisation – to record their stories. But what of the realm of the *síde*, immemorially ancient and yet also timelessly present? Here the saint appears as something of a politician: affable enough when encountered in person, but formulating ruthless cuts behind the scenes. Patrick urges Caílte to do the gentlemanly thing by Scothníam, and he accepts the homage and the hospitality of Donn. At the same time, his mission in Ireland is at least as much a matter of exorcism as of evangelisation; he has come 'to sow belief and devotion and cross-vigils, and *to cast demons and druids out of Ireland*, and to appoint saints and right-eous men, and to erect crosses and stations and altars, and *to suppress idols, and phantoms, and the arts of wizardry*'.[43] The place of the *síde* in this pro-gramme is only made explicit toward the end of the text as it survives. Despite the fact that they had submitted to Patrick and (at least according to one manuscript) accepted his teaching,[44] we are told that 'he will put the Túath Dé Danann into the slopes of hills and crags; unless someone fated to die should see an apparition visiting the earth'.[45] The place of the fairies in popular belief – as *bunadh na gcnoc* or 'people of the hills', rarely seen and regarded as uncanny portents – is accordingly portrayed as the work of the national apostle.

Only two of the Túatha Dé Danann are allowed a place in Ireland's Christian future. One is the princess Aillenn who has been mentioned above. When she first appears, it is to declare her love for Áed, the king of Connacht. Áed is already married, but Patrick gives him permission to marry Aillenn if his current wife should die, while threatening Aillenn with disfigurement should she in any way seek to bring such a death about. The queen does die thereafter, and Aillenn comes again from the *síd*. Patrick not only grants the couple leave to wed, provided that Aillenn 'put her delusive druidical belief from her, and abase herself to the gospel of the King of heaven and earth',[46] but he himself celebrates their marriage, 'and that was the first couple that the Adzehead married in Ireland, as authorities relate'.[47] Marriage, and the

---

7 talman do géba.   **43** Ibid., ll. 1497–1500: *do šilad chreitmhe 7 crabaid [7 croisfighill] 7 do dhíchur deman 7 druadh a hEirinn, 7 do togha naemh 7 fírén 7 [do tocbáil] cros 7 uladh 7 altoiredh, 7 do thairnemh idhul 7 arracht 7 ealadhan ndraidhechta.*   **44** Ibid., ll. 5378–9: *ro slechtsat ule do Pátraic. Conid ann do chreidset Túath dé Danann.* The second of these sentences appears as a marginal addition in Laud 610, and occurs in none of the other manuscripts. Donnchadh Ó Corráin has highlighted the radical ecumenism of this statement ('the king of the Otherworld and his folk … become true believers'), but without adverting to its probably secondary character in the text: 'Legend as critic' in T. Dunne and C. Doherty (eds), *The writer as witness* (1987), pp 23–38 at p. 37.   **45** Stokes, 'Acallamh', ll. 7535–6: *cuirfid Túaith dé Danann ind-étnaib cnocc 7 carracc acht muna faice trú tadhal talman do thaidbsi.*   **46** Ibid., ll. 7828–9: *acht co léiced a creidem doilfi drai[d]echta uaithe 7 co slechtad sí do tšoiscel Ríg nime 7 talman.*   **47** Ibid., ll. 7832–3: *corub hí*

importance of fidelity and stability in marriage, are important themes throughout the *Acallam*; and it has been generally recognised that this aspect of the text reflects the concern with reforming Irish marriage law which was one of the burning issues of the time of the text's composition.[48] It seems odd, however, that Patrick's first performance of this topically crucial sacrament should involve a member of the race that he will soon banish from the surface of Ireland: this episode is evidently intended as a statement of some kind. Perhaps the saint is depicted as granting legitimacy to the idea – age-old, but destined to survive into the modern period – that a king's true spouse is the supernatural personification of the land.[49]

The other Túatha Dé Danann survivor is one of the central figures in the *Acallam* as a whole: Cas Corach, the master musician who comes from the *síde* 'to get knowledge and learning from Caílte, and to seek heaven for my soul from Patrick'.[50] After having met Caílte, he remains the hero's constant companion, sharing his adventures in the mortal realm and in the *síde*; when they finally part, they address one another as fosterfather and fosterson.[51] Caílte introduces Cas Corach to Patrick near the midpoint of the *Acallam*: Patrick praises him and his art, and reiterates this praise throughout the remainder of the text. Cas Corach is the only named exception to Patrick's confinement of the Túatha Dé Danann beneath the earth. Shortly after Áed of Connacht's marriage to the *síd* princess Aillenn, Cas Corach is to marry Áed's sister Échna:[52] so each of the royal siblings finds a spouse from the race of the hollow hills.

Cas Corach's position within the story is clearly of great importance, and deserves more examination than it has to my knowledge yet received.[53] Here it will only be possible to give brief consideration to two aspects of his portrayal. First: not only is Cas Corach, a man of the *síde*, presented as the best of all musicians, but the close connection between music and the *síde* in general is stressed throughout the *Acallam*. Near the beginning of the text, we learn that Finn's chief musician, the diminutive Cnú Deróil, also came to him from the *síde*.[54] Aillén mac Midgna, who burns Tara every Samain until slain by Finn, is likewise a magical musician who lulls all of his hearers to

sin cétlánumain ro pos in Tailgenn inn-Eirinn amal airmid udair.   **48** See the apposite remarks of Dooley and Roe, *Tales*, pp xxviii–xxx. As the editors point out to me, Ruairí Ó hUiginn has argued that similar concerns can be discerned in the Middle Irish version of the Ulster saga *Tochmarc Emire*: 'Rúraíocht agus rómánsaíocht: ceisteanna faoi fhorás an traidisiúin', *Éigse*, 32 (2000), 77–87 at 85–7.   **49** R.A. Breatnach's article 'The lady and the king: a theme of Irish literature', *Studies*, 42 (1953), 321–36 retains its value, especially for its account of the concept's persistence in the later tradition.   **50** Stokes, 'Acallam', ll. 4628–9: *do denum fessa 7 foglumа ac Cailti 7 d'iarraid nime dom anmain ó Patraic.* Elsewhere he speaks only of the first of these aspirations: ibid., ll. 3353–4, 3458, 7277–8.   **51** Ibid., ll. 7891–2.   **52** Their marriage is not described in the surviving text, but is predicted, ibid., ll. 7540–6.   **53** See however the valuable remarks of Dooley and Roe, *Tales*, pp xvii–xx.   **54** Stokes, 'Acallamh', ll. 611–83.

sleep;[55] and the same effect is attributed to the 'soothing music of the *síde*' (*síanargan sidhi*) produced by the mermaid Lí Ban in the copy of the *Acallam* in UCD Franciscan MS A 4.[56] Even Cas Corach's skill is briefly overshadowed by that of Úaine Buide, 'the female musician of all the Land of Promise' (*banairfidech Thíre Tairrngaire uli*), together with the birds of that land: it is said of her that 'anyone would leave the many musics of the world for that music', and Cas Corach himself confesses 'We have heard much music, and we never heard music as good as that'.[57] Intriguingly, it is not only the people of the *síde* who can play the music of the *síde*: it is said of three Leinster princesses that 'women in the anguish of childbirth would sleep at the haunting music of the *síde* that those three maidens used to chant to the company of women'.[58]

Patrick is aware of this music's uncanny provenance, and his praise of it is qualified accordingly: 'It is good indeed ... apart from the soothing lilt of the magic of the *síde* that is in it; and there would be nothing more similar than it is to the music of the King of heaven, were it not for that'. When his scribe Broccán protests that it should not be rejected on that account, the saint agrees with him, but warns against 'excessive belief' in it.[59] Whatever about these scruples, he has no hesitation in promising heaven to Cas Corach and an illustrious future to his profession:

> corub hí in tres eladha ar a fagaib nech a lessugud fa deridh a nEirinn hí, 7 cid mor in doichell bias roim fír th'eladhan, acht co nderna airfided 7 co n-indsi scela, gan doichell reime ... 7 fer lephtha ríg tre bithu re t'eladain, 7 soirbius dóib acht na dernat leisce.[60]

> may it be one of the three arts whereby anyone may obtain his benefit at the end in Ireland. And however great may be the inhospitality toward a practitioner of your art, no inhospitality will be shown to him if he makes music and tells tales ... And practitioners of your art will be the bedfellows of kings forever, and will have prosperity so long as they are not slothful.

He pronounces a similar blessing on Cas Corach and his successors later in the text:

---

55 Ibid., ll. 1664–5.   56 Ibid., p. 303.   57 Ibid., ll. 7192–214: *do tréicfed nech ilcheola in domain ar in céol sin* .... *'Is mor do cheol do chualamur ... 7 ní chualamur céol a commaith sin'*.   58 Ibid., ll. 5552–4: *mná re gur lamnada ro choiteldais leissin céol sirrachtach sidhe ro chandais na tri hingena sin don bantracht*.   59 Ibid., ll. 3481–6: *'Is maith immorro'*, ar Pátraic, *'acht muna beith sianargan in brechta sídhe inti, 7 nocho n[f]uil ní bo chosmala re céol Rig nime inas acht muna beth sin'*. *'Matá ceol a nim'*, ar Brocan, *'cid nach biad i talmain, 7 ni cóir amlaid ind airfited do dichur'*, ar Brocan. *'Ni apraim úm'*, ar Pátraic, *'acht gan rochreidim dó'*.   60 Ibid., ll. 3475–9.

'Buaid n-urlabra ort, a meic', ... '7 cach tres focal adér fer t'eladna comad bind le cach hé, 7 fer leptha ríg díb, 7 caindel cacha hairechta re t'eladhain cháidchi'.[61]

'The virtue of eloquence be upon you, lad', ... 'and may every third word that a practitioner of your art will utter be melodious to everyone; and one of them will be the king's bedfellow; and the candle of every assembly will belong to your art always'.

At the great assembly of Tara, convened at the end of the *Acallam* as we have it, the high king Díarmait mac Cerbaill confers on Cas Corach 'the office of chief sage of Ireland for as long as I shall be in the kingship'.[62]

Harry Roe and Ann Dooley have suggested that Cas Corach's 'successes in poetry, warrior action and love ... are possibly meant to represent the social aspirations of the new secular literary and learned families of medieval Ireland';[63] but something more radical, and indeed more mysterious, seems to be going on. The learned families were proud of their control of expertise in poetry, history, law and medicine. But here the national apostle and the king of Tara join in granting supremacy over all branches of literature and the arts to a musician – a calling whose highest rank was valued, according to *Uraicecht Becc*, lower than all of these professions and also below workers in wood and metal.[64] The author appears to be looking forward to something like a revolution in the cultural hierarchy. And at the head of this revolution he places not the departed heroes, whose tales have now been confided to the manuscripts of the Church; nor for that matter the elite *filid*, who appear indeed not to figure in the *Acallam* at all; but the pupils of the last of the old gods. How we are to interpret this, and how much we are to make of it, are matters for further reflection; but I am in no doubt that these anomalies reflect concerns that lie at the heart of *Acallam na senórach*.

---

61 Ibid., ll. 7750–3. 62 Ibid., ll. 7894–5: *ollamnacht Eirenn ... in comfat rabursa ir-rigi*; cf. l. 7534, where it is said that Cas Corach will receive this dignity 'through the word of Saint Patrick' (*tre breith[ir] naemPátraic*); and l. 7543, where it is foretold that he will receive 'the office of chief sage of Ireland and Scotland' (*ollomnacht Eirenn 7 Alban*) at the assembly. 63 *Tales*, p. 239. 64 D.A. Binchy (ed.), *Corpus iuris hibernici*, 6 vols (1978), v, p. 1616; cf. F. Kelly, *A guide to early Irish law* (1988), p. 64.

Some strands and strains in *Acallam na senórach*

JOSEPH FALAKY NAGY

The title of this essay, which I present in tribute to Professor Ó Coileáin, alludes to the piece that he wrote about the complex mix of oral and literary elements in medieval Irish texts,[1] and about the inescapable but productive 'strain' of staying on the track of these more-disparate-than-not 'strands of the argument' when we examine texts as heterogeneous as *Acallam na senórach*.[2] But, in a bit of bad punning, the 'strands' of the title also refer to the sea- or lake-shore settings where many of the important episodes that happen or are recounted in the *Acallam* take place (including some of the episodes mentioned below), and to which its characters and adventures frequently gravitate.[3] The 'strains', moreover, as of something good (for example, 'strain of music') or something bad ('strain of a disease'), also refer to the precipitates that result from the juxtaposition of (or downright clash between) the varied, sometimes antagonistic ingredients brought together within the confines, or between the outlying 'strands', of this text. Oral and literary, pre-Christian and Christian, Irish and foreign, Otherworldly and this-worldly,

1 S. Ó Coileáin, 'Oral or literary? Some strands of the argument', *Studia Hibernica*, 17–18 (1977–8), 7–35. 2 The edition of the *Acallam na senórach* used here is that of Whitley Stokes, published in W. Stokes and E. Windisch (eds), *Irische Texte*, iv, 1 (1900), based on the earliest surviving recension as found in Oxford, Bodleian Library, MSS Laud 610 and Rawlinson B. 487 and in the Book of Lismore (Chatsworth, Derbyshire). Stokes' edition also incorporates, in square brackets, additions to this text from UCD Franciscan MS A 4. The *Irische Texte* version is now available on line at www.ucc.ie/celt, and a rendering into English by Ann Dooley and Harry Roe was published under the title *Tales of the elders of Ireland* (1999). Translations of excerpted passages included in this paper are my own. Given that it is in effect an altogether different text, the later recension of the *Agallamh* edited by Nessa Ní Shéaghdha (*Agallamh na seanórach*, 3 vols [1942–5]) is not taken into consideration here. 3 For example, the first tale Caílte tells Patrick has to do with the irresistible urge felt by a member of Finn's hunting-warring band (*fian*) to steal the latter's best hunting dogs and take them back to his home across the sea in Britain. This theft brings about a transmarine voyage undertaken by Finn's best men in search of the stolen dogs, an adventure that coincidentally results in the importation to Ireland of the horses henceforth ridden by members of the *fian* (Stokes, 'Acallamh', ll. 166–260). Then, on the other side of the text, a littoral flourish is added to an account of how the Lia Fáil 'works'. In the final recounting of lore before the (unfinished) text ends abruptly, Oisín says of this stone that it would make a sound when a rightful king of Ireland would go upon it (and it would remain mute when anyone else would mount it), and that the sound emitted by the stone would be 'answered' by the three 'waves' or strands that constitute the outer limits of Ireland, as the island is geographically envisioned in the *Acallam* (Stokes, 'Acallamh', ll. 7998–8001: *Ocus intan ticedh rí Eirenn fuirre do ghéised in lecc fái co freacraitis prímthonna Eirenn hí .i. tonn Clídhna 7 tonn Tuaidhe 7 tonn Rudhraigi*).

cleric and layperson, *fían* and *túath*, *gilla* and *óclach* (and *senóir*), to name the more important tensions – the *Acallam*, confronted by opposites such as these that we would expect to refuse to cooperate, actually succeeds in moving some closer together, or even creating the occasional hybrid. It is to this process of reconciliation, to having 'strangers' enter into 'dialogue' with each other, that the *Acallam* of the title primarily refers.

Usually this exchange of ideas and the search for a shared understanding happen between separate interlocutors who are genuinely different from each other – for instance, the old warrior Caílte and the Christian cleric Patrick. Sometimes, however, the *acallam* is carried on among the values espoused by the same person, and a 'monologue' takes on the appearance of a 'dialogue'. We find the most famous example of such introspection in the *Acallam* within the *persona* of Patrick as both missionary and historian: he is conflicted over whether listening to the stories Caílte tells is distracting him from the work of converting Ireland, until his personal angels tell him that listening will be allowed, so long as Patrick sees to it that what he hears is written down and saved for posterity.[4] And, as I have argued elsewhere, the occasional furloughs on which Caílte goes away from Patrick give the old warrior the opportunity to refuel both himself physically and his memory, but they also represent his persistent attraction to the past and its values, and to the world of which he and a handful of other *fían* survivors are the last remnants.[5] There is even more to the ambiguity of the figure of Caílte and to the ambivalence he exhibits, just as he is more than a *fían* member, *de facto* shanachie, and loyal retainer of his deceased lord. 'Stranded' in an era supposedly not his own, the diverse 'strains' in his persona come tumbling forth in the course of the unfolding story of the *Acallam*. Surprisingly, some of these strains as introduced and orchestrated in the text resonate not only with aspects of the 'later past' (the era of Patrick that is the story's setting) but also, as we shall see, with the even later world in which the conceit and the text of the *Acallam* took shape.[6]

4 Stokes, 'Acallamh', ll. 290–303. This angelic encounter stands apart from those recounted in Patrician hagiography, in that the saint is visited here by *two* named angels, and neither is the 'Victor' who usually visits him, alone: J.F. Nagy, *Conversing with angels and ancients* (1997), pp 120–4. Moreover, the doubling of the angelic delegation pales in comparison with the multiplication associated by the *Acallam* (ll. 7735–7) with Ard na nAingel 'the Height of the Angels' in Connacht, where *thousands* of angels are said to have come *thrice* to have *acallam* with the praying Patrick.   5 'Compositional concerns in the *Acallam na senórach*' in D. Ó Corráin et al. (eds), *Sages, saints and storytellers* (1989), pp 149–58.   6 Of course, the premise of Patrick's encounter with warrior-heroes of old was not invented by the author(s) of the *Acallam*. Cú Chulainn, that towering representative of the Ulster Cycle, has his own interview with the evangelising saint, in *Síaburcharpat Con Culainn*, included in *Lebor na hUidre* (*c.*1100) and most likely predating the *Acallam*: R.I. Best and O. Bergin (eds), *Lebor na Huidre* (1929), ll. 9220–548. On the cultural implications of this text, see E. Johnston, 'The salvation of the individual and the salvation of Society' in J.F. Nagy (ed.), *The individual in Celtic literatures* (2001), pp 109–25. Cú

Before examining further the nuances of the *Acallam*'s depiction of Caílte and his fellow *fian* members, I offer what I propose is a useful-to-think-with analog from ancient Greek tradition. Let us visit for a while with the father of history, the fifth-century Greek writer Herodotus, who depicts a world in which the ethos of the 'Heroic Age' reflected in the epics of Homer comes repeatedly under attack from the teeming forces threatening to overwhelm it. The clash, as Herodotus perceives it, is between West and East, Europe and Asia, Greece and Persia. In Book Six of the *Histories*, Herodotus details a key preliminary stage in this conflict, namely, the Persian campaign to crush the rebellion of Miletus and the other Ionian colonies dotting the eastern Mediterranean. Key to Darius the Persian king's success, says Herodotus, was the presence in the Persian fleet of the Phoenicians, who were *prothumótatoi*,[7] the most 'fired-up' among the various ethnic components of the naval expedition. This characterisation of the Phoenicians very much fits in with Herodotus' portrait of this sea-faring people, who make several strategic appearances in the *Histories*. From those appearances, we can infer that their enthusiasm in the campaign against the Ionian colonies came not just from a warlike nature but also from an unerring instinct for business. In the short term, decisively defeating the forces of the Ionian city-states meant winning booty; in the long term, their downfall meant eliminating the Phoenicians' major competitors in trade in the region.[8]

Here are the classical world's exponents *par excellence* of enterprise, restless exploration, exploitation and invention: the sailors, merchants and craftsmen of the Levantine cities of Tyre, Sidon, Byblos and others, known collectively to the Greeks as the *Phoínik* ε ('Purple Ones', probably in references to the dyes they were famous for making and selling). In Herodotus, they are never far from resorting to trickery and piracy. Book One begins with a theory that the troubles between East and West (leading ultimately to the Persian War) began with the serial stealing of kings' daughters. The Phoenicians started it, say the Persians. They came to Greek Argos to ply their wares but ended up stealing the princess Io. Then the Greeks in retaliation stole Europa from Tyre, and Medea from Colchis. East paid back West with the theft of Helen and her abduction to Troy.[9]

In vying to even the score, the Greeks and Phoenicians (including the latter's 'teammates', the Trojans) not only play out a rivalry but come to

Chulainn, however, is returned to the earth in spectral form as a demonstration of Patrick's power. In the *Acallam*, on the other hand, there is no sense that Patrick summons Caílte, Oisín and their companions from beyond the grave, or that their living past their era stems from divine or saintly intervention.   **7** *Histories*, 6.6: A.D. Godley (ed. and trans.), *Herodotus*, 4 vols (1927–41), iii, p. 152.   **8** Sarah P. Morris points out that the 'compliment … makes them the equal of the Athenians, who earned the same superlative before Plataia (in the words of Pausanias: 9.60.3)' in *Daidalos and the origins of Greek art* (1992), p. 372. Other instances of Phoenician participation in naval operations aimed at the Greeks are discussed in the same work, pp 371–7.   **9** *Histories*, 1.1–5: Godley, *Herodotus*, i, pp 2–8.

mirror one another. The theft of Europa, in fact, leads to major interpenetration between the Phoenician and Greek realms, according to Herodotus. Her brother Kadmos comes to the Greek mainland in search of Europa, but to no avail. Abandoning his quest, he founds the city of Thebes in Boeotia. Kadmos and his Phoenician contingent, says the ancient historian, brought with them to their new home a vital cultural tool: their system of writing, which, with some fine-tuning by the natives, became the Greek alphabet.[10] Thus, the figure of the Phoenician plays the role of the exotic Asian 'Other' in the Herodotean scheme, as well as the enthusiastically rapacious enemy of the Greeks. Yet, in the same scheme, the two sides become inextricably caught up in each other's cultural projects, chief among which is *writing*, not only the instrument of and most authoritative 'witness' (the original meaning of Greek *historia*) to Herodotus' achievement, but the bridge between Greek 'super-ego' and Phoenician 'id'.

The ethnonym *Phoínik ϵ* was coined by the Greeks, and there is no evidence that the peoples of the Levant (known as *cana'ani* or *kina'nu* 'Canaanites' in Hebrew, a term that can also mean 'merchants') had any sense of collective identity.[11] And while no one would go so far as to claim that the Phoenicians were a figment of the ancient Greek imagination, they did present the Greeks with the opportunity to realise an emerging cultural *trope*. The classicist Rhys Carpenter observed that the two distinctive designations in the Homeric lexicon for the Phoenicians complement each other: *poludaídaloi* 'having many crafts, skills', as they are described in the Iliad (where Phoenicians are said to produce beautiful artifacts ideally suited for gift-giving, offering sacrifice to the gods, and paying ransom), and *polupaípaloi* 'having many wiles', in the Odyssey (where Phoenicians deviously obtain such objects and even reduce the passengers on their ships to slaves for sale).[12] Building on Carpenter's observation, Irene Winter, a member of a later generation of classicists, formulated her understanding of this 'complex double role played by Homer's Phoenicians' thus:

> On the one hand, they represent the 'different and the foreign' of the traditional enemy, and we must read them in terms of alterity; on the other hand, they represent a projection of the social and economic present, the becoming 'self', and we must read them with all the ambivalence and discomfort, denial even, that contemporary Greeks must have felt about the changes their society was presently undergoing.[13]

10 Ibid., 4.147; 5.57–58: Godley, *Herodotus*, ii, p. 348; iii, pp 62–4. On writing as a Phoenician 'import', see Morris, *Daidalos*, pp 105–6. 11 M.E. Aubet, *The Phoenicians and the west* (2001), p. 10. 12 'Phoenicians in the west', *American Journal of Archaeology*, 62 (1958), 35–53 at 35–6. 13 'Homer's Phoenicians: history, ethnography, or literary trope? [A perspective on early orientalism]' in J.B. Carter and S.P. Morris (eds), *The ages of Homer* (1995), pp 247–71 at

I have chosen the Phoenicians of the ancient Mediterranean world as the mascots of this paper because they supply us with a venerable example of a mythological type we also encounter in the *Acallam* and elsewhere in medieval Celtic literatures.[14] This is a type of character motivated by 'commercial' concerns – unabashedly seeking profit, yet sensitive to the nuances of exchange; knowledgeable about where to obtain rare, precious goods, and familiar with the technologies of craftsmen; quite capable of guile and theft, and well versed in the arts of seduction, especially when it comes to valuable female 'commodities'; engaging in an ambivalent relationship with warrior-heroes and their ethos, to the extent of being indistinguishable from them in some situations; and having the potential to be a culture-hero, an inventor, as well as a practitioner of techniques for preserving and distributing goods for which society is willing to pay a high price.[15] Moreover, the commercial hero is characterised by resilience, the ability to negotiate (etymologically 'do business') with his enemies and rivals, even to the extent of merging with them, or merging his interests with theirs.[16] So far, and throughout the rest of this paper, I refer to this type as a 'he', but in fact there are female reflexes of the commercial hero as well, and it may prove profitable in the future to consider under this rubric the conniving Medb of the Ulster Cycle (who, unlike virtually all other characters featured in that cycle, merits a mention in the *Acallam*),[17] Becfhola, the 'smart shopper' of husbands in *Tochmarc Becfhola*,[18] and the hard-bargaining Elen Luydauc of the Middle Welsh *Breudwyt Macsen Wledic*.[19] The model also provides a new perspective on some famous but seemingly isolated instances of 'commercialism' in the Classical ethnographic record of the Celts and in medieval Celtic texts – a perspective, I hasten to point out, not at all incompatible with the analysis of Georges Dumézil as honed by the Rees brothers in their search for traces of Indo-European ideological structures in the extant Celtic data.[20] The commercial hero can also

---

p. 261.   **14** See also J.F. Nagy, *Mercantile myth in medieval Celtic traditions* (2011). The basis for this or any other argument for a deeply rooted mercantilism in early medieval Irish culture owes an inestimable debt to the groundbreaking work of the historian Charles Doherty, in particular: 'Exchange and trade in early medieval Ireland', *Journal of the Royal Society of Antiquaries of Ireland*, 110 (1980), 67–89.   **15** Writing counts as one of these techniques in the case of Herodotus' Phoenicians, and it resurfaces in the Irish material we will be examining. **16** Perhaps this is the mythical counterpart to Benjamin Hudson's legendary protagonist described in 'The practical hero' in M. Richter and J.-M. Picard (eds), *Ogma* (2002), pp 151–64. See also Philip O'Leary's various explorations of the more devious, opportunistic aspects of heroes and heroism in early Irish literature – for example, 'Verbal deceit in the Ulster Cycle', *Éigse*, 21 (1985), 16–26.   **17** Stokes, 'Acallamh', ll. 3859–70.   **18** M. Bhreathnach (ed. and trans.), 'A new edition of Tochmarc Becfhola', *Ériu*, 35 (1984), 59–91.   **19** Ed. B. Roberts (2005).   **20** The commercial hero has much in common with the 'fifth province' Munster, which, in their analysis of the symbolism of the five 'fifths' of Ireland, Alwyn Rees and Brinley Rees (*Celtic heritage* [1961], pp 143–4) associate with musicians, lower orders of craftsmen, teeming assemblies, and Lug, 'the master of all arts and the institutor of fairs', and the Irish counter-

wade into the swiftly moving streams of contemporary scholarly findings about the Viking settlers in Ireland and their impact, and about how the Irish *literati* utilised the archaic institution of the *fian* and stories about it to interpret new players and circumstances in the complex historical drama unfolding *c.*1000.

Following the 'golden trail' of the commercial hero, as conspicuous as that left by Louernios in the famous Classical account of this Gaulish entrepreneur-politician,[21] we now return to the aforementioned *Acallam*. Whether this work ranks with the artistic achievements attributed to Homer is open to question, but it merits comparison to an Iliad or Odyssey if only because, as we will have the chance to discover, the epically proportioned *Acallam*, like Homeric epic, views its changing historical milieu in terms of displacement, deferment and projection.

The scene in the *Acallam* where Patrick is visited by the two angels, already mentioned, not only supplies the text and its audience with an explanation of how the text itself came to be but also justifies the keen interest in native, local and even pre-Christian traditions displayed in this and many other vernacular productions of medieval Ireland. Another scene soon follows in the *Acallam*, equally definitive and profound in its implications. Patrick summons Caílte and his fellow pagan survivors from Finn's *fian* to receive the sacrament of baptism. He has already exorcised them,[22] but, if the *fian* heroes and their stories are to be entered into the Christian record, the storytellers will have to become *bona fide* members of the church community. The scene is invested with even more gravity when, for the first time, the members of Caílte's 'time-capsule' contingent are named and briefly described. Of special note here is that, although they are said to be a *nónbar* 'party of nine', the names given add up to eleven.[23] Adding Caílte, we have an apostolic twelve, accompanying the Christ-like missionary. Before Patrick pours the holy water over the converts, he poses a question about the sacramental act to their spokesperson Caílte, who does not know the answer – a reversal of what usually happens in the *Acallam*, in which Patrick is typically posing questions about the past to the knowledgeable Caílte, who almost always knows the answer:

part to the Gaulish Mercury, 'the greatest power in commercial affairs', as he is portrayed by Caesar. On a more general front, Émile Benveniste surveys the Indo-European vocabulary pertaining to commerce, 'an occupation without a name' in *Indo-European language and society*, trans. E. Palmer (1973), pp 113–20. I am grateful to my colleague Gary Holland of the University of California, Berkeley, for bringing Benveniste's comments on this subject to my attention. **21** The reference is to Athenaeus, *Deipnosophistai*, 4.37: C.B. Gulick (ed. and trans.), *Athenaeus: the deipnosophists*, 7 vols (1967), ii, p. 194. See P. Mac Cana, 'Notes on the legend of Louernios' in M. Richter and J.-M. Picard (eds), *Ogma* (2002), pp 138–44, and the author's *The poetics of absence in Celtic tradition* (2003), pp 4–8. **22** Stokes, 'Acallamh', ll. 64–71. **23** Ibid., ll. 304–13. The number of survivor-companions is tripled much later in the text, in a scene where they die of grief (ll. 7896–902).

'(In) bfedubair cidh fa tucad dom acallaim sib don (chu)r so?' ar
Pátraic. 'Ni fedumar immorro', ar Cáilte. 'Ar dáigh cu ro sléchtadh
sibh do soiscéla rígh nime 7 talman .i. in firDia forórda'.[24]

'Do you know why you were brought here to talk with me now?' asked
Patrick. 'We don't know', said Cáilte. 'In order that you may submit to
the gospel of the King of Heaven and Earth, the true, glorious God'.

This micro-exchange, explicitly designated an *acallam*, mirrors the text in
which it is embedded, and serves to validate the macro-exchange of the
Acallam as a Christian transaction, just as the divine response to Patrick's
dilemma, delivered by the two angels in the previous scene, justifies his continuing conversation with Cáilte.

As soon as the baptism takes place, our attention shifts back to Cáilte, who
produces an eye-catching item from behind his shield: a chunk of red gold as
long and wide and thick as Patrick's arm. (One source throws in the exoticis-
ing detail that the precious metal was from Arabia).[25] This was the last
túarastal 'stipend' he received from Finn, Cáilte says, and he gives it to
Patrick and the church for the salvation of his and his companions' souls, and
for the salvation of his deceased lord Finn.[26] Here and elsewhere in the
Acallam, the payment given by Finn to the warriors fighting for him, termed
túarastal, usually consists of gold and/or silver. Except in the unique case of
this *fian* hero, who is still carrying his *túarastal* on his person, the text typically envisions such caches of precious metal and other prized *fian* possessions as buried treasure awaiting rediscovery.[27] The impression reasonably to
be derived from this scene, that Cáilte is in effect giving Patrick payment in
exchange for his baptism, may render the proceedings spiritually unedifying
for the modern reader. Yet, in the context of medieval religious practice, this
is less an instance of simony than a demonstration of the centrality of baptism
among the services rendered by the clergy to the laity – services by which the
cleric 'earns' the support of the layperson.[28] Along these lines, a Hiberno-
Latin text attributed to Saint Finnian, described by its editor as 'the earliest
Irish penitential now in existence', states in effect that *monachi* (perhaps in

24 Ibid., ll. 314–17.   25 UCD Franciscan MS A 4 (Stokes, 'Acallamh', ll. 320–1). On the
Middle-Eastern origins of some of the (silver) coinage brought to Ireland by Viking merchants,
see J. Sheehan, 'Early Viking Age silver hoards from Ireland and their Scandinavian elements'
in H.B. Clarke et al. (eds), *Ireland and Scandinavia in the early Viking Age* (1998), pp 166–202
at pp 186–8; see also M.A. Valante, *The Vikings in Ireland* (2008), p. 54.   26 Stokes, 'Acallamh',
ll. 319–26.   27 Perhaps these prizes waiting to be dug up from the landscape of the *Acallam*
correspond to the hidden hoards of silver and gold from the Viking era in Ireland: see Sheehan,
'Early Viking Age silver hoards', pp 167–76.   28 On the the twelfth-century theological and literary subtext to this incident of baptism in the *Acallam*, see M. Ní Mhaonaigh, 'Pagans and
holy men: literary manifestations of twelfth-century reform' in D. Bracken and D. Ó Riain-
Raedel (eds), *Ireland and Europe in the twelfth century* (2006), pp 143–61 at pp 152–3.

the sense of sub-ecclesiastical monastic tenants) should not perform baptisms, since they are not entitled to receive alms.[29] Furthermore, the exchange of goods and services that takes place in the *Acallam* scene not only legitimates the ongoing dialogic adventure of Patrick and Caílte but highlights the mutually beneficial nature of the relationship between Christian saint (who entices the *fian* survivors with the prospect of both heaven and the renewal of their earthly fame) and pagan hero (who proves very helpful to Patrick in many respects). The text specifies that the piece of gold given to Patrick by the new convert weighed 150 ounces – enough gold, we are told, to gild the missionary's bells, psalters and mass books.[30]

The impressive quantity of Caílte's 'pocket change' accords with the picture of *fian* opulence already conveyed by the old *fénnid* ('member of the *fian*') right from the beginning of the *Acallam*, as soon as Patrick starts to inquire about Finn and life in the *fian*. In response to the saint's question as to whether Finn was a good lord, Caílte makes the famous statement of praise (*formolad*) that if the leaves of the forest (Finn's realm) had been of gold, and the waves of silver, Finn would have given them away.[31] Shortly after this, Patrick, picking up on the theme not so much of Finn's generosity but of his having the wherewithal to be the paradigm of the generous lord, asks if the *fian* had been well supplied with cups made of crystal and gold. Indeed they were, replies the old *fénnid*, who proceeds to list the vessels, their names, and their owners, in the first major poem the text includes that focuses on the *fian*

---

29 L. Bieler (ed. and trans.), *The Irish penitentials* (1963), §50, p. 92: *Monachi autem non debent babtizare neque accipere elimosinam. Si autem accipiant elimosinam, cur non babtizabunt?* In another episode of the *Acallam*, Benén, Patrick's right-hand man, points out the *quid pro quo* of a situation in which Patrick grants retroactive salvation to a figure of the past whose treasure in silver Caílte has unearthed from a grave mound and donated to the saint at Benén's suggestion: Stokes, 'Acallamh', ll. 1090–2 (see note by Dooley and Roe, *Tales of the elders*, p. 233). Also of relevance is the *screpall soiscéla* 'gospel scruple' (a unit of value) paid out to Patrick by royal figures who seek the saint's favor (and presumably baptism), on three different occasions in the *Acallam* (ll. 3710–12, 5393–7, 5906–9). On the second of these, Benén specifies that the *screpall* should consist of land (l. 5395); on the other two, it is paid in gold and silver. Compare also Patrick's baptismal fee or *screaball baithis* 'baptism scruple', consisting of three pennies per person, mentioned by the seventeenth-century Irish historian Geoffrey Keating: D. Comyn and P.S. Dinneen (ed. and trans.), *Foras feasa ar Éirinn*, 4 vols (1902–14), iii, p. 377. Arguably, these payments would have been anathema to the clerical proponents of ecclesiastical reforms in twelfth-century Ireland, which forbade the demanding of a fee for baptism: A. Gwynn, *The twelfth-century reform* (1968), p. 60. 30 Stokes, 'Acallamh', ll. 326–8. In this regard, it is perhaps meaningful that *túarastal*, the term used in the *Acallam* to describe the reward members of the *fian* received from their employer Finn, and which Caílte passes on to Patrick, in its original legal context means 'evidence of an eyewitness' (literally 'the act of attending on or to'): see R. Thurneysen, *A grammar of Old Irish* (1946), pp 514, 532; *DIL* s.v. *túarastal*. When the old pagan, baptised by Patrick, receives the ecclesiastical seal of approval, he reciprocates by providing his baptiser with informative and genial company, bearing invaluable witness to the past, and serving as living evidence of what he narrates. 31 Stokes, 'Acallamh', ll. 113–17.

itself.[32] Clearly, the *fian* life of hunting and fighting in the interstices between the human and supernatural world, where *fiana* traditionally dwell, netted a considerable profit for Finn and his colleagues, who lived a life that can only be described as luxurious, at least as we see it in the *Acallam*.

The theme of the *fian* heroes as possessors of distinctive 'collector's items' is not limited to this text. It recurs elsewhere, for instance, in one of the poems preserved in the seventeenth-century *Duanaire Finn* collection, a treasure trove of late medieval popular balladry. Here, in fact, the object, a *síthal* 'sieve, bowl' (from Latin *situla*), serves the same function as the precious metal bequeathed to Patrick by Caílte in the *Acallam* episode mentioned above. The bowl, according to the poem, came from an array of valuables awarded to Finn by an Otherworldly host, and it was given by the *rígfhénnid* to his trusty companion Caílte. The *síthal* later falls into a spring and is lost, but Finn predicts that it will be miraculously recovered by Patrick, then melted down, and used to decorate the saint's gear.[33]

After the episode of Caílte and his companions' baptism, the *Acallam* returns to the business of recording the travel, encounters with the new and the old, and conversations shedding light on the past in which Patrick and company take part. Meanwhile, Caílte, having spent the reserve he had tucked away behind his shield, engages fully in all that takes place but keeps an eye open for opportunities to claim or win treasure. Not long after being accepted fully into Patrick's Christian fold, the aged hero finds a cache with which he more than makes up for what he paid at his baptism. In this profitable adventure, he also shows that he knows how to strike a good bargain as well as to obtain rare items that *per se* might not seem valuable but that in the right context give him the bargaining edge.[34]

During his sojourn with Patrick in Munster, Caílte notices a settlement new since his time and, veering off course by himself, sets out to investigate. He finds the dwelling sparsely occupied, left in the care of two grief-stricken ladies. Asked by Caílte why they are sad, the women explain that their husbands, the sons of the king of Fir Maige, have left them and are bringing home new paramours. As soon as these arrive, the first wives explain, they themselves will have to leave. Caílte notices a large stone near where he is holding the conversation with the women and remembers that it serves as the hiding-place of the stipend (*túarastal*) paid long ago by Finn to another of his warriors in the *fian*. The text itemises what the stipend consists of – once again precious metal, but in much greater quantity and variety than what Caílte had in his possession earlier in the *Acallam*. Inside the stone lie hidden 150 ounces *each* of gold, silver and white bronze (*plus* 150 golden bracelets,

---

32 Ibid., ll. 121–62. 33 Poem XVII in E. MacNeill and G. Murphy (ed. agus trans.), *Duanaire Finn*, 3 vols (1908–53), i, pp 38–45, 140–9. See discussion of this poem in Joseph Flahive's contribution to this volume (below, pp 179–83). 34 Stokes, 'Acallamh', ll. 953–98.

adds the text of the *Acallam* preserved in UCD Franciscan MS A 4). Quickly Caílte concocts a plan, asking the ladies what price (*lúagh*) they would be willing to pay if he were to restore their husbands' love for them. Anything in their possession, they respond, but Caílte's response, that he would ask for the stone, puts them at a loss, for, they say, it is virtually immovable. No problem, says Caílte – lifting the rock will be his concern.

And so a deal is struck. The foraging Caílte collects for and gives to the abandoned wives herbs of the *síd* that were known to the women of the *fían* as having aphrodisiac properties, and tells them to bathe in them. After the husbands return and fall under the spell of the renewed attractiveness of their spouses,[35] Caílte is given possession of the stone, which he pulls out of the ground all by himself and takes away. Although the text tells us that upon rejoining Patrick the old warrior told him all that had happened, the text discreetly drops the stone from the story line, as well as the treasure it contains, and never tells us what use, if any, Caílte ever made of the cache.[36]

At this stage, the text of the *Acallam* in Stokes' edition has not yet reached 1000 lines (which would be approximately one-eighth of the way to the end of the text). Although by now we have heard Caílte tell stories about what members of Finn's *fían* used to do – namely, fight and hunt – we have not seen Caílte himself actually engage in these activities, as he will later on in the *Acallam*. We have, however, already seen him engage in two separate transactions involving the transfer of the possession of precious metals. In the second of these, Caílte *bargains* with the possessors of treasure that he wishes to acquire, using his knowledge of the recondite to provide a suitable item of exchange, that is, the herbal love potion. Pointedly not of a kind with the glittering objects of Caílte's desire, this product nevertheless proves to have great

---

35 The range of the old *fénnid*'s expertise never fails to impress us. This knowledge of sexual chemistry vaguely recalls the hagiographic scenario of a saint's miraculously adding romantic spice to a failed marriage (see R. Sharpe (trans.), *Adomnán of Iona* (1995), p. 341 n. 321), but it also suits the *fénnid* in his celebrated role as a helpful conductor for those undergoing transitional crises: see J.F. Nagy, *The wisdom of the outlaw* (1985), pp 41–79.   36 Later on in the *Acallam*, a much more altruistic Caílte, while travelling away from Patrick in Ulster, sets up the dislodging of a stone concealing a treasure, buried in Finn's time, as a test to see whether Donn, the youthful grandson of one of Caílte's *fían* acquaintances of old, in fact possesses the mettle characteristic of the heroes of the *fían*. After the stone is successfully removed and the treasure revealed, the old warrior gives Donn a third of the treasure (altogether consisting of one vat each of gold and silver, and a third containing cups) and distributes the rest to his Ulster hosts, declaring that he himself does not want any of it. Donn is then called upon by Caílte to assist in the hunt of the *Mucc Slánga*, a magical pig that had not been hunted since Finn's time. The slain pig is subsequently presented to Patrick and the king of Ireland in the company of his assembled court, divided, and consumed. In addition, per Caílte's instructions, Patrick and company are given two items from the unearthed cache: Finn's sword and one of his vessels, decorated with fifty ounces of gold and the same amount of silver, alongside 150 gems. In acknowledgment of Donn's accomplishments and lineage, the king of Ireland appoints him to the leadership of a revived Tara *fían*: Stokes, 'Acallamh', ll. 2174–305.

value, as a means of *restoring relationships* (specifically, between husbands and wives) to what they 'should' be. This value in fact also resides in the precious metal that Caílte both gives and receives. These are referred to in both cases as *túarastal* which, in the idiom of the *Acallam*, refers to the payment by which the leader of the *fian* purchases the loyalty of a member of his band.[37] Thus, what Caílte uses to establish a bond with Patrick and all that the churchman represents, and what he wins in return for reuniting wives with husbands, once served to attach him and his colleagues to Finn and the *fian*, contractually and sentimentally. Consequently, Caílte's employment of wealth at hand (his *túarastal*) for the purpose of establishing a new relationship (between him and the church), and his equally shrewd restoration of existing relationships (the marriages) in order to acquire more wealth (a *fian* colleague's *túarastal*), point to his *fian* associations as effectively as (if not even more so than) any heroic feat of arms or hunting that he accomplishes later in the frame tale of the *Acallam*, or that he describes in his inserted narratives.

The same narrative motifs highlighted in these episodes centred on Caílte – the *fénnid*'s knack for shrewd bargaining, the contractual relationship that obtains within the *fian*, and the disrupted social bond in need of repair – all figure prominently in the most famous *Acallam* episode featuring Finn himself, as told by Caílte later on in the text.[38] This story, telling how Finn emerged from the exile typical of the youth of heroes in Celtic and other traditions, surfaces in the aged *fénnid*'s memory when, on an Otherworldly furlough from Patrick, Caílte is handed the same spear that the youthful hero obtained in order to win his birthright as the leader of the Tara king's *fian*. A costly object riveted with (the ever-popular) Arabian gold, as decorative as it is deadly,[39] the spear is admiringly described as if it were more a good-luck charm used to obtain wealth than a weapon for winning fame in battle:

> Ocus an tsleg dobeirise am laimh-si, a Ilbric, as di dorónad an gním sochair sin d'Eirinn, 7 as lé fuair Finn gach rath riamh.[40]

---

37 *Túarastal* appears frequently in the eleventh-century 'Book of Rights', referring to 'stipends paid by a superior king to his subject kings': M. Dillon (ed. and trans.), *Lebor na cert* (1962), p. xvii. Dillon notes (ibid.) that '[t]he payment of a stipend was not so much an obligation upon the king as was the acceptance of it by his subject'. See also n. 30, above.   38 Stokes, 'Acallamh', ll. 1654–771.   39 In fact, right before this object is introduced into the narrative, Caílte produces another object hidden behind his shield (like the lump of gold he gives Patrick) that both has value and can be used to deadly effect: a *fleasc umhaidhi* 'rod of bronze' thrown almost casually by Caílte to rid his hosts of a pesky Otherworldly bird: Stokes, 'Acallamh', ll. 1645–8.   40 Ibid., ll. 1767–9. *Sochor* 'profit', used here in the genitive as a modifier, is *so-chor* 'good contract, mutually beneficial relationship' – an apt description both of the arrangement between Finn and Fíacha, the owner of the spear who sells it to Finn in the tale embedded here, and of that between Caílte and his Otherworldly host Ilbrecc in the frame narrative. Another example of *sochor*, according to medieval Irish legal literature, is a contract a wife 'is entitled to make … independently of her husband' (F. Kelly, *A guide to early Irish law* [1988], p. 181) –

> The spear you place in my hand, Ilbrecc, [says Caílte,] it is with this
> that the profitable deed was done for Ireland, and it is with it that
> Finn won all the good fortune he ever had.

The old warrior proceeds to tell the story of how the young outlaw came in
from the cold, introduced himself to the king of Ireland, regained the leadership of the Tara *fían* (which had been taken away from his father Cumall),
and made peace with his father's old mortal enemies.

Not only does the enterprising Finn take advantage of the festive time of
the Feast of Tara, when, the text explains, feuding is not allowed, but he
jumps at the chance offered in Conn's proclamation that anyone who is able
to prevent the burning of Tara, a catastrophe that takes place every year at
this time, will be awarded his 'patrimony' (*a dhúthchus*). The fearless inter-
loper accepts the offer, but, to win the proper equipment with which to
accomplish the task he has undertaken, Finn has to engage in further negoti-
ation. Fíacha mac Conga, a friend of Finn's father, offers him a spear that
never misses its target, and that will magically help Finn resist the soporific
music that the Otherworldly fire-breather Aillén always plays before he burns
Tara. The weapon does not come free: 'What payment would you give me
[for the spear]?' asks Fíacha. Finn, unlike the desperate housewives of the Fir
Maige episode who offer everything they have, cagily answers the question
with a question: 'What price are you asking of me?' Fíacha proposes a part-
nership: 'However much good fortune you win with your right hand, a third
of it to me, as well as a third of your planning and counsel'.[41]

Finn accepts the offer, Tara is saved, and Finn's fortune (*rath*)-winning
career is underway, but the spear, named *Birgha*, figures in parallel and further
adventures – not in the *Acallam* but in *Macgnímartha Finn*, an incomplete
account of Finn's boyhood deeds, preserved in only a single manuscript and
perhaps contemporary with or even earlier than the *Acallam*. There is no mention made in the *Macgnímartha* of the Tara/Aillén incident, although one sus-
pects that it was included, or would have been, in a complete version of the
text. There is, however, an episode in which the exiled Finn uses the spear of
his mentor Fíacail mac Conchinn – a figure clearly identical with the *Acallam*'s
'Fíacha mac Conga' – to slay an Otherworldly attacker who has established a
record of yearly mayhem (like the perpetrator of Tara's annual burning
described in the *Acallam*). In this *Macgnímartha* episode, Finn comes upon a
pair of wide-open *síde*, as vulnerable to exploitation as the king of Ireland's
court during the Feast of Tara. The young hero throws Fíacail's spear, here as

---

such as the transaction entered into by the wives of the sons of the king of Fir Maige with
Caílte, in the episode introduced above, p. 98.   **41** Stokes, 'Acallamh', ll. 1711–15: *cá luaighidh-
echt dobértha damsa ... Gá luagh chuingi oram ... Gid beg mór do rath ghéba do lámh dheas [a
trian] damsa 7 trian do chocair 7 do chomairli.*

in the *Acallam* named *Birg(h)a* ('Spit-Spear'), and the missile wondrously finds its target, landing in the *síd*. Not one to lose an object given to him on loan, Finn recovers this valuable weapon by kidnapping a *síd*-woman

> as a hostage to guarantee the return of the spear. She promised the spear would be returned in exchange for her. Finn let the woman go back into the *síd* ... The spear was thrown out after that, and Finn took it to where Fiacail was. 'Good', said Fiacail. 'Let the spear with which you accomplished the wondrous deed belong to you'. Fiacail then said that it was a lucky occasion.[42]

The spear, which goes back and forth between Finn and the *síd* (in the *Macgnímartha*), and which he purchases from Fíacha (in the *Acallam*), serves in yet a third instance as an item of exchange, in the present of the *Acallam* frame tale. Caílte's supernatural host Ilbrecc, after hearing the story of the weapon's instrumentality in the heroic rise of Finn (how, we wonder, did it end up back in the Otherworld, in the possession of Ilbrecc?), invites Caílte to keep the spear at hand, in anticipation of an attack by the forces of the *síd* of Finnachad, led by its lord Lir (or Ler). The assault, Ilbrecc says, will come in retaliation for Caílte's having killed a noisome bird, sent by the chief of the rival *síd* to harass the residents of Ilbrecc's dwelling, in an ongoing feud between the two Otherworldly communities.[43] (Earlier, we were told how Caílte slew this creature with a brass rod he fetched from behind his shield – a gesture reminiscent of his golden payment to Patrick, discussed above.)[44] Lir's forces do indeed arrive, and Caílte, the perennial champion, volunteers to fight with Lir himself, described by Ilbrecc as the most formidable warrior among the Túatha Dé Danann[45] – a remarkable addendum to Lir's reputation in light of the comment made elsewhere in the *Acallam* that he was the oldest member of this supernatural race, even back in Finn's day.[46] His venerability does not protect him from Caílte, who slays him, a feat celebrated in a victory song by Ilbrecc, and the army from the *síd* of Finnachad is subsequently routed. Afterwards, Caílte offers to return the loaned spear, but Ilbrecc refuses to take it back, since Caílte (as the last survivor of Finn's *fían* and the gracious guest who has slain his host's mortal enemy) now has the strongest claim to it. In the wake of the battle, Ilbrecc speaks of the weapon *Birgha* as if it were the spoils of Caílte's combat with Lir, and as if it constituted payment to Caílte for services rendered.[47] Once again, as in the bygone era of the youthful Finn's triumphs, ownership of the

42 Nagy, *The wisdom of the outlaw*, p. 217.   43 Stokes, 'Acallamh', ll. 1769–71.   44 Ibid., ll. 1645–8: *Is ann sin tuc Cáilte a láim a comraidh a sceith, 7 fleasc umhaidhi bái aige, 7 tuc urchar don eon di cu rus-marb, co tarla ar lár in tsídha cuca é.*   45 Ibid., ll. 1793–4: *'In ferr as ferr engnam do Thuathaib dé Danann', ar siat, '.i. Lir Sídha Findachaidh'.*   46 Ibid., ll. 5185–6: *... uair iss é is sine do Thúaith dé Danann.*   47 Ibid., ll. 1820–3: *'Do sleagh duit, a Ilbric', ar Cáilte. 'Nír'*

spear alternates back and forth between *fénnid* and the *áes síde*, old trading part-
ners who never miss a chance to benefit from their relationship.

And yet not every Otherworldly player can emerge from this episode of
Caílte's visit to the *síd* with a net gain. Ilbrecc and Caílte both benefit at the
expense of Lir of Síd Finnachaid, who actually loses his life as a result of the
rediscovery of Finn's old spear. In yet another indication that the sequence of
related events in the *Acallam* is rarely if ever accidental, the killing of the
master of Síd Finnachaid with Finn's recovered weapon harks back to the
story of the first and most important deed that Finn accomplished with the
spear. Aillén, the burner of Tara and Finn's opponent in that story, *comes
from* Síd Finnachaid.[48] Behind both saboteurs, Aillén in the past and the bird
with a fiery tail in the present,[49] stands the mysterious figure of Lir, who is
finally eliminated by Caílte.

It is reasonable to assume that the author of the *Acallam* and the tradition
he was following would have associated this Lir, who in yet another episode of
the *Acallam* fights against Finn and his *síd* allies and then arranges a conclusion to the hostilities,[50] with the 'Lir' who is the father of a much more famous
yet tangential member of the Túatha Dé Danann: Manannán mac Lir.[51] And
yet Lir never appears as a figure of story in medieval Irish literature written
before or contemporary with the *Acallam*. His role in general is limited to that
of an unseen parent or genealogical figure.[52] The closest we have to Lir as an
active participant in the vast world of Irish narrative apart from the *Acallam*, is
in a considerably later text than the latter: the Early Modern Irish *Oidheadh
chloinne Lir*, where a hapless Lir loses his children to the machinations of their

*chomadhas duit a rádh rim', ar Ilbrec, 'ór gin gu beth d'arm im Lir acht an tsleg sin as duitsi
dorachadh, ór comarba dílis dingbála di thú'.* **48** Ibid., ll. 1661–2, 1734. **49** Ibid., l. 1630: *co n-
err teinedh.* **50** He also contributes to the Túatha Dé Danann's collection of goods taken up on
behalf of the three sons of Lugaid Menn in an early episode of the *Acallam*: Stokes, 'Acallamh',
ll. 422–3. Elsewhere in the same text, Lir along with his (unnamed) offspring are arrayed among
the enemies of Finn's supernatural hosts, the sons of Midir, in another struggle for power
among different factions of the Otherworld (ll. 5117–18). It is in this latter episode, the longest
adventure involving Finn told by Caílte in the *Acallam*, that Lir adjudicates between the war-
ring parties, as the oldest member of the Túatha Dé Danann (see above, p. 102). **51** On the
figure of Manannán in medieval Irish literature, see C.W. MacQuarrie, *The biography of the Irish
God of the Sea from The Voyage of Bran (700 A.D.) to Finnegans Wake (1939)* (2004), pp 17–
335. On the significance of the two episodes in the *Acallam* in which Manannán plays a leading
role (Stokes, 'Acallamh', ll. 3647–84, 3729–858), see the author's 'The "Celtic love triangle"
revisited' (forthcoming in *Ériu*). **52** Taking their lead from the entry on Manannán in
Cormac's Glossary, where *mac lir* is explained as *mac don muir* 'son [or youth] of [or from] the
sea' (K. Meyer (ed.), 'Sanas Cormaic' in O. Bergin et al. (eds), *Anecdota from Irish manuscripts*,
iv (1912), p. 78; *DIL* s.v. 1 *ler*; see below), modern scholars often interpret the figure of his
father *Lir* or *Ler* allegorically: see Rees and Rees, *Celtic heritage*, pp 31, 39. Whoever or whatever the *Lir* of Manannán's patronymic originally was, or how it was (re)interpreted by the
author of the Glossary, may have hardly any bearing on the fact that in the *Acallam* a character named Lir is prominently featured.

evil stepmother.[53] The pathetic ineffectuality of this Lir makes the relative activism of the Lir of the *Acallam* stand out all the more.

In these various *Acallam* episodes we have considered, and in many others we could have examined to make the same point, the restless search for profit ranks high among the stimuli behind heroic adventure both past and present, matching in intensity the determination of Finn, his *fian*, and Caílte to maintain their reputations as paradigmatic and industrious practitioners of the fighting, hunting and poetic arts. And so, we have begun to assemble a heroic dossier replete with echoes of Herodotus' and Homer's Phoenicians. The *fian* heroes of the *Acallam*, typologically resembling their Phoenician counterparts, rove on land and sea eagerly looking for profit, for the trading of services or goods to their advantage, and even for opportunities to plunder. Munificence, nobility of spirit, and even nascent spirituality are qualities with which the *Acallam* enthusiastically invests Finn, the leader of the *fian*. Yet the text's idealising presentation of the central character of the Finn/*fian* cycle does not go so far as to block out the frequent displays of Finn and his associates' uncanny knack for acquiring valuable objects and using them to acquire items of even greater value, such cleverness often verging on mendacity. Of course, Finn and his *fian* are native characters and not mysterious foreigners, as the Phoenicians were for the Greeks, and the institution out of which these Irish heroes emerge, a kind of initiatory organisation for young males, has its roots in Indo-European antiquity.[54] Yet the Greek image of the Phoenicians may well be as much a projection of a similarly venerable Indo-European mythological type (combined with an emerging aspect of Greek economic and cultural reality) onto an extra-social 'other', as it is a record of a historical encounter with a foreign people. And while the more popular *fian* characters may be local heroes whose stories

---

53 E. O'Curry (ed. and trans.), 'The fate of the children of Lir', *Atlantis*, 4 (1863), 113–57. The Lir of the *Oidheadh*, along with his family, lives in Síd Finnachaid, which is where they are located in the *Acallam* as well. In their enchanted form, the children of Lir live to see the coming of Christianity and become Christians themselves – a conversion comparable to that of the younger generation of the Túatha Dé Danann in the *Acallam* (ll. 5371–9), which most likely served as one of the sources, if not the model, for the *Oidheadh*. The most recent commentator on this text dates it to perhaps as early as the fifteenth century: C. Breatnach, 'The religious significance of *Oidheadh chloinne Lir*', *Ériu*, 50 (1999), 1–40 at 2, 38–40.

In this text, Manannán is mentioned in passing (without a patronymic), as one of the *síd* residents whose company (specifically, his *teagasg* 'teaching') the children of Lir sorely miss while they are in exile: O'Curry, 'The fate of the children of Lir', 140. The editor comments: 'Manannan, son of Lir, but whether of *Lir of Sidh Finnachaidh*, or not, I am not able to say' (ibid.). That there is more than one Lir in the *síd*-world's cast of characters would appear to be the premise of an episode in another Early Modern Irish text, 'The pursuit of Diarmaid and Gráinne', where Lir of Síd Finnachaid becomes the beloved of Manannán's daughter: N. Ní Shéagdha (ed. and trans.), *Tóruigheacht Dhiarmada agus Ghráinne* (1967), p. 50.

54 For the most recent discussion, including a guide to literature on this topic, see K. McCone, 'The Celtic and Indo-European origins of the *fian*' in S.J. Arbuthnot and G. Parsons (eds), *The Gaelic Finn tradition* (2012), pp 14–30.

are rooted in a narrative landscape, paradoxically, as actors in a perpetual rite of passage, they dwell outside the social realm, maintaining a separate existence. Their otherness is compounded in the *Acallam* by their temporal distance from the present of the narrative, not to mention their strangeness in the eyes of Patrick and medieval Christian Irish culture, and by their intimacy with the Túatha Dé Danann and the world of the *síd*. Furthermore, the curious attraction between the *fían* and the family of Lir brings out key aspects of *fían* identity and function beyond the martial activities with which we usually associate them. Finn and his men, like the seafaring son of Lir, are seekers and purveyors of the valuable and the exotic.

The Phoenicians held up a mirror to Homer's audience, showing the Greeks their own collective 'becoming "self"'[55] as traders in the Mediterranean world themselves. In parallel fashion, the aged Caílte adumbrates a key element of the picture of the evolving present for the audience of the *Acallam* in the stories he so lovingly tells about the past as he knew it. While the focus of these tales as of the text itself is on the landscape, legendary figures and peoples of Ireland, many of Caílte's accounts of adventure feature voyages to and from lands across the sea. Representatives of 'foreign' populations regularly enter the narrative picture, mingling with the 'locals', the (human) sons of Míl and the (supernatural) Túatha Dé Danann, who themselves, according to the legendary tradition well established by the time of the *Acallam*, originally migrated to Ireland. As its designated defenders, Finn and the *fían* mediate between Ireland and these outsiders, who in some cases are seeking social acceptance as insiders, and in others are attempting to move in and violently take over. The cast of outsiders in starring roles includes British youth (such as the dog-thief Artúir, son of the king of Britain);[56] invaders from the Continent (the *allmhuraigh* 'foreigners' against whom Finn and his men fight the Battle of Ventry);[57] the sons of the king of Irúa(i)th (whether this placename

---

55 See p. 93, above.   **56** Stokes, 'Acallamh', ll. 166–260. We recall from earlier in this essay that the account of the adventure to Britain in search of Artúir and the stolen dogs is given prominence by virtue of being the first story told by Caílte in the *Acallam*. The members of the *fían* search-party find Artúir, the dogs, and, by accident, some British horses which they also take. This windfall, the bringing of the horses to the *fían*, and their becoming the official horses of the *fían* heroes are what Caílte ends up emphasising in his telling of the story. The recovered Artúir, meanwhile, re-enters Finn's service without much further ado. This 'foreign' member of the *fían* has something larcenous about him that can alienate the company he keeps, but also accords with the enterprising ethos of his fellow *fénnidi*. On the 'Arthurian' implications of this episode, see P.A. Bernhardt-House, 'Horses, hounds and high kings: a shared Arthurian tradition across the Irish Sea?' in J.F. Nagy (ed.), *Myth in Celtic literatures* (2007), pp 11–21.   **57** Stokes, 'Acallamh', ll. 718–868. The *Géisid cúan* poem that is the subject of the essay by Professor Ó Coileáin ('The setting of *Géisid cúan*' in J. Carey et al. (eds), *Cín Chille Cúile* (2004), pp 234–48; reprinted in this volume) figures in the story told in this passage. With the epic struggle fought on Ventry Strand as background, the story highlights the tragic drowning of the *fían* member Cáel úa Nemnainn (after whom a stretch of the strand is renamed) and

refers to Scandinavia or an Irish portal to the Otherworld),[58] mysteriously seeking both to serve the *fian* and to stay apart from it;[59] marauders from Lochla(i)nn (yet more Vikings?) whom the *fian* (back in Finn's day) is obligated to repel, who survive into the present of the frame of the *Acallam*, and whom the aged Caílte and his latter-day recruits are called upon to defeat;[60] and even the proselytising Patrick himself, a missionary entrepreneur who cleverly establishes a mutually beneficial relationship with Caílte and company, the least likely of converts to Christianity, one would think. Finn, Caílte (his ambassador to the future), and their companions in both the past and the present engage in a variety of relations with these and other sundry foreigners, whose alterity, while rubbing off on the *fian* heroes, is in turn countered or even neutralised by the latter's nativeness. These relations are complex and inconsistent, ranging from the hostile to the wary, exploitative, or friendly. Underlying them all, and Finn and his men's foreign policy in general, is the desire for exchange – that is, the *fian*'s quest to enrich itself by means of engagement with figures who are even more 'other' than the *fian* is. The cast of characters within the *fian*, a group that consists of two factions at times mortally opposed to each other (Clann Baíscne and Clann Morna),[61] can make friends with *anybody* if it is in their interest, and can just as easily turn against its own members.

Recent scholarship dates the composition of the *Acallam* to the early thirteenth century, after the time of the invasion of the Anglo-Normans in 1169.[62] Are we not being offered a picture of the author's present as well as a prediction about the future in this cosmopolitan setting of international encounters leading to the exchange of goods, services, and ideas with transmarine adventurers, who in some cases become as Irish as the Irish themselves?[63] The world of the *fian* in the 'good old days' as recounted by Caílte certainly sounds like the Ireland of the late first and early second millennium as historians have reconstructed it: a world

the subsequent death of his bride Créide, overwhelmed by the grief she expresses in the poem.   **58** On the whereabouts of Irúaith, see P. Mac Cana, 'The influence of the Vikings on Celtic literature' in B. Ó Cuív (ed.), *The impact of the Scandinavian invasions on the Celtic-speaking peoples c.800–1100 A.D.* (1962), pp 78–118 at pp 87–93.   **59** Stokes, 'Acallamh', ll. 5447–514, 5555–88, 5617–631, 6083–269.   **60** Ibid., ll. 3114–95; 6853–7013.   **61** Although these factions are seemingly reconciled at the conclusion of the story of the young Finn's triumph at Tara (ibid., ll. 1762–5; see above, p. 101), the stories Caílte tells are littered with the corpses of the victims of this on-again/off-again feud. True reconciliation only comes about in the present of the frame tale of the *Acallam* (ll. 1952–2305), when Caílte joins forces with the last surviving member of the Clann Morna, Donn mac Áeda, the grandson of one of Clann Baíscne's worst enemies; see note 36, above.   **62** A. Dooley, 'The date and purpose of *Acallam na senórach*', *Éigse*, 34 (2004), 97–126; see Anne Connon's essay (above, pp 53–6).   **63** As Ó Coileáin so elegantly put it: 'the heroes of the *Acallam* inhabit a very different world from that of its predecessors: its history and geography are not those of a firmly ordered society; its fluid landscapes, shifting boundaries, anomalous characters and unsure pedigrees lead outwards to a new world of European romance rather than inwards and backwards to a determined, almost claustrophobic "known" past, that is to say, known and controlled by and in the present': in M. Harmon, *The dialogue of the ancients of Ireland* (2009), pp ix–x at p. x.

of increased contact with foreigners, of flourishing international trade, and of harder-to-define boundaries between 'natives' and 'foreigners', as in the case of the 'foreign Irish' (*Gallgoídil*) who are actually mentioned in the *Acallam*,[64] alongside the peoples of Britain, Scandinavia and the Continent.

In sum, the mythic paradigm of the *fian*, among its other uses, provided Irish literary tradition with the means to engage with the changing world around it, starting with the incursions by and settlements of the Vikings, and the opening-up of Ireland to trade relations and new cultural contacts.[65] Significantly, therefore, Finn and the institution he embodies in the *Acallam* are both old and new. By archaic definition, as in the stories told in the text, the heroes of the *fian* had always 'traded' with the Otherworld and exploited their identity as free-agent outsiders. Through the narrative device of miraculous survival, the *Acallam* brings the *fénnidi* of old into a framing present (though one still anterior to that of the actual world of the author and his audience), from the distanced perspective of which they can delve into and reveal their particular experience of the past. This bygone world, with its opportunities for communication and exchange among far-flung realms, anticipates a world that evolved centuries after the era of Patrick and early Christian Ireland. Paradoxically, the nostalgic 'backward look' toward Finn and his *fian* also looks forward to the milieu in which the *Acallam* was composed.

Thus, the *Acallam* ingeniously succeeds in being among the most conservative and the most forward-looking of medieval Irish literary compositions. Therefore, it is understandable that the text presents the *fian* as both a barely remembered fixture of long ago and an institution that, surprisingly, still exists in the time-frame of the *Acallam* or is revived, under the auspices of the high-king of Ireland, in tandem with his embrace of Christianity as well as with the project of recording the lore Caílte obligingly recalls.[66] The seemingly irresistible

---

64 Stokes, 'Acallamh', ll. 4560, 7951. 65 Historically, *fiana* were not infrequently connected with overseas expeditions: see P. McQuillan, 'Finn, Fothad and *fian*: some early associations', *Proceedings of the Harvard Celtic Colloquium*, 8 (1988), 1–10 at 5–7. 66 Stokes, 'Acallamh', ll. 2285–97. Proinsias Mac Cana argued that the fictional idea of the *fian* as a 'national' institution, and the proto-'nationalism' implicit in this concept, came about in the wake of the Viking era in Ireland, as a way to facilitate the literary embrace of stories about Finn and his *fian*: 'The solution for this martial free enterprise [of *fiana*] was the same as that often applied to modern economic free enterprise: nationalization': '*Fianaigecht* in the pre-Norman period' in B. Almqvist et al. (eds), *The heroic process* (1987), pp 75–99 at p. 98. I would add to Mac Cana's observation that the 'enterprise' as envisioned in stories about *fiana* was in fact *economic* as well as *martial*. Katharine Simms points out that 'galloglasses' – that is, mercenaries whose importance in medieval Irish society and politics rises in the thirteenth and following centuries – no doubt found much with which to identify in the picture of the *fian* presented in the *Acallam* and later texts: 'Images of the galloglass in poems to the MacSweeneys' in S. Duffy (ed.), *The world of the galloglass* (2007), pp 106–123 at pp 112–15. On the later medieval Irish construction of Viking, Norman and hired native or foreign warriors/invaders as counterparts to the heroes of the *fian*, see K. Simms, 'Gaelic warfare in the Middle Ages' in T. Bartlett and K. Jeffery (eds), *A military history of Ireland* (1996), pp 99–115 at pp 101–6.

progression from welcoming most elements of the Finn-/*fian*-centred tradition and its surviving proponents into the category of the culturally acceptable, to turning this tradition into text, is perhaps the most intriguing 'Phoenician' aspect of the relationship between Ireland and the *fian* as envisioned in the *Acallam*.

We recall that Herodotus' Phoenicians, in addition to being eager to go to war against their mercantile competitors, ready to 'seize the day' whenever it comes to profit and advantage, and determined to pay back insult with insult and theft with theft, share with the Greeks perhaps their greatest treasure of all, when they come to Greece and become Greeks themselves: the invention of writing. With this item and medium of exchange, the present enters into a reciprocal relationship with its past, which instructs and informs in exchange for being memorialised in this 'new' form. Writing also makes it possible for authors of the present to leave a down-payment for future generations of readers, an attempt to guarantee that posterity will cherish the inscribed present as *its* past. And so with writing, Homer's epics become a fixed yet still performable cultural heritage of Classical civilisation, and Herodotus compiles his authoritative history of how the Greek world came to be the way it was in his day.

Similarly, the acceptance of Caílte and his band of *fian* survivors into Patrick's Christian fold goes hand in hand with the *introduction of writing* onto the Irish scene. With the baptism of the survivors of the *fian*, nothing stands in the way of recording the already-begun 'dialogue' between past and present, the exchange of differing cultural values, and the importation of the past into the present, all resulting in the creation of what purports to be the first vernacular text, *Acallam na senórach*. In both the ancient Greek encounter with the Phoenicians and in the medieval Irish encounter with the *fian*, writing becomes the means of establishing common ground between the otherwise irreconcilable categories of 'native'/'other', 'inside human society'/'outside human society', 'past'/'present', and even 'this world'/'Otherworld'. The basis of the most profitable cultural transaction, writing proves itself to be the ultimate prize, worth any price – whether the buyer is Greek, Phoenician, or Irish.

These nuanced explorations of the relations between story and historical reality are not to be confused with Heinrich Zimmer's tenuous theory that Finn and the *fian* were modeled after the Viking invaders, and that this story-cycle borrowed heavily from Scandinavian tradition: 'Keltische Beiträge III', *Zeitschrift für deutsches Alterthum und deutsche Litteratur*, 35 (1891), 1–172. Even more imaginative is the thesis to be found in the work of J.L. Villanueva as translated by Henry O'Brien (*Phoenician Ireland* [1833]), that the term *fian* derives from the vocabulary of Phoenicians who settled Ireland long ago (pp 56–7). Villanueva, however, does not go so far as to claim that the *fian* heroes themselves were of Phoenician stock: 'I more incline to the opinion of those who would have the troops of the ancient Irish denominated Fenians, not as though they were Phoenicians or descended from them, but because that they exhibited in their conduct the prowess and fortitude of the Ibero-Phoenicans' (p. 57). Hence it would seem that the enthusiasm for exploit, possessed by those whom Herodotus labeled *pro-thumótatoi*, was a trait cultivated in Villanueva's vision of ancient Ireland as well.

The narrative voice in *Acallam na senórach*

GERALDINE PARSONS

Acallam na senórach (*AS*) has often been invoked in studies of orality and literacy in medieval Irish literature because of the attractively convoluted premise of the tale. This is a work in which oral narratives are depicted as being sought, told and, to some extent, written down. As a whole, it comprises an extended consideration of memory and, therefore, of cultural identity, and of how these concepts are preserved through writing and in oral tradition.[1] A busy, polyphonic narrative, in which multiple speech acts, or layers of storytelling, are depicted, this is a frame-tale, whose frame comprises the conversation of St Patrick and Caílte mac Rónáin as they travel around Ireland.[2] In narratological terms, we see the 'complete' embedding of many short episodes which can be described as 'sub-tales' or 'in-tales'. Taken as a whole, therefore, this work is an 'interpolated' frame; narrative action is intermittently located in the frame, rather than just at the beginning or end of the work as sometimes is the case.[3] This structure means that we must recognise a number of temporal layers within the narrative. There are three 'in-narrative' times, or three periods at which the events narrated occur. Put simply, there is a past, which encompasses (and exceeds) Finn's lifetime.[4] That temporality

It gives me great pleasure to be able to acknowledge a profound debt of gratitude to Seán Ó Coileáin. The scholarly relationships in which such debts accrue tend to fall into two categories. The first encompasses those situations in which one scholar has taught or counselled another. If less tangible, the second group of relationships is no less significant; in these scenarios, the direct influence of an individual is exerted through his/her publications or other public utterances. My relationship to Professor Ó Coileáin is of the latter type and since I have come to know his voice through the written word, I would like to offer him some thoughts on the presentation of a key voice in a narrative which, as he has shown in a series of important studies, confronts the complex interactions of the oral and literary modes. Especially significant in this context are his 'Oral or literary? Some strands of the argument', *Studia Hibernica*, 17–18 (1977–8), 7–35; 'Place and placename in *fianaigheacht*', *Studia Hibernica*, 27 (1993), 45–60; 'The setting of *Géisid cúan*' in J. Carey et al. (eds), *Cín Chille Cúile* (2004), pp 234–48. The last two essays here cited are reprinted elsewhere in this volume.

1 See, in particular, J.F. Nagy, *Conversing with angels and ancients* (1997). 2 On frame-tales, see H. Porter Abbott, *The Cambridge introduction to narrative* (2nd ed., 2008), pp 28–30. *AS* is an extreme example of a 'framing narrative ... that can have a significant effect on its embedded narrative' (p. 29); see G. Parsons, 'The structure of *Acallam na senórach*', *Cambrian Medieval Celtic Studies*, 55 (2008), 11–39. 3 D. Coste and J. Pier, 'Narrative Levels' in P. Hühn et al. (eds), *The living handbook of narratology*, paragraph 22, accessed 22 February, 2012. Rory McTurk has analysed the narrative structure in accordance with the theories of Gérard Genette: '*Acallam na senórach* and Snorri Sturluson's *Edda*' in S. Ó Catháin (ed.), *Northern lights* (2001), pp 178–89. 4 See John

governs the majority of the sub-tales recounted by Caílte and, occasionally, by his erstwhile companion, Oisín. These sub-tales constitute retrospective and piecemeal narratives within the primary 'present' of *AS*, that is, the period in which the conversations between Patrick and Caílte take place. As well as that 'frame-tale present', another rarely perceived and apparently chronologically later time is depicted, namely the timeframe within which we are to imagine the narrator operating. This is a more complicated temporality than the other two; the narrator positions himself somewhat out of time and claims knowledge of what is in his terms the future as well as what are for him the past and present.[5]

The concept of the narrator has long been invoked in the study of medieval Irish poetry, and the operation of the narrator has assumed importance in a number of studies of prose and prosimetric texts as well.[6] Yet, analysis of the functions of narrators within prose/prosimetrum has not been exhaustive. Tomás Ó Cathasaigh initiated recent work on this topic, demonstrating that the narrative voice can shape sagas by acting as 'commentator on the events or the personages or setting of the story'.[7] His view of the role of the narrator of *Fingal Rónáin* – the first and most detailed of his case studies – can be taken as indicative of his findings. While the narrator of *Fingal Rónáin* is judged to be 'fairly discreet' overall, he

> intrudes in three different ways: first, he comments on one of the characters; secondly, he claims knowledge of the thoughts or feelings of

Carey's contribution to the present volume. On the depiction of Finn's death in *Acallam na senórach*, see G. Parsons, 'Breaking the cycle? Accounts of the death of Finn' in S.J. Arbuthnot and G. Parsons (eds), *The Gaelic Finn tradition* (2012), pp 81–96.   5 For the sake of convenience, the male pronoun is used throughout to refer to the narrators under discussion; anthropomorphisation of the narrative voice occurs commonly. For discussion, see U. Margolin, 'Narrator' in P. Hühn et al. (eds), *The living handbook of narratology*, paragraph 22, accessed 13 February, 2013.   6 See, for example, T.O. Clancy on poets' use of 'fictive speakers' which draws on contributions made by James Carney, Máirín Ní Dhonnchadha, Katharine Simms and others: 'Women poets in early medieval Ireland: stating the case' in C. Meek and K. Simms (eds), *'The fragility of her sex'?* (1996), pp 43–72 at pp 49–50. See also M. Tymockzo, 'A poetry of masks: the poet's persona in early Celtic poetry' in K.A. Klar et al. (eds), *A Celtic florilegium* (1996), pp 187–209. Gerard Murphy commented on the narrator's operation in connection to *fianaigecht* ballads in, for example, *The Ossianic lore and romantic tales of medieval Ireland* (2nd ed., 1971), pp 21–2. Recent examples of studies concerned with prose/prosimetric tales which invoke the concept of the narrator include three essays published in J.F. Eska (ed.), *Narrative in Celtic tradition* (2011): J. Findon, 'Fabula, story and text: the case of *Compert Conchobuir*', pp 37–55; E.R. Henken, '"Then was spoken the proverb …": the proverb legend in medieval Celtic literature', pp 100–16 (including discussion of *AS* at pp 104–6); K. Hollo, 'Allegoresis and literary creativity in eighth-century Ireland: the case of *Echtrae Chonnlai*', pp 117–28.   7 T. Ó Cathasaigh, 'Three notes on *Cath Maige Tuired*', *Ériu*, 40 (1989), 61–8 at 66. See also idem, 'The rhetoric of *Fingal Rónáin*', *Celtica*, 17 (1985), 123–44; 'The rhetoric of *Scéla Cano meic Gartnáin*' in D. Ó Corráin et al. (eds), *Sages, saints and storytellers* (1989), pp 233–50.

two of them; and, thirdly, he provides information which does not
advance the action, but which helps us to understand what is going on
in the saga.[8]

In relation to *Cath Maige Tuired*, however, he has identified

another kind of intrusion in Irish saga, which is devoted to comment
… on a telling or on tellings of it. This can take the form of adding an
alternative account of the events, as when the narrator of Recension I
of *TBC*, having told us how Cú Chulainn killed Culann's hound, adds
a quite different account of the event 'according to another (version)'.
This kind of intrusion might be best regarded as redactorial rather than
narratorial.[9]

In their discussions of narratorial roles, Erich Poppe and Hildegard Tristram
have engaged with narratological theory in greater detail. Poppe's careful
analysis of the diminished role of the narrator in Irish adaptations of two
Middle English romances relative to their source texts has yielded the following insights, which he has characterised as tentative: 'In native medieval Irish
narrative, the narrator is in general fairly unintrusive',[10] and '[t]he narrator's
presence in native medieval Irish narrative is, at best, implicit; narrators rarely
comment and hardly ever speak of themselves'.[11] Tristram's work has emphasised the narrative voice as a vital element within medieval Irish tales, a view
which is not incompatible with Poppe's characterisation of the narrator as
unintrusive relative to the narrators of (poetic texts in) other medieval literatures.[12] She has explored the complex discourse strategies employed by the
narrator of the *Táin*, arguing that they convey authorial concern about the
maintenance of audience interest over a lengthy narrative.[13] She has analysed
the narrator of the *Táin* in terms of the employment of diegetic and mimetic
discourse strategies. In diegetic mode, the narrator 'presents the events and
actions of the story by means of 3rd person narration, retarding the action by

8 Ó Cathasaigh, 'The rhetoric', p. 125.   9 Ó Cathasaigh, 'Three notes', p. 67.   10 E. Poppe,
'Narrative structure of medieval Irish adaptations: the case of *Guy* and *Beues*' in H. Fulton (ed.),
Medieval Celtic literature and society (2005), pp 205–29 at p. 215. Similar comments are to be
found in his '*Imtheachta Aeniasa*: Virgil's *Aeneid* in medieval Ireland', *Classics Ireland*, 11 (2004),
74–94; idem, '*Stair Ercuil ocus a bás*: rewriting Hercules in Ireland' in K. Murray (ed.),
Translations from classical literature (2006), pp 37–68.   11 Poppe, 'Narrative structure', p. 217.
Overall, Poppe has adopted a cautious stance regarding the extent of the narrator's presence in
the Irish texts, adaptations and native sagas alike, particularly in some passages of explanation
and evaluation. See pp 213–15, where he invokes Monika Fludernik's concepts of 'on-' and 'off-
plotline'.   12 H.L.C. Tristram, 'Mimesis and diegesis in the *Cattle raid of Cooley*' in J. Carey
et al. (eds), *Ildánach ildírech* (1999), pp 263–76; T. Davenport, *Medieval narrative: an introduction* (2004), pp 35–54.   13 Tristram, 'Mimesis', p. 275.

the use of descriptions, lists or catalogues, enumerations and reported speeches'.[14] 'Mimetic narration' by means of 'metatextual enunciations' by the narrator, she has suggested, is also prominent. In this mode:

> the narrator himself forms no part of the narrative; he himself is no character in it, but he tells the audience in what way he is telling the story, what he knows and thinks about its subject matter; he interrupts the narration by providing titles, closing formulae of episodes, ono-mastic passages, and one verse quotation. He uses abbreviations ('et rel.') for formulaic expressions ... comments upon the progress of the narration, refers back to episodes or events already narrated, refers to variant versions, to triads or triadic expressions, to the 'Cattle Raid' as a tale itself, to other sagas, to episodes as in-tales of the 'Cattle Raid'; the narrator also provides explanations of names, titles and Old Irish words, background information not immediately relevant to the action, and sometimes he also uses Latin words and phrases.[15]

It hardly needs to be said that underpinning these discussions of the narrator is the basic narratological principle that a distinction be maintained between the narrator's voice within the text and the author's personality beyond it.[16] Nonetheless, the remarkable advances currently being made by Anne Connon and Ann Dooley towards establishing the location, date and circumstances in which *Acallam na senórach* was composed render consideration of the work's narrator timely because some likely authors of the text have now been posited.[17] Attempts to locate the *Acallam* in a specific socio-historical context by means of reading it as a statement or series of statements of authorial con-cerns and interests can be finessed in light of Connon and Dooley's research. Early in the text there is a well-known reference to the site which is 'now' called Mainistir Droichit Átha, the monastery of Drogheda, which has often been invoked in such discussions:[18]

---

14 Ibid., pp 269–70.   15 Ibid., pp 270–2.   16 See, for example, Abbott, *The Cambridge intro-duction to narrative*, pp 68–9, including discussion of R. Barthes, 'Introduction to the structural analysis of narratives' in idem, *Image-music-text*, repr. in S. Sontag (ed.), *A Barthes reader* (1981), pp 251–95.   17 A. Dooley, 'The date and purpose of *Acallam na senórach*', *Éigse*, 34 (2004), 97–126. See A. Connon, 'Plotting *Acallam na senórach*: the physical context of the "Mayo" sequence' in S. Sheehan et al. (eds), *Gablánach in scélaigecht* (2013), pp 69–102 at pp 71–5 and 98, and her contribution to the present volume.   18 On the 'X which is now called Y' formula, see P. Mac Cana, 'Placenames and mythology in Irish tradition: places, pilgrimages and things' in G.W. MacLennan (ed.), *Proceedings of the First North American Congress of Celtic Studies* (1988), pp 319–41 at p. 338; Ó Coileáin, 'Place and placename', pp 59–60; N. Ó Muraíle, 'Agallamh na seanórach' in P. Ó Fiannachta (ed.), *An fhiannaíocht, Léachtaí Cholm Cille*, 25 (1995), pp 96–127 at p. 124; R. Ó hUiginn, 'Onomastic formulae in Irish' in M. Ó Flaithearta (ed.), *Proceedings of the Seventh Symposium of Societas Celtologica Nordica* (2007), pp 53–70.

téit Cáilte roime co hIndber mBic Loingsigh a mBregaibh, risi-ráidter Mainistir Droichit Átha isin tan so .i. Bec Loingsech mac Airist itor-chair ann .i. mac ríg Rómán táinic do ghabháil Eirenn co rus-báidh tonn tuile ann hé.[19]

Cáilte goes on to Indber Bic Loingsigh, 'the Estuary of Bec the Exile', in Brega, which is now called Mainistir Droichit Átha, 'the Monastery of Drogheda'; Bec mac Airist the Exile was killed there. The son of the king of the Romans, he came to conquer Ireland until a flood-wave drowned him there.

The 'Monastery of Drogheda' is Mellifont Abbey, which was the first Cistercian house founded in Ireland and is emblematic of reform activity in the Irish church.[20] As a result, this passage has loomed large in readings of the *Acallam* as a witness to the changing relationship of the Church to the learned classes responsible for producing and transmitting its kind of literary text. Dooley, for example, has noted that this reference to Mellifont 'is the first indication we have that the author intends to project a contemporary aspect and agenda on his compendium of tales'.[21] The significance of this pas-sage for the current study is rather that in it the author reveals that he is locating his narrator in something close to his own 'real-time': the narrator's world is one in which the toponym Mainistir Droichit Átha is current.[22] There are intimations here, right at the beginning of the work, that the nar-rator is acquainted with the world of ecclesiastical reform. Questions that can be raised in connection with the author's stance on the status of 'traditional' vernacular learning in this period can, and should, be posed in relation to the narrator as well.

Identifying the narrator within *Acallam na senórach* can be a challenge. The near-lack of punctuation in the manuscript versions of the tale as well as the presentation of Cáilte as a 'second-level' narrator,[23] mean that editors' and translators' decisions regarding the extent of the narrator's presence within

19 W. Stokes (ed. and partial trans.), 'Acallamh na senórach' in W. Stokes and E. Windisch (eds), *Irische Texte*, iv, 1 (Leipzig, 1900), ll. 52–5. Translations of Stokes' edition are my own unless stated otherwise. I will only give literal translations of placenames which are subject to onomastic explanation within the passages. Cf. A. Dooley and H. Roe, *Tales of the elders of Ireland* (1999), p. 4.   20 On Mellifont and reform activity, see M.T. Flanagan, *The transform-ation of the Irish church in the twelfth and thirteenth centuries* (2010), p. 24 et passim.   21 'The date and purpose', p. 98. See also Nagy, *Conversing with angels and ancients*, pp 319–20 for dis-cussion of this 'pointed allusion' to Mellifont.   22 The assumption here, as in the work of scholars who see it as providing a *terminus a quo* for the composition of *AS*, is that the toponym is integral to the text. See M. Dillon (ed.), *Stories from the Acallam* (1970), p. 25, nn. 52–3 for the suggestion that the mention of Mainistir Droichit Átha may be a gloss which has been incorporated into the main text.   23 McTurk, '*Acallam na senórach* and Snorri Sturluson's *Edda*', p. 179.

the text must sometimes be subjective. Yet it is possible to draw some conclusions concerning the operation of the narrator within the text. He fits the pictures of the narrator within Irish saga offered by Ó Cathasaigh, Poppe and Tristram. He is what Gérard Genette termed a heterodiegetic narrator, 'a narrator who has not participated in the circumstances and events about which he or she tells a story'.[24] Measured by some criteria, this is indeed an 'unintrusive' or 'discreet' voice, but it is nonetheless one which contributes a great deal to the reception of the work by an audience.[25] Where those elements of mimetic narration as identified by Tristram, in particular, appear in the *Acallam*, I see them as building up a sense of the narrator's authority over the subject matter he is presenting. Here is a narrator who, if not 'omniscient',[26] asserts a diachronically rich knowledge of Irish history and Gaelic literary tradition. A key element in this assertion of authority in *senchas* is the narrator's demonstration of his knowledge of the past.

There are numerous statements that underline the fact that the narrator has access to a full history of particular characters or places right up to a particular point in time depicted in the frame-tale. These are demonstrations of a knowledge which exceeds the temporal boundaries of the narrated material and as such constitute the convergence of two of the narrative's temporalities: the past and the frame-tale present. The narrator distances himself from both periods. He holds in his hand not only those visible threads of narrative that pertain to the past and frame-tale present temporalities, but also several others which are unseen. The narrator makes clear that he knows what happens in the narrative's principal temporal lacuna, which corresponds to the period between the onset of the decline of the *fian* and Patrick's meeting with Caílte and Oisín. The opening of the narrative offers an indication that the battles of Commar, Gabair and Ollarba took place during this lacuna in the narrated time but otherwise glosses over the gap entirely.[27] As Máirtín Ó Briain pointed out in relation to the Tír na nÓg material, our text is thus in keeping with wider *fianaigecht* tradition, which has remarkably little to say about the period between those battles traditionally dated to the late third century, and the conversion of Ireland in the mid-fifth century.[28] In light of that fact, it is striking that our narrator makes clear that his knowledge of the past of the *fian* transcends his narrated accounts. Many assertions, such as the following, involve the narrator's use of the adverb *ríam*, 'ever':[29] 'the greatest

24 D. Herman (ed.), *The Cambridge companion to narrative* (2007), p. 278; see discussion in H. Porter Abbott, 'Story, plot and narration', ibid., pp 39–51 at pp 42–3, citing G. Genette, *Narrative discourse: an essay in method*, trans. J.E. Levin (1980), pp 212–62.   25 The term 'audience' is used as an umbrella term here, covering those who encounter the text aurally and in written form alike.   26 See Abbott, *The Cambridge introduction to narrative*, pp 73 and 239.   27 Stokes, 'Acallamh', ll. 1–2: *Ar tabhuirtt chatha Chomuir 7 chatha Gabra 7 chatha Ollurbha, 7 ar ndíthugud na Féindi*.   28 M. Ó Briain, 'Some material on Oisín in the Land of Youth' in D. Ó Corráin et al. (eds), *Sages, saints and storytellers* (1989), pp 181–99 at p. 185.   29 See Poppe,

hunting that Finn ever did (*doróine Find riam*) in that place was equal to the hunting that Caílte did that day'.[30]

Indeed, over the narrative as a whole, the narrator claims to possess a full knowledge of a character's deeds and sometimes, although less frequently, their emotions. In other words, in his evaluation of characters' behaviour or feelings, the narrator indicates that he knows more about them than is available to the audience from the discourses of Caílte, Patrick and others. So, while Caílte does not supply his own assessment of being attacked by a giant's dog, the narrator can assert that 'horror and fear of [the hound] seized Caílte, such as had never seized him in battle or in combat'.[31] Moreover, there are also instances of the narrator drawing attention to the temporal gap – the period *ó docuaid in Fiann* – and implying that there is no corresponding gap in his knowledge:

> ní rainic nech do muintir rig Laigen cetguin muice na aighe ac in air-fidech 7 ic a gilla, 7 ní dernad ó docuaid in Fiann selg bud tarthighe ina in tselg sin.[32]

> None of the retinue of the king of Leinster but the musician and his servant managed to draw first blood of a pig or a deer and since the *fian* departed, there had not been a more abundant hunt than that one.

In the following passage, the narrator seems to refer to another lacuna, namely the period after that depicted in the frame-tale present, which is nonetheless in the past for the narrator:

> Conid iat sin da ech 7 carpat ar a raibi Cailte fa deired a nEirinn, 7 géb é ro indisfed in scel sin .i. imthechta Cailti 7 anmanna in da ech d'fiarfaigi de .i. Err 7 Indell a n-anmanna.[33]

> Those are the two horses and the chariot that Caílte used at the end in Ireland, and if anyone telling that tale of the journeys of Caílte be asked the names of the two horses, their names were Err and Indell.

This passage raises some interesting questions about the intended temporal scope of the narrative. Critics of *Acallam na senórach* must always contend with the fact that nothing resembling a convincing ending survives in any of the five extant copies of the text. It may be that the death of Caílte formed

'Narrative structure', p. 215. **30** Stokes, 'Acallamh', ll. 3238–9: *in tselg is mó doróine Find riam issin n-inadh sin ba comeit re in tselg doroni Cailti in lá sin*; cf. Dooley and Roe, *Tales*, p. 98. **31** Stokes, 'Acallamh', ll. 1908–9: *gabus gráin 7 egla Cáilte roimpi nar' ghabh riam a cath ná a comlann*; cf. Dooley and Roe, *Tales*, p. 59. **32** Stokes, 'Acallamh', ll. 4820–2; cf. Dooley and Roe, *Tales*, pp 134–5. **33** Stokes, 'Acallamh', ll. 4909–12; cf. Dooley and Roe, *Tales*, p. 137.

part of a planned, or lost, ending.[34] If so, this passage belongs to the second narrative gap just proposed which would have covered the period up to Caílte's death. If, however, the phrase *fa deired a nEirinn* is taken to refer to the Last Days,[35] this statement takes on a different complexion, bearing witness to the narrator's knowledge of future events. Whichever temporality is in operation, this passage is noteworthy on account of the narrator's acknowledgement of the possibility that others will relate the matter of the sub-tale which he has just recounted. Throughout the *Acallam*, the provision of a definitive account of the deeds of the *fian* is a major authorial concern.[36] The narrator's suggestion of his own expertise concerning the lore connected with Caílte indicates that the author is using the narrative voice to guarantee the comprehensiveness and reliability of this account of the *fian*.

It is not merely with regard to *fianaigecht* tradition, however, that such authority is proposed, as the narrator claims a wider expertise in *senchas*. There are a wealth of examples to chose from in order to illustrate this fact – *Acallam na senórach* contains a strikingly high number of intertextual allusions, where the term 'intertextual' alludes to stories which we know to have been circulating in medieval Ireland in some form, oral or written. Works which are related to the *Acallam* in this way include *Buile Shuibhne*, Ulster Cycle texts such as the *Táin* and a version of the death of Conchobar, and a number of saints' Lives.[37] Patrician tradition too underpins the narrator's discourse:

> Is annsin táncadar rompa co Gleann in scáil soir, risi n-abar Muindter Diugra isin tan-so, áit a raibhe Pátraic a ndaeire ac Milcoin mac húi Buain ac ríg Dhail nAraide.[38]

> Then they proceded eastwards to Gleann in Scáil, 'the Glen of the Phantom', which is now called Muindter Diugra, 'the Retinue of Díucra', where Patrick had been in bondage to Miliuc mac huí Búain, king of Dál nAraide.

Several things are accomplished here. The provision of the characters' itinerary is the fundamental level of narration ongoing and this is 'interrupted' by the provision of onomastic information. A glancing reference to the tradition of St Patrick's slavery, which stretches back to the seventh century, is pres-

---

34 See Parsons, 'The structure of *Acallam na senórach*', 12.   35 Cf. Dooley and Roe, *Tales*, p. 151 and see Stokes, 'Acallamh', ll. 5409–10.   36 Parsons, 'Breaking the cycle?', pp 83–4. 37 See, for example, A. Dooley, 'The deployment of some hagiographical sources in *Acallam na senórach*' in S. Arbuthnot and G. Parsons (eds), *The Gaelic Finn tradition*, pp 97–110, and Dooley and Roe, *Tales*, p. 236 n. 71, p. 237 n. 74, p. 238 n. 80, p. 239 n. 105, p. 240 n. 116, p. 241 nn 160–1, p. 242 n. 162.   38 Stokes, 'Acallamh', ll. 3689–91; cf. Dooley and Roe, *Tales*, p. 112.

ent.[39] In a work which features Patrick so prominently, this is not itself surprising, but it is noticeable that here alone in the protracted portrait of the saint obsessively extracting knowledge and story from the Irish landscape is an allusion, albeit implied, to his status as foreigner, as a Briton in Ireland.[40] The Irish toponymy familiar to Caílte is not natural to Patrick, not only because of the passage of time and the disruptive effects of Christianity's 'new learning' on the transmission of such tradition, but also because he is a stranger. As Joseph Falaky Nagy in particular has shown, *Acallam na senórach* provides, *inter alia*, a meditation on Irish identity and its mode of expression was probably shaped by its author's experience of the early years of the Norman invasion and the influx of foreign ecclesiastics.[41] Therefore, the figure of Patrick, the foreign-born cleric, is surely significant with regard to the author's response to the ecclesiastical landscape which he inhabited. Within *acallam* conventions, however, there is little scope to explore Patrick's symbolic function. An *acallam* depicts a conversation between interlocutors who have opposing – if reconcilable – worldviews.[42] One party (Caílte, for most of the narrative) acts as informant and the other, Patrick, as interrogator. The conventions governing these roles mean that little information is expected to pass in the other direction. This may explain why the saint does not provide Caílte, whom he baptises, with even a basic catechesis. This depiction contrasts, for example, with Tírechán's depiction of Patrick as a teacher of catechumens.[43] As well as proving himself familiar with Patrician tradition, in his short interjection the narrator is deftly and subtly deployed to override a generic convention. He enriches an appreciation of the saint's 'reading' of the landscape and thereby offers some guidance regarding the intended interpretation of the dramatic set-up presented.

The possibility that the narrator claims to know of future, as well as past, events has already been entertained. Within the *Acallam*, the future can be understood in two ways, first in terms of the frame-tale future, by which I mean the period of time which is later than any action in the frame-tale present but which is nonetheless in the present or past of the narrator, and second in terms of the narrator's own future time. Both the passage referring to Patrick's slavery and that alluding to Mellifont provide examples of the frame-tale future.[44] To be grouped with these passages are all the examples of the double-naming of places, a technique to which Ó Coileáin has drawn attention,[45] wherein the later of the two names given is said to be a name current

---

39 The name Miliuc is given in Muirchú's *Life*, preface, chap. 11 and chap. 12: A.B.E. Hood (ed. and trans.), *St. Patrick: his writings and Muirchu's Life* (1978), pp 61, 66.   **40** See comments at Parsons, 'The structure', p. 32, n. 37.   **41** Nagy, *Conversing with angels and ancients*, pp 317–23.   **42** Ibid., p. 3.   **43** L. Bieler (ed. and trans.), *The Patrician texts in the Book of Armagh* (1979), pp 122–67 at §6, §18, §26, §28.   **44** See above, p. 113.   **45** 'Place and placename', pp 59–60; cf. idem, 'The setting of *Géisid cúan*', pp 241–2.

in the narrator's time. The phrases *risa ráiter* and *risa n-abar*, both meaning 'which is called' occur repeatedly in conjunction with the temporal marker *is(s)in tan-so* 'in this time', a phrase used to demarcate the narrator's time from Caílte's extended lifespan, which maps onto the narrative past and frame-tale present and is designated *(iss)in tan sin* '(in) that time'.

The other manifestation of future time within the narrative is in statements wherein the narrator positions himself outside the normal progression of time, claiming knowledge of the future. He makes a series of claims that cumulatively suggest his familiarity with the totality of Irish history, claims which are distinct from predictions or statements of eschatological beliefs.[46] In the following instance, the narrator's knowledge of later times allows him to assert that particular situations are never reversed nor events repeated: 'It was done thus, for he was swallowed up then because of St Patrick's pronouncement and the power to defeat the Leinstermen was not given to any successor of his',[47] and 'That was the last Muc Slángha, "Sow of Healing", that was divided among the men of Ireland'.[48] The narrator is again establishing his credentials for the narration of a definitive version of the deeds of the *fian*, by demonstrating that it is rooted in a maximal account of Irish history.

If the provision of a full and coherent *fianaigecht* narrative was one of the aims of the author of *Acallam na senórach*, then *dinnshenchas* was a tool utilised by him to that end. As Ó Coileáin has shown, place is central to this tale, as the locus of lore and as the inspiration for story-telling.[49] That Caílte's memory will fail is a cause for concern throughout the narrative – the angels sent from Heaven to alleviate Patrick's doubts about the propriety of his conversation with the aged *fénnidi* make clear that Caílte's grasp on the past is weakening and that writing must now be used to preserve the knowledge which is almost uniquely his but which was once commonly held.[50] Later in the narrative, a sympathetic woman of the Otherworld promises to restore his memory. As she expresses it, the purpose of remembrance is to be able to 'read' the natural features one encounters:

[Caílte:] '7 ... atá dail fer nEirenn a cind bliadna do Temraig, 7 ní fétaim-si gan dul d'accallaim mo choiccli 7 mo chomalta .i. Oissin mac Find, 7 tre forchongra in Tailgind do aichin dim dul ann, 7 maithe fer nEirenn a n-aeninadh d'indissin mod 7 morgnim gaili 7 gaiscid na Feinde 7 Find meic Cumaill 7 fer nEirenn archena, 7 do lesugud údar 7

46 See above, pp 114–15.   47 Stokes, 'Acallamh', ll. 4520–2: *Ocus doronad mar sin, uair do sluiced ann hé tre breithir naemPátraic, 7 gan nert do gabail d'fir a inaid ar Laighnech(aib)*; cf. Dooley and Roe, *Tales*, p. 127.   48 Stokes, 'Acallamh', ll. 2303–5: *Ocus ba hí sin Muc Slángha déidhenach do roinned idir feruibh Eirenn*; cf. Dooley and Roe, *Tales*, p. 71.   49 'Place and placename', pp 53–60.   50 Stokes, 'Acallamh', ll. 290–302; cf. Dooley and Roe, *Tales*, pp 11–12.

olloman dona scelaib indesmait-ne ann co dered aimsire'. 'Ocus fil cobair accainde duit', ar in ingen. 'Ca cobair sin?' ar Cailte. 'Deoch cuimnigthi céille d'indlucud duinde duit co Temraig connach tecma duit es nó abhann nó indber nó a cath nó a comlann nach bia a cuimne accut'.[51]

[Caílte:] '... and there is a meeting of the men of Ireland at Tara at the end of the year, and I must go there to converse with my companion and foster-brother, Oisín mac Finn, and because of the summons of the Adze-Head who has commanded me to go there and to tell the nobles of the men of Ireland, gathered in the same place, of the conduct and great deeds of valour and prowess of the *fian* and of Finn mac Cumaill, and of the men of Ireland as well, and to have the stories that we tell there preserved by scholars and sages until the end of time'. 'We have some help for you,' said the girl. 'What help is that?' said Caílte. 'We will bestow upon you a drink for the recalling of meaning, for you to take to Tara, so that you will not happen upon a cataract or river or estuary, or the battle or combat associated with it, that you will not remember'.

The claim that *dinnshenchas* is the gateway to all *senchas* articulates an idea which is implicit in the narrative as a whole. It is important to note, therefore, that the narrator and Caílte assume complementary roles as the preservers of onomastic tradition. While within the frame-tale it is Caílte who can name and explain the landscape, the narrator plays the same role in the Mellifont passage and, to a greater or lesser extent, in relation to all the double-named toponyms put into his mouth. Whereas Caílte, speaking in the frame-tale present, tends to relate how deeds in the past gave rise to names, the narrator can show how toponyms were generated within the frame-tale present, as here:

ro chóirig Cailte in tṡelg 'ar sin, 7 ro chóraig tiug na fer 7 immat na con in t-eolus ro tṡail in dam sin do thiachtain, 7 do chóirig a línta ar allaib 7 ar essaib 7 ar indberaib ind ḟeraind, 7 doriacht in fiad mor da n-indsaighid mara ticed cacha bliadna 7 atchonnairc Cailte in dam allaith ac tuidecht co hAth in daim ar Slaine. Ocus ros-gab Cailte in Coscraig .i. a tṡleg, 7 tuc réo n-urchair don dam 7 sé a lenmain isin lín co tarla fat láma laich don chrann na sleige trít. 'Adar limsa do dergad ar in ndam', ar Coscrach, '7 ca ferr ainm da mbeth ar ind ath ina Ath dergtha in daim?' ainm ind atha ossin anall cossaníu.[52]

Caílte arranged the hunt after that and arranged the crowd of men and the multitude of hounds in the direction in which he expected that stag

---

51 Stokes, 'Acallamh', ll. 7251–61; cf. Dooley and Roe, *Tales*, p. 203.   52 Stokes, 'Acallamh', ll. 4426–36; cf. Dooley and Roe, *Tales*, p. 125. See also, for example, Stokes, 'Acallamh', ll.

to come, and he arranged his nets over the cliffs and cataracts and estu-
aries of the territory. The great deer came towards them as it had done
each year and Caílte saw the wild stag coming to Áth in Daim, 'the Ford
of the Stag', on the Slaney. Caílte took his spear, *in Choscrach*, 'the Triumphant', and cast it at the stag which was stuck in the net so that the
shaft of the spear penetrated him the length of a warrior's arm. 'It seems
to me that the stag is bloodied', said Coscrach, 'and what better name
could the ford have than Áth Dergtha in Daim, "the Ford of the Bloody-
ing of the Stag?"' That is the name of the ford from then until today.

Through the repeated demonstration of his control of *dinnshenchas*, the narrator establishes himself as an authority on the past and as a rival to Caílte on
that basis. Indeed, there is a wider mirroring of the narrator's persona in the
character of Caílte. The latter's position as a secondary narrator within the
text has already been mentioned. The narrator and Caílte employ some of the
same verbal strategies to manage their complex narratives. There is a neat
illustration of this in a passage wherein the term *dála* 'as regards, concerning'
is used four times in rapid succession to indicate the narrative's changing
focalisation – on the first occasion, the king of Munster, a character within
the frame-tale present, introduces a new topic of conversation by use of the
term. Then it is Caílte, within his answer to the king, who uses it twice to
switch between strands of his story. On the fourth occasion, however, it is the
narrator who shifts the narrative focus away from Caílte and onto another
frame-tale character.

> 'Dala in trir óclach sin, a m'anum, a Chailte['], ar rí [Muman] assa
> haithli, 'ind acaibsi do badur nó ind uaib dochuadur?' … [Cailte:] 'Dala
> immorro Find meic Cumaill, rainic reime co Temair Luachra ar scailed
> na Féinde dó, 7 ní roibe don Féind ina farrud acht daescur͘sluag 7 gill-
> ida fedma na Féinne.
> Dala na naenbur sin dorinde Find d'Fiannaib Eirenn d'iarraid da
> mac rig …
> Dala Patraic immorro 7 ríg Muman tangadur secha bodes co Beind
> mbain in retha.[53]

> 'As regards those three warriors, my dear Caílte', said the king of
> Munster after that, 'did they stay with you or depart from you?' …
> [Caílte:] 'As regards Finn mac Cumaill, then, he reached Temair
> Lúachra after the *fian* had separated from him, and none of the *fian*

3438–41, and Dooley and Roe, *Tales*, p. 71.   **53** Stokes, 'Acallamh', ll. 5617–33; Dooley and
Roe, *Tales*, pp 157–8. For discussion of parallel usages of the term *dála* to mark a change of
protagonist, as well as of *dála* as a term which initiates episodes, see Poppe, 'Narrative structure', p. 218.

accompanied him but the common people and the servants of the *fian*.

As regards those nine which Finn has compelled from the *fiana* of Ireland to seek the two sons of the king ...

As regards Patrick and the king of Munster, moreover, they passed southwards to Bend Bán in Retha, 'the White Peak of the Run'.

The term *dála* is commonly used to manage multi-stranded narratives. Poppe has discussed 'the Irish redactor of *Guy* and *Beues* [having] a sense of the episodic macro-structure of his work, which he displays by the demarcation of distinct episodes within it', noting that a *dála* at the beginning of an episode is often balanced by a '*conidh* "so that it/this is" plus summary' at its close.[54] The passages already cited make clear that the narrator of the *Acallam* makes use of both formulae; they do not, however, occur as a pair in the way described by Poppe, while the alternative use of *dála* to mark 'a change of protagonists within episodes' is more prevalent than its use to move the narration from frame- to sub-tale or vice versa.[55]

Conid and *corub*, however, are used frequently in a number of formulations to delineate episodes. The most common usages are in toponymic statements, placed in both Caílte's mouth and that of the narrator, statements which serve to underline the authority of each and to strengthen the association between these figures.[56] Poppe has also discussed the use of *conid* and a noun relating to the scholarly classification of narratives by their chief events, such as *aided* or *loinges*.[57] This usage is very rare in the *Acallam*. The first such construction seems to represent an innovation in the Franciscan manuscripts, which are characterised by their shared distance from the other witnesses in terms of structure and expression.[58] The second example is as follows: 'This is the Hunt of Bend Boirchi and the Colloquy of Lí Bán (*Imaccallaim Li baine*), daughter of Echu mac Eogain, King of Ireland, and Caílte up to that point'.[59] The use of the term *imacallam* here to characterise a distinct episode in the narrative assumes a particular significance in relation to the (apparently synonymous) use of the terms *imacallam* and *acallam* elsewhere in the text. The terms are used twice more to designate instances of colloquies or conversa-

---

54 Poppe, 'Narrative structure', pp 217, 220.   **55** Ibid., pp 218–19.   **56** For such an example of *conid* put in Caílte's mouth, see Stokes, 'Acallamh', ll. 867–8. For an example spoken by the narrator, see ibid., ll. 6442–3.   **57** Poppe, 'Narrative structure', p. 218.   **58** Stokes, 'Acallamh', l. 528. See also UCD Franciscan MS A 20(a), fo. 11v5. The fullest discussion of the witnesses to *AS* is in Ó Muraíle, 'Agallamh na seanórach', pp 110–11. On the use made by Stokes of UCD Franciscan MS A 4, see G. Parsons, 'Whitley Stokes, Standish Hayes O'Grady and *Acallam na senórach*' in E. Boyle and P. Russell (eds), *The tripartite life of Whitley Stokes* (2011), pp 185–95 at pp 194–5. The A 20(a) text is so closely related to that of A 4 that it is regarded as a copy.   **59** Stokes, 'Acallamh', ll. 3246–7: *Conid hi Selg Beindi Boirchi 7 Imaccallaim Li baine, ingine Echach meic Eogain rí[g] Eirenn, 7 Cailti conici sin*. This passage is omitted in Dooley and Roe, *Tales*.

tions which are in some way notable: *Corub hí Accallaim na Senorach ac in chartha a mullach Uisnig sin 7 cachar' chansat d'fis 7 d'eolus d'feraib Eirenn uile ó sin amach*, 'That is the Colloquy of the Ancients at the pillar-stone on the summit of Uisnech as well as everything that they related of knowledge and learning to all the men of Ireland from then on'.[60] Elsewhere, in a sub-tale, it is asked about the length of time Finn and Caílte spent at Slíab Én. It is noted: 'that was a question for the Colloquy of the Ancients' (*Gurub ceist sin ar Imacallaim na Senorach*).[61] Further illustrating the overlaps between the narrative personae operating, the second reference is taken by Ann Dooley and Harry Roe to be spoken by Caílte but an attribution to the narrator is feasible and, to my mind, preferable.[62]

These passages present other challenges of interpretation centred on the term *(im)acallam*, not least because of the modern understanding of it as the title of *AS*.[63] The phrase *Accallaim na senorach* in the first of the two passages appears to refer not to the specific encounter depicted at this point in the frame-tale between Patrick, Caílte, Oisín, Díarmait mac Cerbaill and other kings at Uisnech alone, but to function as a label for the wider conversation depicted as ongoing in the frame-tale.[64] The reference to *ar Imacallaim na senorach* provides support for this interpretation of the phrase's significance, suggesting that the in-narrative understanding of the phrase is as a name for the wider conversation depicted. Such a metatextual awareness of the unfolding narrative is in evidence elsewhere in the text, most notably when the narrator suspends the story of the king of Connacht and his Otherworldly lover, in favour of another narrative strand: 'The girl set off to her *síd* after that, until the story returns its focus to her again'.[65] Such metatextual commentary seems to bring the narrator closer to the position of the author relative to his narrative than does any other narratorial function explored here. Poppe has discussed *dála* and *conid* in terms of redactors' engagement with the narration of translated works. Ó Cathasaigh has conceived of a category of apparently narratorial interjections which may in fact represent a(n) (author-)redactor's work. It is worth considering the extent to which his label 'redactorial' might be applied to the examples presented here from the *Acallam*. It is certainly

---

60 Stokes, 'Acallamh', ll. 2702–3; cf. Dooley and Roe, *Tales*, p. 82.   61 Stokes, 'Acallamh', l. 5363; cf. Dooley and Roe, *Tales*, p. 149.   62 Dooley and Roe, *Tales*, p. 149.   63 The title is not given in any extant manuscript witness.   64 Dooley and Roe, *Tales*, p. 236, n. 69: 'The stories and lore told by the old *Fían* survivors are formally ratified and codified by order of the king and a title to the work, *Acallam na Senórach: The Conversation of the Ancients* ..., given'. Cf. Standish Hayes O'Grady's translation of the passage in question – 'this that you have here [both above and to follow] comprises "the Colloquy with the Ancients" at the pillar-stone on the top of Usnach, as well as all else that by way of knowledge and instruction they uttered to the men of Erin': O'Grady (ed. and trans.), *Silva gadelica*, 2 vols (1892), ii, p. 170.   65 Stokes, 'Acallamh', ll. 6436–7: *Ocus atract in ingen roimpe dochum a sida 'arsin, noco tabair in scel fuirmed doridhissi furri*; cf. Dooley and Roe, *Tales*, p. 181.

the case that the statements highlighted, which seek to shape the experience of readers/auditors of complex narratives by demarcating episodes or drawing attention to the narrative structure in other ways, recall the methods commonly employed to interpret those narratives by those who read and reworked medieval texts. A marginal comment incorporated by Whitley Stokes into his edition demonstrates this fact. The marginal *conid* initiates a summary of an episode which is just concluding and it is followed directly in the main text by a *conid* phrase which functions in the same way:

> [in marg: Conid ann do chreidset Túath dé Danann do Patraicc].
> Conid hé sin scel ro indis Cailte do rig Laigen 7 do Pátraic annsin.
> Ocus tuc Donn mac Midhir feis dithat na háidchi sin.[66]

> [in marg: Then the Túatha Dé Danann gave allegiance to Patrick].
> That is the story that Caílte then told the king of Leinster and Patrick.
> And Donn mac Midir provided that night's hospitality.

Yet, these statements need be redactorial only in that they recall the approaches of contemporary author-redactors. The examples discussed each appear in more than one manuscript witness, not including the Franciscan copies, and so have been understood by two or more scribes as integral to the text of *Acallam na senórach*. I would argue that they were understood as being voiced by the narrator, who is operating in mimetic mode, as when the narrator of the *Táin* provides titles, recalls episodes or events already narrated, and refers back 'to the "Cattle Raid" as a tale itself' as Tristram has argued.[67] In the absence of any linguistic or palaeographical evidence to the contrary, the parallels presented between Caílte's style of narration and that of the narrator encourage the view that our default assumption should be that these passages are integral to the text as we know it, and are to be understood as spoken by the narrator. The careful crafting of the *Acallam* reveals its author to have been mindful of his audiences' engagement with his structurally complicated text.[68] The deployment within this work of a mimetic narrator – operating in the terms set out by Tristram – is part of a wider strategy to direct audience responses to the work.

That *Acallam na senórach* offers an intricate reflection on the interaction of the oral and the literary has long been accepted, but to date the contribution of the narrative voice to this aspect of the tale has not been fully explored. For readers, or those listening to a text read aloud, the narrative voice is inherently intermedial, straddling the divide between oral and written narration. This aspect of the narrator's persona is played upon by the

66 Stokes, 'Acallamh', ll. 5378–81; cf. Dooley and Roe, *Tales*, pp 149–50.   67 See above, pp 111–12.   68 See Parsons, 'The structure'.

author of the text. The narrator is closely associated with Caílte, the in-narrative authority who is depicted as operating in an oral mode. In his handling of a complex frame-tale – his demarcation of episodes, including using terms which are used to categorise tales elsewhere, and other explicit acknowledgements of the narrative's structure – the narrator functions in a manner which is reminiscent of contemporary scholarly engagement with written textual culture. Just as the written record is shown to outstrip oral methods of preserving lore in the *Acallam*, the narrator is shown to surpass his *fénnid* counterpart in terms of the depth of insight he can bring to the narration of an event from the past of the *fian*. It is suggested here that the narratorial persona is built around the notion of authority over the material presented, and that as such it is a function of the authorial intention to provide a definitive account of the deeds of the *fian* and its encounter with Christianity.[69]

69 I wish to thank Dr Kevin Murray and Dr Aidan Doyle for the invitation to contribute to the conference which preceded this volume and those who participated in the discussion which followed the delivery of this paper. I am grateful in particular to Dr Hugh Fogarty for passing on some very helpful references subsequently. Some of the ideas presented here featured in a paper given at 'Ní hansa: extraordinary accounts of mediality in early Irish literature', a workshop held at Universität Zürich in March 2011. I would like to acknowledge my gratitude to the organiser, Ms Sarah Erni, and the other participants of that workshop for their useful comments. I wish too to thank Dr Kate Louise Mathis for allowing me to read part of her unpublished doctoral thesis ('The evolution of Deirdriu in the Ulster Cycle' [University of Edinburgh, 2010]) and Prof. Thomas Owen Clancy for his comments on a draft of this essay. Naturally, its shortcomings are entirely my own.

Gods and heroes: approaching the *Acallam* as ethnography

STIOFÁN Ó CADHLA

In *The history of curiosity*, Justin Stagl argues that research is coeval with mankind. Accounts of the emergence of the disciplines of ethnology and folk-lore bear some resemblence to what some might call mythical thought in so far as they totter perpetually between firsts and lasts. There are many instances that spring to mind: the first ethnographer, folklorist, fieldworker, Christian; the last pagan, Irish speaker, use of cow dung for fuel and so on. In his fateful terminality, Oisín himself is exemplary, even proverbial: *i ndiaidh na féinne/ an deigh nam fiann* or 'after the *fianna*'.[1] The Modern Irish poet Máirtín Ó Direáin likened himself to *Oisín ar na creaga*.[2] Zimmerman describes Caílte as 'the first Irish guide explaining his country to visitors'.[3] In the *Acallam*, Saint Patrick prompts Caílte to relate the story of the *fian*. As may be gleaned from the body of the text, the outline of a basic questionnaire is utilised to this end.[4] What wood is that? Who lies in this grave? Where did the seven handsome sons of Ailill die? This well-conceived conceit succeeds in conjuring up the conversion, repentance and sometimes subtle recalcitrance of the *fian*, the starcrossed heroes of generations of storytellers.

Stagl also quotes Paul Lazarsfeld, asserting that 'the use of the question-naire has a long past which still waits for its recorder'.[5] There are some accounts of the formation of questionnaires, but they begin and end for the most part in the early modern period. DuBois traces the beginnings of 'the genre and enterprise of ethnography' to the monastic *scriptoria* and royal courts of the medieval period.[6] In Ireland, sites such as Clonmacnoise, Armagh, Iona and Kildare, and the *historia*, *annalis* and *chronica* compiled as early as the sixth century come to mind. These appear almost as soon as the Christian mission brought Latin and the technology of writing.[7] In Scandinavia, early descriptions of the cosmology, modes of divination and

---

1 J. Macpherson, *Ossian's poems* (1863), p. 13; cf. T. Ó Máille, *Seanfhocla Chonnacht* (2nd ed., 2010), p. 213 where there is an extensive bibliography for this and similar expressions. See also D. Ó hÓgáin, 'Magic attributes of the hero' in B. Almqvist et al. (eds), *The heroic process* (1987), pp 207–42 at p. 212 and n. 19. 2 'Oisín on the rocks': see 'Deireadh ré', M. Ó Direáin, *Dánta 1939–1979* (1980), p. 51; cf. Gael Linn, *Máirtín Ó Direáin: dánta á léamh ag an bhfile*, CD (2010). 3 G.D. Zimmerman, *The Irish storyteller* (2001), p. 17. 4 The outline is appended to this article. 5 J. Stagl, *A history of curiosity* (1995), p. 1. 6 T.A. DuBois, *An introduction to shamanism* (2009), p. 13. 7 E. Bhreathnach, 'The *seanchas* tradition in late medieval Ireland' in E. Bhreathnach and B. Cunningham (eds), *Writing Irish history* (2007), p. 18.

spirituality of the Sámi emerge in such a context. The idea of the archaic survey, carried out when the life of a community is disturbed, is particularly intriguing. As Stagl reminds us, every human society has its own system of research techniques;[8] it is not a purely Western or Eurocentric phenomenon brought into the field or outwards to the unconscious exotics near and far.

It is worthwhile considering the *Acallam* as something more than a manuscript tale, that is, something more than residuum, antiquity or mere 'folktale'. The very idea of a wholly unalphabetised 'folk' possessing only flawed scraps of a distant, pristine original knowledge is now considered problematic. So too is the very twee Victorian idea of folklore itself, and the unqualified blanket use of motifs as the methodological currency to transact meaning or compile evidence. Often such materials were sporadically collected over relatively short periods of time and in relatively limited areas. Belief, or indeed disbelief, is difficult to quantify or even to identify. I will therefore discuss the *Acallam* from an ethnographic perspective by foregrounding some of these prominent topoi. Some are difficult to contain within the early medieval period as they echo across the millennium in a three-dimensional cultural universe that circumscribes medieval history, mythology, antiquarianism, Celticism, emergent native Irish ethnology and even aspects of popular culture. When Finn, the heroicised god, washes his face, it is almost as if he can see us. What Gearóid Ó Crualaoich calls *friotal na laoch*, the ecstatic voice perhaps, transcends personal and historical time.[9] It has at least an estimated date of 'the later prehistoric (that is, pre-Christian) phase of Irish pseudo-history' but consider for a moment that it may not be just fiction, quaint folklore or remote epic literature.[10]

Patrick Campbell, a native of Argyll in Scotland, visited a group of Mohawk Indians who had fought alongside Highlanders in 1791. He surmised that they were undergoing similar processes of conversion and civilisation as the Highlanders themselves, and the *Acallam* came to his mind. He was troubled by the thought of those who had never heard of Christ and speculated whether they would also go to hell. The Highlander's worries echo Oisín's concern for the *fian* under the new Christian dispensation, an interesting observation as *fian*-warriors were in many ways exemplars or cultural heroes.[11]

Acallam na senórach has enjoyed unrivalled popularity among storytellers, scholars and the population in general. A few remarkable patterns of contiguity have been identified, the modern redactions sometimes resembling those in the manuscripts.[12] Copies were made in the eighteenth and nineteenth cen-

---

8 Stagl, *A history of curiosity*, p. 3.   9 G. Ó Crualaoich, 'An ceol sí agus friotal na laoch', *Comhar* (1992), 94–9 at 98.   10 W. Gillies, 'Heroes and ancestors' in B. Almqvist et al. (eds), *The heroic process* (1987), pp 57–73 at p. 64.   11 M. Newton, 'Celtic cousins or white settlers?' in K.E. Nilsen (ed.), *Rannsachadh na Gàidhlig*, 5 (2008), pp 221–37 at p. 229.   12 J.F. Nagy, *The wisdom of the outlaw* (1985), p. 6.

turies.[13] There are over seventy copies of *Agallamh na seanórach* in the Royal Irish Academy.[14] In the nineteenth century, Clare poet Mícheál Coimín composed a long poem on the theme of Oisín in the Land of Youth.[15] Continuities such as these led Murphy to highlight the 'intricacies of connection between the earliest literature and modern folk tradition'.[16] In one form or another, *fiannaíocht* became a privileged genre among scholars, scribes, storytellers and the wider population. It was, as Pádraig Ó Siochfhradha states, 'the epic of the masses'.[17] It also became something of an elite genre in translation, enjoyed in one guise or another by native and foreign antiquarians, scholars and *literati* such as Blake, Byron, Goethe, Herder and Yeats.[18] Finn Cycle tales were recited with special reverence across Scotland and Ireland with storytellers uncovering their heads to relate them. Certain taboos surrounded the genre which, it was believed, could keep the devil from a house.[19] In Waterford, a storyteller stood upright, presumably in order to narrate *fiannaíocht* in the appropriate fashion.[20] The genre was also favoured among the various obsequies during wakes.[21] There seems to be evidence that *fiannaíocht* may have had a 'culturally intensifying' role in this and other rituals and gatherings.[22] The proverb *an áit a mbíonn Fiannaíocht ní bhíonn diabhlaíocht*, or '*fiannaíocht* and evil are never in the same place', illustrates this perspective. By way of explanation it is said that Saint Patrick was suddenly overcome with guilt while writing stories from Oisín's dictation and threw them on the fire. He heard a voice, however, reminding him that there cannot be any harm in *fiannaíocht* and rescued them again.[23]

Our recent understanding of the relationship between the Christian and the non-Christian in indigenous and popular culture alike is complicated by the coincidence in the modern period of intensive folklore collection with intensive Catholic religiosity. It is difficult not to see these issues as intimately related, and in any case it should be borne in mind, that Christianity itself 'cannot be completely separated from mythical thinking'.[24] There has been some discussion of the handling of indigenous belief and practice in the *Acallam*,[25] with Nagy arguing that the pre-Christian divinities are present in

13 Ibid., p. 168. 14 See V. Morley, *Ó Chéitinn go Raifhtearaí* (2011), p. 11. 15 For details, see E. MacNeill and G. Murphy (ed. and trans.), *Duanaire Finn*, 3 vols (1908–53), iii, p. xxii. 16 Ibid., p. lxx. 17 P. Ó Siochfhradha (ed.), *Laoithe na féinne* (1941), p. vii. 18 D.S. Thomson, 'MacPherson's *Ossian:* ballads to epics' in B. Almqvist et al. (eds), *The heroic process*, pp 243–64 at p. 264. 19 Nagy, *The wisdom of the outlaw*, pp 231–2. 20 N. Breatnach, *Ar bóthar dom* (1998), p. 4. Breatnach describes the storyteller (Tomás Ó Cathail, Sean-Phobal, Co. Waterford) as standing on the hearth, uncovering his head, and reciting the runs in particular with such intensity that he perspired. 21 T. de Bhaldraithe (ed.), *Seanchas Thomáis Laighléis* (1977), p. 133. 22 G. Ó Crualaoich, 'Irish storytelling' in N. Buttimer et al. (eds), *The heritage of Ireland* (2000), pp 171–7, at p. 174. 23 See Ó Máille, *Seanfhocla Chonnacht*, p. 212. 24 M. Eliade, 'Survivals and camouflages of myths' in D. Apostolos-Cappadona (ed.), *Symbolism, the sacred and the arts* (1985), pp 32–52, at p. 33. 25 K. McCone, *Pagan past and Christian present in early Irish literature* (1990), pp 6–7.

the 'liminal ambience' of the narrative.[26] Ní Mhaonaigh claims that the non-Christian occupies a 'comfortable niche'.[27] Caílte has been described as a 'simultaneous inhabitant of past and present worlds',[28] while a modern Connacht belief collected by Douglas Hyde attributes his rearing to the 'fairies'.[29] In more recent years, however, many folklorists and ethnologists are more sensitive to the negotiated and nuanced nature of indigenous spirituality, particularly following an extended period in the late nineteenth and early twentieth centuries of intense religious fervour and even censorship. In historical terms, it appears as if no Christian episcopate had to cope with anything like the large groupings or *túatha* that Saint Patrick and his successors faced. A special relationship was formed with chieftains to establish monasteries and nunneries, and 'as a result there grew a network of Christian communities intimately involved in the life of each local dynastic grouping, fostering Christian life throughout the island all the more powerfully because monasteries were so enmeshed in the pride and pre-Christian traditions of each *tuath*'.[30] It is possible to speak of the *Acallam* as imagining ways in which 'individuals were turned around by Christianity, but also the ways in which they could turn around what Christiantity meant'.[31] Missionaries christianised

> the 'pagan' divine Figures and myths that resisted extirpation. A large number of dragon-slaying Gods or Heroes became St. Georges; storm Gods were transformed into St. Eliases; the countless fertility Goddesses were assimilated to the Virgin or to female Saints.[32]

It is not just a matter of pointing to the most explicit evidence but of tracing the symbolic watermark emblazoned on the backdrop of the story, the back-lighting where belief may or may not be implicit or may even be absent altogether.

For want of a more precise term, the *Acallam* has what could be described as a degree of modern sensibility. This may be related to what Murphy calls the 'new mentality', the emergent form and style of the tenth, eleventh, twelfth and thirteenth centuries when the learned classes were 'busy at antiquarian research'; perhaps the *Acallam* questionnaire illustrates this. There was a refashioning of pseudo-history, and of mythological and warrior traditions in more personalised narratives enhanced by the evocative *dán díreach* metre.[33] In places, it reads like a work produced by an ethnographer

---

26 Nagy, *The wisdom of the outlaw*, p. 5.   27 M. Ní Mhaonaigh, 'Pagans and holy men: literary manifestations of twelfth-century reform' in D. Bracken and D. Ó Riain-Raedel (eds), *Ireland and Europe in the twelfth century* (2006), pp 143–61, at p. 151.   28 G. Parsons, 'The structure of *Acallam na senórach*', *Cambrian Medieval Celtic Studies*, 55 (Summer, 2008), 11–41 at 37.   29 See MacNeill and Murphy, *Duanaire Finn*, iii, p. xx.   30 D. MacCulloch, *A history of Christianity* (2010), p. 331.   31 Ibid., p. 5.   32 Eliade, 'Survivals and camouflages of myths', p. 37.   33 MacNeill and Murphy, *Duanaire Finn*, iii, p. lxxxvi.

with a fresh and creative approach to cultural interpretation and expression. It has been described by Eoin MacNeill as 'rambling'. This perspective may depend too much upon an elite notion of literary taste, and may be contrasted with Ó Riain's view that it is 'a highly artistic composition'.[34] It is possible to view it not just as a window through which we can see the past when 'the past' means that which is ended or over. In another sense it is not over, it is redolent of a particular cultural world or universe. It owes its very form to shared patterns of meaning, assumptions, beliefs and symbolic associations. Throughout the text, we are constantly reminded of the intricate and intimate aspects of indigenous knowledge, to 'local ecology, including plant and animal life; the nature of politics, curing, magic and other ritual'.[35] Carney dismisses the idea that the stories were written down verbatim 'with the scientific approach and attitude of a modern student of ethnography'.[36] The modern student of ethnography is more likely to sympathise with the anthropological or broadly cultural approach and the extent to which the narrative can be considered an auto-ethnographic discourse that encapsulates, more or less, the institutions of the society that created it.[37] In this respect, for example, its value as a source surpasses Giraldus Cambrensis' *Topography of Ireland*.[38] If the symbolic or cosmological superstructure was somehow extracted, the narrative would be compromised. Not all of these are mere fictional, textual or literary tropes, novel archaisms, wild imagination or romance; some are configured within extant effective cultural paradigms. Even if masking or distorting some past social or ethnographic reality, they still speak, or perhaps they speak even more eloquently, of it. As Ó Crualaoich says, it is worth bearing in mind 'both traditional or "insider" or "local" horizons of their semantic significance and the possibility of subsequent, multiple exegetic recontextualizations of these symbols and narratives'.[39] Murphy's 'folkstory-tellers' are not just repeating cognitive photocopies of texts; they are also re-imagining and recreating them vis-à-vis ongoing cultural processes.

In any case, the *Acallam* is presented as a dialogue, conversation or survey, a 'perceptive and epistemological curiosity'.[40] The opening depicts the clergy as wary and frightened at the very appearance and size of the *fian*.[41] This is

---

34 Ibid., i, p. xliv; P. Ó Riain, 'The materials and provenance of "Buile Shuibhne"', *Éigse*, 15, iii (1974), 173–88 at 173. For discussion, see Parsons, 'The structure of *Acallam na senórach*', 11–12.   35 J. Sherzer, *Verbal art in San Blas* (1990), p. 4.   36 J. Carney, *Studies in Irish literature and history* (1955), p. 277; cf. McCone, *Pagan past and Christian present*, p. 7.   37 For examples of creative or auto-ethnography, see H. Glassie, *Passing the time in Ballymenone* (1995), or the special edition of the *Journal of American Folklore*, 118:467 (2005). Other creative approaches, including creative writing, are exemplified in F. de Caro (ed.), *The folklore muse* (2008).   38 J.J. O'Meara, *The first version of the topography of Ireland by Giraldus Cambrensis* (1951).   39 G. Ó Crualaoich, *The book of the cailleach* (2003), p. 71.   40 Stagl, *A history of curiosity*, p. 5.   41 A. Dooley and H. Roe, *Tales of the elders of Ireland* (1999), p. 5; W. Stokes (ed. and partial trans.), 'Acallamh na senórach' in W. Stokes and E. Windisch (eds), *Irische*

very much in keeping with archaic mythologies 'which nearly always portray our progenitors as larger and more long-lived that we are'.[42] Gamble, for example, makes a passing reference to Phelim M'Coal, 'a giant of old'.[43] The story involves a form of travelling, both real and cognitive, within the imaginative world of both the *fian* and the storytellers. The questionnaire incorporates several significant phenomena. The synopsis of the Finn Cycle in the *Handbook of Irish folklore* bears some comparison.[44] The *Acallam* and many of the *laoithe*, although later, have a penchant for lists of things. *Aides memoire*, fragments of evidence, relics, souvenirs, monuments, symbols and stories are central.[45] Many of the two hundred or so stories appropriate and consecrate the artefacts and monuments, mounds and cairns of the ancestors. *Fían*-warriors are like 'Tomb Raider' archaeologists, searching for the monuments or graves of the heroes. The stories they tell are arguably more valuable than the artefacts that inspire them; perhaps this is the point. They dig up the graves, in one case giving the chain of Lug to Saint Patrick, a very symbolic succession.[46] In a further case, the stone container of Finn mac Cumaill is bestowed upon 'holy Patrick' (*nóemPatraic*).[47]

Phenomena such as these often refer to something else and can be used to 'document the structure of culture and society'.[48] The nomadic *fian*-warriors, described sometimes as outlaws or exiles, explore the environment. They move between natural and supernatural worlds bringing an eclectic and wholly encyclopaedic knowledge with them.[49] Of course, such travel is both real and imaginary and may include visions or shamanic insights even where *fian* membership becomes a rite of passage to acquire special knowledge.[50] The literature of rite and ritual is informative on this. Finn, the poet, is initiated but perhaps also initiates the group into what Meade calls 'the future of the society on one hand and open to the origins and ancestral beginnings of the group from the past. For a time, the initiate steps out of being simply himself or herself and becomes an ancestral dreamtime hero or heroine re-entering the origin stories of the culture'.[51] Finn seeks knowledge from nature,

Texte, iv, 1 (1900), ll. 64–78.   **42** G. Schrempp, *The ancient mythology of modern science* (2012), p. 9. Gerard Murphy points out (MacNeill and Murphy, *Duanaire Finn*, iii, p. 197) that this characteristic is also found in modern stories and sometimes attributed to historical people. **43** J. Gamble, *Society and manners in early nineteenth-century Ireland*, edited with an Introduction by B. Mac Suibhne (2011), p. 487.   **44** S. Ó Súilleabháin, *A handbook of Irish folklore* (1942), pp 588–9.   **45** Ó Siochfhradha, *Laoithe na féinne*; there are lists of heroes in 'Anmanna na bpríomh-laoch den fhéinn', pp 64–5; lists of dogs in 'Seilg Locha Léin', pp 67–9 and 'Fiadhach fiann Éireann ar Shliabh Truim', pp 123–4; a list of people and items incinerated in the fire of 'Tóiteán Tighe Finn', pp 186–7; others like 'Caoi Oisín i ndiaidh na féinne' or 'Buile Oisín' list the qualities of the *fian* or the quantities of their possessions, pp 227–44.   **46** Dooley and Roe, *Tales*, p. 64; Stokes, 'Acallamh', ll. 2081–2.   **47** Dooley and Roe, *Tales*, p. 84; Stokes, 'Acallamh', ll. 2761–3.   **48** Stagl, *A history of curiosity*, p. 6.   **49** Ibid., p. 11.   **50** Nagy, *The wisdom of the outlaw*, p. 49.   **51** M. Meade, 'Foreword to the new edition' in M. Eliade, *Rites and symbols of initiation* (1994), pp 5–14 at p. 9.

from the supernatural world, and from locomotion to the monuments of the past or into the ever-present ancestral Otherworld where his own relations and relationships germinate and grow. In such a paradigm, the performative and ritualistic aspects of *fiannaíocht* could highlight the depiction of a fantastic or ideal world, in both archaic and modern narrative streams.

Caílte is detained by Saint Patrick and his clerics in a kind of quarantine, ordained and maintained by a social and cultural institution of hospitality and reciprocity that binds them both. This theme is central to Éamon a' Búrc's narration in the modern period of 'Urchar an daill faoi abhall'. When Oisín chides Saint Patrick for niggardliness, he argues that he is not a proper man as he had not fed anyone adequately in his lifetime.[52] It could be imagined that it is for interrogation that he is, as Stagl puts it, monopolised by his host.[53] There are occasions where it could be said that the saint is initiated into the life of the *fian* by Caílte through the rite of narrative. The value and perception of knowledge is as interesting as the transmission of it. It is understood as vital and communitarian, and is imparted socially in gatherings or in large assemblies 'in the presence of the men of Ireland'.[54] Just as Finn is presented as a proto-Christian, isn't it possible that Saint Patrick has some of the qualities of a proto-Fenian? He displays his own poetical eloquence in recounting the story of Cloch na Cét when told that Finn had foreseen the arrival of Christianity 'with belief in crosses and pious acts',[55] though Roe may have been too confident in suggesting that Ireland was 'totally Christianised'.[56] As a primary cosmological conception of the relationship between this world and the other, the ancestral supernatural world denoted by the Irish *sí*, earlier *síd*, appears to be as central to the *Acallam* as it is to more recent narrative traditions. Latterly, this has often been presented in a rather tawdry manner as a genre of naive 'storytelling', as mere gullible superstition or *piseog* rather than an element of non-Christian belief or religion. As noted above, the intensive collection period in the twentieth century coincided with the heyday of ultramontane Catholicism. One of the results of this was an antagonistic, or at best patronising, view of this ancestral supernatural world. A brief glance at the *Handbook of Irish folklore* demonstrates that the neo-traditional discourse of twentieth-century folkloristics placed the world of the *síd*, appropriately enough, in the chapter concerning 'Mythological Tradition',[57]

---

52 P. Ó Ceannabháin, *Éamon a Búrc: scéalta* (1983), p. 62. Here the saint is called *Pádraig na mBréag* or 'Patrick the Liar'.   **53** Stagl, *A history of curiosity*, p. 12.   **54** Dooley and Roe, *Tales*, p. 220; cf. Stokes, 'Acallamh', ll. 7883–4: *ro indissetar mor d'fís 7 d'fireolus i fiadnaissi fer nÉirenn.* **55** Dooley and Roe, *Tales*, p. 152; cf. Stokes, 'Acallamh', ll. 5418–9: *7 creidem cros 7 crabad inti.* **56** H. Roe, '*Acallamh na senórach*: the confluence of lay and clerical oral traditions' in C.J. Byrne et al. (eds), *Celtic languages and Celtic peoples* (1992), p. 338.   **57** On neo-traditional aspects of modern folkloristics, see S. Ó Cadhla, 'Scribes and storytellers: the ethnographic imagination in nineteenth-century Ireland' in J.M. Wright (ed.), *A companion to Irish literature*, vol. 1 (2010), pp 395–410.

while 'Religious Tradition' was reserved for the Judeo-Christian God and the main saints of Ireland.[58] The *Handbook* goes so far as to call such beliefs (p. 440) 'fictions of the mind':

> Belief in fairies was very strong in Ireland in former times as it was in most countries throughout the world. In Ireland, however, it flourished to an unusual degree owing to the highly developed imaginative powers of our ancestors. It is very difficult to draw a clear line of demarcation between the kingdom of the dead and the fairy world in Irish popular belief. Stories of persons who reappear after death are inextricably confused with tales of the fairies.[59]

The two worlds both mirror and flow into each other. The peripatetic *fian*-warriors travel horizontally but they also travel vertically in and out of the coterminous subterranean Otherworld. The deer of the *síd* are hunted and miracles blend with magic. Proud lonely warriors roam a landscape somewhere between the living and the dead, the old and the new, the Christian and the non-Christian. The *síd* is sometimes treated ambivalently and at other times equated with hell, terror, witches and destruction.[60] In any case, it is the navel where, as Eliade says, in a slightly different but analagous context, they break 'from one plane to another, transcending profane, hetrogeneous space and entering a "pure region"'.[61] Here they can be true to themselves and to the ancestors, or simply be themselves in all of the social, psychological and cultural meanings that this suggests.

The non-Christian sacred landscape is also central to the symbolic topography. Mortal kings and heroes, both Christian and Fenian, mix with immortal kings and heroes. It is worth looking at a few examples. The *síd* or *bruig* is fundamental and features quite early when Saint Patrick inquires how the three sons of the king of Ireland acquired such a vast estate. We learn that it was attained by fasting before the Túatha Dé Danann when Bodb Derg, son of the Dagda, invited them in to the *síd* where the magnificent phantom assembly lavished gifts upon them: females, red gold, garments, a drinking horn, a vat that turns brackish water to wine, swords, strongholds, a cook who is forbidden to refuse food to anyone, and a musician.[62] Each symbol is redolent of power, generosity and the good life lived in harmony with, or perhaps as if in, the Otherworld. A balance between culture and nature is struck. When Túathal and Fíacha divide the country between houses and

58 Ó Súilleabháin, *A handbook of Irish folklore*, pp xxvii–xxix.   59 Ibid., p. 450.   60 Dooley and Roe, *Tales*, pp 175–8; Stokes, 'Acallamh', ll. 6245–358.   61 M. Eliade, *The myth of the eternal return* (1974), p. 15.   62 Dooley and Roe, *Tales*, p. 15; Stokes, 'Acallamh', ll. 410–35. We also learn that that Fiacha's cloak came from the Otherworld or Tír Tairngire: Dooley and Roe, *Tales*, p. 14; Stokes, 'Acallamh', ll. 365–6.

wealth, woods and wilderness, wealth is contrasted unfavourably with free-
dom. Caílte reminds Oisín that he would consider the former the worse bargain.[63] There is an enlightened vision, both real and enchanted, of sociability,
hospitality, generosity, skill, art and craft. Perhaps by alleviating the burden
of historical and moral Christianity, the ancestral supernatural world becomes
integral to the narrative itself.

Negative portrayals of the Otherworld are also present. For example, in
one scene the king of Leinster questions Saint Patrick about the abduction
into the Otherworld of his son Áed by the two *síd*-women, Slat and Mumain.
Only upon his escape, as he confides to Saint Patrick, does he realise the
danger he had been in.[64] Later in the tale, in his dark long hood, he comes
across as an enigmatic figure, perhaps an imaginative likeness of a druid.[65]
The king asks Patrick to break the power of the Túatha Dé Danann over his
son, and the saint does this, guaranteeing the boy 'that he shall get the death
that the King of Heaven and Earth has ordained for him'.[66] Similarly, the
Túatha Dé Danann delay healing Caílte who has refused 'the noble youthfulness of the Túatha Dé Danann'.[67]

Notwithstanding negative elements, denizens of the Otherworld are seen
to possess extraordinary abilities and gifts, and have great prowess, agility and
skill. However, it is not just excellence that emanates from the Otherworld
but that most elusive and invaluable gift of healing. The volatility of the cure
itself is a common feature of such narratives. Libra, the physician, wearing a
woollen cloak from Tír Tairngire, has 'the bottom of his cloak filled with
herbs of healing and of curing'.[68] Caílte and his comrades must restrain him,
preventing him from magically escaping back into the *síd* and, while they are
in his company under the veil of mist, they gain knowledge of the future.
They have a vision of the two sons of Caílte and the two sons of Finn com-
plaining that Finn was missing for a year, leaving them with the decision to
either disband or nominate a new *fian*-chieftain.[69] Caílte resorts to Bé Binn,
daughter of Elcmar, and Bóand, of the River Boyne, to heal his wound.[70] Not
alone is Caílte treated with *materia medica*, with herbs, but music, entertainment and company are also part of the healing procedure and process. Flann
washes his hair so that he has night vision and, an additional benefit, never

---

63 Dooley and Roe, *Tales*, p. 76; Stokes, 'Acallamh', ll. 2482–3.   64 Dooley and Roe, *Tales*, p.
121; Stokes, 'Acallamh', ll. 4097–9.   65 Dooley and Roe, *Tales*, p. 136; Stokes, 'Acallamh', ll.
4889–92.   66 Dooley and Roe, *Tales*, p. 137; cf. Stokes, 'Acallamh', ll. 4928–9: *In bás ro ordaig
Rí nime 7 talmhan do géba.*   67 Dooley and Roe, *Tales*, p. 197; cf. Stokes, 'Acallamh', l. 7038:
sóermacanacht Túaithe dé Danann.   68 Dooley and Roe, *Tales*, p. 145; cf. Stokes, 'Acallamh', ll.
5226–7: *lán ichtair a bruit aice do lossaib leighis 7 ícslainti.* This reminds the folklorist of the
modern discourse on 'fairy doctors', wise men or *fir feasa*, and wise women or *mná feasa*, 'the
still effective representations of cultural knowledge': see Ó Crualaoich, *The book of the cailleach*,
p. 71.   69 Dooley and Roe, *Tales*, p. 146; Stokes, 'Acallamh', ll. 5240–50.   70 Dooley and Roe,
Tales, pp 190–1; Stokes, 'Acallamh', ll. 6804–7.

balds.[71] At Cormac's request, Dub uses his shamanic charm or 'incantation', blending a malign curse and a Christian prayer to banish Aincél, Dígbál and Esbaid.[72] The haberdashers of the *fían* were entertained by three women who had 'a small dulcimer with a bridge of silver and with picks of yellow gold, and women in pangs of childbirth were lulled asleep by the beguiling music of the *síd*'.[73] Caílte uses a charm in the service of Christianity to banish a ravaging flock of birds in the presence of Patrick because as he tells him, 'there was a demon on the bottom of every single blade of grass in Ireland before you, and there is today in Ireland an angel on the bottom of each single blade of grass'.[74]

Another vital facet of the *Acallam* is its interest in music. Giraldus Cambrensis conceded that the Irish were skilled instrumentalists, more skilled 'than any other people'.[75] Saint Patrick asks Caílte the naive question whether the *fían* had music. We know it must have been considered naive since the impatient answer is simply 'Of course' ('*Do bhí imorro*').[76] Caílte proceeds to tell him about Cnú Deróil who was found between the Galtee mountains and Slievenamon, and who had been driven from the *síd* due to the jealousy of his fellow Túatha Dé Danann musicians. In the indigenous philosophy of learning and knowledge, poetry and music are among the highest of all attainments. They are counted as 'one of the three best discoveries' of the *fían* and they essay from the ancestral realms of the imagination.[77] Art and life are as inseparable as Finn and Cnú Deróil.[78] Members of the *fían* traverse the boundaries of this world and the other, they walk the geomantic lines of liminality. As they travel to the battle of Ventry, they meet Cáel Cródae Cétguinech, 'from the dew-covered *Bruig* in the north'. They journey to consult his mother regarding his fairy lover, his bride and a dream that came to him. The narrative recounts: 'we arrived at the door of the *síd* and sang the chant of the *Fían*'. Créde demands a poem from Cáel and he praises her hospitality and wealth saying: 'Her pleasant house is crowded, with women, men and boys,/Druids and musicians, a guardian of doors and ale'.[79] For this, for

---

71 Dooley and Roe, *Tales*, pp 201–2; Stokes, 'Acallamh', ll. 7179–82, 7215–16.   72 Dooley and Roe, *Tales*, pp 175–6; Stokes, 'Acallamh', ll. 6245–69.   73 Dooley and Roe, *Tales*, p. 155; cf. Stokes, 'Acallamh', ll. 5551–4: *do bói timpan becc accu cona leithrind airgit 7 cona deilgib óir buidhe, 7 mná re gur lamnada ro choiteldais lessin céol sirrachtach sidhe.*   74 Dooley and Roe, *Tales*, p. 177; cf. Stokes, 'Acallamh', ll. 6307–8: *ro bói deman a mbun cach énfeornin inti reomut, 7 atá aingel [a] mbun cach énfeornin aniu inti.*   75 O'Meara, *The first version of the topography of Ireland by Giraldus Cambrensis*, p. 87.   76 Dooley and Roe, *Tales*, p. 20; Stokes, 'Acallamh', l. 612.   77 For illustrations of the tenacity of this belief, see S. Ó Duilearga, 'Scéalta sidhe', *Béaloideas*, 1:1 (June, 1927), 95–6; T. Thompson, 'The Irish sí tradition: connections between the disciplines, and what's in a word?', *Journal of Archaeological Method and Theory*, 11:4 (December, 2004), 335–68; P. Ó Héalaí and L. Ó Tuairisc (eds), *Tobar an dúchais* (2007), pp 230–2; R. Uí Ógáin and T. Sherlock (eds), *The otherworld* (2012). The implication is clear in such discourse, the ancestral otherworld is the true dominion of artistic expressions including music, dance and poetry.   78 Dooley and Roe, *Tales*, p. 21; Stokes, 'Acallamh', ll. 628–9.   79 Dooley and Roe, *Tales*, p. 25;

love and pleasure, the battle was suspended and '[t]he couple passed that night in a well-appointed bed and we of the *Fían* were there for seven days, drinking and amusing ourselves, with no shortage of ale or food, though Finn was troubled by the presence of the foreigners at Ventry'.[80]

Later, Cas Corach comes from the *síd* of Bodb Derg, son of the Dagda, 'to learn knowledge and true lore, storytelling and the great deeds of valour of the *Fían* from Caílte'.[81] When he plays his *timpán*, '[i]t is said that badly wounded men would fall asleep from the beguiling music of the *síd* that he played for them'.[82] He is satisfied to take heaven as his reward and the saint, almost going native, promises that only one in a hundred will go to hell, promising the 'men of art' heaven for their poetry and their art. Broccán, the Christian scribe, is impressed but the saint sounds a word of caution about this wonderful music: 'unless indeed the magical melody of the *síd* were in it. If it were not for that, there would be nothing closer to the music of the King of Heaven and Earth than that music'. Broccán is not convinced: 'If there is music in Heaven', he asks, 'why should there not also be music on earth? Thus it is not proper to banish music'. Softening a little, Saint Patrick retorts with the qualification that he did not say that, 'but one should not put too much stock in it'.[83]

Other institutions appear equally important in the framing and presentation of the *Acallam*. For example, the calendar, the quarter days and cross quarter days lend the narrative a temporal framework.[84] Saint Patrick tells Eógan that he is welcome to stay with him 'from the Eve of *Samain* to the Eve of *Belltaine*';[85] such references reflect the fact that 'the primitive Church had already accepted and assimilated a large part of the pre-Christian sacred calendar'.[86] The true quarters or head festivals feature as much as the crooked quarters or cross quarter days, those marking the cosmic cycle of solstices and equinoxes. Among the taboos (*gessa*) of Finn, for example, we may instance: 'Not to sleep with Sadb on summer's shortest night,/Not to travel to Slievenamon at the fires of *Belltaine*'.[87] Often these divisions of the year are

cf. Stokes, 'Acallamh', ll. 776–7: *Aibinn in tech ina tá . idir fira is maca is mná/idir dhruidh ocus aes ceoil . idir dháiliumh is doirseoir.* **80** Dooley and Roe, *Tales*, p. 27; cf. Stokes, 'Acallamh', ll. 820–4: *Is and sin ro faie[s]tar in lánamain sin ar feis leaptha 7 láimhdheraighthi, 7 do bátar ann re secht laithib ag ól 7 ag áibhnes gan esbaidh bhidh ná leanna ná lesaighthe oraind acht mad imnedh ele a(r Finn) .i. allmhuraigh do bheith ac Finntráigh.* **81** Dooley and Roe, *Tales*, p. 101; cf. Stokes, 'Acallamh', ll. 3354–5: *d'foglaim fessa 7 fireolais 7 scelaigechta 7 morgnim gaiscid na Féinne ó Chailti.* **82** Dooley and Roe, *Tales*, p. 130; cf. Stokes, 'Acallamh', ll. 4619–21: *do reir a hindisti do choiteldais fir gonta rissin ceol sirrachtach sidhi dorinde dóib.* **83** Dooley and Roe, *Tales*, p. 106; cf. Stokes, 'Acallamh', ll. 3482–6: *'acht muna beth sianargan in brechta sidhe inti, 7 nocho n[f]uil ní bo chosmala re céol Rig nime inas acht muna beth sin'. 'Matá ceol a nim ... cid nach biad i talmain, 7 ní cóir amlaid ind airfited do dichur' ... 'acht gan rochreidim dó'.* **84** See K. Danaher, 'Irish folk tradition and the Celtic calendar' in R. O'Driscoll (ed.), *The Celtic consciousness* (1981), pp 217–42 at p. 217. **85** Dooley and Roe, *Tales*, p. 106; cf. Stokes, 'Acallamh', ll. 3496–7: *o aídchi tšamna co haídchi belltaine.* **86** Eliade, 'Survivals and camouflages of myths', p. 37. **87** Dooley

the temporal gateways through which the dead and the living pass. Themes of death, rebirth, purification and sacrality are played out during these intervals and interstices. If the *síd* is central, then *Samain*, 'the dead centre of time', is central to the *síd*.[88] Mac Cana tells us that *Samain* 'was charged with peculiar preternatural energy'.[89] Dismissing the 'end of summer' explanation for the term as a folk etymology, Black, drawing upon Whitley Stokes, suggests that it simply means 'a feast or assembly'.[90] The centrality of the feast with its core ancestral significance emphasises the enduring non-Christian indigenous visions of creation that Eliade calls 'cosmic religion'. During *Samain*, the cosmic rhythms and reverberations are felt, the echoes of primordial chaos and cataclysms are heard, and the rites and gestures of consecration are re-enacted repeatedly. In this, you can sense how 'reality manifests itself as force, effectiveness and duration. Hence the outstanding reality is the sacred; for only the sacred *is* in an absolute fashion, acts effectively, creates things and makes them endure'.[91] It is the centre of the stage where almost all action unfolds, and where almost all acts and actions take effect. When Cainén asks Caílte who was killed at the battle of *Samain* he replies that Eochaid died and that Cormac Cas was injured. His injury lasted for thirteen years, with his brain leaking only to be treated in Dún Trí Liag. Aillén, of the Túatha Dé Danann, repeating the mythical example, comes from the north each year to Tara with his dulcimer and puts everyone to sleep. He comes each year at the festival of *Samain* and '[a]ll fell asleep from the magical sound that he made, and he then blew out his breath and sent out a pillar of fire from his mouth'.[92] He does this for twenty-three years. Other references to *Samain* abound: at the grave of Berrach Brecc, Caílte recalls that sages were hosted in her house 'from the Monday of the beginning of *Samain* to the Monday of the beginning of *Imbolc*';[93] this pattern resembles the institution of *céilí*, *scoraíocht*, *cuartaíocht* or rambling house, which lasted from '*Samhain* to *Bealtaine*' or from Halloween to May. And again, Queen Medb of Ulster Cycle fame is said to have come each year during the festival of *Samain* to consult her druids and poets.[94] And a final example: Caílte narrates the story of the Rock of the Weapons 'on which the *Fían* used to sharpen their weapons each year on the day of *Samain*'.[95]

and Roe, *Tales*, p. 87 (not in Stokes, 'Acallamh').   **88** S. Muller, 'Samhain: the dead centre of time', *Sinsear*, 5 (1988), 88–99. See also D. Ó hÓgáin, 'Time', *The lore of Ireland* (2006), p. 472. **89** P. Mac Cana, *Celtic mythology* (1983), p. 127.   **90** R. Black, 'The Gaelic calendar months: some meanings and derivations', *Shadow*, 2, i (1985), 3–13 at 10.   **91** Eliade, *The myth of the eternal return*, p. 11.   **92** Dooley and Roe, *Tales*, p. 52; cf. Stokes, 'Acallamh', ll. 1667–8: *do chodladais cách risin ceol sídhi donith, 7 do šéidedh a anáil fon cairche teinedh.*   **93** Dooley and Roe, p. 65; cf. Stokes, 'Acallamh', ll. 2108–9: *ó luan taite tšamhna co tait[e] n-imbuilg.*   **94** Dooley and Roe, p. 116; Stokes, 'Acallamh', ll. 3863–4: *fa lith laithe na sámna ticed d'acallaim a druad 7 a filed.*   **95** Dooley and Roe, *Tales*, p. 125; cf. Stokes, 'Acallamh', ll. 4465–6: *[in chloch] risa meildis in fiann a n-airm il-laithe na samhna cacha bliadna.*

The description of Slievenamon is worth quoting at length.[96] We are led to believe that the temptation for Caílte to enter was immense as he observed the Otherworldly opulence:

> co facca in síd solusmor co n-ilar chornn 7 chuach 7 chopan buis 7 banóir ann ... atchonnarc ochtur ar .xx. óclach isindara leith don tigh 7 ben chaem chennálaind ar gualaind gach fir díb, 7 seissiur ingen mín maccaemda mongbuide isin leith aili don tig, 7 tuignech futairli forro go formna a ngualann, 7 ingen mín mongbuide i cathair ar laechlar in tighi, 7 cruit ina laim 7 sí 'ga sefnad 7 'ga sírséinm, 7 cach uair do gabad láid doberthea corrn di co n-ibhed deoch as 7 dobered in corn il-laim ind fír dobered dí hé.

> I saw a great bright *síd* with an abundance of horns and chalices and goblets of crystal and white gold within ... [I] saw twenty-eight warriors on one side of the house and a fair-headed, lovely woman beside each man, and six gentle, young, yellow-haired girls on the other side of the house, with shag mantles on their shoulders. A gentle, yellow-haired woman was sitting in a chair in the centre of the house with a harp in her hand and she played many songs .... Each time a song was sung a horn was given to her. She took a drink from it and returned it into the hand of the man who had given it to her.[97]

The gentle yellow-haired girl referred to is the fawn sent by Donn to bring them to him in defence of the Túatha Dé Danann.[98] The invisible hand of the gods and of the ancestral Otherworld guides them. Although mortal, they continue to behave as though they were immortal.

Irish popular religious belief and practice has therefore some intricate and some surprising connections to the cosmic religiosity or syncretism of early Christianity.[99] Asserting the historicity of Jesus, Finn, the indigenous god, hero and poet foretells the coming of Christianity. In relating the naming of Ferns, having buried Fern, he puts his thumb under his tooth and foresees the arrival of the saint associated with that place, Saint Máedóc. Through indigenous divination, Christianity springs magically and recognisably from the non-Christian. Heroes become gods and saints. *Uisce trí theorann* or much prized 'boundary water' from the meeting of three rivers is found at the con-

96 Storyteller Seán Ó Conaill gives a similar description of an otherworld 'cúirt' in the Fenian narrative entitled 'Faircheallach Fhínn Mhu'Cumhaill' in S. Ó Duilearga (ed.), *Leabhar Sheáin Í Chonaill* (1964), p. 205. 'Youthfulness' in the shape of a voluptuous and scantily clad woman with fair hair awaits them at the door of the 'cave'. The entire *fian* fall in love with her. 97 Stokes, 'Acallamh', ll. 5017–32; trans. from Dooley and Roe, *Tales*, p. 140. 98 Dooley and Roe, *Tales*, p. 142; Stokes, 'Acallamh', ll. 5103–4. 99 S. Ó Cadhla, *The holy well tradition* (2002), p. 35; M. MacNeill, *The festival of Lughnasa* (1982).

fluence of the Shannon, Nore and Barrow, where Moling Lúath and Cellach Bráenbile live. Finn notes the healing power of the water, 'the first water in Ireland that the angels of God blessed and the last water in Ireland still to be blessed'.[100] After the fort is destroyed, he foretells the coming of four chosen seers, among them Moling, the saint associated with Suibne Geilt.[101] Popular tradition later interpreted the hypocoristic form Moling as *mo ling*, 'my leaper', sometimes understood as a shamanic spirit embarking on a vision quest similar to the figure of Suibne himself.[102] Interestingly, Ó Riain traces the name Moling back to that of the non-Christian divinity Lug, possibly indexing the pre-Christian festival of Lugnasad.[103] It is there that Finn envisages his own resting place, an interesting end given Finn's affinity, if not oneness, with Lug.[104]

In the end, as Caílte finally falters, the questions grow a little more personal. He gives a final account of Finn, 'the most generous man in the north-western part of the world at giving treasures and wealth and valuables', who listened to the music of the *síd* and the humming of the *fian*.[105] A steadfast ally of Saint Patrick, he uncharacteristically leaves his side early in the tale, apparently restless at the sedentary life of the clerics. He goes '[t]o search out the hills and mounds and the heights where my companions and foster-brothers, the prince-warriors and nobles of the *Fían* once were with me, for I am tired of being in one place'.[106] The hills and mounds beloved of the *fian* are to be replaced by the crosses, penitential stations and altars of Christianity. The nativist hankering is emblematic of the *fian*; it haunts Caílte as upon '[e]very hill and mound and fort he would wander by, it seemed to him that two or three or four or five or a band of the *Fían* would appear, but they were only empty hills and smooth, level plains with no hound or boy or warrior on them'.[107] The *Acallam* is an archaic survey, a vernacular exegesis of Christian and non-Christian in which valuable knowledge is abstracted, generalised, streamlined, recontextualised and integrated into the personal memories of Caílte and Oisín. Ultimately, the ancestors, the denizens of the

---

100 Dooley and Roe, *Tales*, p. 81; cf. Stokes, 'Acallamh', ll. 2644–5: *Is é sin cétuisci ro bennachadur aingil Dé a nEirinn, 7 iss é uisce déidinach béos [bendeochar inti].*   101 Pilgrimages to the well of Saint Moling continue on 17th June and on the Feast of Saint James (25th July). 102 Ó hÓgáin, *The lore of Ireland*, pp 352–3.   103 P. Ó Riain, *A dictionary of Irish saints* (2011), p. 488.   104 For discussion, see E. MacNeill and G. Murphy, *Duanaire Finn*, iii, pp lxxi–lxxxv. 105 Dooley and Roe, *Tales*, p. 184; cf. Stokes, 'Acallamh', ll. 6554–5: *in lam thoirberta sét 7 maíni 7 indmusa iarthair thuaiscirt in betha.* Accounts of the hospitality and conviviality of the Otherworld are mirrored in popular sentiment and expressions. For example, Tomás Ó Criomhthain uses the popular expression: *Tá an ceol sí ar siúl* ('The fairy music has started') when the evening entertainment on a market day had begun to intensify: see S. Ó Coileáin (ed.), *An tOileánach* (2002), p. 133.   106 Dooley and Roe, *Tales*, p. 46; cf. Stokes, 'Acallamh', ll. 1488–90: *'D'iarraid cnoc 7 céite 7 dingnadh in bhaili ir-rabutar mu choicli 7 mu chomaltada 7 in flaithfénnid 7 maithi Fian Eirenn am fochair, ór is fada lim beith a n-aein inad'.*   107 Dooley and Roe, *Tales*, p. 102 (not in Stokes, 'Acallamh').

síd, give Caílte a drink that stimulates and revives his memory, enabling him to remember the past. This expresses the value placed upon knowledge, memory, and recollection as rites of consecration and inscription in themselves.[108] The final *universitas* in Tara confers the sage-ship on Cas Corach while ostensibly putting the rest of the Túatha Dé Danann into the steep slopes of hills and rocks.[109] It is about here that the modern storyteller takes up the story.

APPENDIX

ACALLAM NA SENÓRACH: QUESTIONNAIRE

A selection of significant questions and requests as they appear in
Ann Dooley and Harry Roe, *Tales of the elders of Ireland*

1 Was Finn mac Cumaill, your former lord, a good man? (Patrick)
2 What has kept you warriors alive for all these years? (P.)
3 Were there drinking-horns or goblets, or cups of crystal and shining gold in the houses in which you stayed in the old days? (P.)
4 Did you in the *Fían* have horses and chariot-teams? (P.)
5 Where were they acquired? (P.)
6 Was Goll the son of a king? (P.)
7 Tell us the names of the nobles and warriors who had these horses. (P.)
8 Do you know why you have all been brought to speak with me? (P.)
9 What was the best hunt, whether in Ireland or Scotland, that the *Fían* ever took part in? (P.)
10 Where is that place? (P.)
11 Who lived there then? (P.)
12 How did they acquire such a great estate? (P.)
13 Where do these (nuts and apples) come from, young man? (P.)
14 What is your name? (P.)
15 What is your inheritance? (P.)
16 Whom do you plunder? (P.)
17 What time of day is it now? (P.)
18 Has our dinner not yet arrived? (P.)
19 How many brothers did Finn have? (P.)
20 Who were the parents of Mac Lugach? (P.)
21 Were there musicians with the *Fían*? (P.)
22 (The best musician in Ireland and Scotland), what was his name? (P.)
23 Where did you find him? (P.)
24 What did he look like? (P.)
25 Where do you young men come from? (P.)
26 Why is the hill on which we stand called Fair Hill? (P.)

108 Dooley and Roe, *Tales*, p. 203; Stokes, 'Acallamh', ll. 7258–61.   109 Dooley and Roe, *Tales*, p. 210; Stokes, 'Acallamh', ll. 7533–7.

27 Who are you, young man?/Why have you come here? (P. to Bran)
28 What is your method of hunting? (Caílte to Bran)
29 What is the stronghold in which we find ourselves? (C.)
30 For what reason did Oscar fight his first battle? (P.)
31 Whose grave lies on the hill on which we are standing? (P.)
32 Who is buried in the southern end of this mound? (P. to C.)
33 What caused the destruction of all your *Fían*? (P. to C.)
34 Where did Ailill Ólomm, 'the Bare-Eared', the son of Mug Núadat die? (Cainén)
35 Where did Sadb, daughter of Conn, die? (Cainén)
36 Where did Ferchis the Poet, son of Comán, die? (Cainén)
37 The seven handsome sons of Ailill, where did they die? (Cainén)
38 Why is the ford on this great, level plain called the Ford of the Fall? (Cainén)
39 And the battle of Samain, who perished there? (Cainén)
40 Why is this fort called the Fort of Glas? (Muiredach)
41 Why is it called Almu? (Muiredach)
42 Tell us another story. (P.)
43 Did all the *Fían* believe in the King of Heaven and Earth, or did you know of his existence at all? (P.)
44 What destruction was this? (P.)
45 What wood is that? (P.)
46 Did Díarmait have sons? (Flann)
47 How is your life with the family of your mother? (C.)
48 Who of the *Fían* lies in the earthen mound on which we sit? (C.)
49 Against whom did you ride that quick and difficult race? (C.)
50 What house did we spend that night in? (Derg to C.)
51 Did we give anything to him? (Derg to C.)
52 Who gave the black horse to Finn? (Derg)
53 Was there anyone in the *Fían* as skilful with weapons as you? (Áed)
54 Tell us what spear this is, and which man of the *Fíana* of Ireland owned it? (Ilbrecc)
55 Which opponent in the battle is the most troublesome one for you? (C.)
56 Where did Finn find belief, or did he ever? (Ilbrecc)
57 Where did he find it and how did he find it? (Ilbrecc)
58 What destroyed or carried off that wealth? (C.)
59 Tell me the real reason why he was killed? (Donn to C.)
60 For what reason is this cairn called the Cairn of Garb Daire? (Conall to C.)
61 Who lies in this grave? (Conall to C.)
62 Who were these four women? (Conall to C.)
63 Why was she killed? (Conall to C.)
64 For what reason, dear Caílte, has this shore been named 'the Shore of Conbec'? (Conall to C.)
65 Were those four men who lived in Ireland at the same time, Cormac, son of Art, Finn, Cairbre Lifechair, and Oisín, noble men? (P.)
66 Was Cormac a better man than Finn, and was Cairbre better than Oisín? (Díarmait)
67 Why is it that Finn and his *Fían* never killed the great beast that lives in the

Valley of the Forest of the Fowling in the south, when you cleared Ireland of all other monsters? (Eochaid)

68 Why did the *Fían* come to that lake where they and their hounds were killed by the beast? (Eochaid)

69 How many kings of Ireland gave land to the *Fían*? (Eochaid)

70 What caused the destruction of hunting in the Pine Forest of Finn? (Finn)

71 Why is the ford on the floor of the Pine Forest called the Ford of Fern [Ferns]? (Finn)

72 Who held that fortress there (in the Forest of Badgers)? (Finn)

73 Why is this fortress called Ráth Artrach, 'the Fort of Artrach'; and why is the fort in the north called Ráth Mongaig 'the Fort of Mongach', and why is this enclosure in the south called Les na nÉices 'the Enclosure of the Poets'? (Conall)

74 There are three hills near us and we have no knowledge of the names that they bear. One of them is called the Tomb of the Warriors, another the Mound of the Womenfolk, and the third is called the Tomb of the Boys. There is a spring on that hill and a river flows from it that is called the Stream of the Men. (Conall).

75 Why is this lake called the Lake of the Red Stag? (Colmán)

76 What is the reason for those eight hours for which you arise both day and night? (C. to Colmán)

77 Why is the spring at the end of the lake called the Spring of the Company of Women? (Colmán)

78 What better thing could we ask of you than the lore connected with this fort of Áine? (Eochaid)

79 There are two graves here on the Dundrum Bay. What is their history? (Eochaid)

80 Who is the woman to whom honour and dignity is given beyond all others? (C. to Eochaid)

81 Do you know who the four men of greatest generosity were in Ireland and Scotland? (C. to Eochaid)

82 Why is ... [this mound] called the Mound of the Three, and why is this river called Abann Déisi, 'the River of a Pair', and that place over there the Tomb of the Head of a Hound? (Eochaid)

83 Can you tell us who was in this place before Eógan? (P.)

84 How did that Conán die? (P.)

85 What better thing could I ask than the reason why this cairn is called the Cairn of the Seduction of the Wife of the Son of Lir and for what reason is it called the Cairn of Manannán? (Áed)

86 Which of the *Fían* lived in this place? (P.)

87 Why is one wave called the Wave of Clidna, and why is the other called the Wave of Téite? (Corc)

88 What is the name this field, Caílte? (P.)

89 Why is this valley to the north called the Valley of the Hag? (P.)

90 Why is this hill called the Height of Senach, dear Caílte? (P.)

91 Did he give such wealth to many women? (P.)

92 Tell us, dear Caílte, why this place is named the Rough Washing? (P.)

93 What is your name? (P.)

94 What is the fortress that we see yonder? (P.)

95 Why does he (Coscrach na Cét) have that name? (P.)

96 Why is this mighty stone here on the lawn called the Rock of the Weapons?
    (Coscrach)

97 Can you tell us why this spring here in front of the fort is called the Spring of
    Scáthderg? (Eochaid)

98 Tell us of the hosts and multitudes that the lake-monster of the Lake of Lurgu
    drowned. (Eochaid)

99 Why is this hill called the Mound of Mál and the one to the north called the
    Mound of Aífe? (Eochaid)

100 Great are the two forts, my dear Caílte; who dwelt in them? (Eochaid)

101 Why is that hill over there called the Height of Cúanaide and this one here the
    Height of Cuillenn? (Eochaid)

102 Why is this hill here called the Height of the Hindering of the *Fían*? (Eochaid)

103 For what reason was this stone called the Stone of the Hundreds? (Eógan)

104 For what reason was this little fort called the Fort of the Wonders? (Eógan)

105 For what reason was this fort called the Fort of the Dog's-Head and this enclo-
    sure called the Enclosure of the Company of Women? (Eógan)

106 Why is this fort called the Fort of the Company of Women? (Eógan)

107 What is the very strong pillar of stone yonder in the middle of the rampart? (Eógan)

108 What are those two great graves that we see? (Eógan)

109 What is the high pole at the side of the pillar there in the fort? (Eógan)

110 Why is this place called the White Peak of the Run? (Eógan)

111 Why was this place called Callann and Cuillenn and the hill yonder called the
    Grave of the Youth, and why is this rampart that is surrounding the land and
    territory called the Rampart of the *Fían*? (Eógan)

112 Why is this place called the Oakwood of the Conspiracy and why is this ridge
    called the Ridge of the Dead Woman, and why is this little fort in front of us to
    the south called the Little Fort of the Incantation? (Eógan)

113 For what reason is this place called the Grave of Fíadmór, and why is this hill in
    the west called the Hill of Circall, and the hill next to it called the Hill of
    Congna? (Áed)

114 Where did Finn mac Cumaill come from? (Áed)

115 [From] what tribe of Leinster? (Áed)

116 From what place in that tribe? (Áed)

117 Who were the members of the regular *Fían*? (Áed)

118 Why is this place called the Meadow of Stags and for what reason was it named
    the Meadow of Shame? (Áed)

119 What are these two forts that we are in? (Áed)

120 Why is this place called the Thicket of Witches? (Áed)

121 There are three great rocks at one end of my farm and they are called the Pillars
    of the Three. We do not know what women or men are under them or why they
    have this name. (Blathmac)

122 Why is this enclosure called the Enclosure of the Women? (Blathmac)

123 What are these three forts? (C.)

124 Why is this cairn called the Cairn of the Kin-Slaying, and why is this mound
    outside called the Barrow of the Hounds? (Échna)

125 Who is the best man that ever came from Collamair of Brega? (C.)
126 What are your own tales and adventures from the time I left you until today? (C. to Patrick)
127 Why is this stone called the Stone of the Mistake? (Áed)
128 Can anyone tell us where Finn's cup lies? (Oisín in verse)
129 Can anyone tell us who put Currach's head on the hill by Badamair?
130 Who struck Goll, son of Morna, that morning above the Gowran Pass? (O.)
131 Who killed Cairbre Lifeachair, son of Cormac, in the battle of Gabair? (Díarmait)
132 And Oscar then, who killed him? (Díarmait)
133 And Mac Lugach, who killed him in the battle? (Díarmait)
134 What wonder was on the Stone of Fál? (Díarmait)

Aonghus Ó Callanáin, Leabhar Leasa Móir agus an *Agallamh bheag*

PÁDRAIG Ó MACHÁIN

Foinse luachmhar is ea gach aon lámhscríbhinn Ghaeilge, moch agus déanach, ní hamháin d'eolas ar litríocht na Gaeilge, ach d'eolas chomh maith ar na daoine a chleachtaigh agus a chaomhnaigh í ó thosach deireadh an traidisiúin. Ó leabhar go chéile, déantar sainmhíniú mionchúrsach as an nua, arís agus arís eile, ar an rud is litríocht na Gaeilge ann, agus deintear léiriú ar an gcóngas idir an téacs agus fear a sheachadta. Ach tuiscint agus foighne a chaitheamh leis na foinsí seo, níl teora leis an méid is féidir a chur lenár n-eolas ar chleachtadh na litríochta in gach aon tréimhse dár stair.

Ó tháinig ann do dhigitiú a dhéanamh ar chuid de na foinsí seo le breis agus deich mbliana anuas, tá curtha go bunúsach lenár gcumas an saghas seo staidéir a dhéanamh. Nuair a léiríodh na leathanaigh agus na duilleoga de Leabhar Leasa Móir (LLM feasta) ar an gcuma seo don gcéad uair sa mbliain 2012 ar shuíomh idirlín Irish Script on Screen (www.isos.dias.ie), ní haon bhréag é a rá gur cuireadh an dé athuair i lámhscríbhinn shuaithinseach de chuid an chúigiú haois déag, saothar nach raibh oiread sin tráchta déanta air go dtí sin i gcomórtas lena raibh de phlé déanta ar leabhair a bhí comhaoiseach leis a bheag nó a mhór. Is as an obair sin ar LLM a d'eascair an aiste seo a tiomnaítear do dhuine de na scoláirí agus na fir teagaisc is mó a bhain riamh le contae dúchais na lámhscríbhinne seo.

Meas.tar gur lámhscríbhinn í LLM a cuireadh le chéile i gceantar Thigh Molaige agus Cill Bhriotáin do Mhac Carthaigh Riabhach, Fínghean mac Diarmada, a bhí ina cheann fine *c.*1478–1505.[1] Lasmuigh de bheagán peannaireachta ó scríobhaithe eile thall is abhus, obair aon phríomhscríobhaí amháin atá le sonrú ar LLM don gcuid is mó, agus fágann sin go bhfuil sé le háireamh ar na scríobhaithe is mó saothar sa tréimhse seo, ar an bhfianaise a mhaireann inniu againn pé scéal é. Cé nach eol dúinn a ainm siúd, is eol dúinn ainm scríobhaí amháin den mbeagán eile a chuaigh i bpáirt leis tamall gairid. B'é sin Aonghus Ó Callanáin, a scrígh aon cheann déag de dhuilleoga: 132–4, 194–201. Lasmuigh d'obair Aonghusa, agus de scríobhaí an dáin d'Fhínghean ar dhuilleog 158 (féach thíos), níl ach saothrú scríobhaithe faoisimh le feiscint sa leabhar.

Ní féidir comhdhéanamh LLM a bheachtú inniu, ráite nach bhfuarthas ach duilleoga aonaránacha nuair a deineadh an Leabhar a dhícheangal i lár na

---

1 B. Ó Cuív, 'A poem for Fínghin Mac Carthaigh Riabhach', *Celtica*, 15 (1983), 96–110 ag 96–7.

haoise seo caite,[2] a bhuíochas sin ar lucht ceangail an Leabhair sa naoú haois
déag. Fós féin, is dóichí gur ina stuanna ocht nduilleog a cuireadh an leabhar
le chéile don gcéad uair, nó, ar a laghad, gurbh é sin an bunord a chuir lucht
a dhéanta rompu, dála lámhscríbhinní eile na haimsire sin. Is féidir a áiteamh,
leis, gur iarracht ar chnuasach de mhórtheacsaí a sholáthar, stua ar stua, atá i
leagan amach na lámhscríbhinne. Is dá chomhartha sin na hardlitreacha a
chuireann tús – ar *recto* na nduilleog, agus ag barr an chéad cholúin, níos
minicí ná a mhalairt – le gach téacs acu sin.

Gné is ea í seo a thugann ar dhuine breithniú ar LLM mar leabharlann
so-iompair seachas leabhar socair do-athraithe. Is é is brí leis sin ná go
mbeadh ar chumas duine stua a bhaint den 'leabhar' chun ábhar an stua sin
a léamh nó a scrúdú, agus é a chur thar n-ais ar ball, gan aon díobháil a
dhéanamh don lámhscríbhinn. Ba dhóigh liom go bhféadfaí é seo a thabhairt
fé ndeara ar lámhscríbhinní eile a bhain leis an ré seo chomh maith, ach iad
a scrúdú i gceart: is áirithe, mar shampla, gur tuairisc ar chnuasach de stuanna éagsúla, seachas ar leabhair aonair, atá i gcuid ar a laghad den liosta dá
raibh de leabhair i leabharlann Iarla Chill Dara sa mbliain 1526.[3]

Ní hionann an t-áiteamh seo agus beag is fiú a dhéanamh d'iarrachtaí ar
chiall a bhaint as na cineálacha éagsúla uimhríochta atá le tabhairt fé ndeara
ar leathanaigh LLM,[4] ach gur deacair a shéanadh go bhfuil ord leathan
téamúil sa leagan amach atá ar an leabhar mar atá anois. An stua (132–9) a
bhfuil lámh Aonghusa le feiscint air don gcéad uair, mar shampla, is stua é a
chuireann tús le léiriú a dhéanamh sa leabhar ar an rud is ríogacht ann, tré
scata téacsaí a thabhairt le chéile a bhaineann, don gcuid is mó, le Diarmaid
mac Cearbhaill, Rí Éireann (†565), pearsa thábhachtach sa scéalaíocht a
bhaineann le tréimhse na luath-Chríostaíochta. Duine de shinsir Í Néill an
Deiscirt ab ea Diarmaid, agus ní haon chúram ginealaigh ó thaobh na
gCarthach de, go bhfios dom, atá laistiar dá chraobh siúd de scéalaíocht na
ríthe a roghnú le cur in LLM. Agus an bhaint a bhí aige le Feis Teamhra
agus leis an luath-Chríostaíocht, caithfidh gur measadh gurbh í a chraobh siúd
ab oiriúnaí agus ab eiseamláirí chun gnéithe áirithe de ríogacht agus de sheanchas na hÉireann a chur i láthair.[5]

---

2 R.A.S. Macalister, *The Book of Mac Carthaigh Riabhach otherwise The Book of Lismore* (1950),
lch xiii: 'the folios are now entirely detached, nowhere paired in diplomas'. Bhí sé seo ar aon
dul leis an droch-íde a tugadh do Leabhar na hUidhre: R. Powell, 'Further notes on Lebor na
hUidre', *Ériu*, 21 (1969), 99–102 ag 99.   **3** J.T. Gilbert, *Facsimiles of national manuscripts of
Ireland*, iii (1879), §LXIII; S.H. O'Grady, *Catalogue of Irish manuscripts in the British Museum*,
i (1926), lgh 154–5.   **4** Macalister, *The Book of Mac Carthaigh Riabhach*, lgh xii–xv; B. Ó Cuív,
'Observations on the Book of Lismore', *Proceedings of the Royal Irish Academy*, 83C (1983), 269–
92.   **5** 'Diarmait mac Cerbaill was the last to hold the sacral kingship of Tara. He has also
some title to be ranked as the first Christian high-king of Ireland': F.J. Byrne, *Irish kings and
high-kings* (1973), lch 104. Ní bheadh sé as an áireamh ach oiread go mbeadh caolbhaint ag
athair Fhínghin Mheic Carthaigh a bheith ina Dhiarmaid le Diarmaid mac Cearbhaill a roghnú.

Is féidir suimiú a dhéanamh ar a bhfuil sa stua seo ar an gcuma seo leanas:[6]

132ra1. [Suidiugad teallaig Temra] Críochnaíonn ag 134rb35.

134rb36. [Interrogatio Cinnfháelad] Stadann gan chríoch ag bun an leathanaigh, agus tosnaíonn arís gan bhearna ag 134vb14. Críochnaíonn ag bun 134vb.

134va1. [An Agallamh bheag] Stadann gan chríoch 134vb13. (Tosnaítear an téacs as an nua arís 194r). Maidir leis an dtéacs ó 134vb14 go bun leathanaigh, féach 134rb36 thuas.

135ra1. [Scéal ar Aodh Baclámh agus Diarmaid mac Cearbhaill] Críochnaíonn ag 136rb32.

*136rb33. *Olc bith. arupta. daora fir. saora mna.* 5 líne.

*136rb.y. *Nochu chill acht fuath cilli.* 1 rann.

136va1. [Aided Bresail] Críochnaíonn ag 136va33.

136va34. [Achoimre ar Chath Cúil Dreimhne] Críochnaíonn ag 136vb27.

136vb28. [Achoimre ar Aided Diarmada] Críochnaíonn ag 137ra.z.

137rb1. 'Dubh da Thuath dixit'. *Damad mheisi budh ri reil.* 28 rann.

137va8. *Ceart gach righ co reil.* 60 rann.

*137vb.y. *Toirrsi nocha maith in modh.* 1 rann.

138ra1. [Airne Fíngein] Críochnaíonn ag 139vb33.

*139vb34. [Téacs gairid ar Arastotal] Críochnaíonn ag 139vb.z.

Sa tuairisc thuas, tá réiltín curtha le téacsaí beaga áirithe nach bhfuil d'fheidhm leothu ach an leathanach a líonadh amach agus gan meamram a chur amú. Chomh maith leis na téacsaí forlíonaidh sin, is é gnás na lámhscríbhinne seo go líontar amach leathanaigh, duilleoga agus stuanna le téacsaí tánaisteacha nuair nach mbíonn fáil ar mhórtheacsaí eile, nó díreach ar mhaithe le oiriúnú a dhéanamh do na mórtheacsaí céanna chun go dtosnóidís san áit inar mhian leis an scríobhaí. Aithnítear na mórthéacsaí ó na téacsaí tánaisteacha agus na téacsaí forlíonaidh ar bhonn pailéagrafaíochta le húsáid mhórlitreacha tosaigh ar na mórtheacsaí, nó tríd an spás a fágadh do na litreacha sin. Is iad na mórtheacsaí a measadh a chur sa stua seo, mar sin, ná an *Suidiugad*, *An Agallamh bheag* (*AB* feasta), scéal Aodha Baclámh, agus *Airne Fíngein*. Dob fhéidir a rá, leis, gurb iad sin príomhscéalta na ríogachta sa stua so, fé mar a tuigeadh don dá scríobhaí iad i dtosach báire pé scéal é. I stuanna eile thabharfaí fé ghnéithe den ríogacht a bhain, mar shampla, le cearta dlí (140ra: *Leabhar na gceart*), nó le seanchas a ghaibh go dlúth le ríogacht sinsir na gCarthach (148ra: *Caithréim Cheallacháin Chaisil*).[7] I stua Dhiarmada mic

6 Gheofar cuntas níos mine ag Macalister, *The Book of Mac Carthaigh Riabhach*, lgh xvi–xxv, agus ó údar an ailt seo ar shuíomh idirlín ISOS (www.isos.dias.ie), mar a bhfuil an leagan leictreonach den lámhscríbhinn le fáil.   7 D. Ó Corráin, 'Nationality and kingship in pre-Norman

Cearbhaill áfach, nó stua Ua Néill, más ceadaithe é sin a thabhairt air, díríodh ar réamhstair agus luathstair na nGael. I gcur i láthair na gcúrsaí sin, chítear bonn eile comónta idir cuid de na téacsaí ar a laghad.

Stua é seo atá roinnte ó thaobh peannaireachta de idir Aonghus (132–4) agus an príomhscríobhaí gan ainm (135–9). Dhá théacs a bhí i gceist ag Aonghus a chur sa stua. An chéad cheann ná *Suidiugad teallaig Temra*, cuntas ar conas a deineadh leagadh amach ar na cúigí in aimsir Dhiarmada.[8] In insint Fhiontain mhic Bhóchra do Dhiarmaid sa téacs sin ar a chúlra agus a cháilíochtaí féin i gcomhair na hoibre seo, tá achoimre chonláisteach ar stair na hÉireann roimh Chríost anuas go glacadh na comaoineach ag Fiontan agus a bhás i bhfianaise 'spirat Pátraic 7 Brigde'.[9] Breithníodh coitianta ar aimsir Dhiarmada mar an uair inar deineadh sean-stair na hÉireann a bhreacadh ó Fhiontan,[10] mar gurbh é a bhí 'ag coiméad hseanchusa na hErenn o aimsir dhílend go flaitheas Diarmada meic Cearbhaill'.[11] Suimiú ar ábhar Leabhair Ghabhála atá i gcuid den dtéacs seo, mar sin, agus mara raibh i gceist Leabhar Gabhála féin a chur sa lámh-scríbhinn – agus é ina bhuntéacs d'oiread sin lámhscríbhinní móra meamraim na haimsire sin, Leabhar Fhear Maighe (leabhar a bhfuil gaol aige le LLM) ina dteannta[12] – níorbh aon drochionadaí é eachtraíocht Fhiontain mhic Bhóchra mar atá sa *Suidiugad*. Cuimhnímís ar a thugtha a bhí na Gaeil i gcónaí d'aon suimiú ar an stair a tháinig chúchu i bhfoirm fhileata go háirithe, agus i ré na Nua-Ghaeilge féin dob fheidir cás 'Tuireamh na hÉireann' a lua mar shampla.[13] I ndeireadh an scéil, i bhfoirm aguisín agus i malairt dúigh (féach thíos), tá téacs gaolmhar curtha leis an *Suidiugad*: ceistiú Fhiontain ag Ceannfhaoladh (*Interrogatio Cinnfháelad*). Tosnaíonn Aonghus an t-aguisín seo ag duilleog 134rb36, leanann go deireadh an leathanaigh (deich líne ar fad), agus tosnaíonn arís gairid do lár an dara colún ar *verso* na duilleoige sin (134vb14) agus cuirtear críoch leis ('Finitt') ag deireadh na duilleoige.[14] Idir tús agus leanúint an aguisín sin (134va1–vb13) is ea a faightear an dara téacs a bhí i gceist ag Aonghus a chur sa stua, agus gan é ach ina mhírín aige; sin é an téacs ar baisteadh an 'Agallamh bheag' air agus a pléifear thíos ar ball.

An chéad téacs sa stua mar sin, agus an t-aguisín a cuireadh leis, is seanchas atá iontu a foilsítear i bhfoirm cheist agus freagra – saghas agallmha go deimhin

---

Ireland' in T.W. Moody (eag.), *Nationality and the pursuit of national independence* (1978), lgh 1–35 ag lch 31: 'a paradigm in saga-form of the ideal relationship between a king and his vassal lords'.   8 R.I. Best (eag. agus aistr.), 'The settling of the manor of Tara', *Ériu*, 4 (1908–10), 121–72.   9 Ibid., 160.   10 R.A.S. Macalister (eag. agus aistr.), *Lebor gabála Érenn*, v (1956), lch 24.   11 Leabharlann Náisiúnta na hÉireann LS G 1, duilleog 46r–v.   12 P. Ó Macháin, '"A llebraib imdaib": cleachtadh agus pátrúnacht an léinn, agus déanamh na lámhscríbhinní' in R. Ó hUiginn (eag.), *Léachtaí Cholm Cille, 34: Oidhreacht na lámhscríbhinní* (2004), lgh 148–78 ag lch 159.   13 Féach fianaise 'Friar O'Sullivan of Muckross' in C. O'Rahilly (eag.), *Five seven-teenth-century political poems* (1952), lch 58.   14 Mheas Best, 'The settling of the manor of Tara', 122, 164, go raibh an téacs seo gan chríoch in LLM mar níor thug fé ndeara gur lean ar aghaidh ar an *verso*.

– don gcuid is mó, seanchas a bhaineann le cuid de stair na hÉireann a bhí
ceilte ar dhaoine go dtí sin ach a bhí i seilbh dhuine amháin a tháinig slán ar
slí mhíorúilteach ón seanaimsir. Más mian linn tuiscint níos fearr a fháil ar
leanúnachas agus eagar an ábhair seo an stua, ní gá dúinn ach aghaidh a thabhairt ar an dtéacs deiridh ann, *Airne Fíngein*.[15] Téacs é seo a bhaineann le teacht
ar an saol do Chonn Céadchathach, agus na hiontaisí go léir a nochtadh an
oíche chéanna, chomh maith leis an réimeas torthúil a lean sin. Tréimhse go
maith níos luaithe ná Diarmaid mac Cearbhaill é sin, ach fós tá ceangal ag *Airne
Fíngein* leis an *Suidiugad* sa mhéid go bhfuil filleadh bua na cainte ar Fhiontan
mac Bóchra ar iontaisí na hoíche sin, bua a chaill sé ar chlos 'tondgur na dílenn
dó'.[16] Sa scéal seo, foilsíonn bean sí faisnéis ar an seanaimsir agus ar an aimsir
láithreach d'Fhíngen mac Luchta, Oíche Shamhna i nDruim Fhíngin in oirth-
ear Déise, nuair a théann sé chun coinne bhliantúil a choimeád lé: 'Baí ben
shíde oca acallaim ar gach samain do grés'.[17] Ar aon dul leis an *Suidiugad*, agallamh is ea *Airne Fíngein*. Rothníam ingen Umaill Urscathaig is ainm don bhean
sí, agus is nasc áirithe eile é sin le chéad scéal an stua seo sa mhéid is go ndeintear amach gur ghiolla de chuid Fiontain mhic Bhóchra ab ea Umall.[18]

Ó thaobh struchtúir de, is é an ceangal is mó idir téacs tosaigh agus téacs
deiridh an stua ná pearsa ó shaol eile a bheith ag foilsiú seanchais dhiamhair
na hÉireann i bhfoirm agallmha do dhuine a bhí dall ar an eolas céanna go dtí
sin. Maidir le *Airne Fíngein* de, is é an seanchas a bhíonn le nochtadh ag
Rothníam d'Fhíngen ná na hiontaisí go léir – mar shampla, 'teóra primaicde
Érenn' agus 'Cóic prímróit hÉrenn' – a thiocfaidh chun solais agus a soiléireó-
far an Oíche Shamhna sin. Is é réimeas Chuinn buaic an scéil, conas a ghlac-
ann Fíngen leis mar Rí Éireann, agus an seoladh foirfe a bhíonn fén dtír agus
Conn sa ríogacht. Ní haon ionadh, mar sin, léamh Dan Wiley ar an eachtra
nuair a áitíonn, ainneoin chomh Muimhneach is atá an scéal, gurb é atá in
Airne Fíngein ná 'one of the clearest and most detailed compendia of Dál
Cuinn propaganda to be produced in the early Christian period'.[19] Is fiú a lua,
áfach, go raibh Conn i gcraobh choibhneasa na gCarthach, mar gur óna iníon,
Sadhbh, bean Oilealla Óluim, a shíolraigh Corc mac Luighdheach.[20]

Tá tuairisc na tíre agus í fé shíocháin agus fé bhláth i réimeas an rí chóir,
mar a fhaighmíd é in *Airne Fíngein*, ar na samplaí is achoimre dá bhfuil againn

15 J. Vendryes (eag.), *Airne Fíngein* (Dublin, 1953).   16 Ibid., ll. 67–87.   17 Ibid., ll. 4–5.
Raon cnoc a bhfuil an phríomhchuid de le feiscint idir Baile na hEaglaise agus Rinn Ó
gCuanach thoir, agus an Aird Mhór ó dheas, is ea Drom Fhínghin, agus is uaidh ainmnítear
barúntachtaí 'Decies within Drum' agus 'Decies without Drum': féach P. Canon Power, *Logainmneacha na nDéise* (1952), lch 67; tamall siar, áfach, i mbaile fearainn an Churraigh Riabhaigh
(paróiste An Leasa Móir) atá an t-ardán ar ar baisteadh 'Drom Fhínghin' (ibid., lch 42).
18 Vendryes, *Airne Fíngein*, lch 28.   19 D.M. Wiley, 'The politics of myth in *Airne Fíngein*' in
J.F. Eska (eag.), *Narrative in Celtic tradition* (2011), lgh 276–87 ag lch 287.   20 M.A. O'Brien
(eag.), *Corpus genealogiarum Hiberniae* (1962), lgh 192 (147b36–9) agus 195 (148a5–24); 'ua
Cuirc' a tugtar ar Fhínghean Mac Carthaigh (rann 32*b*) sa dán a pléitear thíos.

den dtéama coitianta so, téama atá ina bhunmhóitíf i gcodanna eile den
litríocht Ghaelach, go háirithe i bhFilíocht na Scol.[21] Pé ní is cúis leis, níl fáil
ar an gcuid deiridh seo den *Airne* ach in LLM amháin. Is fiú an tuairisc a
thabhairt anso, mar sin. Dá ghiorra agus da achoimre é ba dheacair teacht ar
léiriú ba chruinne ar an dtéama seo:

> Is amlaid íarum buí flaith Chuinn, cen chreich, cen gait, cen chron, cen
> galar, cen chuil, cen chreabhar, cen choirrmil, cen fleochad, cen
> rogháeith, cen tsnechta, acht an tréidhi si namá .i. drúct 7 bráen 7
> céo; cen foche, cen chernuban, acht beich duillebhair Temhrach, cen
> chrann crín, cen écin forsnach nduini, cen iluigh, cen ochlánach, cen
> foréicin, cen duini fo dímaín, cen faire, cen ingairi. Ní raba trá Ere in
> inbuid sin ráithi cin mes, ná aidche cin drúct, ná lá cin tes. Ba húr
> gach coill, ba lán gach abhunn d'iasc ó ro soicht glún. Ní buí gaí ná
> scían ná claidem; eachlosca 7 goithnedha rob airm ann. Ní treabtha
> acht caeicdigius ar mís d'erruch 7 no berta na harbair fo thrí cecha
> blíadnae. For bennuib na mbó congairtis caí cuchaireacht. Cét cróbo-
> ing for slait, cét cnó in cech cróboing, nói ndruimne for cech ndéis,
> lulgacha na láeigh i n-a remes. Ba hé fiach na huinge aircit gil da
> mhíach dhéc do chruithneacht 7 da chúagh déc do mhil; cethra scrib-
> aill fichet méit na huingi ind inbaidh sin, ba sedh no téigedh ar in
> mboin. Ba parrthus indtsamlach agus ba tír tairrngire fo scoithshemair
> meala Ére fo smacht flaithusa Cuinn Chétchathaig.[22]

Thus indeed was the reign of Conn: free from raiding, theft, harm,
disease; from fly, gadfly, midge; from drenching, great wind, snow, but
these three things only: dew, rain and mist; free from wasps, from
hornet, save the bees of the shrubbery of Tara; without a withered
tree; without violence against a person, without triumphant crowing,
without groaning, without oppression; with no person idle; without
guarding, without herding. Ireland then, at that time, was never three
months without produce, or a night without dew, or a day without
heat. Every wood was green, every river was full of fish to the height
of one's knee. There was no spear nor knife nor sword; riding-crops
and goads were the [only] weapons in use. Ploughing used to be done
for only a fortnight each month in spring and three crops of corn used
to be yielded every year. On the horns of cows the cuckoos used to
make their song. [There used to be] one hundred clusters on a branch,
one hundred nuts in each cluster; nine segments on each ear of corn;
calves gave milk in his time. The value of an ounce of silver was
twelve bushels of wheat and twelve goblets of honey; an ounce was

---

21 Mar shamplaí, L. McKenna (eag.), *The Book of Magauran* (1947), dán 3.13–16; D. Greene
(eag.), *Duanaire Mhéig Uidhir* (1972), dán 7.23–7.

worth twenty-four scruples that time, the cost of a cow. Ireland under
the authority of the rule of Conn Céadchathach was akin to paradise
and was a promised land covered with the best of honeysuckle.

Is leis an dtuairisc idéalach sin ar rath na tíre a cuirtear críoch leis an stua seo
de LLM.[23]

Tá comhpháirtí na tuairisce sin, maidir le ráiteas nó sainmhíniú ar cad is
ríogacht ann, le fáil sa chéad téacs a leanann iarracht Aonghusa sa stua seo
(135ra). Is téacs é sin atá i láimh an phríomhscríobhaí agus a eachtraíonn i
dtaobh aighnis a d'éirigh idir Diarmaid mac Cearbhaill agus naoimh na
hÉireann, go háirithe Ruadhán agus Bréanainn, scéal ar thug O'Grady 'Stair
ar Aed Baclámh' air.[24] I gceartlár an achrainn seo, tugann Diarmaid fé na
naoimh agus tugann míniú suaithinseach ar cad is ríogacht ann, míniú a thagann le breithiúntas Byrne air, a luadh thuas (n. 5), mar 'the first Christian
high-king of Ireland', gan trácht ar thuairim Adhamhnáin ina leith: *totius
Scotiae regnatorem, Deo auctore ordinatum*:[25]

> Uair Dia féin dobeir gradha flatha 7 firénaig 7 firbreathaigthe do neoch
> .i. gu rabh coimhet a fhírinne ocus a fhlaithimhnasa aigi ar is eadh
> dleaghar do rígh trócaire co ndlúthadh reachta do beith aige 7 síth do
> thuathaibh 7 géill a nglasaibh 7 furtacht truagh 7 bathadh bidhbhadh
> 7 díchur in ethig ar mina derna nech réir righ nimhe ibhus ní gabhthar
> taithlech thall uadha et tusa a Ruadháin ar Diarmaid as tromhat táinic
> lot 7 leadradh mu ríghisea ocus mh'fhírinne re Dia 7 ailimsi Dia gurub
> í th'fhairchesea cétfhairche dhiultfaider a nEirinn 7 gurab é cétneimh-
> eadh frisa téagar.[26]

> For God himself it is that on such or such a one confers the orders of
> prince, of righteous ruler, and of equitable judgement, to the end he
> shall maintain his truthfulness, his princely quality, and his governance.
> Now that to which a king is bound is to have mercy coupled with
> stringency of law, and peace maintained in *túatha*, and hostages in fet-
> ters; to succour the wretched, but to overwhelm enemies; and to banish
> falsehood, for unless on this hither side one do the King of Heaven's
> will, no excuse is accepted from him yonder. And thou, Ruadhán, said
> Dermot: through thee it is that injury and rending of my sway, and of
> mine integrity to Godward is come about; and I pray God that thy

---

22 Vendryes, *Airne Fíngein*, ll. 337–62; LLM 139vb6–27.   **23** Taobh amuigh den dtéacs gairid
forlíonaidh ar Arastotal i bhfiordheireadh 139vb.   **24** S.H. O'Grady (eag. agus aistr.), *Silva
gadelica*, 2 iml. (1892) i, lgh 66–71.   **25** W. Reeves (eag. agus aistr.), *The Life of St Columba
founder of Hy* (1857) lch 68.   **26** LLM 136ra1–12 (mara gcuirtear a mhalairt in úil, is uaimse
na cinnlitreacha, síneadh na nod etc. sna sleachta ón lámhscríbhinn tríd síos); O'Grady, *Silva
gadelica* i, lch 69, ii, lch 73 (aistriú).

diocese be the first in Ireland that shall be renounced, and thy church-lands the first that shall be impugned.

Leanann cnuasach beag de théacsaí tánaisteacha scéal Aodha Baclámh, agus baineann a bhformhór sin chomh maith le seanchas Diarmada. Líontar deireadh duilleog 136r le dhá bhlúire fhorlíonaidh: an dán dár tosach *Olc bith aruptha*,[27] agus rann aonair ina dhiaidh (*Nochu chill acht fuath cilli*). Líontar duilleoga 136v–137ra le trí cinn de théacsaí tánaisteacha a leanann do ghnéithe d'fhaisnéis bheatha Dhiarmada: *Aided Bhreasail*,[28] gearrchúntas ar Chath Chúil Dreimhne, agus gearrchúntas arís ar bhás Dhiarmada.[29] Ag teacht idir na miontéacsaí sin agus *Airne Fíngein*, tá duilleog amháin (137rb–v) ar a bhfuil dhá dhán cháiliúla ina bhfaightear teagasc flatha a bhí bunaithe cuid mhaith ar Thecosca Chormaic. B'in iad na dánta dár tús anso *Da mad mheisi budh ri réil*,[30] dán de chuid Ua Néill, agus *Ceart gach righ co réil*,[31] dánta a faightear ní hamháin i gcuid de na lámhscríbhinní is mó le rá ó ré na meánaoise, ach arbh fhiú le hAodh Ó Dochartaigh iad a chaomhnú i Leabhar Uí Chonchobhair Dhuinn sa seachtú haois déag chomh maith.[32] Tá cuma éagsúil ar láimh scríobhaí an dá dhán seo, agus b'fhéidir gur cúntóir de chuid an phríomhscríobhaí atá i gceist.

Is féidir a rá, mar sin, go bhfaightear léargas ar chuid de phríomhghnéithe na ríogachta sa stua seo de LLM, go háirithe chomh fada is a bhaineann le deagh-rialú, ó thaobh bunúis, teagaisc agus torthaí de. Ní gá go dteastódh aon mhíniú breise uainn ar an ábhar seo a bheith ina chuid suime ag na fir léinn a chuir LLM le chéile. Ba leor a rá gur cuid de chlár intleachtúil an leabhair é. Mar sin féin, an té a léifeadh an dán dár tosach *Ní théd an égean a n-ais-gidh*,[33] dán a cumadh d'Fhínghean Mac Carthaigh agus a cuireadh in LLM ar ball, thabharfadh sé leis go raibh béim ar leith á leagaint sa dán sin ar ríogacht agus cearta an fhíor-rí, agus go mba thábhachtach an t-ábhar le Fínghean agus a lucht leanúna é. Tá leaganacha den bhfocal *rí* féin le fáil ocht n-uaire sa dán; tá sampla amháin ann den aidiacht *ríoghdha* (rann 9b), agus dhá shampla an ceann de na hainmfhocail theibí *ríghi* (23c, 24d) agus *ríoghdhacht* (30a, 37b). I gcomhthéacs an ghéillte nár thug cuid dá mhuintir féin d'Fhínghean ach go

27 Cf. O'Grady, *Silva gadelica*, i, lch 80; W. Stokes, *Lives of saints from the Book of Lismore* (1890), lch xxvi.   28 Stokes, *Lives of saints*, lgh xxvii–xxviii; leagan ó ARÉ LS B iv 2 i gcló in K. Meyer, 'Mitteilungen aus irischen Handschriften', *Zeitschrift für celtische Philologie*, 7 (1910), 305–7.   29 O'Grady, *Silva gadelica* i, lgh 71–2; giota as *Aided Diarmata* is ea an gearrchuntas ar Chath Chúil Dreimhne (ibid., lch 79), agus leagan de dheireadh an scéil chéanna is ea an cuntas ar a bhás. Tá plé ar thionchar *Aided Diarmata* ar *Tromdám Guaire* in S. Ó Coileáin, 'The making of *Tromdám Guaire*', *Ériu*, 28 (1977), 32–70 ag 61–2.   30 T. O'Donoghue (eag. agus aistr.), 'Advice to a prince', *Ériu*, 9 (1921–3), 43–54.   31 T. O'Donoghue (eag. agus aistr.), 'Cert cech ríg co réil' in O. Bergin agus C. Marstrander (eag.), *Miscellany presented to Kuno Meyer* (1912), lgh 258–77.   32 K. Simms, 'The selection of poems for inclusion in the Book of the O'Conor Don' in P. Ó Macháin (eag.), *The Book of the O'Conor Don* (2010), lgh 32–60 ag lgh 49 agus 58.   33 Ó Cuív, 'A poem for Fínghin Mac Carthaigh Riabhach', 96–100.

déanach,[34] b'fhéidir go raibh brí bhreise le léamh ar ábhar an tseanchais sa stua de LLM atá i gceist san alt seo.

Tá ráite thuas go bhfuil macallaí téamúla idir ábhar tosaigh agus deiridh an stua go háirithe sa bhfoilsiú a dheineann pearsa ósréalaíoch ar sheanchas na tíre. Tá sé suimiúil chomh maith go mbaineann ábhar an stua seo le huaireanta cinniúnacha i stair na hÉireann: bunú na gcúigí, tréigint na Teamhrach, agus saolú Chuinn, mar shampla. Tá le tabhairt fé ndeara i gcuid acu, leis, an choimhlint a d'eascair as uair chinniúnach eile, teacht na Críostaíochta.[35] Dob fhéidir a rá gur buntéama de scéalaíocht Dhiarmada mic Cearbhaill is ea é sin, mar, ainneoin é bheith ina Chríostaí agus Ciarán Cluana ina anamchara aige,[36] agus gur áitigh féin gur ó Dhia a tháinig cumhacht na ríogachta chuige, mar a chonaiceamair, bhí go leor den teannas idir é agus naoimh na hÉireann chomh maith, mar is léir in LLM, ní hamháin ar an suimiú ar Chath cáiliúil Chúil Dreimhne, ina mbuaitear air tré ghuí Choluim Chille, ach go háirithe i scéal an achrainn idir é agus Ruadhán, ina bhfaightear ranna frithchléireacha den gcineál seo:

> Díthfaider a fhairche ind
> cacfait coin ina caeimcill
> a mbaili Ruadáin na ráth
> beitit eigme in gach entrath.[37]

His diocese will be destroyed there, dogs will shit in his soft cell, in the homestead of Ruadhán of the *ráth*s at every hour there will be screams.

***

Is ag deireadh chéad scéil an stua, an *Suidiugad*, a tugtar an t-aon cholafan le brí in LLM trí chéile, an ceann a thugann fianaise dúinn ar scríobhaí na coda seo agus a phátrún:

> Suig*iu*dad teall*a*ig *te*amra *con*uicisin // FINITT // aonghu*s* ocall*anain* dos*cr*ibh so do mhag *carr*th*aigh* .i. finghean m*ac* d*iarma*da *agus* b[e]n*nacht* leis dó.[38]

34 Ibid., 109. 35 Tá ceann tógtha de théacsaí (*Aided Diarmata* ina measc) a suíodh san 'long-gone liminal period' seo in R. O'Connor, 'Searching for the moral in *Bruiden Meic Da Réo*', *Ériu*, 56 (2006), 117–43 ag 138–9. 36 J. Fraser, 'The miracle of Ciaran's hand', *Ériu*, 6 (1912), 159–60. 37 LLM 136rb3–4; O'Grady, *Silva gadelica*, i, lch 70. 38 LLM 134rb33–5. Ainneoin a ndeir Ó Cuív ('Observations on the Book of Lismore', lch 270 n. 3), dob é Mícheál Óg Ó Longáin, go bhfios dom, a chéidléigh sloinne Aonghusa i gceart sa tras-scríobh a dhein sé sa mbliain 1817 in Maigh Nuad LS M 15, lch [iii]: P. Ó Fiannachta, *Lámhscríbhinní Gaeilge Choláiste Phádraig, Má Nuad: clár* II (1965), lgh 41–2.

'Suigiudad Teallaig Teamra' thus far. Finit. Aonghus Ó Callanáin has written this for Mág Carthaigh, i.e. Fínghean son of Diarmaid, and a blessing to him with it.

Is cinnte nach mbeadh an méid sin d'eolas tugtha dúinn muireach go raibh fuílleach slí i ndeireadh an cholúin a lig don scríobhaí an calafan a scríobh. Is mar fhorlíonta deireadh leathanaigh a faightear nótaí mar seo in an-chuid de lámhscríbhinní na Gaeilge.[39] Rud a mhíníonn cad ina thaobh go bhfanann cuid mhaith acu gan ainm, dá réir sin, ná gur gné de dheagh-scríobh agus de dheagh-dhéanamh na lámhscríbhinní Gaelacha é go raibh ar chumas na scríobhaithe tomhas cruinn a dhéanamh ar fhaid aon téacs agus ar líon na leathanach nó na gcolún a theastódh chun an téacs sin a thógaint. Cuid den tomhas san, gan amhras, ná leagan amach an téacs san eiseamláir a bhí ós chomhair an scríobhaí, ach, ós rud é nach mbíonn aon dá lámhscríbhinn go hiomlán ar aon dul le chéile, tréith de thréithe na scríobhaithe ab ea an cumas tomhais seo leis.

An col a bhíonn ag scríobhaithe le téacs mór nua a thosnú ag bun leathanaigh, nó gairid dó, tá sé le feiscint in LLM go minic, agus, mar atá ráite thuas, is mó téacs i bhfoirm fhorlíonaidh atá le tabhairt fé ndeara sa Leabhar agus iad curtha isteach chun colún a thabhairt chun críche. I gcás duilleog 134rb, tar éis dó a ainm a chur leis an *Suidiugad*, dealraíonn sé gur fhág Aonghus an chuid eile den gcolún bán agus gur iompaigh an leathanach chun tús a chur ar 134v le téacs nua: an téacs ar a dtugtar *An Agallamh bheag* anois.[40] Ní rófhada a lean sé de, áfach, nó gur stad sé de scríobh an scéil go hobann ag 134vb13, tar éis dhá líne agus leathchéad a chur de. Céad fiche éigin leathanach ina dhiaidh sin – do réir ord an Leabhair mar atá inniu – chuir sé tús leis an scéal ó bhonn athuair i stua eile ar fad (duilleoga 194–200), agus chuir sé i gcrích é an turas seo díreach sarar scrígh sé duilleog amháin (201) de *Acallam na senórach* agus tús á chur aige le scríobh an scéil mhóir dá chomhpháirtí, an príomhscríobhaí.

An chéad iarracht seo Aonghusa ar *AB* a scríobh, músclaíonn sé ceisteanna áirithe maidir leis an gcomhthéacs inar ceapadh an scéal a chur. Orthu sin tá dhá cheist go háirithe: (a) cad ina thaobh gur roghnaíodh scéal Fiannaíochta le dul i ndiaidh *Suidiugad teallaig Temra* agus chun áit lárnach a bheith aige i stua a bhain le scéalaíocht na ríthe agus na ríogachta? (b) Tar éis do lucht déanta an Leabhair an cinneadh sin a dhéanamh, cad a thug ar Aonghus Ó Callanáin éirí go hobann is go luath as an scéal a bhreacadh?

I dtaobh an dara ceist, rud amháin a chuireann castacht sa scéal, maidir le *AB* in LLM de, ná an t-athrú dúigh a tharlaíonn ag an bpointe seo i ndeireadh *Suidiugad* agus i dtús *AB*. Dúch donn atá in úsáid ar dhuilleoga

39 Cf. Ó Macháin, *The Book of the O'Conor Don*, lgh 14–15. **40** Míniú ar bhunús an teidil seo in N. Ní Shéaghdha (eag.), *Agallamh na seanórach*, 3 himl. (1942–5), i, lgh xv–xvi.

132–3 agus ar *recto* 134 anuas go deireadh an chalafain ag 134rb35. Léiríonn an dúch gur iompaigh Aonghus an duilleog agus gur scrígh sé seacht líne de *AB* ar 134va sarar lean sé air i ndúch dubh. Is é an dúch dubh céanna atá le feiscint san *Interrogatio* chomh maith i ndeireadh 134rb36–45. Mar sin, lasmuigh de na seacht línte tosaigh de *AB*, atharrach dúigh atá le feiscint san *Interrogatio* agus sa ghiota de *AB* a scríodh ar 134va8–b13.[41]

Dealraíonn gurbh é a tharla ná gur thosnaigh an dúch donn ag éirí lag agus tréigthe fé dheireadh an *Suidiugad* ach gur lean Aonghus air agus bhreac sé línte tosaigh *AB* ar bharr an *verso* mar threoir dó féin nuair a chuirfeadh sé tús leis an scríobhnóireacht arís. Fén am go raibh dúch nua déanta nó aimsithe aige, bhí beartaithe aige gan dul ar aghaidh le *AB* a bhreacadh. Bhí tomhas cruinn déanta ar an nduilleog, áfach, agus chaithfi leanúint le *AB* go pointe áirithe, agus ansan dul thar n-ais agus an *Interrogatio* a thosnú ag deireadh 134r agus é a chríochnú i ndiaidh an ghiota de *AB* ar 134v, chun deimhin a dhéanamh de go bhféadfadh an príomhscríobhaí tús a chur le 'Aed Baclámh' ar bharr 135r.

I dtéarmaí pailéagrafaíochta mar sin, tá tuairim againn i dtaobh ar tharla don gcéad iarracht ar *AB* a chur in LLM. Maidir len é a roghnú le cur san ionad seo chéad uair – an chéad cheist thuas – cé gur téacsaí iad *AB* agus an *Acallam* a bhaineann le luathré na Nua-Ghaeilge,[42] is fíor a rá, leis, nach gan réamhtheachtaithe ná analóga a deineadh iad a fhoirfiú. Cé gur gnách linn féachaint ar litríocht na bhFiann mar *genre* a d'eascair agus a d'fhorbair laistigh dá théarmaí tagartha féin, ní dócha gur mar sin a d'fhéach fear léinn na meánaoise air. Ní miste cuimhneamh go raibh eagrú agus códú á ndéanamh ar réimsí áirithe litríochta sa dara haois déag: an dinnsheanchas mar atá i Leabhar Laighean, mar shampla, agus go háirithe gramadach agus meadaracht na bhfilí. Is féidir glacadh leis an *Acallam* mar iarracht ar chódú a dhéanamh ar an bhFiannaíocht ar an gcuma chéanna, agus b'é tuairim Ghearóid Uí Mhurchú gur mar chnuasach dinnsheanchais a d'fhéach fear an dara haois déag air.[43] Is dóichí gur bhraith agus gur thuig an fear sin na meánaoise, gan cheist, na macallaí, na tagairtí, agus na nascanna go léir leis an seanlitríocht a bhí ag borradh tré gach aon chuid den dtéacs seo. Fiú ag breithniú dúinn siar air agus sinn lasmuigh den dtraidisiún go hiomlán, tuigimíd go

---

41 Tá athrú dúigh den gcineál ceanann céanna le feiscint ar dhuilleoga 197r agus 199r, cuid Aonghusa fós.   42 M. Dillon (eag.), *Stories from the Acallam* (1970), lch ix: 'Just as Chaucer is the beginning for many students of English literature, so the *Acallam* may be the upper limit of a programme of Modern Irish'; féach A. Dooley, 'The date and purpose of *Acallam na senórach*', *Éigse*, 34 (2004), 97–126. Maidir le *AB*, tá ráite gur scríobhadh é beagáinín níos déanaí ná an *Acallam* féin (argóintí luaite ag J.S. Kühns, 'Some observations on the *Acallam bec*' in S.J. Arbuthnot agus G. Parsons (eag.), *The Gaelic Finn tradition* (2012), lgh 122–38 ag lch 124).   43 E. Knott agus G. Murphy, *Early Irish literature* (1966), lch 161. Tá an ceangal idir códú réimsí áirithe seanchais tugtha fé ndeara ag F.J. Byrne, '*Senchas*: the nature of Gaelic historical tradition', *Historical Studies*, 9 (1974), 137–59 ag 157.

bhféadfaí cás a dhéanamh, mar shampla, gur macasamhail í an *Acallam* de shean-téacsaí a léirigh Pádraig Naofa ina thaistealaí agus an tír á baisteadh aige chomh maith leis na daoine; más cúrsaí dinnsheanchais is cnámh dhroma don *Acallam*, dob fhéidir an rud ceanann céanna a chur i leith *Bethu Phátraic*.[44]

Is é is bunstruchtúr don *Acallam*, agus do *AB* leis, duine eolgaiseach ag tabhairt freagraí, i bhfoirm fhilíochta de ghnáth, ar iliomad ceisteanna ó dhaoine nach mbíonn eolas cruinn acu ar aimsir na Féinne. Ní mar a chéile lucht ceistithe agus éisteachta Chaoilte sa dá scéal, dár ndóigh. San *Acallam* is é Pádraig Naofa an príomhcheisteoir, agus scata maith eile ina dhiaidh. Is dá chara Fionnchadh is mó a nochtann Caoilte a fhaisnéis in *AB*, chomh maith le faisnéis a dhéanamh do mhuintir Dhiarmada mic Cearbhaill, dá dheirfiúr féin Samhnach, agus do Dhubhthach mac hua Lughair 'ríghfhile Laighean';[45] ní bhíonn aon bhaint ag Pádraig leis an gceistiú. Ní bheadh sé as an áireamh go mbeadh fréamhacha an struchtúir seo le rianadh go dtí córas teagaisc agus foghlama atá go maith ar eolas againn ón sean-litríocht, is é sin córas na gceist agus na bhfreagraí. Córas é sin dárbh fhéidir analóga ginearálta a lorg i litríocht na Gréigise ó aimsir Phlato agus Socrates anuas,[46] agus i dtraidisiún *dialogus* na Laidne agus teangacha eile, agus in *katechesis* na hEaglaise féin. Córas ab ea é, fiú agus é i riocht deoranta, a thaithin riamh leis an nGael,[47] agus bíonn solaoidí de, agus d'fhoirm na hiomagallmha i gcoitinne, le fáil in gach aon chraobh den litríocht dúchasach: dlí, gramadach, seanchas, an Fhiannaíocht ó ré roimh an *Acallam*,[48] agus seanchas Phádraig féin.[49] Más féidir linn a leithéid sin de shinsearacht a shonrú inniu ar an litríocht seo, nó a chur i gcás di, cá bhfios cad iad na nascanna, na craobha coibhneasa agus na comh-théamaí a shamhlaigh lucht léinn sa mheánaois dhéanach léi?

Ina theannta sin go léir, ar fhéachaint dúinn ar chineál agus comharthaí sóirt na dtéacsaí atá mórthimpeall air, agus ar chineál *AB* féin, is féidir teacht ar thuairim bhreise i dtaobh seasamh *AB* i súilibh lucht déanta LLM. Is chun tabhairt fén mbearna san insint ar luathsheanchas na nGael, agus é sin a dhéanamh taobh istigh de fhráma na Críostaíochta mar a chraolaigh lucht léinn san Eoraip é, a cumadh Leabhar Gabhála.[50] Braitheadh uaireanta, chun cruth a chur ar sheachadadh na hinsinte sin, nár mhór pearsa nó gné éigin ósréalaíoch nó meitifisiciúil chun míniú a thabhairt ar conas a nochtadh an

44 K. Mulchrone (eag.), *Bethu Phátraic* (1939).   45 LLM 197va1–7. Is ionann é seo, gan amhras, agus Dubthach maccu Lugair a luaitear i gcomhthéacs *Senchas már* agus Pádraig Naofa (féach, mar shampla, Kim McCone, 'Dubthach maccu Lugair and a matter of life and death in the pseudo-historical prologue to the *Senchas már*', *Peritia*, 5 (1986), 1–35).   46 D. Nikulin, *On dialogue* (2006), lgh 5–10.   47 Mar shampla, R.A.Q. Skerrett, 'Fiarfaidhi San Anselmuis', *Celtica*, 7 (1966), 163–87.   48 K. Meyer, *Fianaigecht* (1910), lgh 22–7; B. Ó Cuív (eag.), 'Agallamh Fhinn agus Ailbhe', *Celtica*, 18 (1986), 111–15.   49 B. Ó Cuív, 'The Irish marginalia in Codex Palatino-Vaticanus No. 830', *Éigse*, 24 (1990), 45–67 ag 65.   50 R.M. Scowcroft, 'Leabhar gabhála part I: the growth of the text', *Ériu*, 38 (1987), 79–142; idem, 'Leabhar gabhála part II: the growth of the tradition', *Ériu*, 39 (1988), 1–66.

sean-sheanchas.[51] Is ar an gcuma sin a samhlaíodh *Do fhallsigud Tána bó Cúalnge* le taibhse Fhearghusa mic Róigh in aimsir Dhiarmada mic Cearbhaill, mar shampla;[52] agus ní haon ionadh é gurb iad an triúr sean-údar a luaitear le cuid d'fhilíocht an dinnsheanchais ná Fiontan mac Bóchra, Colum Cille, agus Fionn mac Cumhaill.[53] I gcúrsaí dlí, mar shampla eile, ní hamháin go gcuirtear an téacs i bhfoirm agallmha ar uairibh, ach cuirtear na téacsaí a mbíonn an cruth sin orthu i mbéalaibh daoine ón miotaseolaíocht.[54] Sa mhéid is go gcuirtear Caoilte agus a chairde i láthair mar dhaoine a bhain le ré eile, ré na réamh-Chríostaíochta, b'oiriúnach an téacs é *AB* le cur san ionad seo sa lámhscríbhinn maidir lena dtugtar ann d'fhaisnéis ar an ré eile úd.

Dob fhéidir glacadh le *AB* chomh maith mar fhorlíonadh ar eachtra Fhiontain sa *Suidiugad*. Achoimre ar lucht ghabhála na tíre a bhí i gcuid d'insint Fhiontain; is í an ghabháil dhéanach ar fad, gabháil na dTáilgeann, atá mar aimsir, agus, go pointe áirithe, 'fáth airicc' ag *AB*. Saghas ath-Fhiontan é Caoilte, go háirithe mar a léirítear iad beirt i ndeireadh an dá scéil fé seach: Fiontan agus é spíonta i ndeireadh a ré i gCiarraighe Luachra; Caoilte mar an gcéanna i dTeamhair. Mar thaca leis an méid sin, is beag duine a déarfadh nach raibh ar a laghad cosúlachtaí téamúla idir dánta deiridh Fhiontain ('Fand inniu mo beatha búan' agus 'Am crín indiu i Comor chúan')[55] agus dán deiridh Chaoilte in *AB*, 'Ní maith aniu mhirlabra'.[56] Ní miste cuimhneamh leis ar *Airne Fíngein* agus ar Fhíngen mac Luchta agus ríogacht Chuinn Ceadchathaigh á seachaint aige fé 'dobrón 7 domenma … for imurchor sechnón Éirenn as cech tír 7 díthrub i n-araile'[57] sara mbuaileann fé ar Sliabh Mis sa deireadh, agus sara ngéilleann do Chonn ina dhiaidh sin.

In *Airne Fíngein*, leantar do bhéim Mhuimhneach LLM maidir le log an scéil de, mar sin, díreach mar a bhaineann deireadh an *Suidiugad* le Ciarraighe Luachra, agus mar a thaistealaíonn Caoilte in *AB* ó Ghleann Fleisce soir 're hAbaind Mhóir hi crích Fer Maighi'.[58] Léiríu é sin ar thábhacht suíomhnú na scéalta so in LLM, agus ar thábhacht na logainmníochta dá réir sin in *AB*. Níl amhras ná go bhfuil an ceart ag Seán Ó Coileáin maidir le feidhm nua-rómánsúil cuid, ar a laghad, de na logainmneacha san *Acallam*;[59] san am gcéanna, mar a deir sé féin ag tagairt dó don dán *Géisid cúan* san *Acallam*, bíonn gá fé leith sa bhFiannaíocht le loganna cinnte, so-aitheanta:

51 R. Flower, *The Irish tradition* (1947), lgh 14–15.   52 K. Murray, 'The finding of the *Táin*', *Cambrian Medieval Celtic Studies*, 41 (Summer, 2001), 17–23. Tá dáta agus gnéithe eile den dtéacs seo pléite in Ó Coileáin, 'The making of *Tromdám Guaire*', 48–50.   53 M. O Daly, 'The metrical *dindshenchas*' in J. Carney (eag.), *Early Irish poetry* (1965), lgh 59–72 ag lch 63.   54 L. Breatnach, *A companion to the Corpus iuris Hibernici* (2005), lgh 361–2, 371.   55 Best, 'The settling of the manor of Tara', 154–60.   56 LLM 200va29–b22.   57 Vendryes, *Airne Fíngein*, ll. 299–304 ('sadness and depression … wandering throughout Ireland from every other land and wasteland').   58 LLM 196rb2.   59 S. Ó Coileáin, 'Place and placename in *fianaigheacht*', *Studia Hibernica*, 27 (1993), 45–60 (i gcló arís sa leabhar so). Cf. N. Ó Muraíle, 'Agallamh na seanórach' in P. Ó Fiannachta (eag.), *Léachtaí Cholm Cille*, 25: *An fhiannaíocht* (1995), lgh 96–

Place has become text. This is not at all to deny the actuality of such names. On the contrary, it is necessary that a credible relationship be maintained between the landscape and its evocation: there must be the appearance of recognition to counterbalance the elusiveness of place.[60]

Dá réir sin, nuair a luaitear loganna a bheadh ar eolas ag lucht léite nó éisteachta an scéil, níl amhras ná gur fada a leithéid ón bhfolús is talamh dúchais don Rómánsaíocht mar is eol dúinn í go hidirnáisiúnta.[61] Fiú maran domhan so-aitheanta léarscáilithe amach is amach í an Fhiannaíocht, is fuirist fós é a nascadh, ar bhonn an dinnsheanchais, le mórán saghasanna seanchais a ghaibh roimpi, an naomhsheanchas agus an ríoghsheanchas san áireamh. Dhá thráigh atá á bhfreastal ag an logainmníocht sa bhFiannaíocht mar sin: cinnteacht áirithe suímh agus éiginnteacht agus 'eileachas' na hósréalaíochta. Mar deir Mac Cana:

> The landscape through which they [*sc.* An Fhian] move is ostensibly that of the Irish countryside and is generally furnished with real place-names, yet it exists in a fourth dimension where perception becomes reality and where the secular relativities of time and space are effaced or subverted.[62]

Nuair a thaistil Caoilte soir go críoch Fhear Maighe, ar éigean nár thuig lucht léite agus éisteachta *AB* gurbh i gceantar LLM agus Leabhar Fhear Maighe a bhí sé tagtha.

I gcúrsaí pearsanra is é Diarmaid mac Cearbhaill an ceangal is treise idir an *Suidiugad*, 'Aodh Baclámh' agus *AB*. Ní haon chumadóireacht de chuid údar *AB* é an caidreamh idir Diarmaid agus an Fhiannaíocht, mar gur in aimsir Dhiarmada atá an *Acallam* suite chomh maith;[63] tá macalla den gcaidreamh sin le fáil leis in Dán XLVII de chuid *Duanaire Finn*, ina dtugtar tuairisc ar chlaíomh Chaoilte do Dhiarmaid mac Cearbhaill.[64] Tá tagairt do Dhiarmaid go luath in *AB*, nuair a scarann Caoilte agus Oisín agus nuair a luaitear nár casadh ar a chéile arís iad go haimsir Dhiarmada: 'Ocus nír comruicset in tsheinfhian iarsin acht Cailti 7 Oisin i tigh Diarmada meic Cerbhuill

---

127 ag 120–4 ('Aguisín II: logainmneacha san Agallamh').   **60** S. Ó Coileáin, 'The setting of *Géisid cúan*' in J. Carey et al. (eag.), *Cin Chille Cúile* (2004), lgh 234–48 ag lch 241 (i gcló arís sa leabhar so).   **61** J. Stevens, *Medieval romance: themes and approaches* (1973), lch 169: 'Medieval romance … is … a processional form; and the chief actors move from one *aventure* to another, not through a clearly defined and located countryside, but in a geographical vacuum'. **62** P. Mac Cana, *The cult of the sacred centre* (2011), lch 249; féach lgh 291–2 chomh maith. **63** Féach O'Grady, *Silva gadelica*, i, lgh 143–53; W. Stokes (eag.), 'Acallamh na senórach' in W. Stokes agus E. Windisch (eag.), *Irische Texte*, iv, 1 (1900), ll 2239–701.   **64** E. Mac Neill agus G. Murphy (eag. agus aistr.), *Duanaire Finn*, 3 himl. (1908–53), ii, lch 124; dáta ó lár an dara haois déag atá curtha ag Ó Murchú air (ibid., iii, lch 107).

i Teamhraigh'.[65] Fágann an abairt sin go mbíonn ar an údar ar ball deimhin a dhéanamh de go bhfuil an comhthéacs stairiúil i gceart agus Diarmaid a theacht i gcomharbacht ar Thuathal Maolgharbh i ríogacht na hÉireann: 'Táinic bás Tuathail Mhaoilgairbh foí sin 7 roghabhustur Diarmat mac Cerbaill righi nEirenn'.[66] Cuireann sé sin ar a chumas Diarmaid a thabhairt isteach mar mhionphearsa i ndeireadh an scéil chun réiteach a dhéanamh do Chaoilte a thabhairt go Teamhair. Is é an chuma ina ndeintear é sin ná go dtugann an rí maithiúnas ar dtúis do 'thrí mic Brogáin',[67] uaisle a dtugann Caoilte tamall ina dteannta agus iad ar a gcoimeád ó bhain an rí a dtailte díobh. Fágann an maithiúnas sin Caoilte ina aonar arís. Ina dhiaidh sin, bíonn ar Dhiarmaid féin go pearsanta Caoilte a thabhairt go Teamhair:

> Ro chuir Diarmat mac Cerbhaill Tuathal reachtaire na Teamhra ar ceann Cailti 7 ni thainic leis 7 do chuaidh fein 7 tuc leis he co Ros na Rígh .i. Ros Teamhrach 7 ro fhiarfaigh ca hainm in tinad so ar Cailti Ros Teamhrach ar siat 7 do rindi in laoidh.[68]

> Diarmaid mac Cearbhaill sent Tuathal, steward of Teamhair, to Caoilte and he did not return with him; and he [sc. Diarmaid] himself went and brought him to Ros na Ríogh, i.e. Ros Teamhrach, and Caoilte asked: 'what is this place called?' 'Ros Teamhrach', they said. And he made the lay.

Chomh maith leis an gcomhléiriú ar Chaoilte agus ar Fhiontan, agus leis an scéal a shuíomh i gcomhthéacs stairiúil Dhiarmada mic Cearbhaill, is cinnte go dtiocfadh *AB* leis an léiriú atá sna téacsaí eile sa chomharsanacht a phléann le cineál agus comharthaí sóirt na ríogachta. Tá síocháin na deagh-ríogachta ina chúlra agus ina chuid tábhachtach de mhíniú cás Chaoilte agus Oisín. Díbheirgigh is ea iad, agus dob ea riamh, ach anois níl fanta dá sórt sa tír ach iad féin amháin. Nuair a thugann Caoilte deatach tine na dTáilgeann fé ndeara uaidh mar sin, deir sé leis féin:

> Ingnad leam ar se in deatac út at chiú i Cuillind uair ní fhuil bruigh nait bailedha ann 7 ní fhuilet foghlaidh feadha naid dibercaidh ind Eirind Uair ata Ere in a topur thechtaighthi Ocus fuilet da coicedh Muman ac Aonghus mac Natfraich 7 coicedh Connacht ac Eichean mac Briain meic Eochach Muimheadhóin 7 coicedh Uladh ac

65 LLM 194va34-5 ('and the old *fian* did not meet up again after that, save Caoilte and Oisín in the house of Diarmaid mac Cearbhaill in Teamhair'). Cf. An Craoibhín (eag. agus aistr.), 'An Agallamh bheag', *Lia Fáil*, 1 (1927), 79-107 ag 88.　66 LLM 198vb28-9; maidir leis an gcomharbacht seo, féach O'Brien, *Corpus genealogiarum Hiberniae*, lch 124 (137a10).　67 LLM 199ra8-10: 'Adubairt Diarmat mac Cerbhaill righ Eirenn tabraidh tri mic Brogáin chucum. tucad 7 dorindedh a sígh 7 tucad a crich fein doibh'.　68 LLM 200ra25-9.

Muiredhac Muinnderg 7 coicedh Laighean ac Crimhthan mac Éatna
Ceinnsealaigh 7 braighde Eireann uile ac Laoghure mac Néil i
Temraigh Ocus conac fuilet dibeargaidh nait anmargaidh náit foghlaidh
feadha a nEirinn Ocus ní fhuileat fianna aile a nEirinn acht sinne.[69]

'I am surprised', said he 'at that smoke that I see in Cuilleann since
there is neither house nor homesteads there, and there are neither
highwaymen nor outlaws in Ireland because Ireland is a frozen well,
and [because] the two provinces of Munster belong to Aonghus mac
Nadfraoich, and the province of Connacht to Eichean mac Briain meic
Eochach Muighmheadhón and the province of Ulster to Muireadhach
Muindearg and the province of Leinster to Criomhthan mac Éanna
Ceinnsealaigh and the hostages of Ireland to Laoghaire mac Néill in
Teamhair; and because there are no outlaws, marauders nor highway-
men in Ireland, and there are no other *fian*s in Ireland except our-
selves'.

Tá an tír fé shíocháin mar sin – ina 'topur thechtaighthi'[70] mar deir Caoilte –
agus ní hin é an saol lena mbaineann an Fhiann ná aon fhiann eile. Le dhá
shaol eile a bhaineann siad, agus cuid de luach agus d'ábhar spéise *AB*, agus
an *Acallam* féin gan amhras, ná an insint a tugtar orthu sin: an saol lasmuigh
den ríogacht, agus an saol cianaimsireach atá imithe. Is é an chéad saol acu a
bhaineann le ceist na ríogachta, agus an dara saol agus an caitheamh a bhíonn
ag Caoilte go háirithe ina dhiaidh ('cuimhniughadh na Féine', nó 'smuaineadh
Find agus na Féinde') a thugann blaiseadh den eolchaire agus den uaigneas
don saothar trí chéile.

'Everyman' Gaelach is ea Caoilte san *AB*: imíonn gach aoinne uaidh diaidh
ar ndiaidh go dtí nach mbíonn fágtha ach é féin ina aonar. Téann scaoileadh
ar dtúis ar 'na trí noenbhair', nuair a scarann Caoilte agus Oisín lena chéile;
cailleann Caoilte a ghiolla, Fear Gaire, ar ball, agus bíonn air a fhianbhoth féin
a ullmhú don gcéad uair riamh; imíonn a bhuanchara Fionnchadh uaidh i
dtreo an deiridh ar fad, ionnas nach mbíonn fágtha ach Caoilte amháin, agus
leisce air saol an díbheirgigh a thréigint nó go dtagann Diarmaid mac
Cearbhaill ar a thuairisc. Tugtar bheith istigh i dTeamhair ansin dó, agus é ina
fhoinse sheanchais ag maithe na tíre nó go dtagann Oisín chuige i líne
dhéanach an scéil agus go gcuirtear deireadh ábhar beag obann leis an eachtra.

Mar sin, tá cuntas ar an saol lasmuigh den ríogacht agus géilleadh don
ríogacht sa deireadh, mar a ghéilleann Fíngen do Chonn in *Airne Fíngein*, ar
cheann de théamaí *AB*. Tá cás Fhíngein gan a bheith rófhada in aon chor ó
chás Caoilte sa saol a chaitheann an bheirt ar a seachaint, más ea, i bhfad ó

---

69 LLM 194rb11–20; An Craoibhín, 'An Agallamh bheag', lch 82.   **70** Is é sin, rud nach féidir
a shuathadh; cf. *DIL* s.vv. 2 *téchtaide* agus *téchtaigid*.

lár an fhlaithis.[71] Tharlódh gurbh é sin agus an ceangal le Diarmaid mac Cearbhaill a ba chúis le *AB* a roghnú le cur sa stua seo ar dtúis. Tá feicthe againn cheana féin na nascanna eile a threiseodh leis an rogha sin. Bhí, mar shampla, an tír a bheith fé shíocháin; agus gur daoine ón gcianaimsir iad Caoilte agus Fionnchadh a chaitheann solas ina n-agallamh dóibh ar an am atá thart, díreach mar a tharlaíonn ina n-agallmha i gcás Fhiontain agus Tréfhuilngid agus Diarmaid sa *Suidiugad*, agus Fíngen agus Rothníam in *Airne Fíngein*. Ceangal eile is ea é, mar a luadh thuas, gur in aimsir ghabháil na dTáilgeann ar Éirinn a bhíonn *AB* agus an *Acallam* féin suite, gabháil a bheadh le cur leis na gabhála eile a ríomhaigh Fiontan sa *Suidiugad*.

Luadh cheana gur bunchuid de bheathaisnéis Dhiarmada is ea an teannas agus an t-aighneas a thagann i gceist go minic idir é agus naoimh na hÉireann – Colum Cille go háirithe – agus an frithchléireachas atá le sonrú sa chlampar idir é agus Ruadhán.[72] Cé gur luaithe, nó gur éagsúla, an tsraith Fhiannaíochta atá le tabhairt fé ndeara in *AB* ná frithchléireachas na Fiannaíochta déanaí,[73] agus gur beag rian den aighneas seo atá le fáil san *Acallam*, mar sin féin tá a leithéid de theannas i gceist go caolchúiseach in *AB* sa tseachaint a dheineann Caoilte ar Phádraig tríd síos, agus go deimhin féin sa mhóid a thugann Oisín maidir leis na Táilginn a mharú. Is mó ar fad de bhagairt chaolchúiseach ná coimhlint os aird atá sa mhíréiteach seo idir an Chríostaíocht agus an Fhiann in *AB*, áfach, seachas mar atá i scéalta Dhiarmada, agus is fearrde go mór *AB* an chaolchúis sin.

Pé snaidhm atá, nó a measadh a bheith, idir *AB* agus na scéalta eile sa stua seo, áfach, d'éirigh Aonghus as bheith á scríobh go luath tar éis dó tús a chur leis. B'fhéidir gurbh amhlaidh a d'aithin sé féin agus an príomhscríobhaí, dá mhéid an ceangal idir *AB* agus na scéalta mórthimpeall air, go raibh deifir mhór stíle eatarthu fós agus gurbh fhearr go mór agus go fada *AB* a chur i dteannta *Acallam na senórach*, a raibh cosúlachtaí i bhfad níos soiléire aige leis. Agus, mar atá ráite thuas, is mar sin a deineadh: Aonghus Ó Callanáin a scrígh arís (duilleoga 194–200), agus chuir sé tús le téacs an *Acallam* díreach ina dhiaidh (duilleog 201) sarar lean príomhscríobhaí LLM den scéal mór fada sin ó dhuilleog 202 go deireadh na lámhscríbhinne mar atá sé anois againn.

Dealraíonn sé gur ag Aonghus a bhí teacht ar *AB*, fé mar gur shainscéal dá chuid féin ab ea é. Léiríonn anailís atá déanta agam ar an dá leagan de thosach an scéil in LLM gur mar a chéile iad ó thaobh foclaíochta de. Maidir le forás ceird na peannaireachta i dtraidisiún na lámhscríbhinní Gaeilge, go háirithe i gcúrsaí poncaíochta, tá tábhacht nach beag ag baint le saothrú

71 Maidir le Fíngen bheith ina *deórad*, féach G. Bondarenko, 'King in exile in *Airne Fíngein* "Fíngen's vigil": power and pursuit in early Irish literature', *Études Celtiques*, 36 (2008), 135–48.   72 'Comlond Diarmata meic Cerbaill fri Ruadan' a tugtar ar théacs gaolmhar leis sa Leabhar Breac (ARÉ LS 23 P 16 [1230], lch 260).   73 Mar le forás an téama seo, féach P. Ó Fiannachta, 'The development of the debate between Pádraig and Oisín' in B. Almqvist et al. (eag.), *The heroic process* (1987), lgh 183–205.

Aonghusa in LLM. Scéal thairis é sin san alt seo ach amháin go mbíonn gaol i gcónaí, geall leis, idir poncaíocht agus tuiscint an scríobhaí. Ní hamháin gur mhaith a thuig Aonghus an t-ábhar a bhí á chóipeáil aige,[74] ach is léir domsa gur aithin sé agus a chomhpháirtí gur théacs ar leithligh a bhí ann, agus gur leithleachas é a sháraigh aon phráinn théamúil a spreag iad len é a chur i stua Dhiarmada an chéad uair.

Más cuntas ar ghné na ríogachta ó shúilibh na ndíbheirgeach atá in *AB*, agus más tuairisc leis é ar an gcianaimsir agus ar ghabháil thosaigh na dTáilgeann ar Éirinn, fós féineach is scéal Fiannaíochta é. Tar éis an chéad chinneadh a dhéanamh maidir le *AB* a chur i stua Dhiarmada mic Cearbhaill, agus tar éis d'Aonghus tosnú á bhreacadh ar dhuilleog 134v, rith sé leis na scríobhaithe gurbh fhearr a d'oirfeadh sé d'ionad eile ar fad sa leabhar, agus é mar a bheadh ina réamhscéal ag *Acallam na senórach* ar dhuilleoga 194–200. Caithfidh gur tuigeadh dóibh go raibh tréithe lasmuigh de chúrsaí stíle ag gabháil le *AB* a dhealaigh amach é ó na scéalta eile a bhain le Diarmaid agus Conn Céadchathach.

Ní deacair cuid ar a laghad de na tréithe sin a aithint fós sa lá inniu. Ba dhóigh le duine go mbeadh áit ag leithéid *AB* in aon díolaim a bheadh le tiomsú in onóir taoisigh éirimiúil i ndeireadh na meánaoise in Éirinn. Cuid tosaigh an téacs so, tá sé le háireamh ar na blúirí cumadóireachta is áille i sean-litríocht na Gaeilge. Baineann tosach an scéil le teacht na dTáilgeann, dream atá ina macasamhail ghlan ar an bhFéinn, a sciatha ina lámhaibh acu agus 'fodhord conuire' ar siúl acu agus iad ar bóthar. Ní hiad Caoilte ná Oisín a thugann fé ndeara iad ach Fear Gaire, giolla Chaoilte, nuair a stadann ag sruthán chun deoch a ól: 'Agus gabhais in gilla ac fégain in tshluaig 7 craobh eattura agus a chenn'.[75] Tugann Fear Gaire tuairisc na n-eachtrannach don bhFéinn ar ball nuair a éiríonn leis teacht suas leo, agus aithníonn Oisín láithreach gurb iad na Táilginn atá ann 'ro tharrngairset ar ndraíthi agus Find duind'.

Athrú is ea an léiriú drámatúil sin ar sheift an fharaire mar a faightear sa tsean-scéalaíocht é.[76] Fógra is ea é chomh maith go bhfuilimíd ag plé le reac-aireacht as an ngnáth sa scéal seo. Deineann an t-údar gabháil ar an gcumasc cuí idir uaigneas i ndiaidh an tsean-shaoil atá ar ciumhais imeachta go deo agus an t-iontas agus an alltacht a chuireann na strainséirí ar iarsma seo na Féinne; deineann suimiú, leis, ar an áit imeallach a bheidh ag na Táilginn sa scéal. Teacht na Críostaíochta ina fíorthosach atá á léiriú anseo agus dul as do na seanghnáthaimh. Ach oiread le Fear Gaire, ní bhfaigheann an léitheoir aon radharc ceart ar na gabhálaithe nua seo ach amháin an radharc a gheobhadh duine agus é i bhfolach taobh thiar de chraobh.

---

74 Scéitheann noda comónta idir an dá leagan, agus gnéithe eile sa téacs iomlán ar nós ceartú a–b (cf. duilleog 196va10), gur cinnte gur chóipeáil a bhí i gceist; agus féach Kühns, 'Some observations on the *Acallam bec*', lch 123.   **75** LLM 134va20–21, 194ra19–20; An Craoibhín, 'An Agallamh bheag', lch 80.   **76** J. Carney, *Studies in Irish literature and history* (1955), lgh 305–21.

Tagraíodh thuas don tslí ina gcuirtear pearsa Chaoilte i láthair agus conas a caitear leis mar aonarán nach bhfaigheann faoiseamh ón eolchaire ná ón uaigneas nó go nglacann, ní leis an gCríostaíocht, ach le tearmann na ríogachta mar a cleachtaítear i dTeamhair í. Marab ionann agus an *Acallam*, ní bhíonn aon bhaint lárnach ag Pádraig Naofa le scéal *AB*: tugann Caoilte a mhóid go seachnóidh sé na Táilginn agus sin é díreach a dheineann sé, agus an t-údar leis. Fanann Pádraig agus a bhuíon mar a bheadh scáthanna ar imeall an scéil. An t-aon teangáil dhíreach a bhíonn aige le Caoilte agus Fionnchadh, tarlaíonn nuair a thagann sé orthu agus iad ina gcodladh, agus nuair a baistear ina dhiaidh sin iad.[77]

Cé gur cuid an-tábhachtach den scéal iad, ní ar Phádraig ná ar an gCríostaíocht atá an bhéim mar sin féin. Pé ní is téama bunaidh do *AB* – an tseanaois, eolchaire agus uaigneas, oilithreacht tuirsiúil phearsanta an aonaráin – is scéal meánaoiseach é a ngabhann blaiseadh nua-aimseartha leis, ar nós na scéalta is fearr i litríochtaí eile ón dtréimhse sin. Ainneoin an chrutha dhúchasaigh phrós-mheadrachtúil, dhinnsheanchasúil, tá nuaíocht sa téacs seo chomh maith. Cé go bhfuil carachtar Chaoilte in *AB* ag teacht le léiriú Odysseus i bhfilíocht Homer, mar shampla, duine gur beag athrú a théann air ó thosach deireadh,[78] is léir mar sin féin go bhfuil dul chun cinn áirithe i gceist le Caoilte, taobh amuigh d'athrú na seanaoise. Mar shampla, tarlaíonn ar a laghad cuid de chur ar aghaidh na heachtra i gceann Chaoilte féin ('7 do bui ic a rádh in a mhenmuin'),[79] mar go dtuigeann an t-údar nach 'lasmuigh' i gcónaí a thiteann gnéithe den scéal amach. Ina theannta sin, tá le tuiscint i ndeireadh an scéil nach bhfuil suaimhneas i ndán do Chaoilte ach amháin laistigh de shocaíocht a bhíonn fé réir ag ríogacht Teamhrach. Gan fhios dúinn go léir, Caoilte san áireamh dar leat, sin é ceann scríbe an scéil: gur i dtreo na Teamhrach a bhí a thriall i gcónaí riamh, ar aon dul le Fíngen mac Luchta. Tar éis dó domhan an dinnsheanchais a chur de agus talamh na hÉireann a shiúl, is i lárionad idéalach na ríogachta a dheineann sé a shuaimhneas sa deireadh thiar, díreach mar a ghealladh Filí na Scol dá bpátrúin nárbh fhiú aon sprioc eile ach flaitheas na Teamhrach, flaitheas nárbh ann dó. Ní túisce ann do Chaoilte, taobh istigh den ríogacht dob fhéidir a rá, agus é in ísle brí ar fad, ná go dtagann Oisín chuige gan choinne agus cuirtear deireadh leis an scéal leis an bhfaisnéis obann sin: 'Ro boi tra Cailti i Teamhraigh amhlaidh sin co torracht Oisin hi cind trill 7 proind chaocat cach laithe dó'.[80] Cineál úrscéil é *AB*, *novella* meánaoiseach Gaeilge.

---

77 LLM 197rb22–43; cf. Ní Shéaghdha, *Agallamh*, ii, 41–2. Féach Kühns, 'Some observations on the *Acallam bec*', lgh 130–6.   78 E. Auerbach, *Mimesis* (1968), lch 17.   79 LLM 194rb11; An Craoibhín, 'An Agallamh bheag', lch 82.   80 LLM 200vb24: 'Caoilte was in Teamhair thus until Oisín arrived after a while, [providing] a meal sufficient for fifty for him every day'.

San athrú meoin a tháinig ar scríobhaithe LLM, mar sin, maidir le leagan amach na lámhscríbhinne i gcás *AB* agus an *Acallam*, tá sé soiléir go mba threise tarraingt na scéalaíochta ná an tseanchais. Maireann an t-iarsma den iarracht tosaigh sin ar bhileog 134v, áfach, mar chomhartha ar bhrí eile a samhlaíodh leis an scéal sarar beartaíodh sa deireadh ar é a chur leis an *Acallam*. Léiríonn sé a thabhachtaí is a bhíonn an comhthéacs lámhscríbhinne sa phlé a deintear ar théacsaí Gaeilge, agus conas is féidir leis an gcomhthéacs sin solas breise a chaitheamh ar bhrí an téacs. Chomh fada agus a bhaineann le *AB*, meabhraíonn sé dúinn an suíomh idir eatarthu a bhí ag an bhFiannaíocht i gcónaí: cos amháin sa bhfiorsheanchas aici, idir dhinnsheanchas agus stair na hÉireann roimh theacht na Críostaíochta, agus an chos eile sa bhfiorscéalaíocht, idir charachtracht agus phléisiúr na heachtraíochta. Ba dhé-aitheantas é sin a chinntigh, ní hamháin an t-athrú meoin a tharla do na scríobhaithe maidir leis an áit chóir a ba cheart bheith ag *AB* in LLM; ach chinntigh chomh maith go mairfeadh an Fhiannaíocht, thar aon chineál eile scéalaíochta ón ré úd, i mbéalaibh daoine go dtí ár n-aimsir féin.[81]

---

81 Táim thar a bheith buíoch den Dr Pádraig de Brún as dréacht den aiste seo a léamh agus a phlé liom.

Revisiting the Reeves *Agallamh*

JOSEPH J. FLAHIVE

Some years ago, Nollaig Ó Muráile classified texts of *Agallamh na seanórach* into four major recensions, a division that provides the basic structure of this collection.[1] But, without denying the basic truth and usefulness of this class-ification, I have claimed that:

> succeeding generations of copyists individually modernised, cut, and interpolated more yet as the taste of the scribes or patrons warranted: long before this point in its evolution [the emergence of 'An tAgallamh Nua in the eighteenth-century], it would not have been unfair to describe the *Agallamh* more as a genre than a text.[2]

Of the many text-groups and variants available, the majority of scholarship has focussed on the earliest group, represented by its vellum witnesses: the Oxford manuscripts Laud 610 and Rawlinson B. 487, the Book of Lismore, and Franciscan MS A 4, this last now deposited in University College Dublin archives;[3] these share a plot structure in addition to simple content. An epit-ome, reduced to 10,000 words and simplifying the plot, fittingly known as the *Agallamh bheag* ('Little *Agallamh*'), is also preserved in the Book of Lismore and is discussed in this volume by Pádraig Ó Macháin, while the most modern version, An tAgallamh Nua ('the new *Agallamh*'), is the subject of another paper by Síle Ní Mhurchú in this collection. In this essay, I focus on the third *Agallamh*, a unique text preserved in one original manuscript only, RIA 24 P 5.[4]

The manuscript was first described by Douglas Hyde, who gave it the appellation of the 'Reeves Manuscript' in honour of the antiquarian bishop

---

1 N. Ó Muráile, 'Agallamh na seanórach' in P. Ó Fiannachta (ed.), *Léachtaí Cholm Cille*, 25: *An fhiannaíocht* (1995), pp 96–127 at p. 103.   2 J. Flahive, '*An fhianaigheacht*: the Fenian cycle' in C. Downey and S. Ó Coileáin (eds), *A history of Irish manuscript literature* (forthcoming). 3 There is a fifth manuscript witness, UCD, Franciscan MS A 20(a), but this is generally understood to be a copy of Franciscan MS A 4.   4 As a doctoral student in Edinburgh, I trav-elled frequently to Dublin to consult UCD, Franciscan MS A 20(b), on which my thesis cen-tred ('The relic lays: a study in late Middle-Gaelic *fianaigheacht*', PhD thesis [2004]). On one of these trips, I made my first pilgrimage to the Royal Irish Academy to see the codex contain-ing this *Agallamh*, which also pertained to my studies. Having filled out the manuscript request slip, I brought it to the librarian's desk. In the reply that I received, I was quickly introduced to the interest that the Academy takes in the work of the scholars who visit its halls, as well as the rarity of this particular request: 'No one has asked for that since Nessa'.

William Reeves, from whose library it came to the Academy – although it was known that the manuscript had been collected by Mac Adam before him. Hyde observed that:

> Some peculiarities of the orthography point to a northern origin. It may have been written in Antrim or Derry or Down, and the only known copy of this particular MS. (one volume of which I have) was made by a Belfast man nearly 120 years ago. Almost all Mr Mac Adam's MSS. were picked up by him in the north of Ireland.[5]

The manuscript also bears the names of a William Morgan and Terrance Morgan, of whom no further information has yet been found. Together, these names could suffice to give nearly a complete history of it in the later eighteenth and nineteenth centuries.

An excellent three-volume semi-diplomatic edition of this codex was produced by Nessa Ní Shéaghdha.[6] Her time as cataloguer of Gaelic manuscripts in the Academy, and also in the National Library of Ireland, served Ní Shéadhgha well in this project. On the basis of the hand, she identified the scribe, who signed his name in other manuscripts that he penned as 'Pádruic mac Oghannan' (classically 'mac Adhomhnáin', sometimes anglicised McOnan), a scribe known for three surviving copies of the earlier *Agallamh*, some Ulster Cycle tales including *Cath Muighe Léana* and *Táin bó Cúailnge*, and *An cath cathardha*. His period of activity comprised the last two decades of the seventeenth century.[7] The *Agallamh* manuscript is at times faded and worn, with some assistance to the reader provided by the transcript that Hyde owned. This was penned by Samuel Bryson. Another imperfect, acephalous copy in Bryson's hand survives as RIA MS 23 L 22, which contains the text of pp 135–470 of the 522 surviving in MS 24 P 5. Ní Shéaghdha also consulted it as necessary in her edition. She further identified excerpts from this *Agallamh* in two eighteenth-century National Library manuscripts, G124 and G126,

5 D. Hyde, 'The Reeves manuscript of the *Agallamh na senorach*', *Révue Celtique*, 38 (1921), 289–95 at 290.   6 N. Ní Shéaghdha (ed.), *Agallamh na seanórach*, 3 vols (1942–5). Unfortunately for scholarship, a point has been reached in which there may well be more copies of the microfilm of the original manuscript in the research libraries of the world than survive of the published text, of which only about 500 copies were printed due to paper rationing during the Second World War. For the same reason, her work did not circulate outside Ireland, and the suspension of journals meant that there were no reviews to bring it to scholars' attention. Since then, the work has languished in obscurity, with only rare citation in academic discourse. It is indeed a happy development that, shortly after this paper was delivered, the Irish Texts Society obtained permission to reprint her edition, which will presently make it accessible to a new generation of scholarship.   7 Ní Shéaghdha, *Agallamh*, i, pp xxii–xxiv. The other manuscripts in his hand are RIA 24 P 4, 24 P 28, and 24 L 36; for further details, see her entries on these manuscripts in T.F. O'Rahilly et al., *Catalogue of Irish manuscripts in the Royal Irish Academy*, 28 fascicles (1926–70), MSS 92, 130 and 131, pp 272–5, 383–6.

and in RIA Stowe MS F v 2. None of these provide the damaged beginning or missing end of MS 24 P 5, and all of them are probably derived from it (or possibly from its exemplar).[8]

Although a programmatic outline of the journey of Oisín though Ireland in this circuit would make for a most interesting comparison with the thematically linked progression explored in detail by Ann Dooley,[9] and by Anne Connon in her contribution to this volume and elsewhere,[10] such an approach to the Reeves *Agallamh* is dependent on analysis of the *Agallamh bheag*, most of which remains unpublished.[11] A full edition of the text has been produced by Julia Kühns, but it has not yet been printed.[12] The introduction to her thesis contributes a key observation: the *Agallamh bheag* is not merely an epitome; it introduces significant quantities of narrative verse not present in the earlier version. As Ní Shéaghdha observed, virtually the entire text of the *Agallamh bheag* has been imported, with some stylistic reworking, to form a large portion of the framework of the Reeves *Agallamh*, with additional episodes and poems inserted as thematically appropriate throughout.[13] Furthermore, a large quantity of material from the early *Acallam* that is not present in the shorter work is reintroduced, much of which 'bookends' the *Agallamh bheag* at the start and conclusion, as Hyde's synopsis describes, but verse could also adorn the new text in different places on occasion. The extent of the expansion – encompassing as least as much new material in addition to what was recovered from the medieval text – is such that the *Agallamh bheag* comprises only a tenth of the final text.

Hyde described the Reeves text mostly by comparison with Stokes' edition of the first recension;[14] although he observed that a large section incorporated virtually the entirety of the *Agallamh bheag*, he did not make that difficult-to-access text the basis of his comparative discussion. The same approach was later followed in the published RIA catalogue,[15] which simply lists the embedded poems not found in Stokes. This method, in which the point of reference is the edition of the first recension, obscures the chain of textual dependence and evolution. It is interesting that although Ní

8 Ní Shéaghdha, *Agallamh*, i, pp xx–xxii; see also N. Ní Shéaghdha and P. Ó Macháin, *Catalogue of Irish manuscripts in the National Library of Ireland*, 13 fascicles published (1967–), pp 29–30, 32–3; O'Rahilly et al., *Catalogue of Irish manuscripts in the Royal Irish Academy*, MS 35, pp 113–14. 9 A. Dooley, 'The date and purpose of *Acallam na senórach*', *Éigse*, 34 (2004), 97–126; A. Dooley and H. Roe, *Tales of the elders of Ireland* (1999), pp xx–xxviii. 10 See above pp 21–59; A. Connon, 'Plotting *Acallam na senórach*: the physical context of the "Mayo" sequence' in S. Sheehan et al. (eds), *Gablánach in scélaigecht* (2013), pp 69–102. 11 Hyde published a third of the text with a Modern Irish translation: 'An Agallamh bheag', *Lia Fáil*, 1 (1924), 79–107; this has been translated into English by W. Pennington, 'The little colloquy', *Philological Quarterly*, 9.2 (1930), 97–110. 12 J.S. Kühns, 'An edition and translation of the *Agallamh bheag* in the Book of Lismore', MPhil thesis (2006). 13 Ní Shéaghdha, *Agallamh*, i, p. xxv. 14 W. Stokes (ed. and partial trans.), 'Acallamh na senórach' in W. Stokes and E. Windisch (eds), *Irische Texte*, iv, 1 (1900). 15 MS 93, pp 275–7.

Shéaghdha also discusses the *Agallamh bheag* in her introduction, her discussion has nothing to say concerning the direct link in the line of descent through the evolution of the plot, despite the fact that she did find such a similarity in the opening scenes as to use the beginning of the *Agallamh bheag* to supply the text (three pages in her edition) missing or illegible at the beginning of MS 24 P 5, adjusted by switching the names of Caoilte and Oisín to bring their places in line with the later text.[16]

The circuit of Ireland, *deiseal*, which stands as the framework in the *Agallamh bheag*, still acts as the frame for the *Agallamh*'s second half, and the difference of length is primarily due to larding: the introduction of a longer beginning and several episodes based on the original text, the addition of more verse, and the composition of long *argumenta* for many additional poems. There are two other striking differences, as Hyde noted:

> In all the vellums from which Stokes has edited, it is Caoilte who at the beginning of the story meets Saint Patrick and the Clerics, and it is Oisin who retires into the Sidh (Shee) mound of Ocht Cleitigh where his mother was. Caoilte in the vellums is the hero of the story up to line 2255, when without any motivation or apparent cause, Oisin suddenly comes on the scene in company with Patrick, and the King of Munster.
>
> In the Reeves MS. on the other hand, Oisin it is who at the beginning of the book meets Patrick and is the hero of the story until Caoilte appears, but Caoilte's appearance in the Reeves MSS. [*sic*] is properly led up to, and explained.[17]

Those who study the early *Acallam* are familiar with how the text breaks off in all copies, leaving us only much later tradition and guesswork as to how the dialogue may have concluded, though it is generally agreed to include the deaths of the ancients at Tara. One also encounters the same problem with this text. The poem on Ros Teamhrach is legible until the final quatrains, where it becomes slightly fragmentary; and, at the last verse, the second couplet begins a new and wholly illegible page. Although one can reconstruct the poem from other copies with ease, the remainder of the prose text is too faded. At any rate, in the extant portion, the procession stops at Tara, and the tale most likely did as well shortly thereafter.

The Reeves *Agallamh* comprises a prosimetrum of dissimilar construction to the early one. In Stokes' text, one encounters short poems, often comprising or highlighting lists, such as battles, gravesites, the cups of the *fian*-warriors, and the hounds of Fionn. There are many brief epitaphs and epigrams. Long poems are rare. The frame-tale unfolds through the prose; it incorpo-

---

16 Ní Shéaghdha, *Agallamh*, i, pp xv–xix and 1 n. 1.   17 Hyde, 'The Reeves manuscript', 290.

rates verse interludes, alongside brief prose in-tales, narrated by Caoilte or Oisín, which impart information requested by Patrick and his company. The poems from the first *Acallam* that are retained in the *Agallamh bheag* come through into the Reeves recension, along with those added there. Many more poems from the original *Acallam* are also re-introduced. In contrast to the first version, where prose narrative is supplemented by lyric, elegiac, or versified lists, this text does not unfold simply in prose segments between short poems, though the prosimetric form remains. Instead, the majority of poems are preceded by long prose *argumenta*, describing the action – and there is action – contained in the poem. While the short poems from the *Agallamh bheag* and a few more of that ilk are retained, there are long, narrative lays of a sort not found in the earlier *Acallam*. Many of these contain lore, lists, and learning, which form a narrative that reduplicates in both prose and verse with linguistic concord of many phrases found in both. The prose bears the alliterative style of the later medieval romances in contrast to the greater directness of the verse.

Hyde was optimistic indeed about the antiquity of the tradition of the lays in the *Agallamh*, and imported this into faith in the great age of this version:

> But there are other reasons for believing that it may represent a text quite as old as any of the vellums if not older, for in certain stories where these only tell a part of the tale the Reeves MS. tells the whole story, and while they have often only a few verses of a poem, the Reeves MS. gives a long full poem (some of them are to be found in the Book of Leinster) upon which the prose story is usually founded. Often where the vellums have no poem at all the Reeves MS. has ten or twenty or thirty stanzas, and it seems generally that it is the verses which are the older part, and that it is upon them the prose story is built up.[18]

Although the investigations of the last ninety years have been far less comprehensive than might be desired, modern philology has borne out the antiquity of the lays, if not the prose. The Reeves text cannot predate the *Agallamh bheag*, which is generally dated to shortly after *AS*.[19] For this reason, Ó Muraíle called the Reeves version An tAgallamh Déanach ('the late *Agallamh*'),[20] although this name can be misleading when there is not only the still later Agallamh Nua ('new *Agallamh*'), but also the popular verse dialogue that takes the name *Agallamh Oisín agus Pádraig* 'The dialogue of Oisín and Pádraig', the oldest copy of which is in *Duanaire Finn*, where Gerard Murphy dated it to the sixteenth

---

18 Ibid., 291.   19 See J.S. Kühns, 'Some observations on the *Acallam bec*' in S.J. Arbuthnot and G. Parsons (eds), *The Gaelic Finn tradition* (2012), pp 122–38 at p. 124.   20 Ó Muraíle, 'Agallamh na seanórach', p. 103.

century.[21] The floruit of Mac Oghannáin at the end of the seventeenth century provides the *terminus ante quem*. In her edition of the text, Ní Shéaghdha evaluates the language of the Reeves *Agallamh*; the chief points of reference in this discussion are the Franciscan MS A 4 text and the *Agallamh bheag*. She notes that the 'modern' type of Ossianic verse, which became popular in the sixteenth century, is not included among the lays, though poems of an elegiac character like those in the Book of the Dean of Lismore are; on these grounds she gives an estimated date of composition for the *Agallamh* in the fourteenth or fifteenth century.[22] For the present, this may suffice. More important is the consensus that pre-existing verse is embedded within. As will be explored in greater detail below, some of this is also found in earlier manuscripts; other items employ pre-Classical language. Within the *Agallamh*, the dating of individual poems has as little relation to the medium in which they are found, or to each other, as the age of the sixpences do to the Christmas pudding.

So far, the sketch has been drawn with a broad brush. Although details are very numerous in so lengthy a text, this overview remains to be supplemented with a selection of such details chosen to illustrate different aspects of the work. The listing of its constituent poems that are not found in *Acallam na senórach*, as undertaken by Hyde and also by the Academy catalogue, remains useful.[23] Unfortunately, neither list is complete, for both exclude single quatrains and various other short items. They include the items found in the *Agallamh bheag* alongside those added only in the Reeves *Agallamh* without distinction, obscuring at what stage material might have been introduced into the *Agallamh* tradition. There is a further drawback to the simple approach of listing out the poems' *incipits*, in that *Acallam na senórach* is known in several places to include stray quatrains here and there, but to tell the tale in prose. On the other hand, a full lay is frequently found in the Reeves *Agallamh*; where it is an addition, it will not be revealed by this technique, because the first line of the lay will not match the initial words of the selection of quatrains embedded in the first recension's text: the *Acallam*'s practice of excerpting stanzas for inclusion as ornament to the prose frustrates the method of listing poems and counting the matches. When comparing the texts of the poem 'Aonach anú luidh an rí' found in *Duanaire Finn* with the more conservative versions in the Reeves *Agallamh* and Book of Leinster, Murphy drew attention to the presence of a prose version of the story in the first *Acallam* (ll. 1595–618), which is ornamented by four non-consecutive quatrains taken from the lay.[24] If one were simply to tally the first lines, it would seem that Stokes' *Acallam* has four short poems not found in the Reeves *Agallamh*, and that the latter text incorporates

21 E. MacNeill and G. Murphy (ed. and trans.), *Duanaire Finn*, 3 vols (1908–53), iii, p. 126.
22 Ní Shéaghdha, *Agallamh*, i, §10, esp. pp xxx–xxxi.   23 Hyde, 'The Reeves Manuscript', 291–4; O'Rahilly et al., *Catalogue of Irish manuscripts in the Royal Irish Academy*, p. 277.
24 MacNeill and Murphy, *Duanaire Finn*, iii, p. 26.

a long poem not included in the former. In this case, the lay survives in multiple manuscripts and the text is easily identified; but, if it had perished, any attempt to connect the four stanzas as part of a lost whole would be speculative, and it could not be said with any certainty that these were not independent short compositions – or indeed quotations from several different compositions. There is also another slight problem of deciding what poems are constituent of the original text: there are discrepancies between the copies, especially additions in the Franciscan MS A 4 text. Stokes knit together a composite text for publication that includes materials not found in all the manuscripts. It should suffice to say that the early text as presented by Stokes has passed down to the later one seventy-six poems. The longest of these, 'Ráidh a Chaoilte, cia dá bhfuil' (a lore-poem sometimes titled 'Seanchas na féine'), has fifty-three quatrains here, but only forty-nine in Stokes' edition. The next longest has twenty-nine quatrains. The majority, however, are very short, with a substantial proportion not extending beyond three stanzas.

Comparative listing nevertheless demonstrates the kind of poems introduced, each of which stands as the centrepiece for an extended prose episode.[25] To begin, there are twelve poems found in the *Agallamh bheag* as well as in the Reeves *Agallamh* that are not in the original *Acallam*; only two of these are single quatrains. Six of these poems have more than fourteen quatrains. These poems have a strong learned element, as typified by 'An bhfuil neach uaibh abradh riom', known as 'Ceasta Chaoilte', which contains a series of questions about toponyms extending to seventy-seven quatrains. There is some variation in the quantity of verse in these two versions. The second longest of the poems in this group, 'Dámh thrír thángadar a-le', here extends to thirty-six quatrains, whereas the *Agallamh bheag* only includes twenty-two; another copy of this poem preserved in the Book of Leinster has twenty-three.[26] In contrast, 'Baile na ríogh Ros Teamhrach' has only seventeen stanzas here, whilst the *Agallamh bheag* includes thirty-six; confusingly, an altogether different poem of four quatrains' length with the same *incipit* is found in the *Acallam*, and is reproduced here alongside the longer poem, yet it is absent from the *Agallamh bheag*. Beyond the twelve poems introduced via the *Agallamh bheag*, there are thirty-four further poems in the Reeves *Agallamh* that are not in Stokes' edition of the *Acallam*. Most of these are substantial poems: only three are single stanzas, with a further one that is two quatrains in length.

A number of these reflect toponymic or genealogical learning, like so much of the early *fianaigheacht* corpus collected by Meyer.[27] Unlike the ear-

---

25 Ní Shéaghdha, *Agallamh*, iii, pp 256–61, indexes all verse in the *Agallamh*, with cross-references to Stokes' *Acallam*, the *Agallamh bheag* (abbreviated 'H'), and other notable manuscript copies of individual poems. For the purpose of this discussion, references listed therein are not duplicated.   26 R.I. Best et al. (eds), *The Book of Leinster formerly Lebar na Núachongbála*, 6 vols (1954–83), iv, ll. 29301–412.   27 Meyer, *Fianaigecht* (1910), pp xviii–xxxii; continued in

liest Fenian texts, or, for that matter, the verse in the *Acallam*, the items found here are extended poems, with narrative elements, but still modelled on *dinnshenchas*:

- 'Cnuca, cnoc ós linn Life' (61 qq), describes the site of Cumhall's final battle;
- 'Claidhid fir feart Éadaoine' (10 qq), explaining the grave of Oscar's wife;
- 'Fionn File ba fear go lí' (17 qq), also preserved in *Duanaire Finn*, is a genealogical poem listing Clann Tréanmhóir;
- 'Clointear craobh coibneasa an ríogh' (17 qq), also largely concerns Fenian genealogy;
- 'Do ghon Luichead Aodh na gCéad' (8 qq), also found in *Macgnímartha Finn*, gives details on certain participants in the battle of Cnucha, focussing on Goll;
- A *dinnshenchas* poem beginning 'Snámh Dhá Éan, na heóin dia tá' (55 qq), the first section of which forms part of the *Metrical dinnshenchas*, but here the last stanzas give an additional, alternative explanation of the toponym's origin following the *dúnadh* of the original account;
- The extension of the poem 'Alma Laighean, lios na bhFían' to 45 qq, where the *Acallam* incorporates only 10 quatrains, is worthy of note in this context, even if the poem is not strictly a new addition. It tells of Fionn's *ráth* at Almha, and how he acquired it.

Others, however, are purely narrative lays. A number of these, such as 'Cliodhna chinn-fhionn, búan an béud' on Tonn Chlíodhna, 'Tiaghaid teachta uainn go hAodh' ('Oidheadha Ghuill agus Aodha'), or 'Iongnadh fis tádhbhas damh' ('Oidheadha na féine') have an elegiac tone or focus on death that typifies a strain of late medieval Fenian verse, especially the collection of heroic verse in the Book of the Dean of Lismore as well as Irish lays concerning the Battle of Gabhra, though the identification of graves as a component of *dinnshenchas* is a concern earlier.[28] Narrative poems added or expanded at length are:

'Erschienene Schriften', *Zeitschrift für celtische Philologie*, 8 (1912), 599, an abridged translation of which has been inserted as an addendum to the Dublin Institute of Advanced Studies' reprint of *Fianaigecht*. These lists recently have been re-evaluated by K. Murray, 'Interpreting the evidence: problems with dating the early *fianaigecht* corpus' in S.J. Arbuthnot and G. Parsons (eds), *The Gaelic Finn tradition* (2012), pp 31–49, esp. pp 31–3 and 48–9. **28** D.E. Meek, 'The Gaelic ballads of Scotland: creativity and adaptation' in H. Gaskill (ed.), *Ossian revisited* (1992), pp 19–48 at pp 36–7; idem, '*Duanaire Finn* and Gaelic Scotland' in J. Carey (ed.), *Duanaire Finn: reassessments* (2003), pp 19–38 at pp 34–5. Most noteworthy among the early poems focussed on death is 'Ligi Guill i mMaig Raigni', the earliest witness of which is the Book of Leinster (vol. iv, ll. 28620–964); see D. Ó Murchadha (ed. and trans.), *Lige Guill* (2009).

- 'A chorr úd thall san léana'. Ní Shéaghdha entitled the episode *Oisín is an chorr*, 'Oisín and the crane' (129 qq), which describes Oisín's encounter with an ancient bird, in which they reciprocally narrate a tale. The crane versifies the whole of her life: Oisín responds with a single adventure of his own;
- 'An abhus, a ógláigh fhinn' (31 qq), a narrative poem on Tonn Chlíodhna, the events of which are referred to in the prose of the *Acallam* (perhaps hinting at the pre-existence of the lay), but no verse is given there;
- 'Leaba dese a nDún Gaoithe' (36 qq), a tale of the warrior Dealbh Scóinne and his poisonous sword;
- The acephalous poem '... mar do bhímís uile ann', of which 14 qq remain following the chasm in the manuscript between pp 106 and 107, focuses on the career of Diarmaid Ó Duibhne, ending with his grave, though it may well have been more than an elegy;
- 'Sealcc do-righneadh le Fionn féin' (26 qq) is a chase-lay that results in the reproach of Oscar's valour;
- 'Síothal Chaoilte cia ros-fuair' (121 qq), a long narrative lay on how Fionn obtained a wonderful vessel from the *aos sídhe* after chasing an enchanted boar and proposing marriage to the Otherworldly Scáthach;
- 'Téighim toiscc d'fhulucchadh Finn', a popular lay known as 'Caoilte and the creatures', telling of Caoilte rounding up animals and birds as a ransom for Fionn from imprisonment by an angry Cormac, is here told in 55 qq. Several other short poems on the subject precede it. This poem is told with even greater expansion of the hunt in the Book of the Dean of Lismore.[29] The central episode is also preserved in 29 qq in *Duanaire Finn* beginning 'Maidhim in mhaidin fa ghlonn';[30]
- 'Turas agom dia hAoine' (28 qq), the tale of Caol and Créide;
- 'Aonach anú luidh an rí' (49 qq), known as 'Finn and the phantoms' is presented in full; the *Acallam* includes four quatrains from this poem to adorn its prose summary. It is also found in the Book of Leinster;[31]
- The lay of Bearrach Breac, 'As í cathair na ccéad', appears here as a narrative adventure of 29 qq, only four of which are found in the excerpt in the *Acallam*;
- 'Dámh trír tanccadar a-le' (36 qq), expanded from the *Agallamh bheag*, which presents only twenty-two quatrains. It is not found in the *Acallam*, but its antiquity is guaranteed by its presence in the Book of Leinster.

29 A transcription of the poem is printed in A. MacBain and J. Kennedy (eds), *Reliquiae Celticae*, 2 vols (1892–4), i, pp 72–5; and J.F. Campbell (ed.), *Leabhar na feinne* (1872), pp 139–41. For a normalised text and translation, see Neil Ross (ed. and trans.), *Heroic poetry from the Book of the Dean of Lismore* (1939), pp 40–59. A new Scottish Gaelic Text Society edition by Donald Meek is forthcoming.   30 MacNeill and Murphy, *Duanaire Finn*, i, pp 19–21, 116–8. 31 Best et al. (eds), *The Book of Leinster*, iv, ll. 29089–300.

There are also some learned descriptions, resembling the verse in the *Acallam*, though these poems are not found in it. These tend to be among the shorter additions:

- 'D'aonach Tailltean téighmís-ne' (13 qq) comprises a description of the splendour of the fair of Tailltiu;
- 'Is é so an slabhradh suairc sean' (9 qq) gives the history of Lugh's chain.

Not all the poems included are in syllabic verse. 'Rhetoric' is also represented in the additions of 'Ní fó an feidhm flaith-chogadh' and 'Screadois muc re mór-chonuibh'. The corpus listed here falls into two major categories: a significant core of fully narrative verse and learned classics in the *dinnshenchas* tradition.

One of the issues that arises frequently is the handling of materials inherited from within the tradition. After Caoilte narrates his rescue of Fionn in the poem 'Téighim toiscc d'fhulucchadh Finn', the company proceed to Sídh Ochta Cleitigh, where Oisín meets a crane and converses with her in a long lay, 'A chorr úd thall san léana'.[32] The insertion of the episode concerning a crane (*corr*) at this point clearly builds on a pun, for Caoilte's adventure is a *corr-imirce* 'odd migration' (*AgS* iii, p. 83.14). The crane's narration is the story of her life, the tale of a shape-changing ancient. She reveals herself to be of royal blood, Miadhach, daughter of Eachdhonn Mór. Both she and her foster-sister Morann fell in love with the same man, Ábhartach, and Morann brought this quarrel to Eachdhonn. Although Miadhach renounced her love – for which her father rewarded her with a splendid catalogue of treasures – yet he changed her into a crane. She was then chased into exile by the eagle of Druim Cró. Returning to Ireland, she became the lover of the blackbird of Leitir Bhile, until they parted due to incompatible habitats. Her next love was the pigeon of Aonach Luisean. She then asks Oisín to reciprocate; he proceeds to give not his own history, but a tale of a quest to Lochlann and back to recover the women of the *fian*, who have been taken by Aonghus.

There are no other copies of this poem, and it displays no signs of linguistic antiquity of any significant degree beyond the prose. Nevertheless, its crane motif is one with many echoes. Though these are not easy to unravel, they demonstrate continuities in the materials of the tradition. The ancient crane echoes the tradition of the bag called the *corrbholg*, which first appears in the poem 'A Rí richid, réidig dam' in a mysterious quatrain at

---

32 I presented a text seminar on this poem and the 'Crane-bag' lay in *Duanaire Finn* in the Department of Early and Medieval Irish, University College Cork, in 2005. This discussion makes use of the unpublished materials used in that seminar, and I wish to thank the participants for their ideas, which have shaped my own views on these texts.

the end of the world-history poem, not following on from the previous one due to a lacuna:

> Tricha sét, ní gáes fir buirb, tall Find a cráes in chorrbuilg,
> íar nguin Glonda 'cunn áth oll is Lé[i]th Lúachra na llúathbond.

Thirty jewels – it is not the wisdom of an ignorant man – Finn took out of the jaws of the crane-bag, after he had slain Glonna at the vast ford and Liath Luachra of the swift deeds.[33]

This object also features in *Macgnímartha Finn*, where Goll carries away the *corrbholg* when he kills Cumhall. It is later recovered by Fionn from Liath Luachra, whom he defeats.[34] Although Meyer, aware of later tradition, translated the term as 'crane-bag', perhaps in these early texts 'peculiar/magical bag' should be understood. There is a fragment on this object in *Duanaire Finn*, which Murphy thought was 'of the 13th century, or perhaps the very late Middle Irish period'.[35] In the *Duanaire Finn* poem, Caoilte tells of the *corrbholg* of Tréanmhór, Fionn's father. It was a magical item, made from the skin of Manannán's pet crane. This crane was also a changeling, who lost out in a love-triangle. Here, she bears the name Aoife, and her lover is Ilbhreac. Her rival, Iuchra, tricks her into joining her for a swim, at which Aoife transforms into a crane. Iuchra prophesies Aoife's future avian life, and that after her death, Manannán would fashion a treasure-bag from her skin, capable of holding vast quantities that disappear into it like the ebb and flow of the sea. Manannán then gave it as a gift to Conaire, the legendary high-king. *Cetera desunt.*

This fragment toys with the reader's expectations. With respect to the term *corrbholg*, the prefix *corr-* 'rounded', 'odd-shaped', 'peculiar' is frequent and prolific, but only one ordinary compound, the magical/satirical practice of *corrghuine*, along with its linguistic derivatives (*corrghuineach*, *corrghuineacht*) are found in the lexicon with the sense of *corr* 'crane'.[36] The lay appears to play with the audience's expectations in its explanation. T.F. O'Rahilly understood this as a corruption of something mythologically profound:

---

33 Meyer, *Fianaigecht* (1910), pp 50–51, §28.   34 There are a number of texts and translations: J. O'Donovan (ed. and trans.), 'Mac-gnimartha Finn mac Cumaill: the boyish exploits of Finn mac Cumhaill', *Transactions of the Ossianic Society for the year 1856*, vol. 4 (1859), 281–304; K. Meyer (ed.), 'Macgnimartha Find', *Révue Celtique*, 5 (1881–3), 197–204; idem (trans.), 'The boyish exploits of Finn', *Ériu*, 1 (1904), 180–90; J.F. Nagy (trans.), 'Appendix 1.1: the boyhood deeds of Finn', *The wisdom of the outlaw* (1985), pp 209–18.   35 MacNeill and Murphy, *Duanaire Finn*, iii, p. 20. The lay is printed and translated in ibid., i, pp 21–2, 118–20.   36 See *DIL* 'C' col. 486 s.vv. *corrguine*, *corrguinech*, *corrguinecht*. There are also a handful of poetic compounds listed s.v. *corr* 2 (col. 484), most prominent of which is *corr-clerech* 'crane-cleric', a poetic name for Colum Cille, which builds on both the slenderness of the crane as a metaphor for asceticism and possibly also the endearment *corrucán* 'dear little crane' (s.v., col. 487).

Gilla in Chomded and the compiler of 'Macgnímartha Find' understood the *corrbolg* to be some kind of bag (*bolg*) containing 'jewels' or
precious articles of workmanship; according to the latter text the bag
and its contents belonged to Cumall, father of Finn. Later tradition,
apart from the poem [in *Duanaire Finn*] mentioned above, knows nothing of the *corrbolg*. In our principal source, 'Macgnímartha Find', the
allusions to the *corrbolg* are more or less meaningless as they stand, and
they serve no apparent purpose in the tale. It is clear that in what we
are told concerning the *corrbolg* we have the remnants of a dying tradition, which in the twelfth century was no longer understood. The
analogy of *caladbolg* and *gaí Bulga* places the real meaning of *corrbolg*
beyond doubt. It is a name for the lightning-weapon, belonging to the
Otherworld-deity, which Finn acquired; in other words it is ultimately
identical with the spear of Fiacclach mac Conchinn. *Corrbolg*, therefore, would mean something like 'pointed lightning', i.e. the lightning-
spear; for the adjectival prefix compare *corr-ga*, *corr-shleg*. As the word
bolg, 'lightning', suggests, Finn's connexion with the *corrbolg* probably
belonged exclusively to the traditions of the Builg or Érainn. Liath
Luachra we may take to have been a Munster counterpart of Goll; the
episode in which he is slain by Finn originally told how Finn got possession of the god's lightning-spear and 'slew' the god with it.[37]

Yet it is equally clear that the crane, living or dead, has a deeply rooted place,
and is no mistake. Not only is there a correspondence of the love-triangle of
the transformed ancient in the two lays, but the crane has a deeper significance,
which Anne Ross has explored at length. In the ancient Continental Celtic
world, cranes feature in Gallo-Roman religious art: 'La grue apparaît ... dans
des contextes militaires, et puet ainsi être associée à Mars dans son rôle de dieu
de la guerre' (that is, Gallo-Roman Midir as Mars).[38] Ross' paper traces the
crane as companion of Otherworldly figures/gods, observing that the crane had
a special status and was never eaten; this status is reflected in medieval Celtic
laws. The appearance of a crane is considered an ill omen for battle – an
Otherworldly presence calling the warrior thither, foretelling doom. There are
additional transformations of women into cranes in medieval Irish literature,
including associations of crane-figures with Colum Cille. Cranes in folklore provide protection against evils. Ross assembles a large body of evidence for a long
continuity of the association of cranes with Otherworldly women. The associations of transformations of the rival woman in the love-triangles of each poem
and the Otherworldly motifs of the ancient animals that appear as the bird-
lovers in the *Agallamh* poem, and of the court of Manannán in the *Duanaire*

37 T.F. O'Rahilly, *Early Irish history and mythology* (1946), pp 73–4.   38 A. Ross, 'Esus et les
trois «Grues»', *Études Celtiques*, 9 (1960), 405–38 at 415.

Finn fragment, all evoke aspects of a cohesive tradition, which does not support O'Rahilly's theory, which requires the corruption of forgotten myth.

Yet, the waters are muddy: the mythological theory strikes back from within the *Agallamh* poem in a way that O'Rahilly never considered. The episode related by Oisín in the second half of the lay in the Reeves *Agallamh* is not unrelated to the *corrbholg* theme: the Fenian women have been taken away due to a trick by Aonghus, the Otherworld deity. As the *fian* pursues them overseas, they journey to Lochlann, a place with Otherworldly associations. There, the king, who is magically invincible, is slain with his own sword by Goll, in exactly the manner required by the myth recalled by O'Rahilly. Aonghus then returns the women when they arrive back in Ireland. Is the division between the king and Aonghus merely a late development of an inherited plot? When the two seemingly unrelated tales are read together, suddenly a deep connexion between them is found, like the uncharted waters beneath the earth through which the ancient salmon swims between wells. Both halves of the poem depend for their plot on different aspects of the legend; they comprise a diptych. It is rash to dismiss any part of the tradition as a mistake: indeed, the waters of this tradition run deep, and no attempt will be made here to channel them into facile answers.

Having examined an episode that displays content of definite antiquity, it is fitting to proceed to one that contains text that demonstrably predates its setting. The poem beginning 'Aonach anú luidh an rí', given the title 'Díoghaltas na bhfuath' by Ní Shéaghdha, which has also been named in English 'Find and the phantoms' by Stokes, and 'The headless phantoms' by Murphy, provides an illustrative case. This poem is not found in full in the earlier versions of the *Acallam*, but it was easily drawn in fully alongside the prose account of its plot as the *Agallamh* expanded and developed. Its antiquity is proven by independent preservation in the twelfth-century Book of Leinster and also by evaluation of its language, which Kuno Meyer placed in the eleventh century.[39] An earlier version of the tale also survives in prose, which has been dated to the tenth century – and possibly the ninth – by Meyer,[40] and by Murphy variously to the tenth and twelfth centuries.[41] An interesting comparison is also found in the presence of another copy in *Duanaire Finn*, where the text has been modernised greatly from the Middle Irish original. A sample quatrain demonstrates the extent of textual divergence:[42]

---

39 Meyer, *Fianaigecht*, p. xxv, §XXXI.   **40** Ibid., p. xxiii §XIX. See L.-C. Stern (ed. and trans.), 'Find and the phantoms', *Revue Celtique*, 13 (1892), 5–22.   **41** MacNeill and Murphy, *Duanaire Finn*, iii, pp lix–lx.   **42** In addition to the diplomatic presentation of the text in Best et al. (eds), *The Book of Leinster*, iv, ll. 29089–300, the poem has been edited and translated by W. Stokes, 'Find and the phantoms', *Révue Celtique*, 7 (1886), 289–307; editions of the other copies are in MacNeill and Murphy, *Duanaire Finn*, i, pp 28–30, and Ní Shéaghdha, *Agallamh*, i, pp 173–82. The discussion draws on Flahive, 'The relic lays', pp 79–80.

Book of Leinster

Inn uair do bímmis cind ar chind.
cia nar cobrad acht mád Find.
ropsar marba mór in mod.
meni beth Find a oenor.[43]

When we were face to face, who would not help but Fionn?
we would have been dead men – great the matter – were it not for
Fionn alone.

Duanaire Finn

Mar do bhádhmar cionn ar chionn. cía do fhoirfedh sin acht Fionn
ba ro mharbh sinne dhe. muna bheith Fionn na Féine.[44]

As we were face to face, who should have protected us but Fionn?
we would have been killed by it, were it not for Fionn of the *fían*.

Agallamh na seanórach

In uair do bhám*ar* cionn ar chionn
cia do fhóirfea*d*h sin acht Fionn?
do m*arbhad*h sinn uile dhe
muna bheith Fionn na Féine.[45]

When we were face to face, who should have protected us but Fionn?
we would all have been killed by it, were it not for Fionn of the *fían*.

In this example, alongside the usual orthographical modernisations, multiple
changes have been made towards intelligibility for the readers of the later
manuscripts, not all of which preserve the metrical integrity of the poem, as
the hypometric line *c* of the *Duanaire Finn* text demonstrates.

Over the course of the poem, sometimes either later manuscript will agree
with the Book of Leinster against the other. The tradition of manuscript studies bows to the venerable Book of Leinster, but there are cases where the evidence suggests that seventeenth-century witnesses may preserve original readings
against innovation in the Book of Leinster.[46] In the face of such continual vari-

---

43 Best et al. (eds), *The Book of Leinster*, iv, ll. 29265–68; equivalent to Stokes, 'Find and the
phantoms', ll. 181–4. The editions of this quatrain are identical save for the reduction of the
initial *Inn* to *In* by Stokes. The translations are by the author.   **44** MacNeill and Murphy,
Duanaire Finn, i, p. 30, q. 38 (cf. ibid., p. 129).   **45** Ní Shéaghdha, *Agallamh*, i, p. 180.16–19.
46 The Book of Leinster's treatment of its texts has been the subject of ongoing study. Kevin
Murray provides a guide and discussion in regard to another text in the codex in his edition of

ations, the additional possibility arises that some obvious modernisations could have been introduced independently in both these manuscripts or in their lines of descent, rather than inherited through a modernising intermediary.

In the quatrain examined here, the textual changes represent a move towards simplification and increased intelligibility. These three copies of this poem formed one of the case studies used by John Carey to revisit and evaluate the dating criteria used by Murphy to assess the age of texts in *Duanaire Finn*.[47] Over the course of the poem, *Duanaire Finn* has modernisms in a number of places where the *Agallamh* text is more conservative; these are listed by Carey. In the first quatrain, the Book of Leinster and the *Agallamh* rhyme nominative *rí* : *lí*; but *rí* is used as a genitive in *Duanaire Finn*. A modern verbal ending is introduced in 8*c*, and an English loan-word, *sporais*, in 15*b*. At 12*a*, *Duanaire Finn* alone uses the nominative singular in place of the genitive plural. To these may be also added the preservation of the feminine numeral in *Trí lá teóra hoidhche ar bhlaidh* (*AgS* iii, p. 175.9) against *Trí lá is trí hoidhche go mblaidh* (*Duanaire Finn* i, p. 28, q. 10*a*). However, Carey also observes that the *Agallamh*'s text does tend to introduce independent pronouns. He concludes:

> If the *Duanaire Finn* copy of 'The Headless Phantoms' is considered in isolation, then, I do not see how it could persuasively be dated earlier than the thirteenth century, and an even later date would be difficult to rule out. That it is in fact older than this is of course guaranteed by the Book of Leinster copy, written in the twelfth century: here (and for that matter in the *Agallamh* copy as well) none of the late features just mentioned is to be found.[48]

Although it would be unfair to judge *Duanaire Finn* too harshly here on the basis of a modernised text alongside many well-preserved ones in its collection, this example does highlight the preservation of poems of considerable antiquity embedded within the *Agallamh*, and it provides a yardstick for the evaluation of the treatment of the verse. The presence in the *Agallamh* of this poem, alongside several other poems also preserved in the Book of Leinster, 'Dámh thrír thángadar a-le' and 'Snámh Dhá Éan, na heóin dia tá' (an item in the canonical *dinnshenchas*), and other poems of known antiquity, 'Cnuca, cnoc ós linn Life'[49] and 'Do ghon Luichead Aodh na gCéad', embedded in

---

'The finding of the *Táin*', *Cambrian Medieval Celtic Studies*, 41 (2001), 17–23 at 19, esp. n. 14.
47 'Remarks on dating' in J. Carey (ed.), *Duanaire Finn: reassessments* (2003), pp 1–18 at 16–18.
48 Ibid., p. 17.   49 This poem is not the canonical *dinnshenchas* version, though it shares seven opening quatrains with it, then continues with two on the Fenian battle, a long digression on the kings of Ireland, and placement of Fionn's life within regnal synchronisms. It has been edited separately by M. Power, 'Cnucha cnoc os cionn Life', *Zeitschrift für celtische Philologie*, 11 (1916), 39–55.

Macgnimartha Finn in Oxford, Bodleian Library MS Laud 610,[50] provide testimony that venerable materials previously outside the *Agallamh* tradition were sought for incorporation into this composition; a number of other lays containing signs of earlier phases of the language, of which earlier copies have not been preserved, may also be similar in age.

Having looked in detail at a small bit of text that is found in two other important manuscripts, and allowing for some evaluation of the qualities of this line of transmission of verse texts, a broader comparison of an episode of the *Agallamh* provides other insights into its construction. The episode 'Sítheal Chaoilte' ('Caoilte's dipper') will be considered here.[51] It is constructed around a long narrative lay, here extending to 121 qq, with some Middle Irish linguistic features. The poem is also preserved in *Duanaire Finn* (117 qq), the text of which Murphy dated to *c.*1200; however, he did not collate it with the *Agallamh*'s version, which provides more conservative readings on occasion than those available in the text in *Duanaire Finn*.[52] There are also copies in three late *duanaireadha* (Royal Irish Academy MSS 23 L 34 and 24 M 2, and Maynooth Renehan MS 69); the texts they contain are close to that found in the *Agallamh*.

Oisín opens the lay with a description of the *sítheal* just recovered from a pool at Duibh-cheachair. He proceeds to narrate its history, and recalls Caoilte. With the *fiana* assembled at Assaroe, Forann departs with a third of the retinue. Fionn then proceeds to divide the hunting grounds of Ireland among the remaining troop, sending Oisín to Leinster and Ossory, with Fionn's men hunting in Leath Cuinn. Fionn himself remains behind in Bearnas with Bran and eight of his men, likewise accompanied by their hounds. Soon, a boar appears.[53] The hounds are loosed upon it, but the boar kills them all. The spears of the *fian*-warriors merely glance off his hide. Fionn steps forward, inspiring Bran with a *caithréim* of the boars that he slew. The chase is afoot. As they proceed aptly enough to Gleann Teichidh, 'Glen of the Chase', a churl comes forth to protect the boar, binding Fionn's men, but Fionn and Bran chase the boar up the glen. The churl comes up and takes it, carrying it on his shoulders, but laying Fionn under *geasa* that he

50 Meyer, 'Macgnimartha Find', 197–8. 51 The poem is printed in Ní Shéaghdha, *Agallamh*, iii, pp 21–42, and in MacNeill and Murphy, *Duanaire Finn*, i, pp 38–45. *Sítheal* is the only form used in the *Agallamh* text. According to *DIL*, this was a normal form in Middle Irish, but the classical grammatical tracts prescribe *síothal*. Ní Shéaghdha prints the classical form on the page header and in the index, but does not alter the manuscript reading in the text. *Duanaire Finn* is inconsistent, writing the nominative three ways: *síothal* (1*a*), *sítheal* (7*b*), and most frequently *síthal* (including 86*a*, 112*d*, 117*d*). 52 MacNeill and Murphy, *Duanaire Finn*, iii, pp 36–7. 53 The association of Bearnas, the Barnesmore Gap, with the boar is strong in the tradition of the lays. It is called Bearnus Muici Balair, 'The Gap of Balor's Swine' in lay XIV (MacNeill and Murphy, *Duanaire Finn*, i, p. 30), and the Fenians also hunt boar there in lay LIV (ibid., ii, pp 184–93).

must follow his boar, and they repair across a glen to a *síodh*. The toponyms
of this section diverge between the *Agallamh* and *Duanaire Finn*, but neither
set is identifiable any longer.[54] With a tap of the wand, the churl becomes
Éanán, king of the *síodh*; the boar transforms into his son. They welcome
Fionn into the fairy feast, where he is given a golden *sítheal* and his retinue
are given silver. He is smitten with love for Éanán's daughter – who is none
other than the Otherworldly female warrior Scáthach. Fionn proposes to
marry her, offering a lavish bride-price. She reluctantly agrees, though she
considers the match beneath her. Éanán offers a lavish dowry, restores the
hounds to life, and pays the honour-prices of the *fian*-warriors for his trick.
When they are in their cups, Scáthach takes the harp and plays fairy music
in the mode of *súantarglés*; all sleep. When Fionn awakes in the morning, the
band are back in Bearnas, each with his spear and hound, but they find out
as the *fian*-warriors return in the evening that a night has not elapsed in this
world. The only evidence for the encounter is the treasure, including Fionn's
drinking vessel, which he gives to Caoilte. Seven years later, Caoilte sends his
servant Guaire to fetch him a drink at Duibh-cheachair. Guaire drops the
dipper into the well, whence it cannot be recovered. Fionn prophesies the
coming of Patrick, who will recover it with the help of the salmon of the well,
and by this foreknowledge, Fionn comes to believe in God. Returning to the
frame, Oisín realises sorrowfully that the precious relic of his Fenian past has
outlived its use: its gold and silver will adorn the croziers, bells, and Gospels
of the new age's clerical heroes. This poem's narrative is enclosed in an
ecphrasis of an object whose construction resembles the Ardagh chalice. In it,
the hunts of Ireland, lists of the hounds of the *fian*-warriors, the victories of
Bran, provide a learned element not dissimilar to the short poems of the first
Acallam; nevertheless, here the focus is on the tale.

The *Agallamh*'s version is clearly a witness independent of *Duanaire Finn*.
Though preserving some older or more conservative forms,[55] the *Agallamh*'s
text also has numerous modernisms such as the loss of accusative forms and
the replacement of infixed pronouns with independent ones; furthermore,
analytic verbal forms are rather more commonplace in the *Agallamh* than in
Duanaire Finn, which has a slightly better preserved text, grammatically
speaking, in regard to this poem. The *Agallamh* preserves ten stanzas not in
Duanaire Finn, whilst the latter has seven quatrains not found in the former.

Turning now to the eight-page prose frame (*AgS* iii, pp 13.18–21.7);
although the verse comprises twenty pages, the two are not dissimilar in

---

54 O'Rahilly, *Early Irish history and mythology*, p. 281, wryly commented on excavations aiming
to find Fionn's palace of Almha that 'The Otherworld is impervious to archæological exploration': so are its placenames to onomastics.   55 For example: *do-rochair* (*AgS* iii, p. 28.7);
connmhaigh (*AgS* iii, p. 29.19); *ó't-chiú-sa* (*AgS* iii, p. 42.13); and preservation of hiatus in *faoiis*
(*AgS* iii, p. 23.17).

length due to the very generous spacing of the verse. In fact, the prose is slightly longer. The actual introduction is extraordinarily brief. The *Agallamh* framework of the lay is executed within the first page: Patrick, his retinue and Oisín reach Duibh-cheachair. Oisín volunteers the name of the place, which Patrick proceeds to bless. Therewith, the salmon comes forth from the depths and gives the saint the Fenian vessel. In response to Patrick's question, Oisín narrates the history of the vessel as in the lay, frequently reflecting its phrasing; when he reaches the end, *ro ráidh na roinn* 'he said the verses' (*AgS* iii, p. 21.7). At the conclusion of the recitation, the assembled retinue proceed into the next episode without so much as a comment.

There are no significant archaisms in the prose. The lay, when describing the retinue of Éanán in the *síodh*, uses an independent dative. The couplet of the lay reads:

> do-ríachd 'na ndíaigh, línibh snas,
> caocca sgolócc fionn folt-chass.[56]
> there came after them in neat rows
> fifty scholars with white, curly locks.

It is interesting that the equivalent in *Duanaire Finn*, which has a line of different meaning, preserves the same construction:

> lodar na ndíaigh milibh snas
> caoga macaomh fial foltchas.
> followed these with thousands of charms
> fifty noble ringleted damsels.[57]

The prose reproduces the sense, removing the poetic construction:

> coecca sgolócc sgíamhdha sgúird-leabhor sgíath-chorcra d'fhearthain fáilte risna féinneadhaibh go fior-chonnail.[58]

> fifty scholars adorned with trailing cassocks and purple shields welcomed the *fian*-warriors in truly friendly manner.

The prose redactor may have interpreted *línibh* of the poem above as 'tunics' (*léinibh*) and replaced it with the synonym *sgúird*. From this, he has constructed an alliterating description of their attributes – as he did for the lads preceding the scholars, and the ladies who follow after. The details need not match exactly, and the prose style is sufficient reason to take liberties. Here,

---

56 Ní Shéaghdha, *Agallamh*, iii, p. 32.15–16.   57 MacNeill and Murphy, *Duanaire Finn*, i, p. 42, q. 64*cd* (trans. ibid., p. 145).   58 Ní Shéaghdha, *Agallamh*, iii, p. 19.3–5.

as often, the *argumentum* is a retelling, not a summary. The scribal lack of an eye for detail as he rewrites may be seen at other points. The prose can swarm with pronouns, confusing the reader who does not refer to the text of the lay. In the paragraph beginning at *AgS* iii, p. 18.3, Fionn, the churl, and the boar are all referred to by *é* (and the boar by the infixed pronoun -*s*-) with rapid changes of referent, and *iad* represents both the Fenian hunt and the duo of Fionn and Bran; the careful reader must keep a finger on the lay for verification. Likewise, in the close of the in-tale:

> Iarras C*aoilte* digh uiscce
> ar Ghuaire fa glan t-uixe:
> gabhus in sítheal 'na láimh;
> luidhis lé d'iarr*aid*h úaráin.[59]

> Caoilte asked a drink of water
> from Guaire – the water was clean:
> he took the dipper in his hand;
> he went with it to seek a spring.

Here the prose redactor writes:

> 'Laithe n-aon bámuir-ne sonn a bhfarr*ad*h Fhinn', ol Oisín, '7 ro ghabh íota adhb*hal*-mhór ann sin, 7 siris ar Ghúaire m*a*c Neachtoin dul d'iarr*aid*h dighe dhó'.[60]

> 'Then one day we were in the company of Fionn', said Oisín, 'and a great thirst seized him then, and he asked Guaire son of Neachtain to go to find a drink for him'.

It is not at all clear from the prose tale that it is Caoilte, named in the previous paragraph, who requests the drink. Without the poem to hand, the reader would naturally take Fionn to be the unexpressed direct object of *ro ghabh*.[61]

Despite frequent but minor departures from his verse originals, the redactor has gone to a great deal of trouble. As it stands in this text, the poem has 121 qq. As already noted, it contains some minor modernisms not found in *Duanaire Finn*, alongside some alternative readings, some of which are more conservative, as well as a number of stanzas not found in *Duanaire Finn*; all of which disproves Hyde's suggestion that poems may have found their way from this *Agallamh* into *Duanaire Finn* (obviously copied through an inter-

---

59 Ibid., iii, p. 41.1–4.   60 Ibid., iii, p. 20.   61 *Duanaire Finn*'s copy of the lay confuses the characters at this point also: its equivalent to the first couplet of q. 109 reads *Siris Gúaire digh uisce / ar Chaoilti ba maith tuisge*, reversing the request; this alternative reading is less satisfactory than the one in the *Agallamh*.

mediate manuscript no longer extant).[62] Yet the introduction or prose 'summary' provided for this episode can hardly be described as such. It is not the procession stopping at a place where a *seanóir* recites lore in verse, as in the first *Agallamh*. It extends onto nine pages in the diplomatic edition: it is as long as the poem itself, perhaps slightly more so with its additional quantity of alliterating verbiage and appended description. The redactor considered the poem to be worthy of preservation, a venerable antiquity; but the poems in this *Agallamh* – notably old and often with difficult Middle Irish verbal forms, infixed pronouns, declined accusatives, and obsolete vocabulary – are accompanied by a summary that can exceed them in length, though this is tempered by cases where it leaves out long, presumably tedious, lists (as here with the list of boars slain by Bran, recited to spur him on against the enchanted boar in the poem, but not recounted in prose). This is a prosimetrum *Agallamh* of a wholly different type from the earlier *Acallam*: a prose romance, punctuated by the texts whence the material was mined. The new text is a polished and fashionably ornamented tale with source-poems included as a scholarly apparatus, rather than the original programme of introduction and recitation in which the verse speaks for itself.

In the Reeves *Agallamh*, the terms of the dialogue have shifted. The tastes of another age impose themselves over the verse narratives, adding a layer of the heavy Early Modern prose of the romances: the prose has become a full rewrite in the literary form of a later age. Even if Oisín has grown garrulous as he provides *argumenta* for the Fenian adventures relayed in verse to Saint Patrick, he retains the strength to repeat himself, chanting far more than he did in the earlier *Acallam*. And yet the lays did not die; the prose tale failed to oust them from their place of honour in this work, or in the wider literature, and some of these lays continued to circulate independently of this framework into which they were woven. New poems intended for popular consumption flourished, even if many of the older compositions won less favour. Indeed, the genre of *laoithe fianaigheachta* continued to be productive for the composition of Fenian adventures in narrative verse into the eighteenth century.

If, in the course of this paper, I have recounted a traveller's tale for our honorand about a journey through a great, wild, and remote corner of Irish literature, and suggested some reasons why others may wish to travel thither themselves, I should consider this paper to be a success. The territory, a work of a 100,000 words in prose and verse, is too extensive to attempt to chart here, and 'here be monsters' must be scrawled on more than one corner of this account – and not merely where the *fian* chase an enchanted boar or enter a *bruidhean*. Saint Patrick requests the lore of the name of Duibh-cheachair Droma dá Oss, an unidentified 'Black Pool of the Ridge of Two

---

62 See Hyde, 'The Reeves manuscript', 295.

Fawns' near Assaroe at the start of the 'Caoilte's Dipper' episode (*AgS* iii, p. 14), which we have just explored at some length. This may reflect the young Oisín of the lay, and the ancient who recounts the events. When one looks over to the copy of the poem in *Duanaire Finn*, the place is instead Duibheochair, the 'Black Verge', seemingly reflecting on the depth of the spring. Although the *fian*-warriors never invite us to stop and smell the roses as they roam about Ireland, Seán Ó Coileáin has advised us that as we follow them, we should stop and smell the wild garlic in the spring woodlands, rather than pursue a Creamh-choill in an epic chase through Hogan's *Onomasticon*, into the townlands index, across the Ordnance Survey name books and indices, and into the clear plains of the next fascicule of Locus' *Historical dictionary of Gaelic placenames*.[63] If some of our places are lost from the map, we should recognise that the fairy music accompanying the *Agallamh*'s lays hides in the shadowy woodlands of a thicket of prose. But if we have identified some of the landmarks so far, the map of this vast forest of tales remains to be made.

---

63 'Place and placename in *fianaigheacht*', *Studia Hibernica*, 27 (1993), 45–60 (reprinted in this volume). See also D.E. Meek, 'Placenames and literature: evidence from the Gaelic ballads' in S. Taylor (ed.), *The uses of placenames* (1998), pp 147–68.

An tAgallamh Nua: athleagan déanach d'Agallamh na Seanórach

SÍLE NÍ MHURCHÚ

Is éard atá curtha romham agam a dhéanamh anseo ná cuntas a thabhairt ar thraidisiún lámhscríbhinní an Agallaimh Nua, athleagan déanach d'Agallamh na Seanórach, a bhfuil cóipeanna de le fáil i lámhscríbhinní ó dheireadh an seachtú céad déag agus ó thús an ochtú céad déag go dtí deireadh an naoú céad déag.

I

Tá ceithre leagan dhifriúla d'Agallamh na Seanórach ann:[1] an leagan is luaithe ná an Bun-Agallamh a cuireadh le chéile go déanach sa dara haois déag nó go luath sa tríú aois déag, ceaptar.[2] Tá cur síos ag Ó Muraíle ar cheithre chóip den mBun-Agallamh sna lámhscríbhinní:

> Leabharlann Bodleian, Oxford, LS Laud 610;
> Chatsworth, Leabhar Leasa Móir;
> Leabharlann Bodleian, Oxford, LS Rawlinson B. 487;
> An Coláiste Ollscoile, Baile Átha Cliath, LS Phroinsiasach A 4.

Glactar le LS Phroinsiasach A 20(a) (An Coláiste Ollscoile, Baile Átha Cliath) mar chóip den mBun-Agallamh leis; cóip de LS Phroinsiasach A 4 atá inti.[3] Tá dhá eagrán den mBun-Agallamh i gcló: ceann acu le haistriúchán in *Silva gadelica* ag O'Grady, agus an ceann eile le leath-aistriúchán in *Irische Texte* ag Stokes.[4] Glactar leis go bhfuil leagan Stokes níos cruinne,[5] agus mar sin, is dó

---

1 Bunaithe ar an gcur síos in N. Ó Muraíle, 'Agallamh na seanórach' in P. Ó Fiannachta (eag.), *Léachtaí Cholm Cille*, 25: *An fhiannaíocht* (1995), lgh 96–127 ag lgh 103–14. Is é Ó Muraíle féin a bhaist 'An tAgallamh Nua' ar an leagan sin; 'Agallamh Chaoilte agus Phádraig' nó 'Agallamh na Seanóireadha' a bhíonn air sna lámhscríbhinní de ghnáth.   2 Pléitear tuairimí scoláirí éagsúla maidir le dátú an Bhun-Agallaimh in ibid., lgh 105–8. Féach leis A. Dooley, 'The date and purpose of *Acallam na senórach*', *Éigse*, 34 (2004), 97–126 ag 98–100.   3 Féach M. Dillon et al., *Catalogue of Irish manuscripts in the Franciscan library, Killiney* (1969), lch 41; G. Parsons, 'The structure of *Acallam na senórach*', *Cambrian Medieval Celtic Studies*, 55 (2008), 11–39 ag 12.   4 S.H. O'Grady (eag. agus aistr.), *Silva gadelica*, 2 iml. (1892), i, lgh 92–233; ii, 101–265. W. Stokes (eag. agus leathaistr.), 'Acallamh na senórach' in W. Stokes agus E. Windisch (eag.), *Irische Texte*, iv, 1 (1900).   5 Stokes, 'Acallamh', lch xi; N. Ní Shéaghdha (eag.), *Agallamh na seanórach*, 3 himl. (1942–5), i, lch xiii.

san a thagrófar san aiste seo agus trácht á dhéanamh ar an mBun-Agallamh. Tá eagrán Stokes bunaithe ar LS Laud 610 agus Leabhar Leasa Móir den gcuid is mó, agus thóg sé sleachta gearra as LS A 4 leis.[6]

Ceaptar gur cuireadh le chéile an *Agallamh bheag* tamall i ndiaidh an Bhun-Agallaimh,[7] agus shíl Nessa Ní Shéaghdha gur dócha gur roimh 1500 a cuireadh le chéile an 'Reeves Agallamh' nó an tAgallamh Déanach.[8] Is éard atá ann ná ábhar as an mBun-Agallamh agus as an *Agallamh bheag* fite le chéile mar scéal leanúnach, agus scéalta agus giotaí breise filíochta curtha leo san.[9] Níl ach cóip amháin ann den dtéacs seo: Acadamh Ríoga na hÉireann, Baile Átha Cliath, LS 24 P 5.[10]

Ní thugann Ó Muraíle cur síos ar an Agallamh Nua seachas tagairt a dhéanamh don méid a bhí le rá ag Máirtín Ó Briain mar gheall air: 'essentially a modernised and much abbreviated version of *AS* … found in late eighteenth- and nineteenth-century manuscripts mainly of Munster provenance'.[11] Tá an tAgallamh Nua níos luaithe ná mar a shíl an Brianach, mar a chífear thíos.

II

Rahmenerzählung nó fráma-scéal atá san Agallamh Nua chomh maith céanna leis na leaganacha eile d'Agallamh na Seanórach. Caoilte agus Naomh Pádraig atá ag agallamh lena chéile ann agus cuirtear laoithe agus scéalta éagsúla mar gheall ar Fhionn is na Fianna isteach sa chomhrá seo. Sé cinn d'eipeasóidí atá sna cóipeanna is luaithe den Agallamh Nua:

1. Caithréim Fhinn;[12]
2. Scéal Artúir mhic Bheinne Briot;
3. Breith Mhic Lughach agus Comhairle Fhinn do Mhac Lughach;
4. Scéal Airnéalaigh;
5. Scéal Shálbhuí mhic Fheileachair;
6. Tonn Chlíodhna agus Tonn Téide.[13]

---

6 Stokes, 'Acallamh', lgh x–xii; Ó Muraíle, 'Agallamh', lgh 113–14.   7 Tá cuntas cuimsitheach ar an *Agallamh bheag* in J.S. Kühns, 'Some observations on the *Acallam bec*' in S.J. Arbuthnot agus G. Parsons (eag.), *The Gaelic Finn tradition* (2012), lgh 122–38. Féach an aiste ag Pádraig Ó Macháin sa leabhar seo.   8 Ní Shéaghdha, *Agallamh*, i, lch xxxi. Measann Ó Muraíle ('Agallamh', lch 108) go bhféadfaí dáta níos cruinne a chur leis ach mionstaidéar a dhéanamh ar an dtéacs.   9 Ní Shéaghdha, *Agallamh*, i, lch xxix.   10 Ibid., lch xix. Féach an aiste ag Joseph Flahive sa leabhar seo.   11 M. Ó Briain, 'Some material on Oisín in the Land of Youth' in D. Ó Corráin et al. (eag.), *Sages, saints and storytellers* (1989), lgh 181–99 ag lch 185 (luaite in Ó Muraíle, 'Agallamh', lch 103).   12 Stokes, 'Acallamh', ll. 2468–586. Cuireadh an teideal 'Caithréim Fhinn' ar an gcuid seo den Agallamh Nua i gcuid mhaith de na cóipeanna. Ní i gcónaí a oireann na teidil atá ag Stokes do na heipeasóidí mar atá siad san Agallamh Nua; mar sin, chumas féin na teidil eile.   13 Ibid., ll. 163–263, 536–605, 1064–81, 1082–92, 3726–852.

Faightear an giota seo a leanas i dteannta na n-eipeasóidí a luadh thuas i mórán cóipeanna eile: 'Caoilte i gCúirt Rí Uladh'.[14] D'fhéadfaí é seo a roinnt arís, mar leanas:

1. Téann Caoilte ag seilg ar na Beanna Boirche agus buaileann le Líbhán iníon Eochaidh mhic Eoghain;
2. Cumann Caoilte leathrann agus míníonn cad is brí leis;
3. Scéal Dhuibh mhic Thréin is a mhic, Fial, agus pósadh Áine iníon Fhéil;
4. Teacht Choscartaigh mhic Ainchinn chun seanchas na Féinne a fhoghlaim ó Chaoilte;
5. Scéal Thulach an Trír.[15]

III

Ón uair go bhfuil na ceithre cóipeanna is luaithe den Agallamh Nua difriúil lena chéile, tabharfar cur síos orthu go léir ar leithligh. Tá an chóip is luaithe dár aimsíos den Agallamh Nua i gColáiste na Tríonóide, LS H.5.4 (1376). Eoghan Ó Caoimh a ghraf dá dhearthbáir Fionghuine.[16] Níor cuireadh dáta le téacs an Agallaimh Nua féin ach cuireadh dátaí idir 1699 agus 1702 le téacsanna eile sa lámhscríbhinn. Lámhscríbhinn mheasctha í agus tá scéalta Fiannaíochta eile inti leis. Luaitear sa chatalóg go bhfuil cóip den laoi 'Caithréim Fhinn' ar leathanach 279 agus gur 'fragments of *Agallamh na Seanórach*' atá ina dhiaidh seo ach le ceart, baineann siad seo go léir leis an Agallamh Nua. Tá ciumhaiseanna na leathanach stracaithe i ndeireadh na lámhscríbhinne agus go deimhin, ní mór in aon chor atá fágtha againn de na leathanaigh dheireanacha ar fad. Ina theannta san, tá an chuma ar an scéal nár ceanglaíodh na leathanaigh san ord ceart. Toisc gurb í seo an chóip is luaithe den Agallamh Nua, is fiú cuntas cruinn a thabhairt ar a bhfuil ar gach leathanach sa chuid seo den lámhscríbhinn.

Lgh 277–9:	Teideal: 'Agalla Chaoillte [ ]'
	Réamhrá leis an Agallamh Nua.
Lgh 279.4–286:	Teideal: 'Cathréim Fhin*n* m*h*ic Cu*m*hai[ll]'
	Laoi (31 rann) a thosnaíonn 'Sea*cht* rígh dhéag lánmheabh*air* lio*m*'.

14 Ibid., ll, 3196–412. 15 Ibid., ll. 3196–249, 3250–76, 3277–335, 3336–76, 3377–412. Uaine agus Cas Corach a thugtar ar na carachtair seo (Áine agus Coscartach) sa Bhun-Agallamh. 16 T.K. Abbott and E.J. Gwynn, *Catalogue of Irish manuscripts in the library of Trinity College Dublin* (1921), lgh 231–3. Ghraf Eoghan Ó Caoimh an lámhscríbhinn seo i bpáirt lena mhac Art. Féach B. Ó Conchúir, *Scríobhaithe Chorcaí, 1700–1850* (1982), lgh 32–3. Tá an dá láimh anchosúil lena chéile ach déarfainn gurb é an t-athair a ghraf an tAgallamh Nua.

Lgh 287–290:   Scéal Artúir mhic Bheinne Briot. Stadann go
                hobann ag bun lgh 290.
Lgh 291–7:   Breith mhic Lughach ach go bhfuil an chuid
                thosaigh in easnamh. Tosnaíonn an laoi (11 rann)
                'Comhairle Fhinn do Mhac Lughach' ar lch 293
                agus leanann ar aghaidh go dtí bun lgh 296.
                Tosnaíonn Scéal Airnéalaigh i lár lgh 296 agus
                críochnaíonn ag bun lgh 297.
Lgh 298–9:   Cóip neamhiomlán de Laoi Thailc mhic Threoin
                dar tús '[Cnoc an áir] an cnoc so shi[ar]'.
                Freagraíonn na hocht ranna seo do ranna 47, 58,
                60–65 den laoi atá i gcló ag an Seabhac.[17] Téacs ar
                leithligh é seo.
Lgh 300:   Leanann an tAgallamh Nua ar aghaidh ó dheir-
                eadh lgh 297 le Scéal Shálbhuí mhic Fheileachair.
                Tosnaíonn an scéal Tonn Chlíodhna agus Tonn
                Téide ina dhiaidh seo ar lch 301. Tá na trí ranna
                dar tús '[An triar atáimid] *ar* tuin*n*' atá mar chuid
                den scéal seo ar lch 304. Is léir go bhfuil bileoga in
                easnamh idir lgh 306 agus 307 mar tá cuid den
                scéal in easnamh. Tá an laoi dar tús 'Clíodhna
                chean*n*fh[ionn buan a béad]' ar lgh 307–8.
Lgh 309–11:   Níl fágtha ach blúire beag de na leathanaigh seo. Is
                féidir na hainmneacha Oisín mac Finn agus Caoilte
                a dhéanamh amach ar lch 309; mar sin, is léir gur
                Fiannaíocht atá ann ach ní aithním é.
Lgh 315:   Blúire de Scéal Artúir mhic Bheinne Briot.
Lgh 317:   Blúire de Bhreith Mhic Lughach.
Lgh 318:   Deireadh Scéil Artúir mhic Bheinne Briot.

Is léir mar sin go bhfuil na sé cinn d'eipeasóidí a liostáladh níos luaithe, agus
a fhaightear i gcóipeanna eile den Agallamh Nua, sa chóip seo chomh maith
cé go bhfuil cuid de na leathanaigh geall le bheith doléite.

Tá an chéad chóip eile den Agallamh Nua, LNÉ LS G114, againn ina
iomláine. Uilliam Mac Cairteáin a ghraf an lámhscríbhinn seo sna blianta
1700–3. Níor chuir sé dáta leis an gcóip den Agallamh Nua atá sa lámhscríbhinn ach is ar an 17ú Aibreán 1703 a chríochnaigh sé *Feis Tí Chonáin* a
thagann díreach roimis sa lámhscríbhinn agus d'fhéadfaí glacadh leis gur thart
ar an am céanna a grafadh an dá théacs. Aon lámhscríbhinn amháin ab ea
ARÉ LS 23 H 18 agus LNÉ LSS G113/G114 ar dtús.[18] Deineadh cuid de

17 P. Ó Siochfhradha (eag.), *Laoithe na féinne* (1941), lgh 28–30.   18 N. Ní Shéaghdha,
Catalogue of Irish manuscripts in the National Library of Ireland, iii (1976), lch 128.

na téacsanna sa lámhscríbhinn mhór seo a leagan amach de réir an tsórt ábhair atá iontu. Tá sraith fada de scéalta Rúraíochta sa chuid sin den lámhscríbhinn a dtugtar G113 uirthi anois agus ag tosach na lámhscríbhinne ar a dtugtar anois G114. Tá sraith de scéalta agus de laoithe fiannaíochta in LS G114 ó lch 14 go dtí lch 57 agus tá an tAgallamh Nua ina measc seo ar lgh 31–42. Is éard atá i gcóip seo Uilliam Mhic Cairteáin ná réamhrá agus sé cinn d'eipeasóidí, mar a luadh thuas. Tá an leagan amach céanna ar mhórán de na cóipeanna níos deireanaí den Agallamh Nua, mar atá:

> Leabharlann na Breataine, LS Egerton 211 (1758; Seán Ó Murchú na Ráithíneach, Co. Chorcaí);
>
> Baile Átha Cliath, King's Inns LS 7 (1778; Séamas Ó Murchú, gan log);
>
> COC LS Torna X (1780–1; Seán Ó Coileáin, Tigh Molaige, Co. Chorcaí);
>
> Leabharlann na Breataine, LS Egerton 175 (1821; Edward O'Reilly, gan log);
>
> Mainistir Fhear Maí, Coláiste Cholmáin LS PB 7 (1825; Dáibhí de Barra, Bunastó, Co. Chorcaí);
>
> ARÉ LS 23 O 52 [1132] (1799–81; Séamas Stúndún, Áth an Mhuilinn, Co. Chorcaí / 1836; Diarmuid Ó Conaill, gan log);[19]
>
> ARÉ LS 24 B 27 [645] (*c.*1850; Seosamh Ó Longáin, Co. Chorcaí);
>
> ARÉ LS 23 N 14 [489] (19ú céad; Mícheál Óg Ó Longáin, gan log).

Tá an tríú cóip is luaithe den Agallamh Nua in ARÉ LS 23 C 30 (783) a ghraf Aindrias Mac Cruitín thart ar 1733.[20] Ní thugtar log sa lámhscríbhinn; bhí cónaí air i Maigh Ghlas i mbarúntacht Uí Bhreacáin i gContae an Chláir. Bhí pátrúin éagsúla aige sa chontae,[21] ach ní thugtar aon nod dúinn cár tháinig sé ar théacs an Agallaimh Nua. 'Caithréim Fhinn mhic Cumhaill' an teideal atá ar an Agallamh Nua anseo agus tosaíonn an tAgallamh, gan aon réamhrá, leis an laoi sin. 'Seacht rí déag lánmheabhair liom' an chéad líne agus 31 rann atá inti, mar atá i gColáiste na Tríonóide LS H.5.4. Leantar ar aghaidh, mar is gnáth, ansan le Scéal Artúir mhic Bheinne Briot agus Breith Mhic Lughach ina dhiaidh sin. Stopann an insint go hobann i lár an scéil dheireanaigh sin ag an rann 'Gaine ainm mhic Lughaidh loinn'. Tá ocht gcóip eile den Agallamh Nua ann a leanann an patrún san, mar atá:

---

19 Ghraf an Stúndúnach an chuid thosaigh den Agallamh Nua (lgh 458–64 sa lámhscríbhinn) agus ghraf an Conallach an chuid eile (ó lch 465 ar aghaidh).   20 Tá tras-scríobh a deineadh sa bhfichiú haois ar an Agallamh Nua ón lámhscríbhinn seo in LNÉ LS G554.   21 E. Ní Dheá, 'Scríobhaithe lámhscríbhinní Gaeilge i gContae an Chláir 1700–1900' in M. Lynch and P. Nugent (eag.), *Clare: history and society* (2008), lgh 139–55 ag lch 142.

COC LS 83 (1780; Diarmuid Ó Súilleabháin, Cnoc Rafann, Co.
   Thiobraid Árann);
ARÉ LS 23 M 47 [973] (1789–95; Séamas Ó Caoluidhe, gan log);
LNÉ LS G501 (1794; Tadhg Ó Ceallaigh, An Clochán Beag, Co. an
   Chláir);
ARÉ LS 24 P 29 [1074] (1833–7; Mícheál Óg Ó hAnnracháin, Baile
   Uí Cheit gar do Chill Rois, Co. an Chláir);
ARÉ LS 24 L 27 [813] (1838; Tomás Ó hIceadha, Baile Ghrae (sic),
   Co. Thiobraid Árann);
LNÉ LS G403 (1845–9; Tomás Ó hIceadha, gan log);
ARÉ LS 23 E 11 (1850; Nioclás Ó Cearnaigh, gan log);[22]
LNÉ LS G446 (19ú céad; ní fios cé a ghraf, gan log).

Tá an téacs sna leaganacha seo níos cóngaraí do Choláiste na Tríonóide LS
H.5.4 ná mar atá do LNÉ LS G114.

   An ceathrú cóip is luaithe den Agallamh Nua ná COC LS 107. Seán
Cúndún a ghraf sna blianta 1738–9. Ní mór an t-eolas atá againn ar an
scríobhaí seo. Tuairimíonn Breandán Ó Conchúir gur le tuaisceart Chontae
Chorcaí a bhain sé.[23] Scéalta próis is mó atá sa lámhscríbhinn agus grafadh
cóip den laoi 'Tuarascáil Chatha Gabhra' roimh an Agallamh Nua. Seo an
chóip is luaithe den Agallamh Nua ina bhfaightear 'Caoilte i gCúirt Rí
Uladh', mar a liostáladh thuas. Tagann an chuid seo i ndiaidh na sé cinn
d'eipeasóidí a fhaightear sna cóipeanna eile. Níl aon réamhrá leis an Agallamh
sa lámhscríbhinn seo – tosnaíonn an téacs leis an laoi 'Caithréim Fhinn'. Ní
dóigh liom go síolraíonn an chóip seo ó LNÉ LS G114 mar tá difríochtaí
eatarthu agus in áiteanna, tá an téacs i gCOC LS 107 níos cóngaraí don
mBun-Agallamh. Tá ranna sa laoi 'Caithréim Fhinn' i gCOC LS 107 nach
bhfuil i gColáiste na Tríonóide LS H.5.4 ach atá sa Bhun-Agallamh agus i
LNÉ LS G114; mar sin, ní cóip mar leagan Choláiste na Tríonóide LS H.5.4
a bhí mar fhoinse ag an scríobhaí.

   Formhór na gcóipeanna den Agallamh Nua, is éard atá iontu ná na sé
eipeasóidí tosaigh, mar atá i LNÉ LS G114 agus 'Caoilte i gCúirt Rí Uladh'
ina dhiaidh san. Tá réamhrá mar atá in i LNÉ LS G114 lena bhformhór. Na
lámhscríbhinní ná:

COC LS 107 (1738–9; Seán Cúndún, Co. Chorcaí);
ARÉ LS 23 C 26 [765] (1761; Seán Ó Conaill, Cill Uird, Co. Chorcaí);
ARÉ LS 23 N 18 [981] (1772–3; Eoghan Rua Ó Súilleabháin, Dún ar
   Aill, Co. Chorcaí);
COC LS 124 (1773; Eoghan Rua Ó Súilleabháin, gan log);

---

22 Ar lch 315 sa lámhscríbhinn. Tá cóip dhifriúil den Agallamh Nua sa lámhscríbhinn chéanna
ar lch 405. Féach thíos.   23 Ó Conchúir, *Scríobhaithe Chorcaí*, lch 8.

LNÉ LS G109 (1780; Tomás Mac Muiris Ua Gearailt, Co. Chorcaí);

COC LS 96 (1780; Labhrás Ó Fuartháin, Co. Phort Láirge);

ARÉ LS 24 A 20 [928] (1806; Seán Ó Braonáin, Baile Mhic Aindriú, Co. Chiarraí);

LNÉ LS G161 (1812–13; Uilliam Breathnach, Co. Phort Láirge);

ARÉ LS 24 A 5 [972] (1820–1; Máire Ní Riain, gan log);

Má Nuad, LS Murphy 10 (*c.*1817; Eoghan Tóibín, Co. Chorcaí);

ARÉ LS 24 A 6 (1854; Éamann Ó Mathúna, gan log);

Oxford LS Ir. e. 3 [15] (go luath sa 19ú céad; Uilliam Breathnach, Co. Phort Láirge);

LNÉ LS G423 (19ú céad; Séamas Ó hAodha, Co. Thiobhraid Árann);

ARÉ LS 24 B 13 [322] (19ú céad; Brian Ó Luanaigh, Co. an Chláir).

I gcolafan a chuir sé leis an gcóip den Agallamh Nua (na sé eipeasóidí tosaigh amháin) a ghraf sé in Egerton LS 211, chuir Seán Ó Murchú na Ráithíneach in iúl nach raibh 'Caoilte i gCúirt Rí Uladh' chomh maith nó chomh slachtmhar, b'fhéidir, leis an gcuid eile den Agallamh Nua, dar leis: 'Ag sin d*eireadh* le hAgall*amh* Phád*r*aig *agus* Chaoillte gidh*eadh* ata a do no a trí do stuadhaibh *eile* fá tideal Agall*amh* na Seanó*ireadha, id*ir Chaoilte 7 Righ Ul*adh* nách fuil comh fo*i*rfe ris an m*éid*si'.[24] Bhraithfeá air nárbh fhiú leis 'Caoilte i gCúirt Rí Uladh' a chur lena chóip féin den Agallamh Nua.

IV

Tá dornán beag lámhscríbhinní ann inar cuireadh ábhar breise fós leis an Agallamh Nua. An chéad cheann acu seo ná ARÉ LS 23 N 11 a ghraf Mícheál Mac Peadair Ó Longáin roimh 1766. 'Agallamh Chaoilte, Rígh Ul*adh* 7 Líobháin *inghean* Eathach' an teideal atá ar an Agallamh Nua anseo. Tosnaíonn an téacs le 'Caoilte i gCúirt Rí Uladh' agus leanann ar aghaidh mar is gnách go dtí deireadh na laoi 'Foradh na bhFiann fás anocht' a chanann Caoilte do Choscartach mac Ainchinn (Cas Corach) le linn dó bheith ag foghlaim seanchais uaidh.[25] Tá líne thiubh i ndiaidh fhocail dheireanaigh na laoi seo, rud a thugann le fios, b'fhéidir, gurb é sin deireadh an Agallaimh Nua. Tá laoithe eile a bhaineann leis an mBun-Agallamh scríofa ina dhiaidh seo gan bhriseadh ná teideal. An chéad laoi acu seo ná an laoi dar tús 'Almha Láighean lios na bhFiann'. Deich rann atá sa laoi seo sa Bhun-Agallamh.[26] Seacht rann ar fhichid atá i gcóip Mhichíl mhic Pheadair agus ina measc seo, tá ranna a fhaightear sna laoithe 'Almu I' (a thosnaíonn 'Almu Lagen, les na

---

24 Egerton LS 211, lch 144, ll. 21–4.   **25** An ceathrú roinn de 'Chaoilte i gCúirt Rí Uladh', mar a liostáladh thuas.   **26** Stokes, 'Acallamh', ll. 1262–81.

Fían') agus 'Almu II' (a thosnaíonn 'Almu robo cháem dia cois') sa dinnsean-
chas filíochta.[27] An chéad laoi eile sa lámhscríbhinn ná an laoi dar tús 'Giodh
aoibhinn an dún so thoir'. Tá an laoi seo cóngarach do leagan Stokes,
'Aibhinn gidh an dúnsa thair';[28] tá na ranna atá inti agus an t-ord ina bhfuil
siad mar an gcéanna. Thóg Stokes an chuid seo den mBun-Agallamh ó
Leabhar Leasa Móir ach thóg sé dhá cheann de na ranna sa laoi (ll. 1189–92)
ó LS Phroinsiasach A 4. Ranna iad seo nach bhfuil i gcóip Leabhar Leasa
Móir in aon chor ach féach go bhfuil siad sa chóip den laoi seo in ARÉ LS
23 N 11, rud a thacaíonn le ráiteas Mheidhbhín Ní Úrdail go raibh teacht ag
muintir Longáin ar leagan den mBun-Agallamh nár tháinig go díreach ó
Leabhar Leasa Móir.[29]

Tá breis ábhair fós sa chóip den Agallamh Nua atá in ARÉ LS 23 G 23
(256) a ghraf Mícheál Óg Ó Longáin ar an Laghair, paróiste Charraig na
bhFear, Co. Chorcaí, sa bhliain 1800. Is é atá ann ná an tAgallamh Nua le
réamhrá,[30] na sé eipeasóidí tosaigh agus 'Caoilte i gCúirt Rí Uladh' go dtí an
laoi 'Foradh na bhFiann fás anocht'. Níl ann ach an chéad rann den laoi seo
agus an rann deireanach de leagan Mhichíl mhic Pheadair den laoi 'Almha
Laighean lios na bhFiann', mar atá in ARÉ LS 23 N 11. Ina dhiaidh sin,
ansan, tá na heipeasóidí thíos; tagann an chéad cheann acu seo i ndiaidh na
laoi 'Almha Laigen, lis na fian' sa Bhun-Agallamh:

> Scéal Rí Lochlann;
> Beannaíonn Pádraig Cnoc na Rí agus cruthaíonn sé tobar;
> Garad mac Morna agus na mná.[31]

Stad an Longánach i lár na laoi 'A mhná áille Féinne Finn', a thagann ag
deireadh 'Garad mac Morna agus na mná' agus scríobh sé '7c' san áit ar stad
sé, rud a léiríonn go bhfuil an laoi neamhiomlán. Tá cúpla líne i bprós ansan
a mhíníonn deireadh an scéil agus a chuireann an chéad laoi eile i láthair; seo
achoimre le Mícheál Óg féin, a déarfainn. Críochnaíonn an chóip seo den
Agallamh Nua ansan le cóip iomlán den laoi 'Giodh aoibhinn an dún so
shoir'; tá an chóip seo cosúil le cóip Mhichíl mhic Pheadair in ARÉ LS 23 N
11 a luadh thuas. Tá téacs an Agallaimh Nua anseo gairid go maith don
mBun-Agallamh ach go bhfuil an teanga curtha in oiriúint, mar is gnách san
Agallamh Nua, do lucht comhaimsire. Tá bearnaí beaga sa téacs in áiteanna

---

27 E. Gwynn (eag. agus aistr.), *The metrical dindshenchas*, 5 iml. (1906–35), ii, lgh 73–7 agus
ibid., lch 79. Tá ranna áirithe as 'Almu I' leis sa Bhun-Agallamh: féach K. Murray, 'Interpreting
the evidence: problems with dating the early *fianaigecht* corpus' in S. Arbuthnot agus G.
Parsons, *The Gaelic Finn tradition* (2012), lgh 31–49 ag lch 46.   28 Stokes, 'Acallamh', ll. 1181–
204.   29 M. Ní Úrdail, *The scribe in eighteenth- and nineteenth-century Ireland* (2000), lch 191.
30 Cuireadh ábhar breise leis an réamhrá anso, mar a mhíneofar thíos.   31 Féach Stokes,
'Acallamh', ll. 1281–309, 1310–33, 1334–418.

agus i gcolafan ag deireadh an Agallaimh Nua, míníonn Mícheál Óg gur 'drochghraphadh g*an* amhras' atá déanta aige.[32] Tá an chuma ar an scéal go raibh téacs níos faide mar fhoinse ag an Longánach anseo ach nach raibh aga aige é a chóipeáil ina iomláine ná caitheamh go cáiréiseach leis.

Tá dhá chóip eile ann den Agallamh Nua atá cosúil le cóip ARÉ LS 23 G 23. An chéad cheann acu seo ná ARÉ LS F iv 4 (270) a ghraf Peadar agus Pól Ó Longáin i gCorcaigh sa bhliain 1820. Tá cuid de na laoithe in easnamh anseo agus críochnaíonn an téacs níos túisce. An dara ceann ná COC LS 4 a ghraf Séamas Goodman, cuid di sa Sciobairín, Co. Chorcaí in 1874 agus an chuid eile i gColáiste na Tríonóide in 1881. Tá an leagan amach gairid do leagan amach ARÉ LS 23 G 23 ach ní go hiomlán é agus tá eipeasóid nua ann, 'Scéal Aodh mhic Mhuireadaigh', ina dtugann Pádraig fear thar n-ais ón mbás.[33]

V

Mhínigh Nessa Ní Shéaghdha gurb é a dhein an té a chuir le chéile an tAgallamh Déanach ná an teanga a chur 'beagáinín i n-oireamhaint do lucht a aimsire féin' agus luann sí go bhfuil 'breis leadráin i n-innsint gach sgéil' i gcomparáid leis an mBun-Agallamh.[34] Cuireadh teanga an Agallaimh Nua in oiriúint do lucht comhaimsire leis ach tá sé chomh gonta céanna leis an mBun-Agallamh, agus tá cuid de na heipeasóidí níos giorra fós, mar a mhíneofar thíos. Tríd is tríd, tá téacs an Agallaimh Nua cóngarach go maith don mBun-Agallamh cé go bhfuil línte fánacha ann atá níos cóngaraí don Agallamh Déanach. Sampla maith den sórt seo meascáin an laoi ghearr thíos a chanann Ciabhán san eipeasóid Tonn Chlíodhna agus Tonn Téide. Mar seo atá sa Bhun-Agallamh:

> IN t*r*iar atám ar in tuind
> ron tarla a mbeth*ai*d chumaing,
> mor in baegal beith mar sin
> gan bás faeb*uir* dar rochtain.
>
> Missi *ocus* in dias tar muir
> co lín gaile *ocus* gaiscid,
> damad í cath c*é*tach chrón
> dingébmais c*é*t do gach t슬óg.
>
> O ro chím in tuind-seo thes
> is mor dar ndaghles cheiles,
> is mor in brón brón na t*r*iath
> ar nech ó tá dís co t*r*iar.[35]

32 ARÉ LS 23 G 23, lch 28, l. 21.   33 Stokes, 'Acallamh', ll. 1205–45.   34 Ní Shéaghdha, *Agallamh*, i, lgh xxxi–ii.   35 Stokes, 'Acallamh', ll. 3768–73.

Leagan an Agallaimh Dhéanaigh, mar leanas:

> 'In tríar atáim dīar toinn
> ron-tarla a n-íath ēccomhla[i]nn;
> trúagh liom na*ch* b*hfuil* ar ar ccor
> bás d'imi*r*t ar ar mbíodhbh*haid*h.
>
> Misi 7 mo dhías íar sin
> go líon nglíadh 7 gaiscci*d*h
> dā mb*eith*maoís a cc*ath* g*an* bhrón
> dhingēibhmís cē*ad* do dheagh-s*h*lōgh.
>
> Ō dho-chíam an tuinn si theas,
> is mór cheileas óirne dar leas;
> as adhb*har* bróin in b*h*ur n-iath
> b*h*ur mbās eidi*r* dhias is thríar'.[36]

Leagan an Agallaimh Nua:

> An tri*ar* atámaoid *ar* tuin*n*
> Fuil sin*n* an áit éagcómhlain*n*
> **Mór an baoghal bh***eith* **m***ar* **sin***n*
> **7 gan bás d***ár* mbithrin*n*
>
> Misi 7 **an dias** *ar* **mu***ir*
> Go líon **ngoile** 7 gaisgidh
> **Dá madh a ccath chéadach** cró
> Do dhingeabhmaois c*éad* do dh*eagh*shlógh
>
> Ó roichio*m* an ton*n* so theas
> As mór cheilios d*ár* naimhleas
> **As mór an brón** fuil d*ár* **ttriath**
> *Ár* néag a dó, **dias go tri***ar*.[37]

Feicfear go bhfuil na focail i gcló tiubh níos cóngaraí don mBun-Agallamh agus go bhfuil na focail le líne fúthu níos cóngaraí don Agallamh Déanach. Is é an pátrún céanna atá le feiscint san Agallamh Nua trí chéile – tá an téacs níos cóngaraí don mBun-Agallamh ach tá frásaí gearra anseo is ansiúd atá níos cóngaraí don Agallamh Déanach. Is cosúil go bhfuil an tAgallamh Nua bunaithe ar leagan a shíolraigh ó cheann de chóipeanna an Bhun-Agallaimh agus a raibh athruithe beaga tagtha air le himeacht aimsire; is dócha gur

---

36 Ní Shéaghdha, *Agallamh*, i, lgh 132–3.   37 LNÉ LS G114, lch 40, ll. 8–13.

leagan mar sin leis a bhí mar fhoinse ag an té a chuir le chéile an tAgallamh Déanach.

Tá gach ceann d'eipeasóidí an Agallaimh Nua i gcóip Leabhar Leasa Móir, ach mar a bhí i gceist i gcás ARÉ LS 23 N 11, tá cuid de na léamha breise a thugann Stokes ó LS Phroinsiasach A 4 le fáil san Agallamh Nua, rud a léiríonn nach ó Leabhar Leasa Móir a shíolraíonn sé. Tharlódh sé go bhfuil an tAgallamh Nua níos cóngaraí do LS Phroinsiasach A 4, nó b'fhéidir A20(a), atá níos déanaí ná na cóipeanna eile den mBun-Agallamh ach ba ghá mionchomparáid a dhéanamh idir eipeasóidí an Agallaimh Nua agus gach cóip den mBun-Agallamh chun é seo a dheimhniú. Thuairimigh Nollaig Ó Muraíle go mb'fhéidir go raibh ceangal éigin idir an tAgallamh Nua agus dhá bhlogh d'Agallamh na Seanórach i LNÉ LS G125 agus LNÉ LS G126 a ghraf Seán Mac Solaidh ó Chontae na Mí go luath san ochtú céad déag,[38] ach feictear dom go bhfuil eipeasóidí an Agallaimh Nua mar a fhaightear iad sna lámhscríbhinní seo níos cóngaraí do leaganacha an Agallaimh Dhéanaigh. Tá lear mór laoithe a bhaineann le traidisiún Agallamh na Seanórach i gcoitinne gan aon ghiotaí próis eatarthu in LNÉ LS G125 le Seán Mac Solaidh ach níl aon cheangal ar leith acu seo ach an oiread leis an Agallamh Nua.

VI

Tugtar thíos dhá shliocht as an Agallamh Nua,[39] ceann amháin as na sé eipeasóidí tosaigh agus an ceann eile as 'Caoilte i gCúirt Rí Uladh', agus na sleachta a fhreagraíonn dóibh as an mBun-Agallamh, d'fhonn comparáid a dhéanamh eatarthu.

Giota as Scéal Artúir mhic Bheinne Briot
A

'In rabatar eich nó echra*da* acuibh isin Féin?' 'Do bátar *immorro*', ar Cáilte. '.LLL. serrach aenlárach 7 aeneich'. 'Cánas ar frith sin?' ar Pátraic. 'Adér frit a fírinne, a anum', ar Cáilte.

Oclách do búi ac Finn .i. Artúir mac Benne Brit, 7 ba hedh a lín, trí naenb*air*. *Ocus* dorónad sealg Benne hEdair le F*inn*, 7 ba tuillmech

---

38 Ó Muraíle, 'Agallamh', lch 112. Ag tagairt go ginearálta do thraidisiún lámhscríbhinní Agallamh na Seanórach seachas d'aon leagan ar leith atá Ó Muraíle anseo. Thart ar an mbliain 1710 a bhí Mac Solaidh i mbun pinn: Ní Shéaghdha, *Agallamh*, i, lch xxii.   39 Tugtar téacs na sleachta go léir as cóipeanna éagsúla den Agallamh Nua mar atá sna lámhscríbhinní ach gur cuireadh ceannlitreacha ar chéadlitir abairtí, ainmneacha pearsanta, logainmneacha agus ar an bhfocal Fiann, mura raibh ann cheana féin agus gur tugadh an phoncaíocht chun rialtachta in áiteanna.

toirtech in tṡealg soin, 7 do scáilset dá conuibh 7 do shuidh F*inn* i Carn in ḟéinnedha idir Beinn Edair 7 muir, 7 ba maith lais a m*e*nma ag éisd*echt* re raibchedaigh na ndam ndíscir ndás*ach*tach ic á luathmarb*adh* do chonúibh na Fénne.

Is ann dorala d'Artúir mac Benne Brit beith ic coim*et* in mara idir an (fi)adach 7 muir cu nach snáimhdís in (damhrad) uatha; 7 mar do bhí Artúir amuich i cind in chuain atconnaic trí coin do chonuib F*inn* .i. Bran 7 Sceol*ai*ng 7 Adhnuall. *Ocus* as í comairli arar' cinn [Artúir mac] Benne .i. é fein 7 a trí nónb*air* d'imth*echt* tar muir 7 na coin sin do breith leis 'na tír féin; 7 do críchnaiged in com*air*le sin. Dóigh ámh dochuatar-som tar muincinn mara 7 na trí coin sin leo, 7 ro gabsat cuan 7 cal*ad* ac Innb*er* Mara Gaimiach i crích Breatan, 7 tiag*ait* a tír, 7 lotar rompa co Sliabh Lodáin meic Lir, 7 dorónad sealg in tṡléibi sin acu.[40]

B

An rabhad*ar* eich aguibhsi san bhFein*n* a Chaoillte (*air* Pádr*ai*g). Do bhád*ar* *ar* Caoillte trí chaogad chaogad se*ar*rach aon lár*a* 7 aoineich. Cá háit *ar* fríth iad? (*ar* Pádr*ai*g). Fríth (*air* Caoillte) .i. oglaoch ró bhí ag Fion*n* .i. Ártúr M*ac* Bein*n*e Briot M*ac* Rígh Breatan, 7 bá hé líon a mhuin*n*tire .i. trí naonmh*air* óglaoch. 7 do rin*eadh* sealg Bhin*n*e hÉad*air* lé Fionn an t*an* sin, 7 do hosgladh dona muinicíbh do bhí fá bhrághaid na ccon cconfadhach a doirn*n* ghlacaibh na ngiollan*n*raidh. I*ar* sin ró shuig Fion*n* a cC*arr*n an Fhein*n*eadha id*ir* Bhin*n* Éad*air* 7 mu*ir*, 7 bá maith lé Fion*n* a mheanm*a* ag éiste*ach*t lé ró bhéiceach na ndamh n-all*aidh* ndás*ach*tach agá luathmh*ar*bh*adh* do chonaibh na Fein*n*e, *et* asé ionad a raibh Artúr M*ac* Bein*n*e Briot an lá sin ag déanamh na seilge, a ccean*n* an chuain: 7 ad chon*n*airc trí coin do chonaibh na Fein*n*e 7 Fhin*n* chuige a ndiaigh na ndamh all*aidh* ag snámh an mhar*a* .i. Bran, Sgeolang 7 Adhnuall, 7 do rin*eadh* cómh*air*le ag Ártúr gona thrí naonmh*air* na trí coin sin do bhreith leo a cCríochaibh Breatan, 7 do rángad*ar* riompa t*ar* mu*ir*, gur ghabhsad cuan 7 calathphort ag In*n*bh*ir* Mar*a* Gemath a cCrích Breatan, 7 do ráng*a*d*ar* ríompu go Sliabh Lódáin m*i*c L*ir*, 7 do rin*eadh* sealg 7 fiadh-ach an lán tsléibhe sin leo.[41]

Caoilte i mbun comhrá le Rí Uladh
C

… ro ḟiarfaig rí Ul*ad* do Chail*ti*: 'IS álaind in tal*am* tonnglas toghaide', ar in rí, '7 crét ima tuc*ad* Tul*ach* in tr*ir* ar in tul*ai*g seo, 7 cid fa tuc*ad*

---

40 Stokes, 'Acallamh', ll. 166–86. Tá téacs Stokes anseo bunaithe ar an gcóip i Leabhar Leasa Móir.   41 LNÉ LS G114, lch 34, ll. 4–20.

Abhann deisi ar ind abhaind seo, 7 cid fa tucad Lecht chind *con* ar in inad út thall?' 'Gingub nua in ní dia tá, indessat duit in ní dia tá sin, 7 ní ba sen missi ind uair do lenad*ur* na hanmanna sin ucut .i.

Rí ro bí ar Albain .i. Iruath m*a*c Ailpin, ri Alb*an*, 7 ro bad*ur* tri hingena aici .i. Muiresc 7 Aiffi 7 Aillbi a n-anmanna, 7 tucsat g*ra*dh do t*hr*iur óclach i fiannaib Eir*enn* .i. do t*hr*i m*a*caib Aencherda Berra .i. Ger 7 Glas 7 Guba a n-anmanna, 7 tucsat na hócláig sin grád dóibsium, 7 ro bói comseirc re .xx. bli*adan* eturru, 7 ro élad*ur* fecht n-óen ann, 7 tangad*ur* conici in tulaig-sea, 7 ro thuit a torrthaim suain 7 cotalta f*orr*o annso, 7 issí sin uair 7 aimser ro cuired bruigen uathm*ur* re Find m*a*c C*umaill* 7 re m*a*c Mic con, m*a*ic Maic nia, i cuiced lánalaind Laighen, 7 nocho n-uil airem ac filedaib a torchair dona Fiannaib ann 7 do muintir Fathad Canand, 7 dorocrad*ur* d*ono* ann na t*r*i geraiti gaiscid sin .i. t*r*i m*ei*c Aencherda Berra. *Ocus* dala in t*r*ir in*gen* sin, ro eirged*ur* assa cotlud, 7 do chonncad*ur* t*r*iar óclach don feind da n-indsaigid, 7 ro fiarfaigedar scela díb, 7 indissit in bruigen do thabairt 7 ár na Féine do thabairt ann, 7 t*r*i m*ei*c Aencherda Berra do thoitim.[42]

D

As an*n* sin ró fhiafraidh rígh Ul*adh* do Chaoilte, as aluin*n* an tul*ach* so a Chaoilte *ar* an rígh 7 cr*éad* fá ttugadh Tul*ach* an Trír ui*r*the? 7 cr*éad* uma ttugadh Abhan*n* Deise ar an abhain*n*si? In*n*eosad féin sin duit *ar* Caoilte 7 níor ba sean m*ise* an u*air* do leanad*ar* na hanmana sin iad. Árd rígh ró ghabh*us* ce*annus* Alb*an* dár chómhain*m* Iruath m*a*c Ailpín 7 ró bhád*ar* trí hinghiona aige .i. Mu*i*risg, Aoife 7 Aillbhe a nanmana 7 tugad*ar* grádh do th*r*iar óglách do Fhian*n*uibh É*i*rion*n* .i. do thrí m*a*caibh Aoincheárr*da* Béarra .i. Géar 7 Glas 7 Gubha a nanmona 7 tugad*ar* san grádh dóibhsium & ró bhí cóimhshe*ar*c eadur*tha* re bli*adh*uin 7 ró éalód*ar* na mná fe*ach*t naon an*n*, 7 tángad*ar* riomp*a* g*us* an ttul*ach* so 7 do thuit a laoman*n*a suain 7 codlata ortha an*n*so, 7 así sin u*air* 7 aimsir ró cu*i*readh bruíghean uathadh id*i*r Fhion*n* m*a*c Cúmh*aill*, 7 Fatha Canan*n* m*a*c mic *Con* a ccóig*eadh* Laighean 7 ní bhf*uil* á*i*riomh ag fil*eadh*aibh a mh*éad* torch*air* dFian*n*aibh E*i*rion*n* an*n* 7 do mhuin*n*tir Fhátha Canan*n*, 7 do thuit*eadur* an*n* m*ar* aon re cách .i. trí mic Aoincheárr*da* Be*ar*ra. Dála an t*r*iui*r* inghion sin ró e*i*rgead*ur* as a ccodla, 7 do *ch*oncadur triar óglaoch don Fhéin*n* dá nion*n*suighe, 7 ró fhiafruigh*eadur* na h*i*nghean*a* sgéal*a* na Féin*n*e díobh 7 do in*n*sead*ur* bruighean do thabh*air*t 7 ár na Féin*n*e do chur 7 trí mic Aon*ch*earr*da* Béarra do thuitim an*n*.[43]

42 Stokes, 'Acallamh', ll. 3381–403. Tá téacs Stokes anseo bunaithe ar an gcóip i LS Laud 610.
43 COC LS 107, lch 116, ll. 1–17.

Chífear go bhfuil difríochtaí beaga idir na sleachta. Is cosúil gur botún é 'trí chaogad chaogad' in **B** thuas – 'trí chaogad' nó 'lll' a fhaightear de ghnáth san Agallamh Nua. Luaitear in **B** gurb é Artúir mac Rí Breatan, rud ná luaitear in **A**. Tharlódh sé go rabhthas ag cuimhneamh ar Chath Mhá Mhuchroimhe anseo mar tá taoiseach sa scéal sin darb ainm Mac Beine Briot, mac Rí Breataine;[44] tá tagairt don gcath seo i gcuid de na réamhráite a cuireadh leis an Agallamh Nua, mar a mhínítear thíos. Tá míniúcháin bhreise leis an dtéacs in **B** in áiteanna, mar shampla tugtar míniú breise ar an bhfocal lín/líon – 'líon a mhuintire' atá in **B**; b'fhéidir gur síleadh ná raibh an focal 'líon' ina aonar soiléir. Tá an líne 'ba tuillmech toirtech in tṡealg soin' in easnamh in **B**. Tá an cur síos ar na coin á ligean chun fiaigh difriúil sa dá théacs anseo. Tá **B** níos cóngaraí don Agallamh Déanach anseo sa mhéid is go bhfuil tagairt do na muincí a bhí ar na coin sa dá cheann acu:

> Ro hoslaiceadh leō a muinch<idh> féighe forōrdha flaith-mhaiseacha
> do bhraighd*ibh* chon cc<raosach> ccroibh-dh*ea*rg cconfa*d*hach a gheal-
> ghlacuibh giollanr*aid*he Fhinn.[45]

Cuireadh na focail *ró-bhéiceach* in áit an fhocail neamhchoitianta *raibchedach* ('bellowing') in **B**. Tá an cur síos ar Artúir ag fuadach na gcon beagán difriúil sa dá théacs ach tá na logainmneacha gairid go maith dá chéile. Meascán idir Mhéan-Ghaeilge agus Nua-Ghaeilge Mhoch atá sa Bhun-Agallamh,[46] ach is Nua-Ghaeilge Dhéanach liteartha atá sna sleachta as an Agallamh Nua thuas. Tá litriú an Bhun-Agallaimh mírialta toisc gur scríobhadh na lámhscríbhinní is sine atá ar marthain anois beagnach trí chéad bliain i ndiaidh an téacs féin a chur le chéile; tá mírialtachtaí le feiscint i dteanga an Agallaimh Nua leis toisc gur caomhnaíodh leaganacha a bhaineann le tréimhse níos luaithe in áiteanna. Sampla maith de seo líne as an laoi 'Caithréim Fhinn'. 'Isam eolach 'na faisnéis' atá sa Bhun-Agallamh, agus caomhnaíodh an fhoirm Mheán-Ghaeilge seo den gcopail i LNÉ LS G114: 'Asum eolach ina bhfaisnéis'.[47]

Arís, tá **C** agus **D** gairid go maith dá chéile. Baineadh amach an cheist in **C** mar gheall ar bhunús an tríú logainm, Lecht Chind Con, in **D** mar níl an scéal a mhíníonn é sin san Agallamh Nua.[48] Mar sin, deineadh eagarthóireacht anseo ar théacs an Agallaimh Nua chun a chinntiú go mbeadh sé de réir a

44 M. Ó Dúnlainge (eag.), 'Cath Mhaighe Mochruimhe', *Irisleabhar na Gaedhilge*, 17 §25 (1907), 386. Pléitear Artúir mac Beinne Briot leis in W. Gillies, 'Arthur in Gaelic tradition. Part II: romances and lore', *Cambrian Medieval Celtic Studies*, 3 (1982), 41–75 ag 70–1.   **45** Ní Shéaghdha, *Agallamh*, i, lch 15.   **46** Maidir leis an dáta féach nóta 2 (thuas). Cf. M. Dillon (eag.), *Stories from the Acallam* (1970), lch ix, agus K. Murray, 'Interpreting the evidence', lgh 44–7.   **47** Stokes, 'Acallamh', l. 2546; LNÉ LS G114, lch 32, l. 30. Tá an fhoirm seo den gcopail pléite ag L. Breatnach, 'An Mheán-Ghaeilge' in K. McCone et al. (eag.), *Stair na Gaeilge* (1994), lgh 221–333 ag lch 324.   **48** Le fáil in Stokes, 'Acallamh', ll. 3413–27. Tagann laoi ina luaitear na trí logainmneacha ina dhiaidh sin (ll. 3428–35).

chéile. Fiche bliain a bhí na lánúnacha i gcomhshearc le chéile in **C**, bliain amháin in **D**. 'Laomanna suain' atá in **D** in áit 'torrthaim suain' ach tá an dá nath gairid go maith dá chéile.[49]

Féach go gcaomhnaítear éirim na sleachta thuas in ainneoin na ndifríochtaí beaga idir théacs an Bhun-Agallaimh agus théacs an Agallaimh Nua.

VII

Tá réamhráite le formhór na gcóipeanna den Agallamh Nua ina dtugtar cur síos ar Chaoilte agus Pádraig ag bualadh le chéile den chéad uair. Tá an réamhrá a cuireadh le Coláiste na Tríonóide LS H.5.4 difriúil le gach ceann eile. Tá ciumhais na mbileog sa chuid seo den lámhscríbhinn stracaithe; mar sin, níl an téacs ar fad againn, mar a léiríonn na lúibíní cearnacha thíos.

A: Réamhrá an Agallaimh Nua mar atá i gColáiste na Tríonóide LS H. 5. 4

  3: [ ]g seanmóir an chreidimh [ ]
  4: go ndeachaidh go Connachtaibh [ ]
  5: laidh ná naon *air* bruach lo[ ]
  6: sheisior diarmhar na Feinne 7 [ ]
  7: iomrádh *air* Fhionn Mac Cúmh[ ]
  8: iad ag daghra 7 ag do[ ]
  9: mhain as truagh an Ríghfheinn[ ]
 10: do bhí an Éirinn riamh 7 b[ ]
 11: 7 uagna dó dhul déag g[ ]
 12: óir asé an baiste dor[ ]
 13: mi 7 as leis sgriostar [ ]
 14: tsinnsir 7 ní féidir do[ ]
 15: neamhdha gan c[rei]diomh [ ]

  1: [ ]saoilmaoidne (*air* an Fhiann)
  2: [ ]aibh Rígh ann riamh bá mó iná Fionn
  3: [ ]do bhí *air* Pádraig .i. an rígh [ ]
  4: [ ]neamh 7 talamh 7 a bhfuil
  5: [ ]cíodh trath acht táinig do theag–
  6: [ ]an naoimhchléiricc gur ghabhsad an
  7: [ ]sheisear sin baiste 7 ba mó nó
  8: [ ]irde gach neach díobh 7 iad ina
  9: [ ]air bruach an locha, iná Pádruig
 10: [ ]chléiricc 7 iad ina seasamh éag–
 11: [ ]láthair cúigear díobh iar na mbais–

---

49 Féach *DIL* s.vv. *láem, tairthim.*

12: [ ]r mh*air* a*cht* dias .i. Oisín m*ac*
13: [ ]Caoillte m*ac* Rónáin 7 as ó
14: [ ]*air* Pádr*aig* iomad eólais 7
15: [ ]amhuil a d*earthar* a *m*beatha Phád–
16: [ ]ias Hybernias scripsit stg[?]⁵⁰
17: [ ]Roan[ ] seu Ronano.⁵¹

Go hachomair: tá Pádraig ag craobhscaoileadh an chreidimh; téann sé go
Connachta agus buaileann sé le mórsheisear d'iarmhar na Féinne ar bhruach
locha agus iad ag iomrá ar Fhionn mac Cumhaill; táid fé dhobrón mar go
bhfuil an Rí-fhéinnidh is fearr a bhí in Éirinn caillte; míníonn Pádraig gurb é
an baiste a ghlanann peaca an tsinsir agus nach féidir dul ar neamh gan
glacadh leis an gcreideamh Críostaí; míníonn na Fianna gurb é a dtuiscint féin
nach raibh aon rí ann riamh níos tábhachtaí ná Fionn; míníonn Pádraig gur
fearr fós é an Dia a dhein neamh is talamh; glacann an seachtar le teagasc
Phádraig is baisteann sé iad; luaitear gur mhó iad na Fianna ina suí ná cléir
Phádraig agus iad ina seasamh agus nár mhair ach dias díobh i ndiaidh a
mbaiste; is iad san Oisín mac Finn agus Caoilte mac Rónáin; fuair Pádraig
mórán eolais uatha mar a deirtear i m*Beatha Phádraig*. Tógadh an abairt
Laidine ag deireadh an réamhrá as an bh*Foras Feasa*. Tugtar thíos an
comhthéacs ina bhfuil sé sa téacs sin:

> … Caoilte mac Rónáin, do mhair tuilleadh agus trí chéad bliadhan,
> agus do nocht mórán seanchusa do Phádraic, amhail is follus i
> n-Agallaimh na Seanórach; agus is ar Chaoilte is cóir Roanus, nó
> Ronánus do thabhairt. Óir ní léaghtar i leabhar ar bioth do sheanchus
> Éireann, go ngairthí Roanus nó Ronánus d'Fhionntain; acht gidh air do
> bheir Cambrens, mar gach bréig eile d'á chlaoinsheanchus, é: agus
> amhail do chuir-sean 'Roanus' síos i n-a chroinic i n-áit 'Ronánus',
> scríobhaidh gach aon do na Nua-Ghallaibh scríobhas ar Éirinn
> 'Roanus' ar lorg Chambrens mar ainm ar Fhionntain, do bhrígh gurab
> é, Cambrens, is tarbh tána dhóibh le scríobhadh saoibh-sheanchusa ar
> Éirinn, ar an adhbhar nach fuil a mhalairt do threoraidhe aca. Is
> córaide a mheas gurab ar Chaoilte dobheirthear Ronánus, mar chuirid
> sean-úghdair síos idir oibreachaibh Phádraic gur scríobh sé 'Historia
> Hiberniae ex Roano seu Ronáno': is é, iomorro, sloinneadh an úghdair
> is gnáth do chur ós cionn gach oibre d'á scríobhann neach, mar is
> follus do gach léaghthóir chleachtas úghdair do léaghadh.⁵²

---

50 Líne fhada os cionn stg anso.   51 Lgh 277–8 sa lámhscríbhinn. Tá an dá líne tosaigh ar lch
277 doiléir.   52 D. Comyn and P.S. Dinneen (eag. and aistr.), *Foras feasa ar Éirinn*, 4 iml.
(1902–14), i, lgh 150–2.

Tá Céitinn ag áiteamh anso nach bhfuil i scéal Fhionntain mhic Bhóchna a raibh sé ráite air gur mhair sé i ndiaidh na díleann go dtí aimsir Naomh Pádraig ach 'finnsceul filidheachta'.[53] Luann sé go raibh fear ann a mhair na céadta blian agus a thug seanchas do Phádraig agus gurb é seo Caoilte mac Rónáin agus cáineann sé Cambrensis as leagan míchruinn den scéal a chur ina stair-sean. Tá Céitinn sásta glacadh leis anseo gur phearsa stairiúil é Caoilte mac Rónáin nó, ar a laghad, ní bhaineann an cheist sin leis an argóint atá ar bun aige; pé ní é, creideadh go forleathan in am Chéitinn agus i bhfad ina dhiaidh san gur phearsana stairiúla iad Fionn agus na Fianna.[54] Tá an chuma ar an scéal, mar sin, gur tógadh an giota Laidine seo as an bh*Foras Feasa* agus gur cuireadh in oiriúint é chun comhthéacs stairiúil a sholáthar don Agallamh Nua sa réamhrá atá leis an gcóip i gColáiste na Tríonóide LS H.5.4.

Tá an réamhrá a cuireadh leis an Agallamh Nua in LNÉ LS G114, a ghraf Uilliam Mac Cairteáin sa bhliain 1703, againn ina iomláine:

B: Réamhrá an Agallaimh Nua mar atá in LNÉ LS G114

Iar ccur Catha Gabhra 7 iar ttuitim úrmhór na Fein*n*e ní raibh rath ná Rígh ortha tre mhalla*cht* Airt Aoinfhir M*h*ic Cuin*n* chead chathaicc áird rígh Éirean*n*, noch tug a mhalla*cht* do Fhion*n* 7 dFian*n*aibh Éireann tré gan tea*cht* leis do chur Chatha Mhuíghe Muchroimhe an agh*aidh* Mhic Con. Ion*n*as iar ttea*cht* do Phádr*aig* an Éirin*n* nách mór do mh*air* díobh, a*cht* amháin móirsheisior, 7 as amh*laidh* aithrisios an leabh*ar* dár*ab* ainm Agallamh na Seanó*ireadh*a go raibh Pádr*aig* lá naon an Ulltaibh, 7 é ag dul ag sea*n*móir an tsoisgéil don chóige sin 7 go ttárlad*ar* an móirsheisior sin diarmh*ar* na Fein*n*e ar bruach locha, 7 iad ag déana*mh* doghra ag*us* dobróin mhóir an*n*, 7 ag iomrádh *air* an bhflath fhein*n*eadh Fion*n*, go ttáin*ig* an naomh uasal 7 an tapstal árd-chúmha*cht*ach dá láth*air* 7 buídhion mhór do chléireachaibh ina fhoch*air*, 7 fá haoirde gach neach don mhoirseisior sin 7 iad iná suíghe, iná aon dona cle*ir*eachaibh 7 iad ina seasamh. Táinig t*r*ath do theagasg an naoimh 7 dá sheanmóir dhóibh g*ur* [ghl]acsad baiste uadha, 7 fu*ar*ad*ar* cúigior díobh bás do láth*air* i*ar* na mbaiste, 7 níor mh*air* díobh a*cht* dias .i. Oisín M*a*c Fin*n* 7 Coillte M*a*c Rónáin, 7 as ó Choillte fu*air* Pádraicc iomad eoluis 7 seanch*u*sa, óir do mh*air* an Coillte so iomad do chéad*a*ibh bl*iadh*an, 7 dfaisnéis féin 7 Oisín iom*a*d do sheanch*a*s 7 go háir*ir*ghthe dála na Fein*n*e do Phádraicc amhuil atá an*n* so síos.[55]

---

53 Ibid., i, lch 150. Tugtar cuntas ar Fhionntan mac Bóchna in E. Nic Cárthaigh, 'Surviving the flood: revenants and antediluvian lore in medieval Irish texts' in K. Cawsey and J. Harris (eag.), *Transmission and transformation in the Middle Ages* (2007), lgh 40–64. **54** Mar a luaitear in D. Ó hÓgáin, *Fionn mac Cumhaill* (1998), lch 2. **55** Lch 31 sa lámhscríbhinn. Tá cóip den

Tá anáil an Bhun-Agallaimh le brath ar an dá réamhrá seo as Coláiste na Tríonóide LS H.5.4 (**A**) agus LNÉ LS G114 (**B**). Tá Caoilte agus Oisín agus líon beag laoch fágtha i ndiaidh na Féinne,[56] buaileann siad le Pádraig, baistear iad, luaitear an méad atá sna Fianna.[57] Fós, tá an insint i bhfad níos gonta san Agallamh Nua agus fágtar mórán amach; mar shampla, ní thagraítear do thuras Oisín agus Chaoilte ar Chámha ná don uisce coisricthe a chaith Pádraig ar na Fianna agus a chuir teitheadh ar na deamhain a bhí os a gcionn go dtí san.[58] Arís, ní dheintear sna réamhráite seo argóint ar son a thábhachtaí is atá sé na scéalta a insíonn Caoilte a scríobh síos le go gcaomhnófaí iad, mar a dheintear le linn an chuid thosaigh den gcomhrá sa Bhun-Agallamh – glactar leis sna réamhráite seo go mbeadh suim ag Pádraig i seanchas agus in eachtraí na Féinne.[59] Tagraítear i réamhrá **B** don leabhar 'dárab ainm Agallamh na Seanóireadha' faoi mar gur tráchtaireacht a sheasann taobh amuigh den Agallamh féin atá sa réamhrá seachas dlúthchuid den dtéacs; b'fhéidir go bhfuil anáil líne Chéitinn thuas 'amhail is follus i n-Agallaimh na Seanórach' le braith air seo.

Tá tagairt do thrí chath i líne thosaigh an Bhun-Agallaimh – 'ar tabhuirtt chatha Chomuir 7 chatha Gabra 7 chatha Ollurbha';[60] luaitear cath amháin acu seo i réamhrá **B** thuas agus ní luaitear aon chath acu i réamhrá **A** mura raibh tagairt dóibh sa dá líne tosaigh atá doléite. Deintear tagairt in **B** do mheathlú na Féinne i ndiaidh chath Mhá Mhuchroimhe. Tá leaganacha difriúla ann den scéal Cath Mhá Mhuchroimhe, ina measc 'a later romanticised version' atá difriúil leis an gcuid eile, agus is cosúil gurb é sin an leagan a bhfuil tagairt dó san Agallamh Nua.[61] Tá mórán cóipeanna den dtéacs seo sna lámhscríbhinní déanacha agus cuireadh i gcló in *Irisleabhar na Gaeidhilge* é.[62] Níl ach tagairtí fánacha d'Fhionn mac Cumhaill in eagrán O Daly, ach cuireadh eipeasóid a bhaineann leis an bhFéinn isteach sa leagan déanach agus go deimhin, tuairimíonn Alan Bruford gur mar gheall ar an gceangal seo leis an bhFiannaíocht a bhí tóir ar Chath Mhá Mhuchroimhe go maith isteach sa

---

réamhrá seo as Egerton 175 maille le haistriúchán Béarla i gcló in S.H. O'Grady and R. Flower, *Catalogue of Irish manuscripts in the British Library*, 2 vols (1926), i, lgh 648–9.   **56** Stokes, 'Acallamh', l. 6: *dá naonmar*; mórsheisear in A agus B.   **57** Ibid., ll. 77–8: *ní roichead acht co tana a tháibh nó co formna a ghualand in bhfer ba mó dona cléirchibh don fir dhibh sin 7 iat ina súidhi*; A. Dooley and H. Roe, *Tales of the elders of Ireland* (1999), lch 5: 'for the tallest of the clerics came only to the waist or the shoulder-tops of these great men, who were already sitting down'.   **58** Ibid., ll. 11–46; 64–71.   **59** Féach P. Ó Fiananchta, 'The development of the debate between Pádraig and Oisín' in B. Almqvist et al. (eag.), *The heroic process* (1987), lgh 183–205 ag lgh 185–9.   **60** Stokes, 'Acallamh', ll. 1–2.   **61** M. O Daly (eag.), *Cath Maige Mucrama* (1975), lch 1; W. Stokes (eag. and aistr.), 'The battle of Mag Mucrime', *Revue Celtique*, 13 (1892), 426–74 ag 428. Dar le P. Ua Laoghaire, *Lughaidh mac Con* (Baile Átha Cliath, 1917), lch x, 'sé atá sa leagan déanach den gCath ná '[a] modern recension of various legends connected with Art Mac Cuinn and Lughaidh … [that] has little in common with the old tale' (leagan Nua-Ghaeilge den leagan luath den scéal atá in Ua Laoghaire, *Lughaidh mac Con*).   **62** Don eagrán, féach nóta 44 thuas.

naoú céad déag.[63] Sa leagan déanach seo, roim dhul chun catha dó, téann Art mac Cuinn go hAlmhain chun tacaíocht a lorg ar Fhionn mac Cumhaill. Tá Fionn as baile agus cuirtear in iúl d'Art go bhfuil geallúint tugtha cheana féin ag Fionn nach dtroidfidh sé i gcoinne Mhic Con. Cuireann Art mallacht ar Fhionn is na Fianna ansan.[64] Mínítear i dtairngreacht ina dhiaidh san sa scéal gurb é Cairbre, mac mic Airt, a bhainfidh díoltas amach ar an bhFéinn:

> Cairbre a ainm … is é an mac sin mo dheigh-mhic-se dhígheólas ar an bhFéinn mar do thréigeadar mé re h-ucht an chatha so, agus do bhéaraidh sé féin agus an Fhian cath dá chéile, agus gidh thuiteas eisean ann, ní bhiadh athmhaoine na Féinne ann choidhche.[65]

Luann Cairbre é seo leis sa laoi 'Tuarascáil Chatha Gabhra' agus é ag gríosadh a mhórshlua:

> Adubhairt Cairbre go prap
> 'Cuimhne Mhuchroimhe, cuimhne Airt,
> Tuitim bhur sinnsear maille
> de bhrígh fala na Féinne'.[66]

Mar sin, tagraítear sa réamhrá seo do shnáth eile i dtraidisiúin na Fiannaíochta – an traidisiún a bhaineann le cath Gabhra[67] – chun míniú a thabhairt ar mheathlú na Féinne.

Bhí an dá scríobhaí a ghraf an dá chóip is luaithe den Agallamh Nua, Uilliam Mac Cairteáin agus Eoghan Ó Caoimh, mór lena chéile[68] agus go deimhin, tá cúpla líne i láimh Eoghain in LNÉ LS G114, lámhscríbhinn Uilliam.[69] D'fhéadfadh sé go rabhadar ag obair as lámh a chéile ar an Agallamh Nua[70] ach fós, má tá cosúlachtaí áirithe idir an dá réamhrá agus idir iad agus oscailt an Bhun-Agallaimh, is píosaí neamhspleácha ceapadóireachta iad. Níl réamhrá le gach cóip den Agallamh Nua agus tharlódh sé chomh maith gur cumadh na réamhráite seo níos déanaí ná mar a cuireadh le chéile na heipeasóidí.

---

63 A. Bruford, *Gaelic folktales and medieval romances* (1966), lch 8.   64 M. Ó Dúnlainge (eag.), 'Cath Mhaighe Mochruimhe', *Irisleabhar na Gaedhilge*, 17 (1907), 435.   65 Ibid., 438.   66 Ó Siochfhradha, *Laoithe na féinne*, lch 206, rann 6.   67 Tugtar breac-chuntas ar an dtraidisiún seo in E. MacNeill agus Gerard Murphy (eag. and aistr.), *Duanaire Finn*, 3 iml. (1908–53), iii, lgh 92–3.   68 Ó Conchúir, *Scríobhaithe Chorcaí*, lch 19.   69 Ní Shéaghdha, *Catalogue of Irish manuscripts in the National Library of Ireland*, iii, lch 128.   70 Dhein an tEaspag Mac Sleighne pátrúnacht ar an mbeirt acu leis: B. Ó Conchúir, 'Eoin Baiste Mac Sleighne, Easpag (1693–1712), agus pátrún ar an léann Gaelach' in P. de Brún et al. (eag.), *Folia gadelica* (1983), lgh 88–94 ag lch 90. D'fhéadfadh sé gur tríd Easpag Mac Sleighne, a chuir mórán lámhscríbhinní á n-athscríobh dó féin sa tréimhse seo, a bhí teacht ag an mbeirt ar an Agallamh Nua nó fiú go raibh teacht acu ar leagan níos luaithe d'Agallamh na Seanórach agus gurb iad féin a thiontaigh sleachta áirithe as go Nua-Ghaeilge. Níl aon fhianaise againn air seo, áfach.

In ARÉ LS 23 G 23 le Mícheál Óg Ó Longáin (1800),[71] tugtar breis eolais fós (ar lch 1, ll. 1–15) mar gheall ar chath Gabhra:

Cath Gabhra an cath deireannach tugadh le Fiannuibh Éirionn 7 ní bhfuaras léirsgríobhtha é a ndiaigh na núghdar acht amháin go ccuireadh Seathrún Céitinn síos a seanchas Éireann go comuir é mar atá nár ndiaidh–.

Sámuir inghean dFionn mac Cumhaill fá bean do Chormac Cas mac Oilioll Óluim ó ttángadar síol mBriain et cetera. Fá máthair Thinne 7 Chonnla í 7 tréas an ngáodhal san, do chuingimh Modh Corb mac Cormuic bráthair a mháthar .i. Oisín mac Fínn 7 Clanna Baoisgne dar shárrúghadh Chairbre Lifiochair .i. áirdríghe Éireann agus Aoidhe Chaoimh mic Garra Glúnduibh do Chlannuibh Móirnne 7 is ag clanna Mórna [ ] bhí an bhuannacht an uair sin 7 do bhádar air feadh seacht mbliaghan an easaontacht le Fionn [agus] re Clanna Baoisgine, gon uime sin do gríosadh le Clannaibh Móirnne, Cairbre 7 cóigeadhaig Éireann mar aon leis daithríoghadh Mhogha Chuirb, an dóith go ttiocfa[ ] de sin Clanna Báoisgne d'ionnarba, gon de sin táinig Cath Gabhra 7 ó n[ach] fuil an cath aguinn lena chur annso, cuirfeam athuarusgabháil síos fé mar thug Oisín mac Fínn do Naomh Pádraig é an tan do ghaibh baisde uaidhe.

Ina dhiaidh san, grafadh an laoi 'Tuarascáil Chatha Gabhra' ina dtugtar cur síos ar an gcath céanna.[72] Tógadh na deich línte tosaigh sa dara alt thuas a thugann fáthanna chatha Gabhra ón bh*Foras Feasa*.[73] Is cosúil gur ghlac an Longánach leis gur cuntas fírinneach a bhí ag Céitinn, más cuntas gairid féin é, ach léiríonn sé dearcadh níos amhrasaí i dtaobh na laoi – athuarascáil atá ann seachas bunfhoinse, dar leis. Leanann an réamhrá ar aghaidh mar atá in **B** thuas ina dhiaidh san. Tá an réamhrá a cuireadh le ARÉ LS F iv 4, a ghraf Peadar agus Pól Ó Longáin sa bhliain 1820, agus le COC LS 4 a ghraf Séamas Goodman in 1874 agus 1871, dealraitheach leis seo ach nár cuireadh an laoi 'Tuarascáil Chatha Gabhra' leosan.

Tá forbairt bhreise déanta ar réamhrá an Agallaimh Nua i dtrí cinn de lámhscríbhinní, mar atá ARÉ LSS 24 A 5 (1820–1), 24 A 6 (1854), agus 24 B 13 (19ú céad). Tugaim anso an chóip as ARÉ LS 24 A 6 (lgh 210–1):

Iar ccur Catha Gabhradh le Cairbre mac Cormaic Righ Éirionn, air Fhionn 7 air Fhiannaibh Eirionn, mar ar thuit Osgur 7 maithe 7 mór uaisle na feinne, tre mhallacht Airt aoinfhir mic Cuinn céadchathaicc,

71 Ar dhátaí éagsúla idir 1794 agus 1831 a grafadh an lámhscríbhinn ach tugtar an dáta 1800 i gcolafan ag bun lgh 28 díreach tar éis an Agallaimh Nua.　72 Tá sé seo ar aon dul leis an leagan atá in Ó Siochfhradha, *Laoithe na féinne*, lgh 206–12.　73 Comyn and Dinneen, *Foras feasa ar Éirinn*, ii, lch 352. Níl an tagairt do 'Shíol mBriain' san eagrán.

noch tug a mhalla*cht* dóibh air son gan tea*cht* leis do chur Catha
Muighe Mochruime an agh*aidh* mhic Con, go nach raibh raith ná Righ
orrtha o soin amach, amhuil adeir Fion*n* féin lá an catha, 7 é os cion*n*
Osguir mac Oisín san árr dá chaoin*eadh* –

Malla*cht* Airt aoinfhir go mbuadh
Táinig aniugh réam shluagh
Do dhearbh orm gach nidh
Do chuir mo ghlan tslio*cht* air neimhchrith.

Ion*n*us nách raibh ina mbeatha dfian*n*aibh Eirion*n* re tea*cht*
Phattraicc an Eirin*n* do shiola an chreidimh a*cht* móirsheisior arr araibh
Oisin 7 Caoilte m*a*c Rónáin.

Lá dá raibh Pattr*aig* an Ulta tárlaidh an móirsheise*a*r sin do, 7 iad
na suíghe os bruach locha ag iomrádh *air* Fhion*n* 7 air an bhFein*n*,
agus ag déanamh doilghíos 7 déarchaointe ina ndeóig, go ttáinig
Pádruig fán láithir chútha, 7 beanuigheas dóibh, agus fiadhfrios sgéala
dóibh, no*cht*aid na sean*n*oiridhe do gurab diarm*a*r na Féin*n*e iad,
truadh lin*n*e air Pattraicc an righ Feinn*e* is fearr do bhi an Eirin*n* riamh
.i. Fion*n*, 7 badh mhó clú agus oirdhearcus, do dhul déag gan baiste,
dá ttáinig a bheith sgartha ris an sólás siorruighe, 7 ris an nglóire
fhlathusda gheibhid an drong baistighthear, 7 choimeádus dlíghe 7
ra*cht* an Rígh neamhdha.

Ní shilmidne air na sean*n*oiridhe go raibh Rígh riamh san domhan
rób fhearr iná Fion*n*, 7 dá silidhmis is dó, do dhéanfamaois adhradh 7
onóir, maiseadh air Pattr*aig* atá .i. an Rígh do chúm neamh 7 talamh,
7 gach a bhfuil eatartha, 7 nach féidir le neach onóir iomchuibhe do
dhéanamh dhó gan baiste air ttúis, oir asé an baiste dhéanus an creidiomh, 7 an creidiomh sin creidiomh Criosd. Cidh trá*cht* do bhaist
Padruicc an móirsheisior sin, 7 éaguid cúigear diob do láithir, agus nior
mhair doibh a*cht* Oisin 7 Caoilte m*a*c Rónáin agus rug Páttr*aig* leis iad,
7 níor sgar riú an ccein mhaireadar. Agus is ó Chaoilte fuair iomad
eoluis agus sean*n*achuis amhuil is follus san leabhar dá ngoirthear
Agallamh na Seanoiridhe, 7 go nabruid úghdair an tseanchusa na
briatha so Sanctus Patricus Historias Hibernicus scripsit ex Ronana.

Leagtar béim anseo arís ar mheathlú na Féinne i ndiaidh chath Mhá
Mhuchroimhe agus tugtar rann as an laoi 'Tuarascáil Chatha Gabhra' ina
dtag-raíonn Fionn don mallacht a chuir Art ar an bhFéinn.[74] Deintear breis
forbartha ar an gcomhrá mar gheall ar an dá rí – Dia agus Fionn. Tá eilim-
intí as réamhráite **A** agus **B** thuas sa réamhrá seo – tharlódh go raibh teacht
ag an nduine a chéadchum an réamhrá seo ar an dá cheann acu agus go
ndeineadh iarracht iad a thabhairt chun aontachta anseo.

74 Féach Ó Siochfhradha, *Laoithe na féinne*, lch 209, rann 55.

Ní mhínítear sa Bhun-Agallamh conas a tharla sé gur mhair Oisín agus
Caoilte na céadta blian i ndiaidh na Féinne. Mheas Gerard Murphy gur
fágadh an cheist seo amach d'aon ghnó mar gur theastaigh ón té a chuir le
chéile an Bun-Agallamh díriú ar na heilimintí réalaíocha den scéal seachas ar
na heilimintí draíochtúla.[75] Tá dhá chóip den Agallamh Nua in ARÉ LS 23
E 11 a ghraf Nioclás Ó Cearnaigh sa bhliain 1850. Chuir an Cearnach leagan
de scéal Oisín i dTír na nÓg le ceann de na cóipeanna chun an bhearna idir
an dá thréimhse ama – Oisín i measc na Féinne agus ina diaidh – a líonadh.

Tosnaíonn an chóip sin leis an réamhrá mar atá in **B** thuas agus ansan,
leanann ar aghaidh mar seo (lch 405, l. 19 – lch 406, l. 13):

A deiridh drong re seanchus go abé fath fa mair Oisin deis na Feine go
teacht Phattruic inn Éirinn. Lá naen de raibh i nUltaibh *ar* bruach
Locha Deirg do chonarc ingean aláinn do rug bárr *air* mhnáibh in
domhain i sgéimh 7 i naillne deilbhe 7 innealta *air* bruach an locha
cheadna a ngar do. Do dhruid sisi inn a dháil, 7 dubairt de
bhriathraibh caemha ceart-bhinne. Is dóigh liom, a óglaoich, gur brón-
ach thú oir ró throm do osnadha, 7 is buan do chaoi 7 do gheargul, *air*
si. Is eadh amh, *air* Oisin, oir marbhadh iomad den bhfein a ccath
Gabhra, 7 ní mhairionn do láth*air* de chlannaibh Baesgne acht me féin
7 fir-bheagan, 7 do guilfinn deora fola. Níor bho ingnáth é déis mo
chomhdaltadh 7 mo cháirde ionmuin. Is briathar dhamh, *air* an ingean,
gur tu féin Oisin mac an rígh feineadh, Is me go deimhin, *air* Oisin. Is
adhbh*ar* argardais tarrladh dhuit, oir is ad dheighin ro thancas do
chum cabhair 7 furtacht do fhághail dhuit, 7 sólás do-innsighte don
drong daendha do tabhairt dhuit, da ma bhithir de mo réir, *ar* sí. Cia
thusa féin? *air* Oisin. Meise *ar* si, ingean rígh Thíre na n-Óg. Feileogan
m'ainm 7 tarrsa liom g*an* spás 7 ní aithreach duit do thuras, oir bo ro
dhoilg le'm athair do chor deis ár do mhuintire 7 na Feine 7 do
ghreasaigh mise ad ionsaighe, ionas go ngabhthar leat an duais 7 luach-
saethair do ghaisge 7 do ghoile 7 do mhaith-ghníomh go nuige seo, *ar*
si, 7 triallam gan obadh gan fhoill go duithche an aeibhneis.

Tá mórán leaganacha ann den scéal seo agus tá anailís déanta orthu ag Máirtín
Ó Briain. Baineann an scéal thuas leis na leaganacha sin den scéal ina dtagann
spéirbhean chun Oisín a mhealladh go Tír na nÓg.[76] Ní luann an Brianach go
dtagraítear do chath Gabhra in aon cheann acu seo, mar a deineadh thuas;
mar sin, déarfainn gurb shin athrú a cuireadh i bhfeidhm ar an scéal anseo
chun é a chur in oiriúint don gcomhthéacs ina bhfuil sé i réamhrá an
Agallaimh Nua. Déarfainn gur dócha gurb é an Cearnach féin a dhein an cur

---

75 G. Murphy, *The Ossianic lore and romantic tales of medieval Ireland* (1971), lgh 26–7.   76 Ó
Briain, 'Some material on Oisín in the Land of Youth', lgh 187–92 (lch 190 ach go háirithe).

in oiriúint seo – bhí teist na samhlaíochta air – agus cuireadh ina leith, mar shampla, gur chum sé féin cuid de na tairngreachtaí a chuir sé i gcló sa bhliain 1856 sa leabhar *The Prophecies of SS. Columbkille, Maeltamlacht, Ultan, Seadhna, Coireall, Bearcan, etc*, agus chum sé filíocht dá chuid féin leis.[77]

Ní luaitear cad a bhí ar siúl ag Caoilte le linn na headarlúide seo cé gurb é siúd a bhíonn ag comhrá le Pádraig san Agallamh Nua. Fágann seo nach bhfuil scéal Thír na nÓg iomlán oirúnach don gcomhthéacs inar chuir an Cearnach é ach ba dheacair pearsa Chaoilte a shníomh isteach in eachtra Oisín i dTír na nÓg gan an scéal a chur as a riocht ar fad. Leanann scéal Thír na nÓg ar aghaidh mar is gnách agus tugtar cuntas ar Thír na nÓg agus ar Oisín ag filleadh ar Éirinn ina dhiaidh san. Nuair a bhuaileann Oisín le Naomh Pádraig tar éis dó teacht ar ais ó Thír na nÓg, glacann sé baiste uaidh agus mínítear ansan go raibh sé 'a bhfoch*air* Pattraicc cian aimsire go ttug fios 7 sgealaidheacht dho *air* Fhianaibh Éirionn 7 *air* rachtaibh geintleachta 7 draoidheachta na hÉirionn'.[78] Nochtann an Cearnach tuairim eile mar gheall ar an Agallamh ansan:

> Atá fós *air* na dhearbhtha re seanchuidhibh airidhe oile gur mórsheisior druadh 7 luchta adhradh daimh 7 beitheigheach oile da ngoirthaoi dháimh, do tharrla do Phattraicc *air* bhruach an locha, 7 gur gabhad teagasg an fior-chreidimh uad 7 gur bhaist an naemh iad, 7 gur fhaisneis do iomad seanchusa 7 go háiridhe dala na Feine 7 rún geintleacht 7 iol-iomadh ealadhna atá nois *air* ndigh de bhrigh gur múchadh an t-iomlán re Pattraic 7 a chléircibh d'eagla go ttuitheamh cách de siu*c*air do chum geintlea*ch*ta ris.[79]

Luaitear anseo go mb'fhéidir nach nglacfadh Críostaí mar Phádraig le gach scéal a tháinig anuas ó ré na págántachta agus go ndéanfaí cinsireacht orthu dá réir sin. Seo ceist a dtugtar aghaidh uirthi sa Bhun-Agallamh féin agus, mar a mhíníonn Pádraig Ó Fiannachta, chuir mórán scoláirí ó shin suim i ndearcadh na scríbhneoirí agus scríobhaithe luatha a bhí ag feidhmiú i *milieu* eaglasta i leith na scéalta agus na filíochta a bhí tagtha chucu ó ré na réamh-Chríostaíochta.[80] Leanann an tAgallamh Nua ar aghaidh mar is gnách ina dhiaidh seo sa lámhscríbhinn; níl réamhrá mar seo le haon chóip eile den dtéacs.

Cuirtear tús mar sin leis an gcomhrá idir Chaoilte agus Pádraig sna réamhráite. Tá níos mó éagsúlachta sna réamhráite ná mar atá sna coda eile den Agallamh Nua; is cosúil gur tuigeadh nár dhlúthchuid den dtéacs féin a bhí ann agus go bhféadfadh daoine blúirí a chur leis nó é a athrú chun a dtuairimí féin mar gheall ar stairiúlacht an Agallaimh a chur in iúl, nó chun

---

77 D. Breathnach agus M. Ní Mhurchú, *1782–1881 Beathaisnéis* (1999), lgh 85–6. Féach anois www.ainm.ie. 78 ARÉ LS 23 E 11, lch 409, ll. 2–3. 79 Ibid., ll. 4–10. 80 Féach Ó Fiannachta, 'The development', lgh 183–9.

comhthéacs a sholáthar don Agallamh Nua i measc na scéalta agus na laoithe fiannaíochta eile a bhí ar eolas acu.

VIII

Tá an fráma san Agallamh Nua níos simplí ná an fráma mar atá sa Bhun-Agallamh – cuireann Pádraig ceisteanna ar Chaoilte agus freagraíonn Caoilte iad; ní mór eile a thiteann amach sa bhfráma féin. Féachadh thuas ar chuid de na difríochtaí teanga agus miondifríochtaí eile idir sleachta as an mBun-Agallamh agus as an Agallamh Nua. Tabharfar cuntas anseo ar leagan amach na n-eipeasóidí féin – tá giotaí áirithe in easnamh ós na heipeasóidí san Agallamh Nua agus tá cuid acu i gcomhthéacs atá difriúil lena gcomhthéacs sa Bhun-Agallamh. Ón uair go bhfuil difríochtaí níos mó idir na leaganacha de na laoithe 'Caithréim Fhinn' agus 'Comhairle Fhinn do Mhac Lughach', tabharfar cuntas orthu seo ar leithligh níos faide síos.

COMPARÁID: AN tAGALLAMH NUA MAR ATÁ I LNÉ LS G114
AGUS AN BUN-AGALLAMH

Scéal Artúir mhic Bheinne Briot.
- Sa Bhun-Agallamh, tugtar eolas breise ar na laochra de chuid na Féinne a théann sa tóir ar Artúir; tá an t-eolas seo ar lár san Agallamh Nua;
- Tá rann ag Stokes ina ndeineann Artúir síocháin le Fionn; san Agallamh Nua mínítear i bprós gur dhein Artúir síocháin leis an bhFéinn;
- Ag deireadh an scéil seo, sa Bhun-Agallamh, iarrann Pádraig ar Chaoilte úinéirí na gcapall a fuair an Fhiann san eachtra seo a ainmniú. Níl an chuid seo san Agallamh Nua.[81]

Breith Mhic Lughach agus Comhairle Fhinn do Mhac Lughach
Tá an prós san Agallamh Nua gairid go maith do leagan an Bhun-Agallaimh. Tá an laoi 'Comhairle Fhinn do Mhac Lughach' difriúil go maith – féach thíos.

Scéal Airnéalaigh
Tá an dá leagan cosúil lena chéile ach go bhfuil an rann sa Bhun-Agallamh in easnamh san Agallamh Nua.[82]

---

81 Stokes, 'Acallamh', ll. 205–27; 253–4; 261–85. 82 Ibid., ll. 1077–8.

Scéal Shálbhuí mhic Fheileachair

Tá an dá leagan cosúil lena chéile ach go bhuil an rann sa Bhun-Agallamh in easnamh san Agallamh Nua.[83] Luaitear san Agallamh Nua gur 'ga reatha' ('a flying spear?') a mharaigh Sálbhuí, rud nach luaitear sa Bhun-Agallamh. Tá an scéal lom go maith sa dá Agallamh acu.

Tonn Chlíodhna agus Tonn Téide

Tá an dá leagan den scéal seo gairid go maith dá chéile agus is é an dála céanna é ag an dá leagan den laoi 'Clidna cheinfind búan in bét'/'Clíodhna cheannfhionn buan a béad' a thagann ag deireadh an scéil. Ach, stadann an laoi san Agallamh Nua go hobann ag deireadh an tseachtú rainn – 10 rann atá i leagan an Bhun-Agallaimh – agus san Agallamh Nua, ní mhínítear cad a tharlaíonn ina dhiaidh san do Chiabhán atá ar deoraíocht ón bhFéinn agus a bhfuil a ghrá geal Clíodhna tar éis bás a fháil. Go deimhin, is tagairt dhiúltach an tagairt dheireanach do Chiabhán san Agallamh Nua – luaitear sa laoi gur trí cheilg a thug sé Clíodhna leis agus thuigfeá gur mar phionós a fágadh é ina aonar go dearóil, b'fhéidir. Is anseo a stadann an tAgallamh Nua ar fad, gan aon mhíniú ná clabhsúr eile sna cóipeanna sin nach bhfuil iontu ach na sé eipeasóidí tosaigh. Tá Ciabhán ar aon dul le Caoilte sa bhfráma – tá an bheirt acu ar scarúint ón bhFéinn agus lán de chumha; mar sin, b'fhéidir gur shamhlaigh daoine gur dheireadh oiriúnach é seo don dtéacs ar fad. Sna leaganacha den Agallamh Nua inar cuireadh breis eipeasóidí i ndiaidh na heipeasóide seo, ní thugtar míniú ach an oiread – filltear ar chomhrá an fhráma, ní thráchtann Pádraig ná Caoilte ar an méid atá ráite agus téitear ar aghaidh go dtí an chéad scéal eile. Sa Bhun-Agallamh, i ndiaidh na laoi, filleann Ciabhán ar Éirinn agus buaileann leis an bhFéinn. Faigheann a athair, Eochaidh Imdhearg, Rí Uladh, bás an oíche chéanna agus deineann Fionn rí de Chiabhán ina áit. Críochnaíonn leagan an Agallaimh Nua mar sin ar nóta níos éiginnte ná leagan an Bhun-Agallaimh den scéal.[84]

Caoilte i gCúirt Rí Uladh sa Bhun-Agallamh agus i gCOC LS 107

Sa Bhun-Agallamh agus san Agallamh Déanach, is in aimsir Phádraig a bhuaileann Caoilte le Rí Uladh agus tugann Caoilte cuntas do Rí Uladh ar sheanchas Rath Áine agus ar an seanchas a bhain le fearta Airt agus Eoghain, mic Fhionntain rí Chonnacht.[85] Téann siad ag fiach ar na Beanna Boirche ansan. Tugtar cuntas ar eachtraí a thiteann amach in aimsir Phádraig, agus cuntas ó Chaoilte ar scéalta a thit amach san am atá thart, nuair a mhair Fionn is na Fianna. San Agallamh Nua, deintear simpliú ar an bhfráma agus

---

83 Ibid., ll. 1086–7.   84 Tá deireadh na leaganacha go léir eile d'Agallamh na Seanórach caillte nó, i gcás na hAgallmha Bige, chomh grod sin go bhfuil an chuma ar an scéal go bhfuil an téacs neamhiomlán. Féach Parsons, 'The structure of *Acallam na senórach*', lch 12 agus Kühns, 'Some observations', lch 123.   85 Ibid., ll. 3047–195; Ní Shéaghdha, *Agallamh*, ii, lch 125 et seq.

insítear na scéalta fé mar gur san am atá thart, roimh theacht Phádraig, a thiteadar go léir amach. I gcuid de na cóipeanna, bíonn giota beag comhrá roimh na heipeasóidí seo ina n-iarrann Pádraig ar Chaoilte na scéalta a insint dó ach i gCOC LS 107, tosnaíonn an chuid seo den Agallamh go giorraisc díreach tar éis na laoi 'Tonn Chlíodhna', mar leanas: 'As ann sin *iomorro* do bhí rígh Ul*adh* 7 Caoilte ag móirfhéachuin an mh*ara* ...'. Tá an líne seo in eagrán Stokes.[86]

Seilg ar na Beanna Boirche agus Líbhán
Tá an chuid seo an-chosúil le leagan Stokes, seachas na difríochtaí beaga a leanas. Tá an laoi 'Canas a tic in tond tuile' in easnamh san Agallamh Nua. Ní thugtar ainm ar shleá Chaoilte; 'An Choscrach' a thugtar air sa Bhun-Agallamh. Go 'Ráith Náis' seachas go Rath na Sciath/Rath Imill a théann Caoilte agus Líbhán i ndiaidh na seilge.[87]

Cumann Caoilte leathrann
Tá sé seo an-ghar do leagan Stokes.

Dubh mac Tréin, a mhac Fial, agus pósadh Áine
Tá sé seo an-ghar do leagan Stokes.

Teacht Choscraigh mhic Ainchinn
Cas Corach mac Caincinde a thagann fé dhéin Chaoilte chun seanchas a fhoghlaim sa Bhun-Agallamh;[88] Coscrach mac Ainchinn a thugtar air san Agallamh Nua.[89] Tá an laoi 'Foradh na bhFiann fás anocht' a thagann ag deireadh an scéil seo gairid do leagan an Bhun-Agallaimh.

Scéal Thulach an Trír
Sa Bhun-Agallamh, iarrann Pádraig ar Chaoilte an bunús atá leis na logainmneacha Tulach an Trír, Abhainn Déise agus Leacht Chinn Chon a mhíniú dó. Tá an scéal seo san Agallamh Nua mar atá ag Stokes ach gur fágadh amach an scéal ar Leacht Chinn Chon agus an laoi sa Bhun-Agallamh ina luaitear na trí logainmneacha atá Caoilte tar éis a mhíniú.[90] Críochnaíonn an tAgallamh Nua go gonta, mar leanas: 'Gon*n* iad sin na sgéala ró fhiaf*r*aighis díom a rígh Ul*adh*'.[91]

86 Stokes, 'Acallamh', ll. 3210–12. 87 Ibid., ll. 3224–33; 3237; 3245. Tá *Argain Ratha Náis* ar cheann de na scéalta a liostáileadh in *Do nemthigud filed* i Leabhar Laighean: E. O'Curry, *Lectures on the manuscript materials of ancient Irish history* (1861), lch 591. N'fheadar an bhfuil aon bhaint aige sin le Ráith Náis san Agallamh Nua. 88 Stokes, 'Acallamh', l. 3345. 89 Ní foláir nó comhtháthaíodh *cas* agus *corach* le chéile agus bhí an focal nua múnlaithe ar an aidiacht *coscrach*; bhí túschonsan 'Caincinde' comhbháite le 'c' deiridh 'mac', sa tslí gur ceapadh gur 'mac Ainchinn' a bhí i gceist. 90 Ibid., ll. 3413–26; 3428–35. 91 COC LS 107, lch 116, ll.

Caithréim Fhinn

Na cóipeanna den Agallamh Nua nach bhfuil aon réamhrá leo, tosnaíonn siad leis an laoi seo. Tá 49 rann sa laoi seo sa Bhun-Agallamh,[92] rud a fhágann go bhfuil an leagan san níos faide ná leagan an Agallaimh Nua; 53 rann atá ann san Agallamh Déanach.[93] Sa Bhun-Agallamh, tá Caoilte, Oisín agus Pádraig i gcomhthionól le Rí Éireann. Fiafraíonn Rí Éireann dóibh cé mhéid rí a thug talamh don bhFéinn agus tugann siad freagra ar an gceist seo sa laoi. Tá an freagra seo bunaithe, dar le Dooley agus Roe, ar thraidisiún bréagstairiúil ós na meánaoiseanna – feidhmíonn sé san *Acallam* mar 'a kind of founding charter for the *Fían* institution'.[94] Moltar Fionn mac Cumhaill sa dara leath den laoi. San Agallamh Nua, tá an chuid tosaigh den laoi ina dtugtar cur síos ar stair na Féinne in easnamh agus dírítear go hiomlán ar Fhionn mac Cumhaill féin.

Tosnaíonn formhór na gcóipeanna leis an rann 'Dursan leamsa an t-eó óir' agus tá 36 rann iontu; cuid de na cóipeanna, tosnaíonn siad leis an séú rann, 'Seacht rí déag, lán mheabhair liom' agus 31 rann atá iontu seo.[95]

G114	Stokes
1	23, ll. 1, 2 agus 44, ll. 1, 2.[96]
2	níl an chéad leathrann ann; 23, ll. 3, 4.
3	24
4	26
5	níl ann
6	27
7	25
8	37
9	níl ann
10	41
11	38
12	39
13	28
14	29
15	32
16	33
17	30

25–6. **92** Stokes, 'Acallamh', ll. 2486–586. **93** Ní Shéaghdha, *Agallamh*, ii, lgh 75–84. **94** Dooley and Roe, *Tales*, lch 237 (76). **95** Tá an laoi seo in eagar ag Ó Siochfhradha, *Laoithe na féinne*, lgh 268–70. 'Mion-laoithe' a thugann Ó Siochfhradha ar na laoithe sa chuid seo den leabhar, .i. laoithe nach raibh 'ag fás chun aondachta' laistigh d'Agallamh Oisín agus Phádraig ach a fhaightear i dteannta laoithe Agallamh Oisín agus Phádraig de ghnáth sna lámhscríbhinní agus atá 'ar comh-aithne' leo, dar leis (ibid., lch viii). **96** Cuir i gcomparáid: '*Ár mionn mór ár muinntior mhaith / Ár neo ár nurradh ár nárdfhlaith*' (LNÉ LS G114, lch 31, rann 1, ll. 3–4) agus *Ni mairit in muinter maith / ní mairenn Find in fír[f]laith* (Stokes, 'Acallamh', l. 2573).

18   31
19–30   níl na ranna seo ag Stokes
31   34
32   35
33   níl ann
34   rann as Scéal Artúir mhic Bheinne Briot[97]
35–6   níl ann.

Tá ranna i leagan Stokes nach bhfuil san Agallamh Nua, tá ranna san Agallamh Nua nach bhfuil ag Stokes, tá ranna áirithe tar éis titim isteach ina chéile san Agallamh Nua .i. dhá leathrann ó ranna difriúla curtha le chéile.

Cuireadh an rann a fhaightear i Scéal Artúir mhic Bheinne Briot sa Bhun-Agallamh (luaite thuas) agus ina dtugtar cur síos ar fhlaithiúlacht Oisín le 'Caithréim Fhinn' san Agallamh Nua.[98] Baineadh amach ainm Oisín san Agallamh Nua agus tá sé le tuiscint gur don bhFéinn i gcoitinne atáthar ag tagairt ann. Tá deireadh na leaganacha difriúil lena chéile ach cuirtear an smaoineamh céanna in iúl iontu, .i. nach féidir cuntas iomlán a thabhairt ar na maitheasaí go léir a bhí i bhFionn:

Stokes: I N-abraim do thestaib Find
             dar in Rí[g] fuil os mo chind,
             ba ferr som fos co ba tri
             cid mor in ní raidim-sí.[99]

G114:   Dá mbeidís seacht tteangtha am cheann
             Go bráth noch a ttiocfadh leam
             Ar fhlaithios fhir na learg lán
             Maithios an Rígh do ró rádh

             As misi Coillte croidhe
             Déis na laoch gan lúthmhaire
             Coimirce Rígh an talmhan tinn
             Do anmain an Rígh ráidhim.[100]

Tagann dhá rann eile i ndiaidh rann Stokes thuas ina ndeintear tagairt do bhás Fhinn agus do shealbhachas talún, mar atá i gceist ag tosach an leagain seo den laoi. Críochnaíonn leagan an Agallaimh Nua ar an rann thuas ina dtarraingíonn Caoilte aird ar an gcás ina bhfuil sé féin agus ina n-iarrann sé neamh d'Fhionn; faightear ranna mar seo ag deireadh mórán de na laoithe fiannaíochta nach mbaineann leis an Agallamh Nua cé gur gnáithí gurb é Oisín a chanann iad san.

---

97 Ibid., ll. 221–2.   98 Féach leis Ní Shéaghdha, *Agallamh*, i, lch 19.   99 Stokes, 'Acallamh', ll. 2580–1.   100 LNÉ LS G114, lch 33, ll. 33–4.

I leagan an Bhun-Agallaimh, tá sraith de phéírí ranna sa laoi ina n-ainmnítear na cúig draoithe is fearr a bhí riamh ann (ranna 28–9), na cúig lia is fearr a bhí riamh ann (30–31), na cúig filí is fearr a bhí riamh ann (32–3), an cúigear is gaoisiúla a bhí riamh in aon tigh in Éirinn (34–5), na cúig laochra is tréine dá raibh riamh ann (36–7), an cúigear is féile dá raibh riamh ann (38–9), agus na cúig flatha is fearr a bhí riamh ann (40–1). Tá Fionn mac Cumhaill ar dhuine de gach cúigear acu nó i bhfocail eile, bhí sé ina mháistir ar gach ceard agus na buanna is tábhachtaí, bhíodar aige. Baineadh úsáid as an múnla céanna i leagan an Agallaimh Nua chun ranna breise a chumadh (ranna 19–30). Ainmnítear na cúig gaibhne is fearr sa tír (19–20), na cúig ceardaithe is fearr (21–22), na cúig tiompánaithe is fearr (23–4), na cúig crutairí is fearr (26), an cúigear is fearr chun suirí (27–8), an cúigear is eolaí ar chúrsaí mara (29–30), agus arís tá Fionn mac Cumhaill ar dhuine de gach cúigear acu seo.[101] Formhór na n-ainmneacha a liostáiltear sna ranna seo, is mion- agus mór-charachtair iad i dtéacsanna eile leis agus, ina theannta san, chleacht a bhformhór na ceardanna a luaitear leo sa laoi, rud a léiríonn go raibh eolas leathan ar litríocht na Gaeilge ag an té a chum iad. Tabharfar cúpla sampla thíos.

Na crutairí ná Lughaidh Lámhfhada, Craiftine, Seanach Ó Doighre, Cnú Dhearóil agus Fionn. Crutaire a bhí ag Fionn é Cnú Dhearóil. Tá tagairtí dó sa Bhun-Agallamh, san Agallamh Déanach agus sna laoithe fiannaíochta.[102] Is é Lughaidh Lámhfhada, rí Thuatha Dé Danann, athair Chnú Dhearóil agus ba chrutaire é leis;[103] luaitear i gcath déanach Maige Tuiread go raibh an chrutaireacht ar cheann den iliomad ceard a bhí aige.[104] Tá tagairtí do Chraiftine crutaire in áiteanna éagsúla.[105] Tá tagairt sa Bhun-Agallamh do cheoltóirí na Féinne a chuaigh chun ceol sí a fhoghlaim ó Chnú Dhearóil; ina measc san tá 'mac Senaig … Senach … dá Dhaighre … Cuán'.[106] In *Eachtra an cheithearnaigh chaolriabhaigh*, luaitear lucht seinnte ceoil sí agus orthu san a luaitear, tá 'Sennach Ó Doirge'.[107] Tharlódh sé gur thit an dá ainm a bhí sa Bhun-Agallamh isteach lena chéile le himeacht aimsire.

Na suirígh ná Cearmad Milbheoil, Naoise mac Uisneach, Fiamhain mac Foraidh, Diarmuid Ó Duibhne agus Fionn. Mharaigh Lug Cearmad toisc gur

101 Tá na ranna seo go léir in eagrán an tSeabhaic: Ó Siochfhradha, *Laoithe na féinne*, lgh 268–70. Tá an léiriú a thugtar ar Fhionn anseo inchurtha leis an gcur síos a fhaighimid ar Lugh i g*Cath Maige Tuired* ina dtugtar an buafhocal *samildánach* 'multi-skilled' dó: féach E. Gray (eag. agus aistr.), *Cath Maige Tuired* (1983), lgh 38–42, §§55–74. 102 Féach Stokes, 'Acallamh', ll. 630–83; Ní Shéaghdha, *Agallamh*, i, lch 53; MacNeill agus Murphy, *Duanaire Finn*, iii, lch 352. 103 Ibid., 378. 104 Mar shampla, féach W. Stokes (eag. agus aistr.), 'The second battle of Moytura', *Revue Celtique*, 13 (1891), 52–130 ag 76. 105 Comyn and Dinneen, *Foras feasa ar Éirinn*, iv, lch 237. 106 Stokes, 'Acallamh', ll. 652–3. 107 O'Grady, *Silva gadelica*, i, lgh 276–89 ('Echtra in chetharnaig chaoilriabaig nó chetharnaig úi Dhomnaill do réir dhruinge'), ag lch 277. 'Seannach Ó Doire' an litriú atá ag É. Ua Muirgheasa (eag.), *Ceithearnach Uí Dhomhnaill nó eachtra an cheithearnaigh chaoil-riabhaigh* (1912), lch 2.

luigh Cearmad lena bhean agus is dócha gur mar gheall air seo a áirítear mar shuiríoch é.[108] Ní gá na tagairtí do Naoise mac Uisneach agus do Dhiarmuid Ó Duibhne a mhíniú. Is deacra a thuiscint cén fáth gur ainmníodh Fiamhain mac Foraidh anso. Maítear gur col ceathracha, clann dhá dheirféar, iad Oisín agus Fiamhain mac Foraidh i laoi XLVI i n*Duanaire Finn*.[109] Tá Fiamhain ar dhuine de na laochra a áirítear ar liosta oidheadha na Tána.[110] Tugtar teidil éagsúla ar an scéal sna liostaí (más ag tagairt don insint chéanna atá), mar atá *Aided Fhiamain, Forbais Dūin Binne, Orgain Dūine Binne, Echtra Fiamain* agus *Aithed Mugaine re Fiamain*, agus deineann Thurneysen amach gur dócha gurb é a tharla sa scéal ná gur fhuadaigh Fiamhain bean Chonchubhair, gur mharaigh Cú Chulainn Fiamhain ina dhún san, Dún Binne, agus gur fuasclaíodh an bhean.[111] An í seo an chúis gur chuir an té a chum an rann Fiamhain i measc na suiríoch? Tá tagairt do Fhiamhain mac Foraidh agus do Naoise mac Uisneach sa scéal *Tochmarc Emire* – luaitear go bhfuil an bheirt acu agus fir óga eile ina dteannta ag foghlaim cleasa cogaidh le Scáthach sa Bhreatain nuair a thagann Cú Chulainn chucu.[112] Tá amhras ar Meyer an é seo an Fiamhain céanna,[113] ach tharlódh sé gur mar gheall ar an dá ainm a bheith in aice a chéile sa scéal san a cuireadh in aice a chéile iad sa rann seo leis.

An 'cúigear eolach mara mín' ná Manannán, Curcóg iníon Mhanannáin, Ciabhán Casmhongach, an Breacán Buileach agus Fionn. Manannán mac Lir an dia mara an chéad duine acu seo, gan amhras. Is iníon le Manannán í Curcóg sa scéal *Altram tige dá medar*.[114] Tá eachtra mara Chiabháin Chasmhongaigh sa Bhun-Agallamh agus san Agallamh Nua araon, mar a luadh thuas. Is dócha gurb é Breacán Buileach an Breacán a bádh sa ghuairneán idir Éirinn agus Albain ar ar tugadh Coire Bhreacáin ina dhiaidh san.[115]

Deineadh forbairt ar an laoi 'Caithréim Fhinn' san Agallamh Déanach leis ach ní mór na cosúlachtaí atá idir an leagan seo agus leagan an Agallaimh Nua.

Comhairle Fhinn do Mhac Lughach

Tá leagan an Agallaimh Nua, 'A Mhic Lughach comhairle gabh', gairid go maith do leagan an Bhun-Agallaimh, 'A Meic Lugach, toluib snas', ach tá ord

---

108 O. Bergin (eag. agus aistr.), 'How the Dagda got his magic staff' in R.S. Loomis (eag.), *Medieval studies in memory of Gertrude Schoepperle Loomis* (1927), lgh 399–409 ag lch 404. 109 MacNeill agus Murphy, *Duanaire Finn*, ii, lch 122. 110 K. Meyer (eag. agus aistr.), *The death tales of the Ulster heroes* (1906), lch vii. 111 R. Thurneysen, *Die irische Helden- und Königsage bis zum siebzehnten Jahrhundert* (1921), lch 447; féach P. Mac Cana, *The learned tales of medieval Ireland* (1980), lch 93. 112 K. Meyer (eag.), 'Mitteilungen aus irischen Handschriften: *Tochmarc Emire la Coinculaind*', *Zeitschrift für celtische Philologie*, 3 (1901), 226– 63 (229–63) ag 250. 113 Meyer, *The death tales*, lch vii. 114 L. Duncan (eag. agus aistr.), 'Altram tige dá medar', *Ériu*, 11 (1932), 184–225 ag 193. 115 Luaitear é i *Sanas Cormaic*: W. Stokes (eag.), *Three Irish glossaries* (1862), lgh 13–14; K. Meyer, (eag.), 'Sanas Cormaic' in O. Bergin et al. (eag.), *Anecdota from Irish manuscripts*, iv (1912), lgh 27–8 §323. Cf. Gwynn, *The metrical dindshenchas*, iv, lgh 80–7.

na ranna beagán difriúil agus tá rann amháin nua ann. Tá eagrán an tSeabhaic cosúil le leagan an Agallaimh Nua.[116]

Tá 13 rann i leagan Stokes den laoi seo a tógadh as Leabhar Leasa Móir.[117]

G114	Stokes
1	1
2	2
3	4
4	3
5	6
6	7
7	9
8	12
9	10
10	níl ag Stokes
11	11
12	13

Tá cuid mhaith difríochtaí idir na línte sa laoi seo ag Stokes agus san Agallamh Nua ó thaobh na teanga agus an fhoclóra de.

Is deacair cur chuige an duine nó na ndaoine a chuir le chéile na cóipeanna difriúla den Agallamh Nua a mheas toisc nach fios cé na bunfhoinsí a bhí á n-úsáid acu. Fós, tá an prós agus mórán de na laoithe an-ghairid don mBun-Agallamh ó thaobh foclóra agus comhréire de ach gur athraíodh an teanga chun blas comhaimseartha a chur ar an iomlán. Fágadh amach blúirí as an mBun-Agallamh ach eolas breise nach mbaineann leis an scéal atá á insint nó ranna a dheineann achoimre ar an méid a thagann rompu atá iontu seo; mar sin, ní chuireann a n-easnamh isteach ar leanúnachas na scéalta san Agallamh Nua. Ní mór a cuireadh leis na heipeasóidí. Ar an dtaobh eile den scéal, tá an dá laoi is faide san Agallamh Nua difriúil go maith le leaganacha an Bhun-Agallaimh. Léirítear cur chuige difriúil ar fad sna hathruithe a tháinig ar 'Chaithréim Fhinn': ceapadh ranna nua le cur leis an laoi seo i slí chruthaitheach atá inchurtha leis na forbairtí a deineadh ar laoithe fiannaíochta nach mbaineann leis an Agallamh le himeacht na mblianta.[118] Níl na hathruithe a tháinig ar an laoi 'Comhairle Fhinn do Mhac Lughach' chomh suntasach san ach tá ord na ranna difriúil agus tá athrú nach beag tagtha ar

---

116 Áiríonn an Seabhac é seo leis mar 'mhion-laoi': féach nóta 95 thuas: Ó Siochfhradha, *Laoithe na féinne*, lgh 184–5. Féach leis Stokes, 'Acallamh', ll. 580–605, agus Ní Shéaghdha, *Agallamh*, i, lgh 47–9. 117 Tógadh rann amháin (§11) as LS Phroinsiasach A 4: Stokes, 'Acallamh', ll. 600–1. Níl §§5 agus 8 in ARÉ LS G114. 118 Mar shampla, na ranna breise a cuireadh le 'Laoi an bhrait': féach S. Ní Mhurchú, *'Agallamh Oisín agus Phádraig*: composition and transmission' in S.J. Arbuthnot and G. Parsons (eag.), *The Gaelic Finn tradition* (2012), lgh 195–208 ag lch 202.

mhórán de na línte. Tharlódh sé, mar sin, gur as foinsí difriúla leis an gcuid
eile a tógadh na laoithe seo, go raibh athruithe tagtha orthu go neamhspleách
ar an Agallamh Nua, agus gur bhain údar nó údair an Agallaimh Nua úsáid
astu seo in ionad iarracht a dhéanamh ar leaganacha a bheadh níos dílse don
mBun-Agallamh a chur ar fáil. Faightear an dá laoi seo go neamhspleách ar
an Agallamh Nua sna lámhscríbhinní cé gur cosúil gur tháinig na cóipeanna
neamhspleácha seo ón Agallamh Nua féin nó ó Leabhar Leasa Móir, i ndiaidh
a theacht chun solais dó arís sa bhliain 1814.

IX

Ní fios cén méid den mBun-Agallamh ar a raibh teacht ag an nduine nó ag
na daoine a chuir le chéile na cóipeanna difriúla den Agallamh Nua agus fiú,
an d'aon ghnó a cuireadh deireadh níos gonta le cuid de na scéalta san
Agallamh Nua nó an é nach raibh teacht ar na scéalta ina n-iomláine nuair a
bhí sé á chur le chéile. Na sé eipeasóidí tosaigh, ní thagann siad go léir i ndiaidh a chéile sa Bhun-Agallamh, seachas Scéal Airnéalaigh agus Scéal
Shálbhuí; mar sin, shamhlófá gur deineadh rogha ag pointe éigin na scéalta
sin a chóipeáil agus scéalta eile a fhágaint ar lár.

Tá pátrúin téamacha le feiscint sna sé heachtraí tosaigh. Baineann a
bhformhór le hóglaochra uaisle atá ag fáil oiliúna ó Fhionn agus ós na Fianna,
mar atá Artúir mac Beinne Briot mac Rí Breatan (2); Mac Lughach, garmhac
Fhinn mhic Cumhaill (3); Airnéalach mac Rí Laighean (4); Sálbhuí mac
Feileachair mac Rí Mumhan (5); agus Ciabhán mac Eachaigh Mhuindeirg mac
Rí Uladh (6). Tarraingíonn a bhformhór trioblóid orthu féin:[119] fuadaíonn Artúir
Bran, Sceolaing agus Adhnuall, na gadhair is ansa le Fionn; cuireann Mac
Lughach isteach ar an bhFéinn mar nach n-iompraíonn sé é féin mar is ceart;
teipeann ar Airnéalach íocaíocht a thabhairt in am d'fhile a chum dán dó; tugann
mná na Féinne go léir grá do Chiabhán thar aon fhear eile, rud a chuireann olc
ar an gcuid eile den bhFéinn. Ina theannta san, feidhmíonn an chéad laoi san
Agallamh Nua, 'Caithréim Fhinn', mar shampla a léiríonn meon agus iompar
Fhinn mhic Cumhaill, ceannaire agus laoch *par excellence*. An é mar sin go raibh
feidhm theagascach leis an rogha eipeasóidí san Agallamh Nua mar go leagtar
béim ann ar thréithe agus ar iompar atá de dhíth ar cheannaire?

Tagann na heipeasóidí go léir a bhaineann le 'Caoilte i gCúirt Rí Uladh' i
ndiaidh a chéile leis sa Bhun-Agallamh; ach arís, baineann siad le daoine óga
atá ar imeall an tsochaí agus atá fós gan áit bhuan a bhaint amach ann:[120]

---

119 Seo téama coitianta in *Acallam na senórach* trí chéile: féach J.F. Nagy, 'Compositional concerns in the *Acallam na senórach*' in D. Ó Corráin et al. (eag.), *Sages, saints and storytellers*
(1989), lgh 149–58 ag lch 153. 120 Pléitear an ghné seo den bhFiannaíocht in J.F. Nagy, *The
wisdom of the outlaw* (Berkeley, 1985), lgh 60–79.

Líbhán, bean óg atá ag snámh na farraige ó d'imigh Fionn mac Cumhaill; Áine iníon Fhéil, an duine deireanach dá shliocht nach bhfuil scéal a sinsir aici go dtí go n-insíonn Caoilte di é; Coscrach mac Ainchinn, scológ ós na Tuatha Dé Danann atá ag iarraidh seanchas a fhoghlaim ó Chaoilte; triúr mac Aonchearda Béarra a mharaítear agus iad i mbun catha agus triúr iníon Rí Alban a fhaigheann bás de chumha mar gur thugadar grá don dtriúr fear san ('Scéal Thulach an Trír'). Leagtar an-bhéim sna scéalta seo go léir ar an oidhreacht, ar an leanúnachas ó ghlúin go glúin agus ar chaomhnú an chórais bhéascna. Téamaí iad sin a dtéitear i ngleic leo i ngach leagan d'Agallamh na Seanórach gan amhras, ach is ceisteanna leis iad, ní foláir, a bhí ag dó na geirbe go mór ar dhaoine thart ar an am gur grafadh na cóipeanna is luaithe den Agallamh Nua, i ndiaidh 'tonnbhriseadh an tseanghnáthaimh' agus arís, b'fhéidir, i ndiaidh theacht na bpéindlithe sa seachtú céad déag. Pé cúis a bhí le rogha na n-eipeasóidí, is léir ón méid cóipeanna a deineadh den Agallamh Nua go raibh tóir air mar théacs. Grafadh sna lámhscríbhinní é in aice le scéalta rómán-saíochta agus laoithe fiannaíochta, agus ní foláir nó gur thug sé pléisiúr, misneach agus lón samhlaíochta do lucht a léite agus a chloiste.

The setting of *Géisid cúan*

SEÁN Ó COILEÁIN

The poem *Géisid cúan* ('The haven roars'), which occurs in *Acallam na senórach*, is well known and has been edited, translated and discussed on several occasions. It is included in the various editions of the *Acallam* itself, those of Standish H. O'Grady,[1] Whitley Stokes[2] and Nessa Ní Shéaghdha;[3] it forms part of the text of *Cath Fionntrágha* edited by Kuno Meyer[4] and Cecile O'Rahilly;[5] it has been anthologised and annotated by Eleanor Knott,[6] Gerard Murphy[7] and Myles Dillon;[8] in addition to the translations of the poem supplied by O'Grady, Meyer and Murphy, we have others by such as Seán O'Faoláin,[9] Rachel Bromwich,[10] Ruth Lehmann[11] and Thomas Kinsella;[12] it has been the subject of some comment by Proinsias Mac Cana[13] and Joseph Nagy,[14] and has had the critical attention of James Carney.[15] More recently it has been translated by Ann Dooley and Harry Roe, along with the rest of the *Acallam*,[16] and has been newly rendered by Ann Dooley for the *Field Day anthology* with a feminist interpretation.[17] Very few poems in the Irish language have been favoured with such scholarly endeavour or have been so widely appreciated.

But our greatest debt for our knowledge and awareness of the poem is to the unknown compiler-editor-author of the *Acallam* itself, since even the ver-

Reprinted from John Carey, Máire Herbert and Kevin Murray (eds), *Cín Chille Cúile: texts, saints and places. Essays in honour of Pádraig Ó Riain* (Aberystwyth, 2004), pp 234–48, with kind permission of Prof. John Koch. The presentation and referencing system have been brought into line with the norms of the volume; however, no changes have been made to the content of the essay.

1 S.H. O'Grady (ed. and trans.), *Silva gadelica*, 2 vols (1892), i, pp 94–233 at p. 113; ii, pp 101–265 at p. 122.　2 W. Stokes (ed. and partial trans.), 'Acallamh na senórach' in W. Stokes and E. Windisch (eds), *Irische Texte*, iv, 1 (1900), ll. 843–64.　3 N. Ní Shéaghdha (ed.), *Agallamh na seanórach*, 3 vols (1942–5), i, pp 70–1.　4 K. Meyer (ed. and trans.), *The cath Finntrága* (1885), ll. 995–1034.　5 C. O'Rahilly (ed.), *Cath Finntrágha* (1962), ll. 1426–66.　6 E. Knott, *An introduction to Irish syllabic poetry of the period 1200–1600* (1928), pp 27–8.　7 G. Murphy, *Early Irish lyrics* (1956), pp 148–51, no. 49.　8 M. Dillon (ed.), *Stories from the Acallam* (1970), ll. 464–507.　9 S. O'Faoláin, *The silver branch* (1938), pp 82–3.　10 R. Bromwich, 'The continuity of the Gaelic tradition in eighteenth-century Ireland', *Yorkshire Celtic Studies*, 4 (1947–8), 2–28, at 17–18.　11 R.P.M. Lehmann, *Early Irish verse* (1982), pp 88–90.　12 T. Kinsella, *The new Oxford book of Irish verse* (1986), pp 79–80.　13 P. Mac Cana, 'Aspects of the theme of king and goddess in Irish literature', *Études Celtiques*, 7 (1955–56), part ii, 356–413 at 390–3, 399–400.　14 J.F. Nagy, *The wisdom of the outlaw* (1985), pp 72–3.　15 J. Carney, 'Two poems from Acallam na senórach' in J. Carney and D. Greene (eds), *Celtic studies* (1968), pp 22–32 at pp 23–6.　16 A. Dooley and H. Roe, *Tales of the elders of Ireland* (1999), pp 27–8, with commentary at pp xxv–xxvi and pp 231–2.　17 A. Bourke et al. (eds), *The Field Day anthology of Irish writing*, vol. 4 (2002), pp 228–31.

sion of the poem contained in *Cath Fionntrágha* would seem to derive from
that source. More than that, it is to him we owe the setting and interpretation which, prior to Carney, had been unquestioningly accepted by every subsequent editor and commentator: that the poem was a lament spoken by
Créd/Créide for her husband Cáel, whom she had recently wedded, on his
being drowned on the last day of the battle of Ventry. The general principle
according to which Carney, always suspicious of the ways of editors of every
sort, early and late, would challenge this representation is an excellent one: in
cases such as this, where a poem occurs in a prose context, 'we cannot always
assume that prose and verse were a unity from the beginning, although this,
of course, may often be so'.[18] The poem itself is the thing which must continue to determine its own interpretation, although clearly in the manner of
providing a frame of reference a twelfth-century editor must also continue to
have a considerable advantage over a twentieth-century critic, and it is far
from certain that the evidence adduced by Carney is sufficient to disestablish
the earlier link, let alone establish another in its place. He would regard the
poem as 'a conventional bardic elegy'[19] according to the *topos* of the poet as
lover or spouse of his patron, discovered and traced in the literature, for the
most part very convincingly, by Carney himself. Here he would propose that:

> There is no original relationship between the prose and the verse.
> Sometime about AD 1100 in South Kerry, a man of some importance
> called Cael son of Crimthann was drowned. A poet who had been
> closely associated with him wrote a lament in which he referred to him
> as *in laech ro laiged lim …*, 'the warrior who used to lie with me'; he also
> says *is ed rom-mer mét a aéb.* The language and the feeling of the poem
> were such that a saga-writer could quite easily take it and work it into a
> story framework where it appeared to be an emotional statement by a
> woman on her dead husband or lover. But the interweaving of the old
> poetry and the newly created prose was not done very skilfully.[20]

Leaving aside the matter of the 'saga-writer's' skill for the moment, we shall
concentrate on the daring proposition that 'sometime about AD 1100 in south
Kerry, a man of some importance called Cael son of Crimthann was
drowned'. This consists of three elements: (i) the date, which is approximately
that suggested by the language of the poem; (ii) the 'man of some importance', Cáel son of Crimthann, unknown to the annals, genealogies and historical literature generally – not a fatal flaw in itself but a salutary reminder
that, in as far as the evidence goes, he has no existence outside of
fianaigheacht, although Carney might counter that this results from editorial

18 Carney, 'Two poems', p. 22.   19 Ibid., p. 25.   20 Ibid., p. 24.

misplacement in the first instance; (iii) 'South Kerry', as he would have it, from the site of Ventry Harbour. It is remarkable that, having questioned everything else, Carney should have persisted with the location of the poem, or rather with that of its prose context, since it is most unlikely that it would have been hit upon from the evidence of the poem itself. Nor should it still, in my opinion, whether or not we regard the context as relevant, for this story world is not as nearly constrained as that by which we generally seek to measure it. In fact, it is as much through heedlessness to their nature and significance as through being in thrall to their remote counterpart, who made no such claim, although he may have appeared to do so, that modern editors have tended to assume that, if only the evidence were forthcoming, the places could be shown to be somewhere in the Ventry area; actually, as nearly always, the evidence *is* forthcoming and would appear to point in a quite different direction.

So, for instance, Knott states that 'most of the places referred to are unidentifiable as yet, but they obviously belong to the Kerry district', although her single tentative identification, that of Druim Caín with 'Dromkeen townland, near Listowel' in north Kerry, some fifty miles distant from Ventry, hardly supports the case.[21] Gerard Murphy who, although he was very familiar with the area, describes Ventry in the notes to the poem as being in 'south-west Kerry', which is at least an improvement on Carney's 'south Kerry', appears to follow Knott in remarking of Druim Caín that it is 'perhaps Drumkeen townland, near Listowel, Co. Kerry'.[22] Of Druim Dá Léis which immediately follows in the index, he says 'perhaps Drumlesh, near Ennistimon, Co. Clare', which is even further remote; yet one feels that had this Drumlesh been situated near the east coast rather than the west, or in Donegal rather than in Clare, it would not have occurred to him to suggest the identification. The controlling assumption is again evident in the entry for Tulach Léis: 'unidentified hill (perhaps in west Kerry)'.[23] 'Unidentified place' is the only comment on Druim Dá Thrén, Leitir Laíg and Druim Sílenn but the influence of the apparent story geography is again evident in the entry for Loch Dá Chonn, Cáel's place of origin according to the poem and therefore 'situated probably in Leinster';[24] the *Acallam* had previously described him as having come *asin Brug braenach atuaid*,[25] most likely from Brug na Bóinne, although the comfort of that knowledge must be lessened by the suspicion that, in view of its primary Otherworld affiliation, it is likely to be of little use when it comes to establishing physical relationships in this. On the same grounds Murphy would presumably also regard Doire Dá Dos, from whence his mother came, as being somewhere in Leinster, although it is omitted from the index. Apart from noting that the placenames Doire Dá Dos and Druim

21 Knott, *Irish syllabic poetry*, p. 87.   22 Murphy, *Early Irish lyrics*, index s.n.   23 Ibid., index s.n.   24 Ibid., index s.nn.   25 Stokes, 'Acallamh', l. 745.

Caín also occur in *Duanaire Finn*, where they are likewise unidentified, Cecile O'Rahilly has nothing to add to the information provided by Murphy, nor does she remark upon it in any way; Myles Dillon shows no interest in the question, merely listing the names without identification or comment.

Only a single placename in the poem can, with any plausibility, be attached to a west-Kerry location, namely Rinn Dá Bharc, of which Murphy states that it is 'today Rinn na Bairce (Reenverc) in Ventry parish',[26] referring us further to Pádraig Ó Siochfhradha (An Seabhac), *Tríocha-céad Chorca Dhuibhne*, who had made the equation previously.[27] What appears to be the more correct form, 'Rinn na Báirce', occurs elsewhere in Miss O'Rahilly's edition of *Cath Fionntrágha*: *7 bárc mór rígh an domhain do gabh in cuan ar tús conadh Rinn na Báirci a ainm ó sin ale.*[28] Peig Sayers substitutes the synonymous 'Pointe' for 'Rinn' in her own explanation of how the place acquired its name; it runs in Kenneth Jackson's eccentric (and, in some instances, clearly inexact) semi-phonetic transcription: *deirtear gur b'í an bhárc go raibh Daire Donn ínte an chéad lóng do'n aramáil sin do tháinig go Cuan Fíóntrá a' troid le Fión mhic Cúil is le n-a chuid gaiscíoch. Do lean Póinte na Báirce an ainim sin ar an áit riamh ó shoin.*[29] In fact the form 'Rinn Dá Bharc' does not seem to be attested outside of the poem, so that any connection with the Ordnance Survey 'Reenverc' or the other forms cited by Ó Siochfhradha from the 1584 Inquisition ('Ringvarkye') and the Desmond Survey (Renverky *alias* Renwerky), carried out at approximately the same time, though now available only in a late nineteenth-century translation, is open to doubt. Having cited the forms of the name that occur in *Cath Fionntrágha* and the *Acallam*, viz. 'Rinn na Bairce' and 'Rinn Dá Bhárc', Ó Siochfhradha continues: *Chloisinn ag seanchaidhthe an ainm chéadna ar an áit ach ní fios dom an tré chlos scéil na scríbhinne bhí sé aca nó ó oideas sean-chuimhne.*[30] Clearly, neither form was in general use in his time. Apart from this tenuous link, there is no other placename in the poem that can be claimed to belong in the area. And there are other difficulties: for instance, Professor Seán Ó Cinnéide, who has done a detailed survey of the placenames of this his native area, advises me that he has met with no example of the common element 'Leitir' there, nor is any recorded by Ó Siochfhradha, so casting doubt on the likelihood of Leitir Laíg being in the vicinity. This lack of evidence is particularly significant with regard to an area in all of which Irish was the spoken language down to very recent times and in part of which it is still the dominant language; furthermore, its placenames have been exhaustively detailed by one (Ó Siochfhradha) born in the neighbourhood and familiar with all aspects of its oral and liter-

---

26 Murphy, *Early Irish lyrics*, index s.n. 27 (1939), p. 65. 28 O'Rahilly, *Cath Finntrágha*, ll. 96–7. Murphy's 'Rinn na Bairce' derives from Ó Siochfhradha who in turn had it from Meyer, *Cath Finntrága*, l. 72. 29 K. Jackson, 'Dhá scéal ón mBlascaod', *Béaloideas* 4, iii (1934), 301–11 at 306. 30 *Tríocha-céad Chorca Dhuibhne*, p. 65.

ary heritage; indeed it could be claimed, with some justification, that no other district in Ireland has been as minutely examined in respect of its traditions so that scarcely any are likely to have remained undiscovered.

There is one placename in the poem whose origin, it seems to me, can be traced with a great deal more assurance, for it can be shown that Druim Sílenn is probably to be associated with Loch Sílenn in Mag Femin, 'the plain extending from Cashel southwards to the Suir',[31] and the fact that such an obvious association has not already been made is no doubt due to the kind of preconception described earlier, which managed to persist despite the lack of any real tangible evidence, making it impossible to move outside the ill-defined but nonetheless strongly-felt sphere of influence centred at Ventry. Among other sources *The annals of Inisfallen*, s.a. 573, describe how Loch Sílenn came to be named Loch Cenn from the heads of those slain in the battle of Femen:

> Inde est Cennach 7 Loch Cend i Maig Femin de capitibus eorum qui in bello occisi sunt ... Loch Sílend ainm ind Locha sein ar thús.
> Loch Sílend
>   is mairg nod n–ib ara biad!
> ro llín Corpre di chennaib
>   conid crú co rice a grian.

Mac Airt translates the quatrain:

> Loch Sílenn,
>   Alas for him who drinks it with his food!
> Cairpre has filled it with heads
>   So that it is gore to its bottom.[32]

'Alas for him who drinks it on account of its food!' might be a better translation of the second line, for, although the preposition *ar* can express a wide range of meanings, that of accompaniment, as Mac Airt's translation would require, does not appear to be among them. 'Loch Cenn', in turn, has given modern Lough Kent, the addition of the final -*t* being explained according to T.F. O'Rahilly 'when we find that people of the name of Kent were hereditary proprietors in the neighbourhood'.[33] There being no lake within the present boundaries of the three townlands that go to make up Lough Kent, O'Rahilly, who had at first thought the lake might have 'long since been

31 T.F. O'Rahilly, 'Notes on Irish placenames', *Hermathena*, 48 (1933), 196–220, at 209.
32 S. Mac Airt (ed. and trans.), *The annals of Inisfallen* (1951), pp 76–7. John V. Kelleher's graceful rendition (*Too small for stovewood, too big for kindling* (1979), p. 9) is worth quoting: Loch Sílenn. Evil drink with a man's food! Cairbre has filled it with heads. Down to its sand it is blood. 33 O'Rahilly, 'Notes on Irish placenames', 210.

drained', later suggested that it may continue to exist under the name of 'Rockwell Lake, in which are some small islands, about half a mile to the north of Lough Kent'.[34] But it is not the location that primarily concerns us at this point (other than to note that, if we are right, it must have something to tell us about the true nature of the placenames in *Géisid cúan*), but rather the relevance of 'Loch Sílenn' to the 'Druim Sílenn' of the poem. This appears from a passage in the *dinnshenchas* of Mag Femin from the Book of Leinster:

> Daim Dile tuargaibset cend
> Forsin maig ac Loch Śilend.[35]

This we may translate, generally following Gwynn, as 'The oxen of Díl appeared (lit. 'raised [their] head')/on the plain by Loch Sílenn'. There is much variation, if not outright confusion, in the literary sources between *dam Dile/Díle* ('the ox of Dil/Díl') – the short 'i' is guaranteed by the metre in one instance, but that is not fully to deny the alternative – and *dam dílenn* ('a mighty, i.e. antediluvian?, ox').[36] It is the latter that figures in *Géisid cúan*:

> marb eilit Droma Sílenn;
> géisid dam dílenn dá héis.[37]

Here the pairing of *(eilit) Droma Sílenn* with *dam dílenn*, was surely suggested by the *daim Dile, (ac) Loch Śilend* of the *dinnshenchas* poem. It is not a matter of geography at all but of direct borrowing from a germane source, and the impression that the placenames of the poem cannot be regarded as reflecting a pre-determined landscape is confirmed when they are viewed as a group in relation to one another rather than separately in terms of a given geographical area. Perhaps reflecting its different source, indirect literary rather than direct topographic, 'Loch Sílenn' remains exceptional in not fully describing itself, as, for instance, names like 'Doire Dá Dos' ('the oakwood of two thickets') and 'Leitir Laíg' ('the hillside of the calf'), which are self-contained as well as forming part of a broader system of reference to nature, itself uncircumscribed as to particular point of realisation.[38]

Apart from his reference to 'South Kerry', Carney does not attempt to situate the places named in the poem. In view of his poet-patron thesis requiring a historical event and, it would seem to follow, a more-or-less realistic if not local terrain, I would argue that he was remiss in not attempting to do so. But

---

34 Ibid., 220. **35** E.J. Gwynn (ed. and trans.), *The metrical dindshenchas*, 5 vols (1906–35), iii, pp 204–5; cf. ibid., iv, pp 258–9. **36** *DIL* s.v. 1. *dam* ('D' 59.28–47). **37** Murphy, *Early Irish lyrics*, p. 148, §4. **38** The argument here closely follows that of an earlier article: S. Ó Coileáin, 'Place and placename in *fianaigheacht*', *Studia Hibernica*, 27 (1993), 45–60 (reprinted elsewhere in this volume).

he has observed the system of interrelationships, which is finally more important, and the following note brings us very close to the heart of the matter:

> The poet is using placenames for pathetic effect, and finds those with
> the numeral *dá* particularly apt (*Rinn Dá Bhárc, Loch Dá Chonn, Druim
> Dá Thrén, Druim Dá Léis, Daire Dá Dos*). I would suggest that the
> poet's intention in using placenames with *dá* may carry a poetic impli-
> cation that things are properly in pairs, and that with Cael's death a
> unity between him and the poet has been broken.[39]

This is a very acute observation that needs no qualification except to say that the
pairing now severed is more likely to be that of Cáel and Créd/Créide than of
poet and patron: the emotional effect is generated among the story *personae* rather
than to be understood in a transferred, metaphorical sense as Carney would have
it. This requires that the prose context be retained, at least in terms of our
understanding of the poem, if not as actual text; in other words, in setting the
scene, the author of the *Acallam* was working from within an acknowledged
frame of reference. But in selecting (or inventing) the placenames to serve his
poetic purpose he was not constrained by more mundane considerations.

The binding effect of the placename element, '*dá*' (which the poet would
have understood as 'two', whatever its etymology), recalls an earlier claim
made by Carney when comparing the story of Diarmaid and Gráinne with
what he calls the 'Primitive *Tristan*': that the function of a placename 'Doire
Dá Bhoth', which he translates as 'Oakgrove of two bothys', 'as doubtless to
make clear that they did not sleep together on account of Diarmait's loyalty
to Finn. (The hero and heroine sleeping together in this unsatisfactory
manner was a feature of the Primitive *Tristan*)'.[40] This appears to me to be
rather too ingenious. Far from preserving an archaic feature, Doire Dá Bhoth
would seem to have been either a misreading by Standish H. O'Grady, on
whose edition Carney then depended, or a late scribal innovation in one of his
now-lost originals; the earliest version of the text, itself not very early, since
edited by Nessa Ní Shéaghdha, has Doire Dá Bhaoth ('The oakwood/thicket
of two fools') whose implications, if there are any, scarcely merit comment.[41]

The preponderance of placenames of the pattern, X *Dá* Y, in *Géisid cúan*
undoubtedly has an artificial, that is literary, quality. Place has become text.
This is not at all to deny the actuality of such names. On the contrary, it is

---

39 Carney, 'Two poems', p. 30 n. 5.   40 J. Carney, *Studies in Irish literature and history* (1955),
p. 218.   41 S.H. O'Grady (ed. and trans.), 'Tóruigheacht Dhiarmuda agus Ghráinne',
Transactions of the Ossianic Society, vol. 3 (1857), e.g. pp 80–1; N. Ní Shéaghdha (ed. and
trans.), *Tóruigheacht Dhiarmada agus Ghráinne* (1967), e.g. pp 32–3. This Doire Dá Bhaoth
cannot possibly be the place of that name recorded as being in or near Fir Rois in P. Ó Riain
et al. (eds), *Historical dictionary of Gaelic placenames*, i (2003) s.n. Áth Doire Dhá Bhaoth.

necessary that a credible relationship be maintained between the landscape and its evocation: there must be the appearance of recognition to counterbalance the elusiveness of place. Olden counted 226 names of this type (some of which belong to the category of what he calls 'personal appellations') at the end of the nineteenth century,[42] and no doubt many more could be added, but the matter will suffice to indicate what P.W. Joyce had earlier called 'a distinctly market predilection to designate persons or places where circumstances permitted it, by epithets expressive of the idea of duality'.[43] Carney would follow Knott in including *Dá Lí* among them; Murphy reads *coinfiad dá lí* and translates 'a two-coloured fox', a particularly apt description it may be remarked. But in literature it is not a matter of 'either or' but of 'both and'; we cannot suppose the description to be entirely absent from the suggestion of place any more than we can suppose the suggestion of place to be entirely absent from the description; caught between denotation and connotation, each brings with it its own textual and contextual force. There is a real sense in which *coinfiad dá lí/ Coinfiad Dá Lí* is as much a placename as *Druim Dá Thrén/ druim dá thrén* is a description; while we are logically required to detach *coinfiad* from *Dá Lí* in the latter's capacity as placename, regarding X and Y as being in separate categories in this instance, the separation does not endure in terms of overall effect. Placenames of the type *Dá Lí*, or [X] *Dá* Y, while not unknown – one could instance *'á Dhrom* (Ardgroom) beside *Drom 'á Liag* (Drimoleague) from West Cork – are relatively uncommon and stylistically invite formal completion, while, as it were, retaining the right to reassert themselves in their toponymic function.

Whether compounded with *Dá* or otherwise, all the placenames of the text, with the exception of Loch Silenn already discussed, are immediately transparent. Of Tulach Léis we might comment that by far the best-known place of the name is now Tullylease, far inland in North Cork, a situation hardly appropriate to the lines:

> Caínce corr
> Do-ní tonn trom Tulcha Léis.[44]

'The heavy wave of Tulach Léis makes a strange melody'.

42 T. Olden, 'Remarks supplementary to Dr. Joyce's paper on the occurrence of the number *two* in Irish proper names', *Proceedings of the Royal Irish Academy*, 4, 3rd series (1898), 636–43. 43 P.W. Joyce, *Irish names of place*, vol. 1 (1869), p. 247. This question has since been revisited (with varying conclusions) by J. Pokorny, 'Da- in irischen Ortsnamen', *Zeitschrift für celtische Philologie*, 14 (1923), 270–1; H. Morris, '"Da" in Irish placenames', *Journal of the County Louth Archaeological Society*, 6 (1925–8), 131–4; F. McCann (P. Mac Cana), 'Da in placenames', *Bulletin of the Ulster Place-name Society*, 1, 1st series (1952–3), 14–15, 72; D. Flanagan, 'A reappraisal of da in Irish placenames, i', *Bulletin of the Ulster Place-name Society*, 3, 2nd series (1980–81), 71–3. The publication of the promised second part of the last-named article was prevented by the author's untimely death. 44 Murphy, *Early Irish lyrics*, p. 150, §10.

But it is far from certain that situation would have determined the choice of
name or indeed influenced it in any way. This is a world in which places are
detachable from names and names from places, where the importance of place
while being seemingly affirmed is in fact simultaneously being denied. There
is no contradiction – the evidence is not solid enough for that, the landscape
too ethereal – but there is no necessary agreement either. Language takes pri-
ority over location; the catalogue of names is essentially mesmeric rather than
directional. It is only on returning to the prose text of the *Acallam*, ironically
that rejected by Carney, that we find landmarks such as *Tráig Chaíl* which
bind the world of story firmly to the real and then in a manner insufficient
to persuade even Geoffrey Keating of the credibility of the tale: *is follus nach
fuil agus nach raibhe meas staire fírinnighe ag na seanchadhaibh ar Chath
Fionntrágha, acht gurab dearbh leo gurab finnscéul filidheachta do cumadh mar
chaitheamh aimsire é.*[45] No doubt in rejecting it and its like, the *seanchaidhe*
were also influenced by that sense of unreality, so redolent of *fianaigheacht*,
which is as undefined by place and distance as it is by time and circumstance.

Neither, of course, would Carney hold any historical brief for *Cath
Fionntrágha*, but in separating *Géisid cúan* from the ambiance of any version
of the story he is expressing a very different sense of the poem's atmosphere
and essence. But having removed it from an environment with the ethos of
which it would seem to me to be in perfect accord, he neglects to establish it
elsewhere, as would be surely required on his own (historical) terms, except
by way of a kind of critical edict that could be applied to almost any love
poem for which we lack certain knowledge of the precise circumstances of
composition. If some question must remain as to whether the poem belongs
in the *Acallam*, it must remain even more uncertain that it will adhere to a
context for which there is no evidence at all. Perhaps the most significant
point he makes against leaving the poem where we find it is the Christian
allusion in the line that refers to Cáel as being, at the time of the lament, *is
cros úasa chinn*[46] ('with a cross above his head'); Carney observes that 'Irish
poets were never given to this kind of anachronism',[47] but, while this will generally hold true, it may not be so remarkable when regarded as part of a work
that it is notably short on chronology to begin with, if it is permissible to
judge by criteria which have been shown by the text itself not to apply. Apart
from the likelihood that he may not have been greatly concerned at such
things in any event, the author of the *Acallam* had set himself a very complex
task: not only must he negotiate effectively between his own time and a
remote past, transferring to that past for resolution the conflict inherent in his
materials and cultural inheritance, but, at a selected point in the past, Caílte,

---

45 P.S. Dinneen and D. Comyn (ed. and trans.), *Foras feasa ar Éirinn*, 4 vols (1902–14), i, p.
50; cf. ibid., ii, p. 326. 46 Murphy, *Early Irish lyrics*, pp 148–9, §5. 47 Carney, 'Two poems',
p. 24.

in the role of secondary author, must adduce in a fifth-century Christian present a still earlier pagan past in accordance with the always dominant requirements of primary author and audience; Caílte cannot be allowed to know in
his past what he knows in his present and the author of the *Acallam* is not
properly allowed to know anything that occurred between that present and his
own. The system was certain to break down and for the historical period
there is ample evidence that it did. Carney's argument would require that the
more fundamental division between pagan and Christian be strictly observed.
But the appeal must always be not to logical consistency in terms of the
author's conceit as viewed from beyond the affective range of the text, but to
the sensibilities of those who, while sharing in that conceit, share also in the
less definable knowledge of the freedoms and limitations with which it will be
allowed to function in the totality of their imaginative experience. The
modern critic is rather in the position of the prescriptive grammarian who,
having struggled to acquire a language, then seeks to determine how it ought
to be spoken. For both language and literature the rule must be that something is not a problem unless it is felt to be a problem, and for the author of
the *Acallam* and his audience, as for most of those who have come to appreciate the poem in more recent times, this clearly was not. To narrow the
scale, we could similarly object that Cáel is not yet buried at the time he is
said to be *is cros úasa chinn*, but such an objection would properly be dis-
missed as the quibbling that it is; affective truth is not limited in this way.
Incidentally the RIA Dictionary (*DIL*), which would not claim to be comprehensive in this – for instance, it does not cite our text or that of *Turas
acam día háine* (below) – has a number of examples from *fianaigheacht* of the
word *cros* being used with reference to the pre-Christian order in the sense of
cross or cross-shaped object as well as in the transferred sense of prohibition
in the phrase *tar crois*; for instance it cites *cros óir 7 cros airgid* which occurs
as a variant in Stokes edition of the *Acallam* at l. 5839.

Speaking of the prose introduction, whose relevance he would attempt to
dismiss, Carney notes the reference to the external soul: 7 *do bhadar
bethaduigh eile 7 comhsaegal acu re Cael* 'and there were other creatures whose
lifespan was the same as that of Cael'.[48] Of this he says: 'with the introduction of this idea we are obviously in touch with a more popular type of thinking than that which lies behind the poem'.[49] It is true that the motif which
occurs in various guises is well attested in folklore and is particularly associated with Aarne-Thompson, Type 302.[50] But it is no less a feature of traditional Irish literature at all periods, from *Aided Con Roí* onwards,[51] and indeed

---

48 Stokes, 'Acallamh', ll. 834–5.   49 Carney, 'Two poems', pp 24–5.   50 A. Aarne and S.
Thompson, *The types of the folktale* (1964), pp 93–4. Occurrences of the individual motif are
catalogued in S. Thompson, *Motif-index of folk literature*, vol. 2 (1956), pp 493–6, E710 ff.; cf.
T.P. Cross, *Motif-index of early Irish literature* ([1952]), pp 220–1.   51 R.I. Best (ed. and trans.),

has been discussed at some length by Carney in another context,[52] although
he curiously ignores its occurrence in *Tóraigheacht Dhiarmada agus Ghráinne*
where Diarmaid is assigned the same lifespan as the boar in the slaying of
which he effectively slays himself;[53] the motif is also suggested in the story of
Cian and the worm elsewhere in the *Tóraigheacht*.[54] The closest analogue to
the manner of Diarmaid's death is to be found not in Irish literature, nor in
the Tristan material, but in the account of the death of Meleager in Ovid's
Metamorphoses, Book viii. There Meleager, having slain the boar, slays the two
sons of Thestius, his own maternal uncles, who would deprive Atalanta of the
spoils he offers her. Meleager's mother, Althaea,

> in the temple of the gods was offering thanksgiving for her son's vic-
> tory, when she saw the corpses of her brothers carried in. She beat her
> breast and filled the city with woeful lamentation, and changed her
> gold-spangled robes for black. But when she learned who was their
> murderer, her grief all fell away and was changed from tears to the
> passion for vengeance.
>
> There was a billet of wood which, when the daughter of Thestius
> lay in childbirth, the three sisters threw into the fire and, spinning the
> threads of life with firm-pressed thumb, they sang: 'An equal span of
> life we give to thee and to this wood, O babe new-born'. When the
> three goddesses had sung this prophecy and vanished, the mother
> snatched the blazing brand from the fire, and quenched it in water.
> Long had it lain hidden away in a secret place and, guarded safe, had
> safeguarded your life, O youth. And now the mother brought out this
> billet and bade her servants make a heap of pine-knots and fine kin-
> dling, and lit the pile with cruel flame. Then four times she made to
> throw the billet in the flames and four times she held her hand.[55]

Finally the sister in her overcomes, whereupon she flings the brand into the
flames; as it is consumed, Meleager

> feels his vitals scorching with hidden fire ... The fire and his pains
> increase and then die down. Both fire and pain go out together; his
> spirit gradually slips away into the thin air as white ashes gradually
> overspread the glowing coals.[56]

'The tragic death of Cúrói mac Dári', *Ériu*, 2 (1905), 18–35; R. Thurneysen (ed. and trans.),
'Die Sage von CuRoi', *Zeitschrift für celtische Philologie*, 9 (1913), 189–234 at 192 §10. For commentary, see J. Baudiš, 'CúRói and CúChulinn', *Ériu*, 7 (1914), 200–9, an article that is of considerably more value than one might suppose from the comments of T.F. O'Rahilly, *Early Irish
history and mythology* (1946), pp 321–2. **52** Carney, *Studies in Irish literature and history*, pp
204–6; cf. p. 194n. **53** Ní Shéaghdha, *Tóruigheacht Dhiarmada agus Ghráinne*, esp. ll. 1516–31,
1559–66. **54** Ibid., ll. 980–1099. **55** F.J. Miller (ed. and trans.), *Ovid: metamorphoses* (1977),
i, pp 437–9. **56** Ibid., p. 443.

While the external soul is here located in the brand rather than in the animal itself, we have the interesting parallel of the boar hunt followed by the death of the hero through the destruction of the object in which his life force resides; in each case, human agency, depending on the outcome of a debate on opposing allegiances, is finally responsible. It is not suggested that the stories of Diarmaid and Meleager are directly related through literary borrowing, although it is possible that they may be independent realisations of a far-flung tale type, just as *Aided Con Roí* may be an early Irish form of Aarne-Thompson 302 which has a woman, whom the ogre has carried off against her will, betray the secret of his external soul to a hero who is thereby enabled to slay him. But the question to be resolved here is not whether we can establish a relationship on the basis of a story complex but whether a specific motif, namely that of the external soul, can be regarded as indicating 'a more popular type of thinking'; if nothing else, the passage from Ovid, who is not usually associated with such thinking, may be taken as evidence against the view, which would seem to have little enough to recommend it already.

On one level, at least, the relationship of the death of Meleager, as related by Ovid, to that of Diarmaid, as described in *Tóraigheacht Dhiarmada agus Ghráinne*, is not dissimilar to that which Seamus Heaney proposes to exist between Ovid's account of the death of Orpheus in the *Metamorphoses* and the underlying, only partially expressed concerns of *Cúirt an mheán oíche*, which he views as being psychosexual in nature. It is not so much that the maenads' rending of Orpheus is consciously invoked by Merriman, or even that it was known to him, but that the 'power [of the *Cúirt*] is augmented by being located within the force-field of an archetype'.[57] In the *Cúirt*, the threatened punishment of the poet is not carried out: in Heaney's words, 'what O'Tuama calls the archaic feelings are effectively aborted by the dream convention'.[58] The fact that the pattern is completed in Ovid makes that comparison legitimate, regardless of any direct or indirect textual link. Each expression of the myth is adumbrated by the whole which itself is an abstract concept formed of its various partial mainfestations, rather like the relationship of *langue* to *parole*, except that the language is now a mythic one; it is an overarching continuum formed of scattered discontinuities.

It is not the intention to discuss the companion poem *Turas acam día haine*[59] at any length, since much of the argument would repeat what has been said earlier. For example the Christian references implicit in *Día haine* and *Cnoc na Cros* fall into the same category as the phrase *is cros úasa chinn* in *Géisid cúan* and invite like comment. Carney's statement with regard to Murphy's translation of the opening lines of the poem that 'in Ireland, as is well known, it is considered lucky to move into a new house on Friday'[60] is

---

57 S. Heaney, *The redress of poetry* (1995), pp 60–2.   58 Ibid.   59 Murphy, *Early Irish lyrics*, pp 140–7, no. 48.   60 Carney, 'Two poems', p. 27.

at least questionable, nor is it really supported by the note in which he quotes Seán Ó Súilleabháin of the Irish Folklore Commission (as it was then styled) as supporting authority: it is not so much a matter of beginning things as of moving to a new house, Créd's in this instance. According to the *Acallam*, if we allow the most elementary sense of direction, the poet has travelled south-westwards from Ardpatrick in Co. Limerick to the neighbourhood of the Paps and is now *re hucht in tsléibe an-airtúaid*,[61] 'facing the mountain from the north east', that is somewhere in the neighbourhood of present-day Rathmore. If folk tradition has any bearing on the matter, and it is an unreliable guide at the best of times, it is to the effect that one should not remove northwards on a Monday or southwards on a Friday, and there are proscriptions against *Imrighe (Aistriú) an Luain ó thuaidh / Is imrighe (aistriú) na hAoine ó dheas*.[62]

In transferring the events and places of the poem to a factual setting Carney fails to meet the most basic evidential requirements. It is hardly enough for a critic, even for one of his stature, simply to say that 'the poet lives in a place called Sruthar, which must lie south-west of the Paps Mountains ... He decides to visit a wealthy lady called Créd. She lived in the Paps Mountains ... near Loch Cuire. The precise spot is called *Cnoc na cCros*'.[63] Historical or other sources are not aware of any poet who lived in a place called Sruthar or of any 'wealthy woman called Créd' who lived in the Paps – indeed, in view of the terrain, it is unlikely that any wealthy person has ever lived there, not above ground at any rate! And in this area of Sliabh Luachra, almost as steeped in Irish-language tradition as Corca Dhuibhne, we would look in vain for Sruthar or Loch Cuire or Cnoc na Cros. But it is not so much the lack of detailed evidence as of the approach being overly deter-ministic, as appears to me: a fluid world cannot be mapped precisely in a con-ventional way.

Which may appear to be a curious way to conclude a tribute to one who has himself contributed so much to mapping a more tangible world.

---

61 Murphy, *Early Irish Lyrics*, p. 140, no. 48, l. 4.   62 See, for example, An Seabhac, *Seanfhocail na Muimhneach* (1926), p. 188, §§1541–2; cf. G. Henderson, *Survivals in belief among the Celts* (1911), p. 293: 'It is not right to change residence going from north to south except on Monday, and when going from south to north one should go on Saturday'.   63 Carney, 'Two poems', p. 28. For another example of Carney's propensity to create real people and places from inadequate literary sources, see his treatment of the poem *It é saigte gona súain* in 'The so-called "Lament of Créidhe"', *Éigse* 13, iii (1970), 227–42 at 230–1, and compare my comments thereon in 'Some problems of story and history', *Ériu*, 32 (1981), 115–36 at 134–5.

Bibliography

Aarne, Antti and Stith Thompson, *The types of the folktale*, Folklore Fellows Communications no. 184 (2nd revision; Helsinki, 1964).

Abbott, H. Porter, 'Story, plot and narration' in D. Herman (ed.), *The Cambridge companion to narrative* (2007), pp 39–51.

—, *The Cambridge introduction to narrative* (2nd ed. Cambridge, 2008).

Abbott, T.K. and E.J. Gwynn, *Catalogue of Irish manuscripts in the library of Trinity College Dublin* (Dublin, 1921).

Almqvist, Bo, Séamas Ó Catháin and Pádraig Ó Héalaí (eds), *The heroic process: form, function and fantasy in folk epic* (Dublin, 1987). The Fenian essays from this collection were also printed with the same pagination in *Béaloideas* 54–5 (1986–7), and separately as *Fiannaíocht: essays on the Fenian tradition of Ireland and Scotland* (An Cumann le Béaloideas Éireann, 1987).

Arbuthnot, Sharon J. and Geraldine Parsons (eds), *The Gaelic Finn tradition* (Dublin, 2012).

Arthurs, John B., 'The legends of placenames', *Ulster Folklife*, 1 (1955), 37–42.

Aubet, Maria Eugenia, *The Phoenicians and the west: politics, colonies and trade*, trans. Mary Turton (2nd ed. Cambridge, 2001).

Auerbach, Erich, *Mimesis: the representation of reality in western literature*, trans. Willard R. Trask (Princeton, 1968).

Bailey, M.J., 'John V. Kelleher, retired Harvard professor', *Boston Globe*, 11 January 2004.

Barthes, Roland, 'Introduction to the structural analysis of narratives' in idem, *Image-music-text*, repr. in Susan Sontag (ed.), *A Barthes reader* (New York, 1981), pp 251–95.

Baudiš, J., 'CúRói and CúChulinn', *Ériu*, 7 (1914), 200–9.

Baumgarten, Rolf, 'A Hiberno-Isidorian etymology', *Peritia*, 2 (1983), 225–8.

—, 'Placenames, etymology and the structure of *fianaigecht*' in B. Almqvist et al. (eds), *The heroic process* (1987), pp 1–24.

—, 'Etymological aetiology in Irish tradition', *Ériu*, 41 (1990), 115–22.

Bell, Alexander, *L'estoire des Engleis by Geffrei Gaimer*, Anglo-Norman Texts 14–16 (Oxford, 1960).

Benjamin, Walter, 'The storyteller' in Dorothy J. Hale (ed.), *The novel: anthology of criticism and theory* (Malden, MA, 2006), pp 362–77.

Benveniste, Émile, *Indo-European language and society*, trans. Elizabeth Palmer (London, 1973).

Bergin, Osborn (ed. and trans.), 'How the Dagda got his magic staff' in R.S. Loomis (ed.), *Medieval studies in memory of Gertrude Schoepperle Loomis* (Paris and New York, 1927), pp 399–409.

Bernhardt-House, Phillip A., 'Horses, hounds and high kings: a shared Arthurian tradition across the Irish Sea?' in Joseph Falaky Nagy (ed.), *Myth in Celtic literatures: CSANA Yearbook*, 6 (Dublin, 2007), pp 11–21.

Best, R.I. (ed. and trans.), 'The tragic death of Cúrói mac Dári', *Ériu*, 2 (1905), 18–35.
— (ed. and trans.), 'The graves of the kings at Clonmacnois', *Ériu*, 2 (1905), 163–71.
— (ed. and trans.), 'The settling of the manor of Tara', *Ériu*, 4 (1908–10), 121–72.
— and Osborn Bergin (eds), *Lebor na Huidre: Book of the Dun Cow* (Dublin, 1929).
—, Osborn Bergin, M.A. O'Brien and Anne Sullivan (eds), *The book of Leinster, formerly Lebar na Núachongbála*, 6 vols (Dublin, 1954–83).
Bhreathnach, Edel, 'The *seanchas* tradition in late medieval Ireland' in Edel Bhreathnach and Bernadette Cunningham (eds), *Writing Irish history: the Four Masters and their world* (Dublin, 2007).
Bhreathnach, Máire (ed. and trans.), 'A new edition of Tochmarc Becfhola', *Ériu*, 35 (1984), 59–91.
Bieler, Ludwig (ed. and trans.), *The Irish penitentials* (Dublin, 1963).
— (ed.), *Four Latin lives of Saint Patrick* (Dublin, 1971).
— (ed. and trans.), *The Patrician texts in the Book of Armagh* (with a contribution by Fergus Kelly), Scriptores Latini Hiberniae 10 (Dublin, 1979).
Binchy, Daniel A. (ed.), *Corpus iuris hibernici*, 6 vols (Dublin, 1978).
Black, Ronald, 'The Gaelic calendar months: some meanings and derivations', *Shadow*, 2:1 (1985), 2–13.
Bliss, W.H. (ed.), *Calendar of entries in the papal registers relating to Great Britain and Ireland, i: 1198–1304* (London, 1893).
Bondarenko, Grigory, 'King in exile in *Airne Fíngein* "Fíngen's vigil": power and pursuit in early Irish literature', *Études Celtiques*, 36 (2008), 135–48.
Borsje, Jacqueline, Ann Dooley and Gregory Toner (eds), *Celtic cosmology: perspectives from Ireland and Scotland* (Toronto, forthcoming, 2013).
Bourke, Angela, Siobhán Kilfeather, Maria Luddy, Margaret Mac Curtain, Geraldine Meaney, Máirín Ní Dhonnchadha, Mary O'Dowd and Clair Wills (eds), *The Field Day anthology of Irish writing*, vol. 4: *Irish women's writing and traditions* (Cork, 2002).
Breathnach, Diarmuid and Máire Ní Mhurchú, *1782–1881 Beathaisnéis [Maille le forlíonadh le 1882–1982 beathaisnéis agus le hinnéacs (1782–1999)]* (Baile Átha Cliath, 1999).
Breatnach, Caoimhín, 'The religious significance of *Oidheadh chloinne Lir*', *Ériu*, 50 (1999), 1–40.
Breatnach, Liam (ed. and trans.), *Uraicecht na ríar* (Dublin, 1987).
—, 'An Mheán-Ghaeilge' in K. McCone et al. (eds), *Stair na Gaeilge* (1994), pp 221–333.
—, *A companion to the Corpus iuris Hibernici* (Dublin, 2005).
Breatnach, N., *Ar bóthar dom* (Rinn Ó gCuanach, 1998).
Breatnach, R.A., 'The lady and the king: a theme of Irish literature', *Studies*, 42 (1953), 321–36.
Briggs, Charles L., *Competence in performance: the creativity of tradition in Mexicano verbal art* (Philadelphia, 1988).
Bromwich, Rachel, 'The continuity of the Gaelic tradition in eighteenth-century Ireland', *Yorkshire Celtic Studies*, 4 (1947–8), 2–28.
Bruckner, Matilda Tomaryn, 'Speaking through animals in Marie de France's *Lais* and *Fables*' in L.E. Whalen (ed.), *A companion to Marie de France* (2011), pp 157–85.

Bruford, Alan, *Gaelic folktales and medieval romances: a study of the early modern Irish romantic tales and their oral derivatives* (Dublin, 1966).

Bullough-Davies, Constance, 'The form of the Breton lay', *Medium Ævum*, 42 (1973), 18–31.

Byrne, Francis John, *Irish kings and high-kings* (London, 1973).

—, '*Senchas*: the nature of Gaelic historical tradition', *Historical Studies*, 9 (Belfast, 1974), 137–59.

Campbell, John Francis (ed.), *Leabhar na feinne: heroic Gaelic ballads collected in Scotland, chiefly from 1512 to 1871* (London, 1872; repr. Shannon, 1972).

Caplan, Harry (ed. and trans.), *Cicero: rhetorica ad Herennium*, Loeb Classical Library (Cambridge, MA, 1954).

Carey, John, 'The finding of Arthur's grave: a story from Clonmacnoise?' in John Carey, John T. Koch and Pierre-Yves Lambert (eds), *Ildánach ildírech: a festschrift for Proinsias Mac Cana* (Andover and Aberystwyth, 1999), 1–14.

— (ed.), *Duanaire Finn: reassessments*, Irish Texts Society, Subsidiary Series 11 (Dublin, 2003).

—, 'Remarks on dating' in idem (ed.), *Duanaire Finn: reassessments* (2003), pp 1–18.

—, *Ireland and the grail* (Aberystwyth, 2007).

—, *A single ray of the sun: religious speculation in early Ireland* (2nd ed.; Aberystwyth, 2011).

Carney, James (ed.), *Topographical poems by Seaán Mór Ó Dubhagáin and Giolla-na-naomh Ó Huidhrín* (Dublin, 1943).

—, *Studies in Irish literature and history* (Dublin, 1955).

—, 'Two poems from Acallam na senórach' in James Carney and David Greene (eds), *Celtic studies: essays in memory of Angus Matheson* (London, 1968), pp 22–32.

—, 'The so-called "Lament of Créidhe"', *Éigse*, 13, iii (1970), 227–42.

—, 'Language and literature to 1169' in Dáibhí Ó Cróinín (ed.), *A new history of Ireland*, vol. 1: *Prehistoric and early Ireland* (Oxford, 2005), pp 451–510.

Carpenter, Rhys, 'Phoenicians in the west', *American Journal of Archaeology*, 62 (1958), 35–53.

Chadwick, Hector Munro and Nora Kershaw Chadwick, *The growth of literature*, vol. 1 (Cambridge, 1932).

Clancy, Thomas Owen, 'Women poets in early medieval Ireland: stating the case' in Christine Meek and Katharine Simms (eds), *'The fragility of her sex'? Medieval Irishwomen in their European context* (Dublin, 1996), pp 43–72.

Comyn, David and Patrick S. Dinneen (ed. and trans.), *Foras feasa ar Éirinn: the history of Ireland by Geoffrey Keating D.D.*, 4 vols, Irish Texts Society 4, 8, 9, 15 (London, 1902–14).

Connon, Anne, 'Plotting *Acallam na senórach*: the physical context of the "Mayo" sequence' in Sarah Sheehan, Joanne Findon and Westley Follett (eds), *Gablánach in scélaigecht: Celtic studies in honour of Ann Dooley* (Dublin, 2013), pp 69–102.

Coste, Didier and John Pier, 'Narrative levels' in P. Hühn et al. (eds), *The living handbook of narratology*.

Craoibhín, an: *see* Hyde, Douglas.

Cross, Tom Peete, *Motif-index of early Irish literature* (Bloomington, [1952]).

Danaher, Kevin, 'Irish folk tradition and the Celtic calendar' in Robert O'Driscoll (ed.), *The Celtic consciousness* (New York, 1981), pp 217–42.

Davenport, Tony, *Medieval narrative: an introduction* (Oxford, 2004), pp 35–54.

de Barra, Pádraig (ed.), *Agallamh na seanóirí*, 2 vols (Baile Átha Cliath/Maigh Eo, 1984–6).

de Bhaldraithe, Tomás (ed.), *Seanchas Thomáis Laighléis* (Dublin, 1977).

de Caro, Frank, *The folklore muse: poetry, fiction and other reflections by folklorists* (Utah, 2008).

de Vries, Ranke (ed. and trans.), *Two texts on Loch nEchach: De causis torchi Corc' Óche and Aided Echach maic Maireda*, Irish Texts Society 65 (Dublin, 2012).

Dillon, Myles (ed. and trans.), 'The inauguration of O'Conor' in J.A. Watt, John B. Morrall and Francis X. Martin (eds), *Medieval studies presented to Aubrey Gwynn* (Dublin, 1961), pp 186–202.

— (ed. and trans.), *Lebor na cert*, Irish Texts Society, 46 (Dublin, 1962).

— (ed.), *Stories from the Acallam*, Mediaeval and Modern Irish Series 23 (Dublin, 1970).

—, Canice Mooney and Pádraig de Brún, *Catalogue of Irish manuscripts in the Franciscan library, Killiney* (Dublin, 1969).

Doherty, Charles, 'Exchange and trade in early medieval Ireland', *Journal of the Royal Society of Antiquaries of Ireland*, 110 (1980), 67–89.

Dooley, Ann, 'The date and purpose of *Acallam na senórach*', *Éigse*, 34 (2004), 97–126.

—, 'The deployment of some hagiographical sources in *Acallam na senórach*' in S.J. Arbuthnot and G. Parsons (eds), *The Gaelic Finn tradition* (2012), pp 97–110.

— and Harry Roe, *Tales of the elders of Ireland: a new translation of Acallam na senórach* (Oxford, 1999).

DuBois, Thomas A., *An introduction to shamanism* (Cambridge, 2009).

Duncan, Lilian (ed. and trans.), 'Altram tige dá medar', *Ériu*, 11 (1932), 184–225.

Echard, Siân (ed.), *The Arthur of medieval literature: the development and dissemination of the Arthurian legend in medieval Latin* (London, 2011).

Eliade, Mircea, *The myth of the eternal return* (Princeton, 1974).

—, 'Survivals and camouflages of myths' in Diane Apostolos-Cappadona (ed.), *Symbolism, the sacred and the arts* (New York, 1985), pp 32–52.

Erickson, Carolly, *The medieval vision. Essays in history and perception* (Oxford, 1976).

Eska, Joseph F. (ed.), *Narrative in Celtic tradition: essays in honor of Edgar M. Slotkin*, *CSANA Yearbook*, 8–9 (Hamilton, 2011).

Evans, J. Gwenogvryn (ed.), *The White Book Mabinogion* (Pwllheli, 1907); reprinted with introduction by R.M. Jones as *Llyfr Gwyn Rhydderch* (Cardiff, 1973).

Findon, Joanne, 'Fabula, story and text: the case of *Compert Conchobuir*' in J.F. Eska (ed.), *Narrative in Celtic tradition* (2011), pp 37–55.

Flahive, Joseph J., 'The relic lays: a study in late Middle-Gaelic *fianaigheacht*', PhD thesis (University of Edinburgh, 2004).

—, '*An fhianaigheacht*: the Fenian cycle' in Clodagh Downey and Seán Ó Coileáin (eds), *A history of Irish manuscript literature* (forthcoming).

Flanagan, Deirdre, 'A reappraisal of da in Irish placenames, i', *Bulletin of the Ulster Place-name Society*, 3, 2nd series (1980–1), 71–3.

Flanagan, Marie Therese, *Irish royal charters: texts and contexts* (Oxford, 2005).

—, *The transformation of the Irish church in the twelfth and thirteenth centuries*, Studies in Celtic History 29 (Woodbridge, 2010).

Flower, Robin, *The Irish tradition* (Oxford, 1947).

Fraser, J., 'The miracle of Ciaran's hand', *Ériu*, 6 (1912), 159–60.

Freeman, A. Martin (ed. and trans.), *The annals in Cotton MS. Titus A. XXV* (Paris, 1929); originally published in *Revue Celtique* 41, 301–30; 42, 283–305; 43, 358–84; 44, 336–61 (1924–7).

— (ed.), *The compossicion booke of Connought* (Dublin, 1936).

— (ed. and trans.), *Annála Connacht: the annals of Connacht (A.D. 1224–1544)* (Dublin, 1944).

Frye, Northrop, *The anatomy of criticism* (Princeton, 1957).

—, *The secular scripture. A study of the structure of romance* (Harvard, 1976).

Gael Linn, *Máirtín Ó Direáin: dánta á léamh ag an bhfile*, CD (Dublin, 2010).

Gamble, John, *Society and manners in early nineteenth-century Ireland*, edited with an Introduction by Breandán Mac Suibhne (Dublin, 2011).

Genette, Gérard, *Narrative discourse: an essay in method*, trans. Jane E. Levin (Ithaca, 1980).

Gilbert, J.T., *Facsimiles of national manuscripts of Ireland*, iii (London, 1879).

Gillies, William, 'Arthur in Gaelic tradition. Part II: romances and lore', *Cambrian Medieval Celtic Studies*, 3 (Summer, 1982), 41–75.

—, 'Heroes and ancestors' in B. Almqvist et al. (eds), *The heroic process* (1987), pp 57–73.

Ginzberg, Louis, *The legends of the Jews*, trans. Henrietta Szold, 7 vols (Philadelphia, 1909).

Glassie, Henry, *Passing the time in Ballymenone: culture and history of an Ulster community* (Blomington, IN, 1995).

Godley, A.D. (ed. and trans.), *Herodotus*, Loeb Classical Library, 4 vols (New York, 1927–41).

Gray, Elizabeth (ed. and trans), *Cath Maige Tuired: the second battle of Mag Tuired*, Irish Texts Society 52 (London, 1983).

Greene, David (ed.), *Duanaire Mhéig Uidhir* (Dublin, 1972).

Griffith, M.C. (ed.), *Calendar of Irish patent rolls of James I* (Dublin, 1965).

Gulick, Charles Burton (ed. and trans.), *Athenaeus: the deipnosophists*, Loeb Classical Library, 7 vols (Cambridge MA, 1967).

Gwynn, Aubrey, *The twelfth-century reform* (Dublin, 1968).

— and R. Neville Handcock, *Medieval religious houses: Ireland* (London, 1970).

Gwynn, Edward J. (ed. and trans.), 'The burning of Finn's house', *Ériu*, 1 (1904), 13–37 (with an addendum by J.H. Lloyd).

— (ed. and trans.), *The metrical dindshenchas*, 5 vols, Todd Lecture Series 7–12 (Dublin, 1906–35; repr. 1991).

Haines, John, *Satire in the songs of Renart le Nouvel* (Paris, 2011).

Harper, Sally, 'So how many Irishmen went to Glen Achlach? Early accounts of the formation of *Cerdd Dafod*', *Cambrian Medieval Celtic Studies*, 42 (Winter, 2001), 1–25.

Harris, Joseph (ed.), *The ballad and oral literature* (Harvard, 1991).

Hatto, Arthur T. (trans.), *Gottfried von Strassburg: Tristan* (London, 1967).

Hazard, Benjamin and Kenneth W. Nicholls, *Annales Dominicani de Roscoman* (www.ucc.ie/celt/published/L100015A).

Heaney, Seamus, *The redress of poetry* (Oxford, 1995).

Henderson, George, *Survivals in belief among the Celts* (Glasgow, 1911).

Henken, Elissa R., '"Then was spoken the proverb ...": the proverb legend in medieval Celtic literature' in J.F. Eska (ed.), *Narrative in Celtic tradition* (2011), pp 100–16.

Hennessy, William M. (ed. and trans.), *Chronicum Scotorum. A chronicle of Irish affairs from the earliest times to A.D. 1135*, Rolls Series (London, 1866).

— (ed. and trans.), *Annals of Loch Cé. A chronicle of Irish affairs from A.D. 1014 to A.D. 1590*, 2 vols, Rolls Series (London, 1871; repr. Caisleán an Bhúrcaigh, 2000).

— and Bartholomew Mac Carthy (ed. and trans.), *Annála Uladh: annals of Ulster*, 4 vols (Dublin, 1887–1901; facs. repr. with a new Introduction by Nollaig Ó Muraíle, Dublin, 1998).

Herbert, Máire, '*Fled Dúin na nGéd*: a reappraisal', *Cambridge Medieval Celtic Studies*, 18 (1989), 75–87.

Herman, David (ed.), *The Cambridge companion to narrative* (Cambridge, 2007).

Hogan, Edmund, *Onomasticon Goedelicum locorum et tribuum Hiberniae et Scotiae: an index with identifications, to the Gaelic names of places and tribes* (Dublin, 1910; repr. 1993).

Hollo, Kaarina, 'Allegoresis and literary creativity in eighth-century Ireland: the case of *Echtrae Chonnlai*' in J.F. Eska (ed.), *Narrative in Celtic tradition* (2011), pp 117–28.

Hood, A.B.E. (ed. and trans.), *St Patrick: his writings and Muirchu's Life*, Arthurian Period Sources 9 (London, 1978).

Hudson, Benjamin, 'The practical hero' in M. Richter and J.-M. Picard (eds), *Ogma* (2002), pp 151–64.

Hühn, Peter et al. (eds), *The living handbook of narratology* (Hamburg): www.lhn.uni-hamburg.de).

Hyde, Douglas, 'The Reeves manuscript of the *Agallamh na senorach*', *Révue Celtique*, 38 (1921), 289–95.

— [An Craoibhín] (ed. and trans.), 'An Agallamh bheag', *Lia Fáil*, 1 (1927), 79–107.

The Irish fiants of the Tudor sovereigns during the reigns of Henry VIII, Edward VI, Philp and Mary, and Elizabeth I, with a new Introduction by Kenneth Nicholls and preface by Tomás G. Ó Canann, 4 vols (Dublin, 1875–90; repr. 1994).

Iser, Wolfang, *The fictive and the imaginary: charting literary anthropology* (Baltimore and London, 1993).

Jackson, Kenneth, 'Dhá scéal ón mBlascaod', *Béaloideas* 4:3 (Meitheamh, 1934), 301–11.

Johnston, Elva, 'The salvation of the individual and the salvation of society' in Joseph Falaky Nagy (ed.), *The individual in Celtic literatures: CSANA Yearbook, 1* (Dublin, 2001), pp 109–25.

Joyce, Patrick W., *Irish names of place*, vol. 1 (Dublin, 1869).

Kelleher, John V., *Too small for stovewood, too big for kindling* (Dublin, 1979).

Kelly, Fergus, *A guide to early Irish law* (Dublin, 1988).

Kenney, James F., *The sources for the early history of Ireland: ecclesiastical* (New York, 1929).

Kinoshita, Sharon, and Peggy McCracken, *Marie de France, a critical companion* (Cambridge, 2012).

Kinsella, Thomas (trans.), *The Tain* (Oxford, 1970).

—, 'Foreword to illustrated guide to placenames of the *Táin*', *Ireland of the Welcomes*, 24:6 (Nov.–Dec. 1975), 20.

—, *The new Oxford book of Irish verse* (Oxford, 1986).

Klausner, David (ed.), *Wales*, Records of Early English Drama (London and Toronto, 2005).

Knott, Eleanor, *An introduction to Irish syllabic poetry of the period 1200–1600* (Cork, 1928).

— (ed.), *Togail bruidne Da Derga* (Dublin, 1936; repr. 1975).

— and Gerard Murphy, *Early Irish literature* (London, 1966).

Knox, H.T., 'Occupation of the county of Galway by the Anglo-Normans after 1237', *Journal of the Royal Society of Antiquaries of Ireland*, 31 (1901), 365–70.

Kühns, Julia S., 'An edition and translation of the *Agallamh bheag* in the Book of Lismore', MPhil. thesis (University of Glasgow, 2006).

—, 'Some observations on the *Acallam bec*' in S.J. Arbuthnot and G. Parsons (eds), *The Gaelic Finn tradition* (2012), pp 122–38.

Lehmann, Ruth P.M., *Early Irish verse* (Texas, 1982).

Lloyd, J.H., '*Formaoil na bhfiann*: a country of the Clann Morna', *Journal of the Galway Archaeological and Historical Society*, 9 (1915–6), 112–4.

Mac Airt, Seán (ed. and trans.), *The annals of Inisfallen (MS Rawlinson B. 503)* (Dublin, 1951).

— and Gearóid Mac Niocaill (ed. and trans.), *The annals of Ulster (to A.D. 1131)* (Dublin, 1983).

Macalister, R.A.S., *The Book of Mac Carthaigh Riabhach otherwise The Book of Lismore*, Facsimiles in collotype of Irish manuscripts, v (Dublin, 1950)

— (ed. and trans.), *Lebor gabála Érenn: the book of the taking of Ireland*, v (Dublin, 1956).

MacBain, Alexander and John Kennedy (eds), *Reliquiae Celticae: texts, papers and studies in Gaelic literature and philosophy left by the late Rev Alexander Cameron Ll.D.*, 2 vols (Inverness, 1892–4).

Mac Cana, Proinsias, 'Aspects of the theme of king and goddess in Irish literature', *Études Celtiques*, 7 (1955–6), part i, 76–114; part ii, 356–413; *Études Celtiques*, 8 (1958–9), part iii, 59–65.

—, 'The influence of the Vikings on Celtic literature' in Brian Ó Cuív (ed.), *The impact of the Scandinavian invasions on the Celtic-speaking peoples c.800–1100 A.D.* (Dublin, 1962), pp 78–118.

—, *Celtic mythology* (London, 1968).

—, *The learned tales of medieval Ireland* (Dublin, 1980).

—, '*Fianaigecht* in the pre-Norman period' in B. Almqvist et al. (eds), *The heroic process* (1987), pp 75–99.

—, 'Placenames and mythology in Irish tradition: places, pilgrimages and things' in Gordon W. MacLennan (ed.), *Proceedings of the First North American Congress of Celtic Studies held at Ottawa from 26th–30th March, 1986* (Ottawa, 1988), pp 319–41.

—, 'Notes on the legend of Louernios' in M. Richter and J.-M. Picard (eds), *Ogma* (2002), pp 138–44.

—, 'The *ingen moel*', *Ériu*, 52 (2002), 217–27.

—, *The cult of the sacred centre: essays on Celtic ideology* (Dublin, 2011).

McCann, F. (Proinsias Mac Cana), 'Da in placenames', *Bulletin of the Ulster Placename Society*, 1, 1st series (1952–3), 14–15, 72.

McCone, Kim, 'Dubthach maccu Lugair and a matter of life and death in the pseudo-historical prologue to the *Senchas már*', *Peritia*, 5 (1986), 1–35.

—, 'Werewolves, cyclopes, *díberga* and *fianna*: juvenile delinquency in early Ireland', *Cambridge Medieval Celtic Studies*, 12 (1986), 1–22.

—, *Pagan past and Christian present in early Irish literature* (Maynooth, 1990).

— (ed. and trans.), *Echtrae Chonnlai and the beginnings of vernacular narrative writing in Ireland* (Maynooth, 2000).

—, 'The Celtic and Indo-European origins of the *fian*' in S.J. Arbuthnot and G. Parsons (eds), *The Gaelic Finn tradition* (2012), pp 14–30.

—, Damian McManus, Cathal Ó Háinle, Nicholas Williams and Liam Breatnach (eds), *Stair na Gaeilge in ómós do Pádraig Ó Fiannachta* (Maigh Nuad, 1994).

MacCulloch, Diarmaid, *A history of Christianity* (London, 2010).

McKenna, Lambert (ed.), *Dioghluim dána* (Dublin, 1938).

— (ed.), *The Book of Magauran* (Dublin, 1947).

Mac Mathúna, Séamus (ed. and trans.), *Immram Brain: Bran's journey to the Land of the Women* (Tübingen, 1985).

MacNeill, Eoin and Gerard Murphy (ed. and trans.), *Duanaire Finn: the book of the lays of Fionn*, 3 vols, Irish Texts Society 7, 28, 43 (London 1908–53).

MacNeill, Máire. *The festival of Lughnasa: a study of the survival of the Celtic festival of the beginning of the harvest* (Oxford, 1962).

Macpherson, James, *The poems of Ossian* (Boston, 1863).

MacQuarrie, Charles W., *The biography of the Irish God of the Sea from The Voyage of Bran (700 A.D.) to Finnegans Wake (1939)* (Lewiston, 2004).

McQuillan, Peter, 'Finn, Fothad and *fian*: some early associations', *Proceedings of the Harvard Celtic Colloquium*, 8 (1988), 1–10.

McTurk, Rory, '*Acallam na senórach* and Snorri Sturluson's *Edda*' in Séamas Ó Catháin (ed.), *Northern lights: following folklore in north-western Europe. Aistí in adhnó do Bho Almqvist: essays in honour of Bo Almqvist* (Dublin, 2001), pp 178–89.

Mannhardt, William., 'Request' in Alan Dundes (ed.), *International folkloristics* (New York, 1999), pp 15–25.

Margolin, Uri, 'Narrator' in P. Hühn et al. (eds), *The living handbook of narratology*.

Mathis, Kate Louise, 'The evolution of Deirdriu in the Ulster Cycle', PhD (University of Edinburgh, 2010).

Meade, Michael, 'Foreword to the new edition' in Mircea Eliade, *Rites and symbols of initiation: the mysteries of birth and rebirth* (Putnam, 1994).

Meek, Donald E., 'The Gaelic ballads of Scotland: creativity and adaptation' in Howard Gaskill (ed.), *Ossian revisited* (Edinburgh, 1992), pp 19–48.

—, 'Placenames and literature: evidence from the Gaelic ballads' in Simon Taylor (ed.), *The uses of placenames* (Edinburgh, 1998), pp 147–68.

—, '*Duanaire Finn* and Gaelic Scotland' in J. Carey (ed.), *Duanaire Finn: reassessments* (2003), pp 19–38.

Meyer, Kuno (ed.), 'Macgnimartha Find', *Révue Celtique*, 5 (1881–3), 197–204.

— (ed. and trans.), *The cath Finntrága or battle of Ventry edited from MS. Rawl. B. 487, in the Bodleian library*, Anecdota Oxoniensa, Mediaeval and Modern Series, 1.4 (Oxford, 1885).

— (ed. and trans.), *The vision of Mac Conglinne: a Middle Irish wonder tale* (London, 1892).

— (ed.), 'Mitteilungen aus irischen Handschriften: *Tochmarc Emire la Coinculaind*', *Zeitschrift für celtische Philologie*, 3 (1901), 226–63.

— (trans.), 'The boyish exploits of Finn', *Ériu*, 1 (1904), 180–90.

— (ed. and trans.), *The death tales of the Ulster heroes*, Todd Lecture Series 14 (Dublin, 1906).

— (ed. and trans.), *The triads of Ireland*, Todd Lecture Series 13 (Dublin, 1906).

—, 'Die Wiederauffindung der Táin bó Cúalnge', *Archiv für celtische Lexikographie*, 3 (1907), 2–7.

— (ed.), 'Stories from the Edinburgh MS. XXVI (Kilbride Collection No 22)' in O.J. Bergin, R.I. Best, Kuno Meyer and J.G. O'Keeffe (eds), *Anecdota from Irish manuscripts*, iii (1910), pp 7–10.

—, 'Mitteilungen aus irischen Handschriften', *Zeitschrift für celtische Philologie*, 7 (1910), 305–7.

—, *Fianaigecht: being a collection of hitherto inedited Irish poems and tales relating to Finn and his fiana*, Todd Lecture Series 14 (Dublin, 1910).

— (ed.), 'Sanas Cormaic: an Old-Irish glossary' in O.J. Bergin, R.I. Best, Kuno Meyer and J.G. O'Keeffe (eds), *Anecdota from Irish manuscripts*, iv (Halle/Dublin, 1912).

— (ed.), 'Mitteilungen aus irischen Handschriften', *Zeitschrift für celtische Philologie*, 8 (1912), 102–20, 195–232, 559–65.

— [Meyer, Kuno], 'Erschienene Schriften', *Zeitschrift für celtische Philologie*, 8 (1912), 599.

— (ed.), 'Ferchuitred Medba' in O.J. Bergin, R.I. Best, Kuno Meyer and J.G. O'Keeffe (eds), *Anecdota from Irish manuscripts*, v (Dublin, 1913), pp 17–22.

Miller, Frank J. (ed. and trans.), *Ovid: metamorphoses*, Loeb Classical Library, 2 vols (3rd ed., Cambridge, MA, 1977).

Morley, Vincent, *Ó Chéitinn go Raiftearaí: mar a cumadh stair na hÉireann* (Baile Átha Cliath, 2011).

Morris, Henry, '"Da" in Irish placenames', *Journal of the County Louth Archaeological Society*, 6 (1925–8), 131–4.

Morris, Sarah P., *Daidalos and the origins of Greek art* (Princeton, 1992).

Mulchrone, Kathleen (ed.), *Bethu Phátraic. The tripartite Life of Patrick* (Dublin and London, 1939).

Müller, Sylvie, 'Samhain: the dead centre of time', *Sinsear*, 5 (1988), 88–99.

Murphy, Gerard, *Saga and myth in ancient Ireland* (Dublin, 1955).

—, *The Ossianic lore and romantic tales of medieval Ireland: fianaíocht and rómánsaíocht* (Dublin, 1955; revised ed. Cork, 1971).

—, *Early Irish lyrics* (Oxford, 1956).

—, 'Irish storytelling after the coming of the Normans' in Brian Ó Cuív (ed.), *Seven centuries of Irish learning: 1000–1700* (Dublin, 1961), pp 72–86.

Murray, Kevin, 'The finding of the *Táin*', *Cambrian Medieval Celtic Studies*, 41 (Summer, 2001), 17–23.

—, 'Interpreting the evidence: problems with dating the early *fianaigecht* corpus' in S.J. Arbuthnot and G. Parsons (eds), *The Gaelic Finn tradition* (2012), pp 31–49.

Nagy, Joseph Falaky, *The wisdom of the outlaw: the boyhood deeds of Finn in Gaelic narrative tradition* (Berkeley/Los Angeles/London, 1985)

—, 'Compositional concerns in the *Acallam na senórach*' in D. Ó Corráin et al. (eds), *Sages, saints and storytellers* (1989), pp 149–58.

—, *Conversing with angels and ancients: literary myths of medieval Ireland* (Cornell, 1997).

—, *The poetics of absence in Celtic tradition*, Sir Thomas Parry-Williams Memorial Lecture, 2002 (Aberystwyth, 2003).

—, 'Life in the fast lane: the *Acallam na senórach*' in Helen Fulton (ed.), *Medieval Celtic literature and society* (Dublin, 2005), pp 117–31.

—, *Mercantile myth in medieval Celtic traditions*, H.M. Chadwick Memorial Lectures 20 (Cambridge, 2011).

—, 'The "Celtic love triangle" revisited', *Ériu* (forthcoming).

Newton, Michael, 'Celtic cousins or white settlers? Scottish Highlanders and first nations' in Kenneth E. Nilsen (ed.), *Rannsachadh na Gàidhlig*, 5 (Novia Scotia, 2008), pp 221–37.

Nic Cárthaigh, Emma, 'Surviving the flood: revenants and antediluvian lore in medieval Irish texts' in Kathleen Cawsey and Jason Harris (eds), *Transmission and transformation in the Middle Ages: texts and contexts* (Dublin, 2007), pp 40–64.

Ní Dheá, Eilís, 'Scríobhaithe lámhscríbhinní Gaeilge i gContae an Chláir 1700–1900' in M. Lynch and P. Nugent (eds), *Clare history and society: interdiscipilinary essays on the history of an Irish county* (Dublin, 2008), pp 139–55.

Ní Mhaonaigh, Máire, 'Pagans and holy men: literary manifestations of twelfth-century reform' in Damian Bracken and Dagmar Ó Riain Raedel (eds), *Ireland and Europe in the twelfth century: reform and renewal* (Dublin, 2006), pp 143–61.

Ní Mhurchú, Síle, '*Agallamh Oisín agus Phádraig*: composition and transmission' in S.J. Arbuthnot and G. Parsons (eds), *The Gaelic Finn tradition* (2012), pp 195–208.

Ní Shéaghdha, Nessa (ed.), *Agallamh na seanórach*, 3 vols, Leabhair ó Láimhsgríbhnibh 7, 10, 15 (Baile Átha Cliath, 1942–5).

— (ed. and trans.), *Tóruigheacht Dhiarmada agus Ghráinne: the pursuit of Diarmaid and Gráinne*, Irish Texts Society, 48 (Dublin, 1967).

— and Pádraig Ó Macháin, *Catalogue of Irish manuscripts in the National Library of Ireland*, 13 fascicles published (Dublin, 1967–).

Ní Úrdail, Meidhbhín, *The scribe in eighteenth- and nineteenth-century Ireland: motivations and milieu* (Münster, 2000).

Nikulin, Dmitri, *On dialogue* (Lanham/Oxford, 2006).

Nuner, Robert D., 'The verbal system of the *Agallamh na senórach*', *Zeitschrift für celtische Philologie*, 27 (1958–59), 230–310.

Nutt, Alfred, *Ossian and Ossianic literature*, 2nd edition (London, 1910).

Ó Briain, Máirtín, 'Some material on Oisín in the Land of Youth' in D. Ó Corráin et al. (eds), *Sages, saints and storytellers* (1989), pp 181–99.

—, 'Snáithín san uisge: loisc agus léig a luaigh le sruth' in Máirtín Ó Briain agus Pádraig Ó Héalaí (eds), *Téada dúchais: aistí in ómós don Ollamh Breandán Ó Madagáin* (Indreabhán, 2002), pp 245–72.

O'Brien, Michael A. (ed.), *Corpus genealogiarium Hiberniae* (Dublin, 1962).

Ó Cadhla, Stiofán, *The holy well tradition* (Dublin, 2002).

—, 'Scribes and storytellers: the ethnographic imagination in nineteenth-century Ireland' in Julia M. Wright (ed.), *A companion to Irish literature*, vol. 1 (Oxford, 2010), pp 395–410.

—, 'Seanchas na fiosrachta agus léann an dúchais' in Stiofán Ó Cadhla and Diarmuid Ó Giolláin (eds), *Léann an dúchais: aistí in ómós do Ghearóid Ó Crualaoich* (Cork, 2012), pp 79–97.

Ó Cathasaigh, Tomás, 'The rhetoric of *Fingal Rónáin*', *Celtica*, 17 (1985), 123–44.

—, 'The rhetoric of *Scéla Cano meic Gartnáin*' in D. Ó Corráin et al. (eds), *Sages, saints and storytellers* (1989), pp 233–50.

—, 'Three notes on *Cath Maige Tuired*', *Ériu*, 40 (1989), 61–8.

Ó Ceannabháin, Peadar, *Éamon a Búrc: scéalta* (Dublin, 1983).

Ó Coileáin, Seán, Review of *The making of Homeric verse: the collected papers of Milman Parry*, ed. Adam Parry, *Studia Hibernica*, 13 (1973), 171–8.

—, 'The structure of a literary cycle', *Ériu*, 25 (1974), 88–125.

—, 'The making of *Tromdám Guaire*', *Ériu*, 28 (1977), 32–70.

—, 'Oral or literary? Some strands of the argument', *Studia Hibernica*, 17–18 (1977–8), 7–35.

—, 'Some problems of story and history', *Ériu*, 32 (1981), 115–36.

—, 'Irish literature' in Joseph R. Strayer (ed.), *Dictionary of the Middle Ages*, vol. 6 (New York, 1985), pp 521–33.

—, 'The Irish lament: an oral genre', *Studia Hibernica*, 24 (1988), 97–117.

—, 'Place and placename in *fianaigheacht*', *Studia Hibernica*, 27 (1993), 45–60 (republished in this volume).

—, 'Preface' in Maurice Harmon, *The dialogue of the ancients of Ireland: a new translation of Acallam na senórach* (Dublin, 2009), pp ix–x (reprint of idem, 'Preface' in Maurice Harmon (trans.), *The colloquy of the old men* (Dublin, 2001), pp vii–ix).

— (ed.), *An tOileánach: Tomás Ó Criomhthain* (Dublin, 2002).

—, 'Society and scholarship: Irish in the modern world' in Máire Herbert and Kevin Murray (eds), *Retrospect and prospect in Celtic Studies: Proceedings of the Eleventh International Congress of Celtic Studies* (Dublin, 2003), pp 45–58.

—, 'The setting of *Géisid cúan*' in John Carey, Máire Herbert and Kevin Murray (eds), *Cín Chille Cúile: texts, saints and places. Essays in honour of Pádraig Ó Riain* (Aberystwyth, 2004), pp 234–48 (reprinted in this volume).

Ó Conchúir, Breandán, *Scríobhaithe Chorcaí, 1700–1850* (Baile Átha Cliath, 1982).

—, 'Eoin Baiste Mac Sleighne, Easpag (1693–1712), agus pátrún ar an léann Gaelach' in Pádraig de Brún, Seán Ó Coileáin and Pádraig Ó Riain (eds), *Folia gadelica: essays presented by former students to R.A. Breatnach* (Cork, 1983), pp 88–94.

O'Connor, Ralph, 'Searching for the moral in *Bruiden Meic Da Réo*', *Ériu*, 56 (2006), 117–43.

Ó Corráin, Donnchadh, 'Nationality and kingship in pre-Norman Ireland' in T.W. Moody (ed.), *Nationality and the pursuit of national independence* (Belfast, 1978), pp 1–35.

—, 'Legend as critic' in Tom Dunne and Charles Doherty (eds), *The writer as witness: literature as historical evidence* (Cork, 1987), pp 23–38.

—, Liam Breatnach and Kim McCone (eds), *Sages, saints and storytellers: Celtic studies in honour of Professor James Carney* (Maynooth, 1989).

Ó Crualaoich, Gearóid, 'An ceol sí agus friotal na laoch', *Comhar* (Bealtaine 1992), 94–9.

—, 'Irish storytelling' in Neil Buttimer, Colin Rynne and Helen Guerin (eds), *The heritage of Ireland* (Cork, 2000), pp 171–7.

—, *The book of the cailleach* (Cork, 2003).

Ó Cuív, Brian, 'A poem for Fínghin Mac Carthaigh Riabhach', *Celtica*, 15 (1983), 96–110.

—, 'Observations on the Book of Lismore', *Proceedings of the Royal Irish Academy*, 83C (1983), 269–92.

— (ed.), 'Agallamh Fhinn agus Ailbhe', *Celtica*, 18 (1986), 111–15.

—, 'The Irish marginalia in Codex Palatino-Vaticanus No. 830', *Éigse*, 24 (1990), 45–67.

O'Curry, Eugene, *Lectures on the manuscript materials of ancient Irish history* (Dublin, 1861).

— (ed. and trans.), 'The fate of the children of Lir', *Atlantis*, 4 (1863), 113–57.

O Daly, Máirín, 'The metrical dindshenchas' in James Carney (ed.), *Early Irish poetry* (Cork, 1965), pp 59–72.

—, (ed. and trans.), *Cath Maige Mucrama: the battle of Mag Mucrama*, Irish Texts Society 50 (Dublin, 1975).

Ó Direáin, Máirtín, *Dánta, 1939–1979* (Dublin, 1980).

O'Donoghue, Tadhg (ed. and trans.), 'Cert cech ríg co réil' in Osborn Bergin and Carl Marstrander (eds), *Miscellany presented to Kuno Meyer* (Halle, 1912), pp 258–77.

— (ed. and trans.), 'Advice to a prince', *Ériu*, 9 (1921–3), 43–54.

O'Donovan, John (ed. and trans.), *Annála ríoghachta Éireann: annals of the kingdom of Ireland by the Four Masters*, 7 vols (Dublin, 1848–51; 2nd ed. 1856; facs. repr. with Introduction and Appendix by K.W. Nicholls, Dublin, 1990).

— (ed. and trans.), 'Mac-gnimartha Finn mac Cumaill: the boyish exploits of Finn mac Cumhaill', *Transactions of the Ossianic Society for the year 1856*, vol. 4 (1859), 281–304.

Ó Drisceoil, Proinsias, *Seán Ó Dálaigh: éigse agus iomarbhá* (Cork, 2007).

Ó Duilearga, Séamas, 'Scéalta sidhe', *Béaloideas*, 1, iv (June, 1927), 95–6.

— (ed.), *Leabhar Sheáin Í Chonaill* (Dublin, 1964).

Ó Dúnlainge, Micheál (ed.), 'Cath Mhaighe Mochruimhe', *Irisleabhar na Gaedhilge*, 17 §25 (Meán Fómhair 1907) – 18 §4 (Aibreán 1908).

O'Faoláin, Seán, *The silver branch* (London, 1938).

Ó Fiannachta, Pádraig, *Lámhscríbhinní Gaeilge Choláiste Phádraig, Má Nuad: clár II* (Maigh Nuad, 1965), pp 41–2.

—, 'The development of the debate between Pádraig and Oisín' in B. Almqvist et al. (eds), *The heroic process* (1987), pp 183–205.

— (ed.), *Léachtaí Cholm Cille*, 25: *An fhiannaíocht* (Má Nuad, 1995).

Ó Flannghaile, Tomás (ed. and trans.), *Laoi Oisín ar Thír na n-Óg* (Dublin, [1910]).

O'Grady, Standish Hayes (ed. and trans.), 'Tóruigheacht Dhiarmuda agus Ghráinne', *Transactions of the Ossianic Society for the year 1855*, vol. 3 (Dublin, 1857), pp 40–211.

— (ed. and trans), *Silva gadelica (I–XXXI): a collection of tales in Irish with extracts illustrating persons and places*, 2 vols (London, 1892).

— and Robin Flower, *Catalogue of Irish manuscripts in the British Library (formerly British Museum)*, 2 vols (London, 1926; repr. Dublin, 1992).

Ó Héalaí, Pádraig, and Lochlainn Ó Tuairisc (eds), *Tobar an dúchais: béaloideas as Conamara agus Corca Dhuibhne* (An Daingean, 2007).

Ó hÓgáin, Dáithí, 'Magic attributes of the hero' in B. Almqvist et al. (eds), *The heroic process* (1987), pp 207–42.

—, *Fionn mac Cumhaill: images of the Gaelic hero* (Dublin, 1988).

—, *The lore of Ireland: an encyclopedia of myth, legend and romance* (Cork, 2006).

Ó hUiginn, Ruairí, 'Rúraíocht agus rómánsaíocht: ceisteanna faoi fhorás an traid-isiúin', *Éigse*, 32 (2000), 77–87.

—, 'Onomastic formulae in Irish' in Micheál Ó Flaithearta (ed.), *Proceedings of the Seventh Symposium of Societas Celtologica Nordica* (Uppsala, 2007), pp 53–70.

Olden, Thomas, 'Remarks supplementary to Dr. Joyce's paper on the occurrence of the number *two* in Irish proper names', *Proceedings of the Royal Irish Academy*, 4, 3rd series (1898), 636–43.

O'Leary, Philip, 'Verbal deceit in the Ulster Cycle', *Éigse*, 21 (1985), 16–26.

O'Looney, Brian (ed. and trans.), 'Tír na n-Óg: the Land of Youth', *Transactions of the Ossianic Society*, 4 (1859), 227–79.

Ó Macháin, Pádraig, '"A llebraib imdaib": cleachtadh agus pátrúnacht an léinn, agus déanamh na lámhscríbhinní' in Ruairí Ó hUiginn (ed.), *Léachtaí Cholm Cille*, 34: *Oidhreacht na lámhscríbhinní* (Maigh Nuad, 2004), pp 148–78.

—, 'Two documents relating to Ó Conchubhair Donn', *Ériu*, 57 (2007), 113–9.

Ó Máille, Tomás, *Seanfhocla Chonnacht*, 2 vols (1948–52); 2nd edition, ed. D. Uí Bhraonáin (Dublin, 2010).

O'Meara, John J. (ed.), 'Giraldus Cambrensis in Topographia Hibernie. Text of the first recension', *Proceedings of the Royal Irish Academy*, 52C (1948–50), 113–78.

— (trans.), *The topography of Ireland by Giraldus Cambrensis* (Dublin, 1949).

—, *The first version of the topography of Ireland by Giraldus Cambrensis* (Dundalk, 1951).

Ó Muraíle, Nollaig, 'Agallamh na seanórach' in Pádraig Ó Fiannachta (ed.), *An fhiannaíocht, Léachtaí Cholm Cille*, 25 (Má Nuad, 1995), pp 96–127.

Ó Murchadha, Diarmuid (ed. and trans.), *Lige Guill: the grave of Goll. A Fenian poem from the Book of Leinster*, Irish Texts Society 62 (London, 2009).

O'Neill, Joseph (ed. and trans.), 'Cath Boinde', *Ériu*, 2 (1905), 173–85.

Ong, Walter, *Orality and literacy: the technologizing of the word* (London and New York, 1982).

O'Rahilly, Cecile (ed.), *Five seventeenth-century political poems* (Dublin, 1952).

— (ed.), *Cath Finntrágha*, Mediaeval and Modern Irish Series 20 (Dublin, 1962).

O'Rahilly, Thomas F. (ed.), *Measgra dánta* (Cork, 1927).

—, 'Notes on Irish placenames', *Hermathena*, 48 (1933), 196–220.

—, *Early Irish history and mythology* (Dublin, 1946).

— et al. (eds), *Catalogue of Irish manuscripts in the Royal Irish Academy*, 28 fascicles (Dublin, 1926–70).

Ó Riain, Pádraig, 'The materials and provenance of "Buile Shuibhne"', *Éigse*, 15, iii (1974), 173–88.

— (ed.), *Corpus genealogiarum sanctorum Hiberniae* (Dublin, 1986).

—, *A dictionary of Irish saints* (Dublin, 2011).

—, Diarmaid Ó Murchadha, and Kevin Murray, *Historical dictionary of Gaelic place-names: Foclóir stairiúil áitainmneacha na Gaeilge*, Irish Texts Society, 4 fascicles (London, 2003–).

O'Riordan, Michelle, *Irish bardic poetry and rhetorical reality* (Cork, 2007).

Ó Siochfhradha, Pádraig ['An Seabhac'], *Seanfhocail na Muimhneach* (Baile Átha Cliath, 1926).

—, *Tríocha-céad Chorca Dhuibhne* (Baile Átha Cliath, 1939).

— (ed.), *Laoithe na féinne* (Baile Átha Cliath, 1941).

Oskamp, H.P.A. (ed. and trans), *The voyage of Máel Dúin* (Groningen, 1970).

Ó Súilleabháin, Seán, *A handbook of Irish folklore* (Dublin, 1942).

Padel, Oliver, *Arthur in medieval Welsh literature* (Cardiff, 2000).

Parsons, Geraldine, 'A reading of *Acallam na senórach* as a literary text', PhD (Cambridge, 2007).

—, 'The structure of *Acallam na senórach*', *Cambrian Medieval Celtic Studies*, 55 (Summer, 2008), 11–39.

—, 'Whitley Stokes, Standish Hayes O'Grady and *Acallam na senórach*' in Elizabeth Boyle and Paul Russell (eds), *The tripartite life of Whitley Stokes (1830–1909)* (Dublin, 2011), pp 185–95.

—, 'Breaking the cycle? Accounts of the death of Finn' in S.J. Arbuthnot and G. Parsons (eds), *The Gaelic Finn tradition* (2012), pp 81–96.

Pennington, Walter (trans.), 'The little colloquy', *Philological Quarterly*, 9.2 (1930), 97–110.

Petty, William, *Hiberniae delineatio: atlas of Ireland* (London, 1685; repr. Newcastle upon Tyne, 1968).

Plummer, Charles (ed.), *Vitae sanctorum Hiberniae*, 2 vols (Oxford, 1910).

— (ed. and trans.), *Bethada naem nÉrenn: Lives of Irish saints*, 2 vols (Oxford, 1922).

Pokorny, Julius, 'Da- in irischen Ortsnamen', *Zeitschrift für celtische Philologie*, 14 (1923), 270–1.

Poppe, Erich, '*Imtheachta Aeniasa*: Virgil's *Aeneid* in medieval Ireland', *Classics Ireland*, 11 (2004), 74–94.

—, 'Narrative structure of medieval Irish adaptations: the case of *Guy* and *Beues*' in Helen Fulton (ed.), *Medieval Celtic literature and society* (Dublin, 2005), pp 205–29.

—, '*Stair Ercuil ocus a bás*: rewriting Hercules in Ireland' in Kevin Murray (ed.), *Translations from classical literature: Imtheachta Æniasa and Stair Ercuil ocus a bás*, Irish Texts Society, Subsidiary Series, 17 (London, 2006), pp 37–68.

Powell, Roger, 'Further notes on Lebor na hUidre', *Ériu*, 21 (1969), 99–102.

Power, Maura, 'Cnucha cnoc os cionn Life', *Zeitschrift für celtische Philologie*, 11 (1916), 39–55.

Power, P. Canon, *Log-ainmneacha na nDéise: the placenames of Decies* (2nd ed.; Cork 1952).

Quin, Ernest Gordon (general editor), *Dictionary of the Irish language based mainly on Old and Middle Irish materials* (Dublin, 1913–76; compact edition 1983); available online at http://edil.qub.ac.uk

Rees, Alwyn and Brinley Rees, *Celtic heritage: ancient tradition in Ireland and Wales* (London, 1961).

Reeves, William (ed. and trans.), *The Life of St Columba founder of Hy* (Dublin, 1857).

Richter, Michael and Jean-Michel Picard (eds), *Ogma: essays in Celtic studies presented to Professor Próinséas Ní Chatháin* (Dublin, 2002).

Roberts, Brynley (ed.), *Breudwyt Macsen Wledic* (Dublin, 2005).

Robinson, Tim, *Connemara, a little Gaelic kingdom* (Dublin, 2011).

Roe, Harry, '*Acallamh na senórach*: the confluence of lay and clerical oral traditions' in Cyril J. Byrne, Margaret Harry and Pádraig Ó Siadhail (eds), *Celtic languages and Celtic peoples: Proceedings of the Second North American Congress of Celtic Studies* (Halifax, Nova Scotia, 1992), pp 331–46.

Roider, Ulrike (ed. and trans.), *De chophur in da muccida*, Innsbrucker Beiträge zur Sprachwissenschaft 28 (Innsbruck, 1979).

Ross, Anne, 'Esus et les trois «Grues»', *Études Celtiques*, 9 (1960), 405–38.

Ross, Neil (ed. and trans.), *Heroic poetry from the Book of the Dean of Lismore*, Scottish Gaelic Texts Society 3 (Edinburgh, 1939).

Rychner, Jean (ed.), *Les lais de Marie de France* (Paris,1969).

Schrempp, Gregory, *The ancient mythology of modern science* (McGill-Queens UP, 2002).

Scowcroft, R. Mark, '*Leabhar gabhála* part I: the growth of the text', *Ériu*, 38 (1987), 79–142.

—, '*Leabhar gabhála* part II: the growth of the tradition', *Ériu*, 39 (1988), 1–66.

Seabhac, an: *see* Ó Siochfhradha, Pádraig.

Sharpe, Richard (trans.), *Adomnán of Iona: Life of St Columba* (London 1995).

Sheehan, John, 'Early Viking Age silver hoards from Ireland and their Scandinavian elements' in Howard B. Clarke, Máire Ní Mhaonaigh and Raghnall Ó Floinn (eds), *Ireland and Scandinavia in the early Viking Age* (Dublin, 1998), pp 166–202.

Sherzer, Joel, *Verbal art in San Blas* (Cambridge, 1991).

Shields, Hugh, *Narrative singing in Ireland: lays, ballads, come-all-yes and other songs* (Dublin, 1993).

Simington, Robert C. (ed.), *Books of survey and distribution, being abstracts of various surveys and instruments of title, 1636–1703*, 4 vols (Dublin, 1949–67).

Simms, Katharine, '"Gabh umad a Fheidhlimidh": a fifteenth-century inauguration ode', *Ériu*, 31 (1980), 132–45.

—, 'Gaelic warfare in the Middle Ages' in Thomas Bartlett and Keith Jeffery (eds), *A military history of Ireland* (Cambridge, 1996), pp 99–115.

—, 'Images of the galloglass in poems to the MacSweeneys' in Seán Duffy (ed.), *The world of the galloglass: kings, warlords and warriors in Ireland and Scotland, 1200–1600* (Dublin, 2007), pp 106–23.

—, 'The selection of poems for inclusion in the Book of the O'Conor Don' in Pádraig Ó Macháin (ed.), *The Book of the O'Conor Don: essays on an Irish manuscript* (Dublin, 2010), pp 32–60.

Sims-Williams, Patrick, *Irish influence on medieval Welsh literature* (Oxford, 2011).

Sjoestedt, Marie-Louise, *Gods and heroes of the Celts*, trans. Myles Dillon (London, 1949; repr. Berkeley, 1982).

Skerrett, R.A.Q., 'Fiarfaidhi San Anselmuis', *Celtica*, 7 (1966), 163–87.

Stagl, Justin, *A history of curiosity: the theory of travel 1550–1800* (London, 1995).

Stern, Ludwig-Christian (ed. and trans.), 'Find and the phantoms', *Revue Celtique*, 13 (1892), 5–22.

Stevens, John, *Medieval romance: themes and approaches* (London, 1973).

Stokes, Whitley (ed.), *Three Irish glossaries* (London, 1862).

— (ed. and trans.), *Three Middle-Irish homilies on the lives of Saints Patrick, Brigit and Columba* (Calcutta, 1877).

— (ed. and trans.), 'Find and the phantoms', *Révue Celtique*, 7 (1886), 289–307.

— (ed. and trans.), *The tripartite Life of Patrick, with other documents relating to the saint*, Rolls Series 89, 2 vols (London, 1887).

— (ed. and trans.), *Lives of saints from the Book of Lismore* (Oxford, 1890).

— (ed. and trans.), 'The second battle of Moytura', *Revue Celtique*, 13 (1891), 55–130, 306–8.

— (ed. and trans.), 'The battle of Mag Mucrime', *Revue Celtique*, 13 (1892), 426–74.

— (ed. and trans.), 'The prose tales in the Rennes dindshenchas', *Révue Celtique* 15 (1894), 272–336, 418–84; and 16 (1895), 31–83, 135–67, 269–312.

— (ed. and trans.), 'The annals of Tigernach', *Revue Celtique*, 16 (1895), 374–419, 17 (1896), 6–33, 119–263, 337–420, 18 (1897), 9–59, 150–97, 267–303; repr. 2 vols (Felinfach, 1993).

— (ed. and partial trans.), 'Acallamh na senórach' in Whitley Stokes and Ernst Windisch (eds), *Irische Texte*, iv, 1 (Leipzig, 1900).

Stolz, Benjamin A. and Richard S. Shannon III (eds), *Oral literature and the formula* (Ann Arbor, 1976).

Sweetman, H.S. (ed.), *Calendar of documents relating to Ireland, 1252–84*, vol. 2 of 5 (London, 1877).

Thompson, Stith, *Motif-index of folk literature*, vol. 2 (Copenhagen, 1956).

Thompson, Tok, 'The Irish *sí* tradition: connections between the disciplines, and what's in a word?', *Journal of Archaeological Method and Theory*, 11:4 (December 2004), 335–68.

Thomson, Derick S. (ed.), *Branwen Merch Lyr* (Dublin, 1961).

—, 'MacPherson's *Ossian:* ballads to epics' in B. Almqvist et al. (eds), *The heroic process* (1987), pp 243–64.

Thorpe, Lewis, *The history of the kings of Britain* (London, 1966).

Thurneysen, Rudolf (ed. and trans.), 'Die Sage von CuRoi', *Zeitschrift für celtische Philologie*, 9 (1913), 189–234.

—, *Die irische Helden- und Königsage bis zum siebzehnten Jahrhundert* (Halle [Salle], 1921).

—, *A grammar of Old Irish*, trans. Daniel A. Binchy and Osborn Bergin (Dublin, 1946).

Tristram, Hildegard L.C., 'Mimesis and diegesis in the *Cattle raid of Cooley*' in John Carey, John T. Koch and Pierre-Yves Lambert (eds), *Ildánach ildírech: a Festschrift for Proinsias Mac Cana* (Andover, MA, and Aberystwyth, 1999), pp 263–76.

Twemlow, J.A. (ed.), *Calendar of entries in the papal registers relating to Great Britain and Ireland*, vol. x, 1447–55 (London, 1915).

Tymockzo, Maria, 'A poetry of masks: the poet's persona in early Celtic poetry' in Kathryn A. Klar, Eve E. Sweetser and Claire Thomas (eds), *A Celtic florilegium: studies in memory of Brendan O Hehir* (Lawrence, MA, 1996), pp 187–209.

Ua Laoghaire, Peadar, *Lughaidh mac Con* (Baile Átha Cliath, 1917).

Ua Muirgheasa, Énrí (ed.), *Ceithearnach Uí Dhomhnaill nó eachtra an cheithearnaigh chaoil-riabhaigh* (Baile Átha Cliath, 1912).

Uí Ógáin, Ríonach and Tom Sherlock (eds), *The otherworld: music and song from Irish tradition* (Dublin, 2012).

Valante, Mary A., *The Vikings in Ireland: settlement, trade and urbanization* (Dublin, 2008).

Vendryes, Joseph (ed.), *Airne Fíngein* (Dublin, 1953).

Villanueva, J.L., *Phoenician Ireland*, trans. Henry O'Brien (London, 1833).

Whalen, Logan E. (ed.), *A companion to Marie de France* (Leiden/Boston, 2011).

—, 'The prologues and the epilogues of Marie de France' in idem (ed.), *A companion to Marie de France* (2011), pp 1–30.

Wilde, William, *Lough Corrib, its shores and islands: with notices of Lough Mask* (Dublin, 1867).

Wiley, Dan M., 'The politics of myth in *Airne Fíngein*' in J.F. Eska (ed.), *Narrative in Celtic tradition* (2011), pp 276–87.

Williams, Bernadette (ed.), *The 'Annals of Multyfarnham': Roscommon and Connacht provenance* (Dublin, 2012).

Williams, Nicholas (ed. and trans.), *The poems of Giolla Brighde Mac Con Midhe*, Irish Texts Society 51 (London, 1980).

Winter, Irene, 'Homer's Phoenicians: history, ethnography, or literary trope? [A perspective on early orientalism]' in Jane B. Carter and Sarah P. Morris (eds), *The ages of Homer: a tribute to Emily Townsend Vermeule* (Austin, 1995), pp 247–71.

Zimmer, Heinrich, 'Keltische Beiträge III', *Zeitschrift für deutsches Alterthum und deutsche Litteratur*, 35 (1891), 1–172.

Zimmerman, Georges Denis, *The Irish storyteller* (Dublin, 2001).

Contributors

JOHN CAREY is Head of the Department of Early and Medieval Irish, University College Cork.

ANNE CONNON lectures in History at Ohio Dominican University, Columbus.

ANN DOOLEY is Professor Emerita in the Celtic Studies Program, University of Toronto.

AIDAN DOYLE lectures in the Department of Modern Irish, University College Cork.

JOSEPH J. FLAHIVE works for the *Eriu* Trust and for the *Locus* Project, University College Cork.

KEVIN MURRAY lectures in the Department of Early and Medieval Irish, University College Cork.

JOSEPH FALAKY NAGY is Professor in the Department of English, University of California, Los Angeles.

SÍLE NÍ MHURCHÚ is an O'Donovan Scholar in the School of Celtic Studies, Dublin Institute for Advanced Studies.

STIOFÁN Ó CADHLA is Head of the Department of Folklore, University College Cork.

SEÁN Ó COILEÁIN is Professor Emeritus of Modern Irish, University College Cork.

GEARÓID Ó CRUALAOICH is Professor Emeritus of Folklore and Ethnology, University College Cork.

PÁDRAIG Ó MACHÁIN is Professor of Modern Irish, University College Cork.

GERALDINE PARSONS lectures in Celtic and Gaelic, University of Glasgow.

Index

When medieval and modern spellings of the same word are present, the most common form utilised in the volume has been chosen as headword. Common names and terms which are frequently attested (such as *Acallam na Senórach*, *Agallamh na Seanórach*, *Agallamh Bheag*, Caílte, *fianaigecht/fiannaíocht*, Finn, and Oisín) have not been indexed.